Police Promotion Handbooks
5 Road Traffic

Baker & Wilkie's Police Promotion Handbooks

Police Promotion Handbooks

Road Traffic

Seventh edition

by E. R. Baker OBE, QPM, LL.B
formerly Deputy Chief Constable
South Wales Constabulary

and F. B. Dodge
Chief Inspector South Wales Constabulary

London
Butterworths
1980

England London	Butterworth & Co (Publishers) Ltd 88 Kingsway, WC2B 6AB
Australia Sydney	Butterworths Pty Ltd 586 Pacific Highway, Chatswood, NSW 2067 Also at Melbourne, Brisbane, Adelaide and Perth
Canada Toronto	Butterworth & Co (Canada) Ltd 2265 Midland Avenue, Scarborough, M1P 4S1
New Zealand Wellington	Butterworths of New Zealand Ltd 77–85 Customhouse Quay
South Africa Durban	Butterworth & Co (South Africa) (Pty) Ltd 152–154 Gale Street
USA Boston	Butterworth (Publishers) Inc 10 Tower Office Park, Woburn, Mass 01801

© Butterworth & Co (Publishers) Ltd 1980

ISBN 0 406 84162 4

Reprinted 1981

Reprinted in Singapore by
Tien Wah Press (Pte) Ltd.

Preface

This handbook, as with the others in the series, is based on the syllabus for the police promotion examinations and is designed to enable a student to acquire both the fundamental knowledge and the technique of answering questions necessary to pass the examinations, the latter by the lay-out of the text and the exclusion of unnecessary verbiage and detail. A special feature, which police students will find particularly useful, is that the text relating to subjects confined to the examinations for promotion to inspector is plainly marked as such.

This edition, the seventh, incorporates the many additions to and changes in road traffic law since the sixth edition was published in 1977, notably the harmonisation with EEC regulations and rules of the law relating to drivers' hours and keeping of records, the use and regulation of minibuses and community buses, the extension of certain traffic provisions to Crown roads, new provisions concerning rear fog lamps, amendments to the 1971 lighting regulations, and the effect of the consolidating regulations of 1978 relating to the construction and use of motor vehicles.

E. R. BAKER
F. B. DODGE

December 1979

Contents

CHAPTER 15. GOODS VEHICLES

CHAPTER 16. HOURS OF DRIVING AND RECORDS

CHAPTER 17. ROAD ACCIDENTS: DUTIES OF DRIVERS

CHAPTER 18. MOTOR VEHICLES (CONSTRUCTION AND USE) REGULATIONS 1978

CHAPTER 19. MOTOR CYCLES AND PEDAL CYCLES

CHAPTER 20. MISCELLANEOUS PROVISIONS

Abbreviations

The following abbreviations are used in this book:

AA	Automobile Association
Ag Imp	agricultural implement
Ag Tlr	agricultural trailer
AIL	abnormal indivisible load
AP	authorised person (under RTA 1972, s. 160: see p. 324)
AV	articulated vehicle
AWW	arrest without warrant
BDV	broken down vehicle being towed in consequence of break-down
B/Emp	employer issuing a DRB (see p. 225)
BFG	British forces in Germany (driving licence: see p. 153)
BSI	British Standards Institution
C & U	construction and use
COP	chief officer of police
CJA	Criminal Justice Act
DHSS	Department of Health and Social Security
DPV	dual purpose vehicle
DRB	driver's record book (see p. 225)
E/dr	employee driver (see p. 225)
EEC	European Economic Community
EP	engineering plant
exc	exceeding
FP	fixed penalty (see p. 291)
GB	Great Britain
GLC	Greater London Council
GV	goods vehicle
HCV	heavy commercial vehicle
HD	horse drawn vehicle, not an Ag Imp
HGV	heavy goods vehicle
HGVDL	heavy goods vehicle driver's licence
HM	Her Majesty's
HMC	heavy motor car
HO	Home Office
HP	horsepower

I	triable on indictment
IC	invalid carriage
Ind T	industrial tractor
Int	interval between one WD and the next (see p. 350)
IO	indictable offence
IS	illuminating surface (see p. 107)
kph	kilometres per hour
LA	local authority
LCJ	Lord Chief Justice
LGV	large goods vehicle (see p. 204)
LH	licence holder
LI	land implement
LIC	land implement conveyor
L Loco	land locomotive
Loco	locomotive
LPV	large passenger vehicle (see p. 107)
LT	land tractor
LV	living van
MC	motor car
MOH	medical officer of health
MOT	Ministry of Transport (test)
MPD	Metropolitan Police District
mph	miles per hour
MPV	mechanically propelled vehicle
MT	motor tractor
MV	motor vehicle
NCB	National Coal Board
n/e	not exceeding
NIP	notice of intended prosecution
OAP Act	Offences against the Person Act
OC	operating centre (under Transport Act 1968: see p. 207)
O/dr	owner-driver (see p. 225)
OL	operator's licence (under Transport Act 1968: see p. 207)
o/l	overall length
o/w	overall width
P	provisional powers (under RTA 1972, s. 164: see p. 29)
PCV	pedestrian controlled vehicle
pl	permitted lamps (see p. 131)
PO	Post Office
PPV	private premises vehicle
PSV	public service vehicle
PV	passenger vehicle
pw	plated weight
RAC	Royal Automobile Club
RAF	Royal Air Force
RB	registration book
RM	registration mark
RNLI	Royal National Lifeboat Institution
rpw	relevant plated weight (see p. 205)

RR	road roller
RSAC	Royal Scottish Automobile Club
RSL	road service licence
RT	vehicle designed and constructed to carry round timber
RTA	Road Traffic Act(s)
RTR Act	Road Traffic Regulation Act
S	triable summarily
San Tlr	sanitation trailer (as San V)
San V	sanitation vehicle (i.e. used for street cleansing, collecting refuse, clearing cesspits, etc.)
SGV	small goods vehicle (see p. 204)
S of S	Secretary of State
ST	special trailer (see p. 107)
TA	Transport Act
TL	trade licence
TPC Acts	Town Police Clauses Acts
TRO	traffic regulation order
UK	United Kingdom
US	United States
u/w	unladen weight
VAT	value added tax
VE	vehicle examiner (see p. 324)
VPE	vehicle proceeding to port for export
WD	working day (see p. 225)
WT	works truck
W Tlr	works trailer
WW	working week (see p. 225)

Important

 Police students should note that material in the text which is edge-marked as here indicated relates to subjects listed only in the syllabus for the examination for promotion to inspector.

Chapter 1 **General review of statutes relating to road traffic**

1. Pre-1930 legislation

Generally speaking no statute prior to 1930 dealing with traffic on roads and highways and directly embracing mechanically propelled vehicles as such remains on the statute book. All, prior to that year, relate to traffic of the pre-motor car era—pedestrians, equestrians, drovers, shepherds, the drivers of animal-drawn wagons, carts and carriages, etc. By s. 195 of the RTA 1972, however, any reference to a carriage in any statute, or regulation or byelaw made under a statute, includes a motor vehicle or a trailer.

(1) Highway Act 1835

(as to exemption of an IC, see p. 302)

a) Section 72: footpaths by side of road, and set apart for foot passengers—It is an offence if any person *wilfully:*

a) rides on such a footpath, or

b) leads or drives any cattle, etc.* carriage on it, or

c) tethers any cattle, etc.* on a highway so as to permit the tethered animal to be on such a footpath.

b) Section 76: names on carts, etc.—Owner's true name, with place of trade or abode, in legible letters (at least 1″ long) to be *painted* on off-side of cart, wagon or other such carriage (i.e. of same kind—vehicles for carrying heavy goods at slow pace). Section 76 does not cover motor vehicles or their trailers.

OFFENCES—OWNER IS LIABLE FOR:

a) using (or allowing use) without name, etc. on wagon as above, or

b) suffering name, etc. to become illegible, or

c) painting false or fictitious particulars (or causing this).

---

* Includes horse, ass, sheep, mule and swine.

c) Section 77: driving more than one cart—One person is not to drive more than two carts at once, but can drive two if each is not drawn by more than one horse and horse of hinder cart is attached by a rein n/e 4 ft long to back of foremost cart.

d) Section 78: offences by drivers, riders, etc.—The following are offences:

I) NO PROPER CONTROL—Driver, unless control is exercised by reins, being on the carriage or horse drawing it without some other person being on foot or horseback to guide the horse(s).

II) CAUSING HURT OR DAMAGE—By negligence or wilful misbehaviour on highway causing hurt or damage to any person, horse, cattle or goods conveyed in any carriage passing along or on the highway.

III) QUITTING WAGON, ETC.—That is, by:

a) going on other side of hedge or fence enclosing the road on which his wagon, etc. remains, or

b) negligently or wilfully being at such a distance from carriage (or in such situation) while on a highway as to have no control over the animal(s) drawing it.

IV) OBSTRUCTION—By:

a) leaving cart or carriage on highway so as to obstruct passage thereof;

b) *any person* in any manner preventing any other person passing him or any horses or cattle or carriage under his care on a highway.

V) KEEPING TO NEAR SIDE—By:

a) *driver* of carriage, wagon, horses or other beasts of burden, meeting any other carriage, wagon, etc. and not keeping his carriage, beast, etc. to the near side of highway;

b) *any person* who by negligence or wilful misbehaviour prevents or hinders the free passage of any person, wagon, cart or horses or beasts of burden on any highway, or does not keep his carriage, wagon, or beasts of burden to the near side to allow free passage.

VI) DANGEROUS DRIVING AND RIDING—That is, any person riding or driving any horse or beast or driving any sort of carriage to do so furiously so as to endanger life or limb of any person on the highway.

Offences are summary offences. The Act applies everywhere.

(2) Town Police Clauses Act 1847

Section 28 creates offences much the same as those in s. 78 of the Highway Act 1835, and provides that a constable can arrest any person offending against the section within his view, though such procedure would rarely be necessary in relation to 'traffic' offences (as distinct from the 'street nuisance' offences also contained in the section). For the MPD similar provisions are contained in the Metropolitan Police Act 1839, s. 54.

(3) Offences against the Person Act 1861, s. 35

Whosoever having charge of any carriage or vehicle, by wanton or furious driving or racing, or other wilful misconduct or neglect, causes bodily harm to any person, commits an offence.

This charge is often coupled with one of reckless driving or cycling under the RTA 1972, when personal injury is caused. The 1972 Act allies this charge to those in the Act by providing that breaches of the Highway Code can be relied on as evidence tending to establish or negative liability in such a charge (s. 37).

(4) Licensing Act 1872, s. 12

DRUNK IN CHARGE

For any person to be drunk while in charge on any highway or other public place of any carriage, horse, or cattle is an offence (AWW: summary offence).

This section does not apply to motor vehicles or pedal cycles where liability to charges under the RTA 1972, ss. 5 or 19 exists, but it would seem to apply to an IC deemed not to be a MV under the RTA—see p. 302.

(5) Public Health Act 1925, s. 74 (2)

DANGEROUS RIDING OR DRIVING

If any person rides or drives so as to endanger the life or limb of any person or to the common danger of passengers in any street (not within MPD) he may be arrested without warrant by any constable who witnesses the occurrence and any person who commits the offence is liable to a fine.

2. Post-1930 legislation

NOTE TO STUDENTS

A student of road traffic law will find it of tremendous value if, before embarking on a detailed study of the subject, he masters the following summary of the main subjects with which the various Acts are concerned, as well as the interpretations and meanings included in the next chapter.

1) **Road Traffic Act 1930** *(powers of local authorities re public service vehicles)*—The only sections of this Act which remain in force relate to the power of local authorities to run public service vehicles.

2) Road and Rail Traffic Act 1933 *(railway crossings)* —This Act is repealed, except for s. 42 which permits gates on a level crossing across a public road to be kept closed across the railway instead of across the road, either constantly or during specified periods, except when rail traffic is passing through. Any gatekeeper not complying with such a direction commits a summary offence.

3) Highways Act 1959 *(functions of highway authorities and highway offences)* —This Act consolidates, with amendments, most of the law relating to the functions of highway authorities in connection with highways, streets and bridges, e.g. maintenance, improvement, removal of nuisances or sources of danger, drainage, etc. The only part of particular police importance is Part VII which deals with offences relating to:

a) *causing damage to highways,* and things connected with a highway (wall, embankment, turf, tree, hedge, shrub, cattle grid, gate, post, traffic sign, milestone, direction sign, etc.);

b) *wilful obstructions of highway;*

c) *straying animals;*

d) *putting wires or ropes* across the highway.

4) Road Traffic Act 1960—Almost all of this Act has been repealed and replaced by the Act of 1972, but Part III dealing with public service vehicles remains.

5) Road Traffic Regulation Act 1967—This is the main Act relating to the control of the use of roads, particularly in relation to the following matters:

a) the making of orders by the S of S and local authority, i.e. traffic regulation orders, experimental orders, etc.;

b) pedestrian crossings, school crossings and street playgrounds;

c) the provision of parking places on and off highways, with and without payment, and offences relating to parking places;

d) removal of 'offending' vehicles from roads and parking places;

e) traffic signs;

f) speed limits;

g) traffic wardens;

h) payment of fixed penalties as alternative to prosecution for certain lighting, obstruction and parking offences.

6) Transport Act 1968—This Act deals with the regulation of the carriage of goods by road, and restrictions on hours of driving of certain goods vehicles and passenger vehicles.

7) Chronically Sick and Disabled Persons Act 1970—This Act exempts from almost all Road Traffic Acts and Regulations invalid carriages which conform with certain requirements.

8) Vehicles (Excise) Act 1971—This Act consolidates all vehicle excise legislation.

9) Road Traffic Act 1972—This replaces the 1960 Act as the 'principal' Act relating to road traffic matters. The Act covers the following main subjects:

a) offences connected with driving motor vehicles and riding pedal cycles (reckless, careless, drink or drugs, racing, etc.);

b) offences concerning driving of motor vehicles (causing death, driving under age, use of footpaths, driving off road, etc.);

c) general traffic offences, e.g. non-compliance with traffic directions, leaving in dangerous position, duties in case of accident, tampering with vehicles, control of dogs on roads, protective headgear;

d) general provisions re construction and use of vehicles and equipment;

e) lighting of vehicles;

f) licensing of drivers (general and for heavy goods vehicles), driving instruction, tests, disqualification, endorsements;

g) insurance requirements;

h) powers of the police and duties of owners and drivers.

10) Road Traffic (Foreign Vehicles) Act 1972—The Act secures the observance of certain statutory provisions relating to road traffic by foreign goods vehicles and public service vehicles. See chapter 23.

11) Road Traffic Act 1974—This Act amended the Road Traffic Regulation Act 1967, the Road Traffic Act 1972, and other Acts, notably with regard to regulation of traffic by the police for traffic surveys, extending the 'type approval' scheme to all vehicles and to vehicle parts, licensing of drivers, and varying penalties. Other provisions impose on vehicle owners liabilities in respect of certain fixed penalty offences and excess parking charges, and make amendments relating to parking on verges and footways. The only section applicable to Northern Ireland is s. 20 which requires authorised insurers to be members of the Motor Insurers' Bureau.

12) International Road Haulage Permits Act 1975—The Act makes provision with regard to the forgery, carriage and production of licences, permits, authorisations and other documents relating to the international carriage of goods by road.

13) PSV (Arrest of Offenders) Act 1975—This authorises the arrest without warrant of persons suspected of contravening regulations about the conduct of passengers on PSVs.

14) Road Traffic (Drivers' Ages and Hours of Work) Act 1976—This Act amended the RTA 1972 with regard to driving licences and the minimum ages for driving.

15) Minibus Act 1977—This authorises the use of certain motor vehicles by bodies concerned with education, religion, social welfare and other activities for the benefit of the community.

16) Transport Act 1978—This Act deals with community bus services, car sharing, control of off street parking, and passenger transport policies in country areas.

17) Regulations—Whenever provisions of a statute are repealed and replaced by another, it is almost always the case that regulations made under the repealed provisions are continued in force by the new statute. It is not uncommon therefore to find regulations ante-dating the statute under which they are enforced.

Chapter 2 **Interpretations, definitions and meanings**

At the commencement of his studies of specific Acts of Parliament the student should master the definitions which expressions used in them have been given by the 'interpretation' sections or clauses of the Acts concerned. Included in this chapter are summarised definitions of general application which have special meanings for the purpose of the Road Traffic Acts (i.e. those which have meanings that do not coincide with what would normally be attributed to them) as well as interpretations which have been attached to them by 'case-law'. Other statutory definitions, not of general application, are given in the text to which the special meanings are related.

1. Motor vehicle

Road Traffic Act 1972, s. 190

Motor vehicle

'Motor vehicle' means a mechanically propelled vehicle (MPV) intended or adapted for use on roads. As to when an IC or a grass mower is not a MV see pp. 302 and 12 respectively.

COMMENT

a) 'Mechanically propelled' covers any source of mechanical power (petrol, gas, oil, steam, electricity).

b) The main principle is that a MPV constructed as such, remains a MPV until its whole character has been changed in such a way that there is no reasonable prospect of it ever being mobile again, for temporary loss of mechanical power (e.g. lack of fuel, breakdown) does not affect the character of the vehicle.

Saycell v Bool (1948) (no petrol)

No petrol in the tank. Owner released the brake and set the vehicle in motion by pushing it from the top of an incline and then got into the driving seat and steered the vehicle downhill operating the brakes, although the engine was not running. *Held:* that he was driving a MPV.

R v Paul (1952) (flat battery)

A car is still a motor vehicle though incapable of being started because of a flat battery.

Lawrence v Howlett (1952) (parts removed)

An auto cycle being ridden on a road simply as a pedal cycle, while the auxiliary motor is not working because the cylinder, piston and connecting rod have been removed, is not a motor vehicle and it does not require policy of insurance.

Floyd v Bush (1953) (engine not used)

Defendant pedalled away a motor assisted cycle belonging to another person. He was held to have been rightly convicted of taking and driving away a motor vehicle without the consent of the owner, and driving (he had caused it to move) without a driving licence and insurance. An auto cycle even though the engine is not used is a motor vehicle.

Newberry v Simmonds (1961)

Held that a car did *not* cease to be a mechanically propelled vehicle on the mere removal of the engine if the evidence admitted the possibility of it being replaced and the motive power restored.

Smart v Allan and another (1962)

Vehicle was bought as scrap, had no gearbox or battery, incomplete engine and had been towed to that place. *Held:* there was no conceivable prospect of it ever being made mobile again and it had ceased to be a mechanically propelled vehicle.

Law v Thomas (1964)

A broken down motor vehicle which can be repaired in a matter of minutes still remains a mechanically propelled vehicle.

Cobb v Whorton (1971)

A MV being towed is still a MPV and it can also be deemed a trailer.

Binks v Department of the Environment (1975)

Where as the result of severe damage a motor car could not be used, it was held still to be a MV because the owner intended to get it repaired.

c) 'Intended or adapted for use on roads'—the only doubt which can arise is in respect of a MPV not primarily intended or adapted for use on roads being designed for special purposes. In the absence of evidence of regular use on roads, it would seem that the test is whether a reasonable man would contemplate general use of the roads as one of the uses of the vehicle (*Burns v Currell* (1963)).

Daley v Hargreaves (1961)
The High Court held that a 'dumper' is not intended or adapted for use on
a road but stated that it might have found differently had there been
evidence of such suitability.

Burns v Currell (1963)
Where there was no evidence of regular use on a road a 'go-kart' was held
not to be a motor vehicle, though it might be otherwise if there was such
evidence. The test is whether a reasonable man looking at it would say
that one of its uses would be for the road.

Chalgray Ltd v Aspley (1965)
The fact that a dumper used on a building site occasionally emerged onto
the highway did not alone make it a motor vehicle.

Nichol v Leach and Lindsell (1972)
A scrap mini-car was rebuilt for autocross racing and towed to a race
meeting. *Held:* the car was produced as an ordinary car and did not cease
to be a MV because the present owners did not intend to use it on a road
under its own power.

2. Classification of motor vehicles

1) A heavy locomotive		A MPV not constructed itself to carry a load, other than water, fuel, accumulators and other equipment used for propulsion, loose tools and loose equipment, *its unladen weight* (u/w)	—(1) exc: 11½ tons
2) A light locomotive	is		—(2) exc: 7¼ but not 11½ tons
3) A motor tractor			—(3) n/e 7¼ tons

4) Motor car—This means a MPV (not a motor cycle or invalid carriage)
constructed itself to carry a load* or passengers, its u/w:

a) if constructed solely to carry *passengers* and effects,
   adapted for not more than seven passengers (ex driver)
   and having pneumatic tyres .... n/e 3 tons
b) if constructed or adapted for *conveyance* of goods* of
   any kind .... n/e 3 tons

---

* Where a MV is fitted with a special appliance (e.g. a crane or welding plant)
essentially a permanent fixture, the fixture is not a load but part of the vehicle. A MV so
constructed that a trailer may by partial superimposition be attached to the vehicle so
that a substantial part of the trailer's weight is borne by the vehicle is deemed constructed
to carry a load. (See 'Articulated vehicle', p. 10).

but if propelled by gas and carrying gas containers or gas
plant and materials for producing gas .... n/e 3½ tons

c) in any other case .... n/e 2½ tons

Keeble v Miller (1950)
The word 'constructed' means constructed at the material time, i.e. at the
time of the offence, not as originally constructed.

5) Heavy motor car—This means a MPV (not being a motor
car) constructed itself to carry a load*or passengers, u/w   exc. 2½ tons

6) Motor cycle—This means a MPV (not being an invalid
carriage) with less than four wheels and u/w .... n/e 8 cwts

7) Invalid carriage—See p. 302.

NOTE
A hover vehicle is a MV but does not fall within any of the above classes (see p.
11).

3. Particular types of vehicles

1) Agricultural trailer—This is a trailer owned by a person engaged in agriculture and not used on a road to convey burden other than agricultural produce
or articles required for agriculture.

2) Articulated vehicle—This means a HMC or MC with a trailer so attached to
it that part of the trailer is superimposed upon it and when the trailer is
uniformly loaded not less than 20 per cent of the weight of the load is borne by
the drawing vehicle.

NOTE
When together the combination is regarded as a MV plus trailer and not as
one vehicle (RTA 1972, s. 191).

But the following exceptions apply:

I) LICENSING—no extra duty is payable with regard to the drawing of the trailer
part.

II) SPEED LIMITS—applicable to a vehicle not drawing a trailer, unless the AV is
itself drawing a trailer.

III) LIGHTING EQUIPMENT AND REFLECTORS—The trailer unit is not required to
carry obligatory front and rear lamps or reflectors during daylight. It must,
however, have rear lights and red reflectors during hours of darkness.

IV) BEING TOWED AWAY IN CONSEQUENCE OF A BREAKDOWN IF THE TRAILER PART IS
UNLADEN—the AV being regarded then as one vehicle (i.e. ohe trailer).

---

* See previous page.

3) Carriage—A MV or trailer is a carriage within the meaning of any statute, or any rule, regulation or byelaw (RTA 1972, s. 195).

4) Close coupled trailer—This means that the wheels on the same side of the trailer at all times remain parallel to the longitudinal axis of the vehicle (its centre line), the distances between their centres of contact with the road n/e 1 metre.

5) Dual purpose vehicle—See p. 81.

6) A hover vehicle—(designed to be supported on a cushion of air and not wheels). This is a MV but is not to be regarded as being within any of the classifications on pp. 9–10, i.e. the law as to MV generally applies but not that limited to motor vehicles of a particular classification (RTA 1972, s. 192). It is not to be treated as a MV for the purposes of any enactment prior to the Hovercraft Act 1968 (SI 1972 No. 674).

7) Industrial tractor—This is a MT not being LT, of u/w n/e 7370 kgs, designed and used primarily for road construction or maintenance (including fitments required for the work) and by construction incapable of exceeding 20 mph on level and under own power.

8) Land implement—This means any implement or machinery used with a land locomotive or land tractor (see below) for purposes of agriculture, grass cutting, forestry, land levelling, dredging, etc. including a living van and any trailer carrying only necessary gear or equipment of the drawing vehicle.

9) Land implement conveyor—This is a trailer, u/w n/e 510 kgs, specially designed to convey not more than one land implement and marked with u/w, all tyres pneumatic and drawn by a land locomotive or land tractor.

10) Land locomotive—This is a locomotive designed and used primarily for work on land in agriculture, forestry, land levelling, dredging or similar operations, driven on a road only to and from site of work and then hauling nothing other than LI or LIC.

11) Land tractor—This is a tractor, u/w n/e 7370 kgs, designed and used primarily for work on land in agriculture, grass cutting, forestry, land levelling or dredging, which is:

a) the property of a person engaged in agriculture or forestry or a contractor engaged in business for farms or forestry, and

b) not constructed or adapted to carry a load other than:
i) necessary requirements for propulsion and loose tools;
ii) a load which does not render it liable for excise duty as a goods vehicle (see p. 149); or
iii) a fixed implement used for farm or forestry work.

12) Locomotive—This includes heavy loco. and light loco.

13) Moped—This is a motor cycle with engine n/e 50 cc, equipped with pedals whereby it is capable of being propelled—but for the definition which applies to mopeds in relation to ages for driving, see p. 161.

14) Pedestrian controlled vehicle—This is a MV controlled by a pedestrian and not constructed or adapted for use for the carriage of a driver or passenger.

NOTE
A grass cutter (or any other MPV which may be specified by regulations) controlled by a pedestrian is not to be treated as a motor vehicle provided it is constructed or adapted:

a) for use only under pedestrian control, or

b) for control by a pedestrian or by a person carried on it, but in such a case only while it is not being controlled by a person carried on it (RTA 1967, s. 103).

15) Trailer—This is a vehicle drawn by a MV. A motor cycle sidecar complying with the regulations (see p. 266) is a part of the motor cycle and not a trailer.

16) Tracklaying vehicle—This is one so designed and constructed that its weight is transmitted to the road either by making continuous tracks or by a combination of wheels and continuous tracks so that weight transmitted to the road by tracks is not less than half the weight of the vehicle.

17) Tramcar—This is any carriage used on a road under the Light Railways Act 1896.

18) Trolley vehicle—This is a MPV adapted for use on roads without rails and moved by an external source of power.

19) Works Truck—This is a MV (other than a straddle carrier) designed for use in private premises and used on a road only in delivering goods from or to such premises or to or from a vehicle on a road in the immediate neighbourhood, or in passing from one part of such premises to another, or to other private premises in the immediate neighbourhood or in connection with road works while at the immediate neighbourhood of such road works.

Greaves & Son Ltd v Peam (1972)
If the two premises are six-tenths of a mile apart they cannot be said to be in the immediate neighbourhood of each other.

20) Works trailer—This is a trailer designed for the same purposes as a works truck.

4. Other definitions

1) Bridleway—A way over which public have no other right of way than on foot, on horseback, or leading a horse, whether there is or is not a right to drive other animals along it.

2) Chief officer of police—The chief constable or, in London, the Commissioner of Police either of the metropolis or of the City of London.

3) Combination of vehicles—All the vehicles linked together when a MV draws trailer(s), including any other MV assisting in propulsion.

4) Driver—This includes, where there is a separate steersman, that person as well as any other person engaged in driving the MV: 'drive' is construed accordingly (s. 196).

Exceptions:

a) causing death by reckless driving;

b) offences relating to parking on highways where charges are made.

Comment—The legal definition goes no further—it does not define 'drive' or 'driving'. The general principle appears to be (when not two drivers) that the driver must not only be steering the vehicle but doing something more, i.e. either to control its propulsion or to stop it.

Wallace v Major (1946)
A person merely steering a broken-down vehicle which is being towed is not a driver and cannot be charged with driving recklessly. (It might be otherwise if the person is also controlling the vehicle by means of the brakes, etc.) Section 196 applies only where separate persons, performing the duties of steersman and driver respectively, are on one and the same vehicle.

R v Roberts (1965)
A man does not drive a MV unless he is in the driving seat or in control of the steering wheel and, also, has something to do with the propulsion of the vehicle.

R v Maddinagh (1974)
A man pushing a car, with both feet on the road and one hand inside the car on the steering wheel, is not driving it. There must be a distinction between pushing a car and driving it. The dividing line will not always be easy to draw and the distinction will often turn on the extent and degree to which the defendant was relying on the use of the driver's controls, e.g. though the above facts do not constitute driving, it might be otherwise if the man had one foot in the car in order to make more effective use of the controls.

R v Arnold (1964)
The accused's vehicle, without the engine running, was being pushed slowly forward by another MV. *Held:* steering alone does not amount to driving—on the same principle as that in *Wallace v Major* (1946), above.

Saycell v Bool (1948)
Held: the defendant was driving the motor vehicle when steering it *and* operating the brakes as it proceeded downhill with no petrol in the tank and without the engine started.

Langman v Valentine (1952)
Where an unlicensed driver was in the driving seat, and the supervisor instructor also had effective control of the car and was able to (and did in fact) steer, stop and start, it was held that it was possible for both to be regarded as driving it.

Tyler v Whatmore (1975)
A man was sitting in the driving seat and his girl friend was sitting next to him. She was leaning across him and steering the car. *Held:* both were driving.

Evans v Walkden (1956)
In *Langman v Valentine* above, the instructor had his hands on the brake and steering wheel. Where a licensed person merely sat beside a young boy (who was in the driving seat) and, though able to reach the steering wheel and footbrake, did not have a hand on the wheel or brake, he was held not to be the driver as he was not in control of the car.

Hill v Baxter (1957)
There might be cases in which a person at the steering wheel of a moving car could be said not to be driving at all, e.g. overcome by sudden illness, struck by a stone or attacked by a swarm of bees. See further on p. 26.

NOTE
'Drink and drive' cases have extended the meaning of 'drive' for the purposes of these offences (see p. 43).

5) First used—The date of first use is the earliest of the undermentioned dates in respect of the vehicle:

a) if registered, date of first registration;

b) date of manufacture in the case of:
  i) vehicle used under trade licence otherwise than for demonstration, test, or delivery to distributor, retailer, purchaser, or hirer;
  ii) Crown (or former Crown) vehicles;
  iii) vehicles belonging (or which belonged to) visiting forces;
  iv) vehicle imported into GB after use on roads elsewhere;
  v) vehicle used otherwise than on roads after being sold or supplied by retail and before being registered.

6) Footpath—A way over which the public have right of way on foot only.

7) Kilogramme—A metric weight equivalent to 2·205 lbs.

8) Kilometre—A metric measure equivalent to approximately ⅝ of one mile.

9) Metre—A metric measure equivalent to 3·28 ft.

10) Owner—In relation to a vehicle subject to a hiring or hire-purchase agreement, generally means the person in possession of that vehicle under the agreement, but for the purpose of the RTA 1972, ss. 162 and 167 (information re insurance) it includes each party to the agreement.

11) Road—This is any highway and any other road to which the public has access, and includes any bridges (RTA 1972, s. 196). By s. 26 of the British

Transport Commission Act 1961, dock roads are roads for the purposes of many sections of the RTA 1972.

I) HELD TO BE A ROAD

Bryant v Marx (1932)
The footpath as well as the carriageway is part of a road.

Harrison v Hill (1932)
A farm road leading from a highway to a farm house and which offered no physical obstruction (e.g. gate, rope, notice) to any member of the public generally (although the farmer who maintained the road sometimes turned away people using it) was held to be a road. Followed in *Cox v White* (1975).

Bugge v Taylor (1940)
The public had no right of access to the forecourt of an hotel which was private property, but it was used in fact by the public not only to reach the hotel but also as a shortcut from one street to another, even with vehicles on occasions. The forecourt was held to be a road.

McCrone v Rigby (1952)
A highway remains a highway though temporarily roped off.

Newcastle Corporation v Walton (1957)
A quayside was held to be a road where the public were free to walk or motor without hindrance or other prohibition.

Worth v Brooks (1959)
A grass verge between the pavement and the bordering hedge or fence was held to be part of a road.

Kellett v Daisy (1975)
A Crown road is a road for purposes of the RTA 1972 at least as far as standards of driving are concerned, even though no Order under s. 149 of the Transport Act 1968 applies to it—see p. 16.

II) HELD NOT TO BE A ROAD

O'Brien v Trafalgar Insurance Co (1945)
A road inside a factory which only pass-holders could enter, and then only through gates guarded by police, is not a road to which the public has access.

Thomas v Dando (1951)
Held: the forecourt of a shop which was not separated from the road by either wall or rail, which only permitted access to the shop by customers but was not otherwise habitually used by the public, was not a road.

Henderson v Bernard (1955)
A courtyard leading off a highway to serve private premises was held not to be a road.

Baxter v Middlesex CC (1956)
Distinguished from *Bugge v Taylor* (1940), and held not to be a road on the facts, because the forecourt permitted access only to the hotel and

was not otherwise used by the public to pass or repass from one place to another.

Griffin v Squires (1958)

The fact that the public has access to a car park does not make the car park a road.

R v Beaumont (1964)

The fact that a large number of persons in a particular class of people (caravan dwellers, anglers, picnickers) were permitted by the farmer to use an occupation road (leading to his farm) at the entrance to which there was a 10 mph speed limit sign, two notices saying 'Trespassers will be prosecuted' and a gate permanently open, did not make it a road, for this is not evidence of unrestricted use by the general public.

Knaggs v Elson (1965)

Notices at the entrance to a cul-de-sac leading to thirty-six houses read 'No Parking'. *Held:* to bring the cul-de-sac within the meaning of 'road', evidence is needed that it was used by the public generally.

An analysis of the above (and many other) cases suggests that the following might provide a useful formula to apply in determining what is or is not a 'road' within the meaning of s. 196. A road must fall into one or other of the following categories, i.e.:

a) *be a highway*—i.e. a way provided and maintained for public travelling, and linking up one town or village with another or others (roads appearing on road maps);

b) *be a public thoroughfare,* i.e. a road or 'made-up' way (whether publicly or privately owned) used by the public generally to get from one *place in a district to another;*

c) *if not a thoroughfare* (e.g. a cul-de-sac, a farmer's occupation road) it is not a road unless it is made up as such and there is completely unrestricted access to it at the time by the public generally: evidence of public use is essential *(Deacon v A. T. (a minor)* (1976)).

III) VEHICLES (EXCISE) ACT 1971 (re excise licences)—Roads repairable at public expense.

12) Special road—This is one provided or being made under the Special Roads Act 1949, or s. 11 of the Highways Act 1959 (e.g. a motorway or any part of one).

13) Crown roads—Roads belonging to the Crown (e.g. in Royal Parks) are not normally roads for the purposes of the RTA, but special regulations may apply to them. By s. 149 of the TA 1968 all (or any) such roads may be made subject to road traffic enactments by special order.

With regard to roads in Royal Parks an Order has been made authorising the provisions of pedestrian crossings, and with reference to offences on these roads (contrary to park regulations) providing park constables (appointed for park duties under the Parks Regulation Act 1892) with the same powers as constables in connection with fixed penalties, obtaining information as to drivers and owners, and evidence by certificate as to the identity of drivers or owners of vehicles.

14) Tonne—1000 kg, slightly less than the British ton.

15) Tyres

I) PNEUMATIC TYRE—See p. 268.

II) OF SOFT OR ELASTIC MATERIAL—Made of such material and either:

a) continuous round the circumference of the wheel, or

b) fitted in sections so that as far as practicable no space is left between ends of sections.

III) A WIDE TYRE—Pneumatic tyre with area of contact with road not less than 300 mm in width (across the width of the tyre).

16) Unladen weight—This is the weight of a vehicle inclusive of the body and parts (the heavier where alternative bodies or parts are used) which are necessarily or ordinarily used with the vehicle when working on a road, but excluding weight of water, fuel or accumulators used to supply power and of loose tools and loose equipment.

17) Weights—Where a weight is applicable to a vehicle this, generally, has to be marked either on a plate carried on the vehicle or on the vehicle itself. Where this does not apply the appropriate weight is determined by multiplying the unladen weight by a number prescribed by the S of S in relation to the class of vehicle.

18) Kerbside weight—This means, in relation to a MV, the weight of the vehicle (including a towing bracket with which the vehicle is normally equipped) when it carries:

a) no person thereon, and

b) a full supply of fuel in its tank, an adequate supply of other liquids incidental to its propulsion, and no load other than loose tools and equipment with which the vehicle is equipped.

5. Using, causing or permitting use

In many offences under the Road Traffic Acts, and particularly those under the C & U Regulations, liability is placed upon any person using the vehicle in respect of which the offence is committed, or permitting or causing the use.

(1) Using

The person driving is 'using', and so also is the owner of the MV (or trailer) if it is being driven or 'used' for the personal purposes of the owner, i.e. where the driver is so doing on behalf of the owner (as agent or servant). For example, the owner 'uses' where his MV is being driven by an employee for the owner's business, say, of furniture removal, but does not where the purpose of the use is not his own, e.g. for the driver's own pleasure or business. Proof of use is sufficient, for the prohibitions under the Regulations are absolute and no evidence of mens rea is necessary; but note *Hart v Bex* (1957), below.

Griffiths v Studebaker (1924)
A car driven by an employee carried an excessive number of passengers even though he had been instructed not to do so. The company was convicted of *using* it.

Watson v Paterson (1949)
The owner is deemed to have been *'using'* in the absence of evidence to the contrary.

Reynold v Austin (1951)
If a MV is being lawfully used by an owner he does not become liable for unlawful use of the MV without his knowledge by persons who are not his employees nor acting on his behalf.

Andrews v Kershaw (1951)
A vehicle is in use when it is stationary on a road for loading or unloading.

Green v Burnett (1954)
An employee driver drove a MV on its owner's business with defective brakes. He had received instructions to get repairs carried out whenever required. The owner was guilty of 'using' even though he was unaware of the defect. Neither mens rea, blameworthiness nor negligence is relevant for consideration except with regard to punishment.

Hart v Bex (1957)
Where a defect in a braking system suddenly occurred on a journey, with no negligence or blame on the part of the driver or employer, the High Court advised that in such cases the police should refrain from prosecution or the court should give an absolute discharge, for there is no moral blame.

L. F. Dove Ltd v Tarvin (1964)
A customer borrowed a car from a garage to use on his own business. The garage did not thereby use the car even though the tyres were defective when the car was handed over. See *Carmichael & Sons v Cottle,* below.

Carmichael & Sons v Cottle (1970)
The hirer of a motor car uses it, but not the car hire firm, for the hirer is not their servant. The hire firm might, however, be guilty of causing or permitting use.

Crawford v Houghton (1972)
The owner is using when his servant is driving, but not so when the driving is by a person other than his servant, though with his knowledge and at his request. The owner may be guilty of permitting.

Garrett v Hooper (1972)

Partners A and B owned a motor vehicle. A was driving when committing a C & U offence. B, not present, was also convicted of 'using'. *Held:* B was not guilty of using but may have been guilty of 'causing' or 'permitting'.

Cobb˙v Williams (1973)

The owner of a vehicle who rides in it as a passenger when it is driven by another person 'uses' the vehicle.

A fair summary of the principles underlying the above decisions as to *'using'* would appear to be—

a) the driver always 'uses', and so does his employer if the vehicle is being driven within the scope of employment;

b) the owner of the vehicle (although not driving) is 'using' if the vehicle is being operated on his behalf;

c) 'using', therefore, involves vicarious liability but does not require evidence of 'mens rea', though complete absence of blame or negligence should be taken into account in deciding whether or not to prosecute;

d) only in cases other than (a) or (b) is there need to consider charges of 'causing' or 'permitting'.

(2) Causing use

In support of a charge of causing the use of a vehicle there must be evidence—

a) that the defendant had the authority to cause the vehicle to be used;

b) that in fact or by inference from the circumstances (including his control over the vehicle) he directed or ordered the use of the vehicle, and

c) that mens rea was present, e.g. knowledge of fault, or negligence in discharging responsibilities.

Patterson v Smart (1936)

Where it could not be proved that the employer induced or directed it or in any way failed in his duty, he was not guilty of causing his driver to drive for an excessive period—no mens rea.

John T. Ellis v Hinds (1947)

An employer neither causes nor permits the use of his vehicle which is used by his servant without authority or on his own account—no mens rea.

Rushton v Martin (1952)

The general manager of five depots, at each of which there is a vehicle superintendent, is not guilty of causing a vehicle to be on a road in a dangerous condition where he has no knowledge that it is on the road or dangerous, for he has no opportunity to exercise local control.

Shave v Rosner (1954)

The owner drove away his van from a garage where the staff had negligently failed to tighten hub nuts on a wheel after repair. *Held:* the garage proprietor was not guilty of 'causing', because as soon as the owner took over the van he ceased to have control and dominion over it and had done nothing which was the active cause of the owner driving it on the road.

Ellis v Smith (1962)

A bus driver who left a bus to go off duty without handing it over to his relief driver was held to have caused the bus to stand so as to make an obstruction.

Milstead v Sexton (1964)

Towing a motor vehicle is causing it to be used.

(3) Permitting use

This also implies an authority or degree of control over the use of the vehicle, but is an allowing of the use, rather than the more positive liability of directing or ordering use. It is a failure to exercise properly the responsibility not to agree to the use of a vehicle until reasonably satisfied that the law is not being contravened by so doing.

McLeod v Buchanan (1940)

Whereas 'to cause' involved an express or positive mandate to the other person from the person causing, permitting may be inferred if the other person is given such control of the vehicle as to carry with it a discretion or liberty to use it in the manner so used.

Lloyd v Singleton (1953)

Any person besides the owner who has control on the owner's behalf can permit its use, e.g. a chauffeur or manager of a company (permitting uninsured person to drive).

The following cases indicate that the general rule is that a degree of mens rea is necessary to prove 'permitting', i.e.:

a) actual knowledge (of the non-compliance of the vehicle), or

b) a failure to take adequate steps to prevent in some cases, or

c) wilful neglect or obvious disregard of duty, e.g. grossly inadequate discharge of responsibilities from which 'constructive' knowledge could be inferred.

Newell v Cook (1936)

Where the owner had no reason to know or to suspect or to be on guard, he was not guilty of permitting his vehicle to be used as an express carriage without a licence.

Evans v Dell (1937)
Where the owner did not know or did not deliberately refrain from making enquiries or shut his eyes to the obvious, he was not guilty of permitting the use of his vehicle as a stage carriage.

Browning v Watson (1953)
Where a company neglected to instruct its staff or take other adequate precautions against misuse of a motor coach, it was held guilty of permitting the offence. Mens rea here—neglect of duty.

James & Son v Smee (1954)
Where a company's vehicle had been sent out in good condition and the brakes had become defective by negligence of the employees whilst on the journey, the company was not guilty of permitting as there was no evidence that a responsible officer of the company permitted the use of the vehicle in that state. No mens rea.

Hutchings v Giles (1955)
An owner, who did not know the brakes were defective, allowed his servant to take the van on a road. *Held:* he was *not guilty* of 'permitting' because the prosecution must prove that he actually knew of the defect.

Wilson v Bird (1963)
Actual knowledge is not needed if proof of shutting one's eyes to the obvious is shown, i.e. constructive knowledge.

Fransman v Sexton (1965)
Knowledge is not imputed by mere negligence. Something more is required, such as recklessly sending out a vehicle and either risking or not caring what would happen.

Hill & Sons Ltd v CC of Hampshire (1972)
'Permit' involves knowledge or deliberate blindness to obvious facts which it would be inconvenient to know, or recklessness as to the facts.

Sheldon Deliveries Ltd v Willis (1972)
On a charge of permitting use of an uninsured MV, knowledge or wilful blindness must be proved.

NOTE
This last case follows the recent trend in which the courts have moved away from the previous decisions which made the offence an 'absolute' one, requiring no evidence of mens rea.

The main differences, therefore, between the offences of 'using' and those of 'causing' and 'permitting' are that 'using' requires no evidence of mens rea and introduces vicarious liability (i.e. the absolute responsibility of owners and employers for the acts of employees or any person using vehicles for them) while the other offences require some evidence of mens rea and for that reason there is no absolute vicarious liability for acts of others.

NOTE

The cases cited above on the subject of 'using, causing and permitting use' have been selected as illustration of what would appear to be the present trend. The student may well come across cases which conflict (or appear to conflict) with those cited, but these will generally be found to be of a comparatively early date and can be regarded as being no longer applicable.

Chapter 3 Reckless riding or driving

1. Summary of offences

I: on indictment
S: summarily
P: provisional powers under s. 164 (see p. 29)

	OFFENCE	PLACE	TRIAL	AWW
a) Motor vehicles only (but not tram-cars)	Road Traffic Act 1972: i) s. 1: causing death by reckless driving	Road	I	See p. 31
	ii) s. 2: reckless driving	Road	I or S	P
b) Any carriage or vehicle including motor vehicles and pedal cycles	i) Offences against the Person Act 1861, s. 35: cause bodily harm by wanton or furious driving or by racing	Any-where	I	See p. 3
	ii) Public Health Act 1925*, s. 74: so as to endanger life or limb of any person, or to common danger	Street	S	Yes, if found committing†
	iii) Highways Act 1835, s. 78: drive furiously so as to endanger life or limb	Any high-way	S	No
	iv) Town Police Clauses Act 1847, s. 28: drive furiously to annoyance, obstruction or danger	Place of public access	S	Yes, if found committing†
c) Pedal cycles only	Road Traffic Act 1972, s. 17: reckless riding	Road	S	P

* Not in MPD where the Metropolitan Police Act 1839, s. 54 applies instead.
† If by summons, information has to be laid by local authority.

	OFFENCE	PLACE	TRIAL	AWW
d) Animals	i) Highway Act 1835, s. 78: ride or drive horse or beast furiously so as to endanger life or limb	Any highway	S	No
	ii) Town Police Clauses Act 1847, s. 28: ride or drive horse or cattle furiously to cause obstruction, annoyance or danger	Place of public access	S	Yes, if found committing†

NOTES

a) For motor vehicles and pedal cycles, recourse should be made to Road Traffic Acts only unless there is a special reason otherwise, e.g. not on a road but **(b)(i)** or **(b)(iv)** may apply.

b) Law relating to notices of intended prosecution applies only to Road Traffic Act offences.

2. Road Traffic Act 1972, s. 2—motor vehicles

OFFENCE

It is an offence to drive a MV on a road recklessly.

(1) Introduction

Until amended by the Criminal Law Act 1977 this section detailed two offences—reckless driving and dangerous driving. To prove reckless driving evidence is required of knowledge on the part of the driver of a particular danger or hazard and a complete disregard of the extra care which he should accordingly have exercised. Dangerous driving, on the other hand, did not require proof of a mental element. It is understandable, therefore, that the prosecution almost always preferred the more straightforward charge (so far as evidence is concerned) of dangerous driving, and that prosecutions for reckless driving have been comparatively rare. Another unforeseen development was that prosecutions and courts, in view of the ever increasing back-log of cases awaiting trial, were perhaps more ready than they would otherwise

† If by summons, information has to be laid by local authority.

have been to take short cuts by accepting pleas of guilty to the lesser charge of careless driving and not proceeding with the more serious charge of dangerous driving. This in itself was not altogether unjustifiable for whether driving is dangerous or careless is a matter of degree, no mens rea having to be determined in either case, and the range of penalties available on conviction for careless driving was adequate for dangerous driving which was not reckless. The trouble was that little regard was being paid to the offence of reckless driving and too many reckless drivers were being dealt with under s. 3. The new arrangement seems far more logical. Driving which causes danger arises from not taking proper care in driving and should be prosecuted under s. 3 unless there is present an additional element, a mental element which must have existed and cannot be ignored, which is dealt with below.

(2) Meaning of 'recklessly'

The term is not defined by the Act, nor is there a precise definition of it to be found in any statute or the common law, though decided cases do indicate two factors which must be present to make any conduct reckless, namely:

a) knowledge of an appreciable danger (to oneself or any other person) in pursuing a course of action, and

b) the deliberate taking of that action despite that risk.

On this basis the tests which have to be applied to driving a MV may be stated as follows:

a) Do the circumstances supply evidence of a knowledge on the part of the driver of the existence of a particular and serious danger, or at least strongly indicate that he must have had that knowledge?*

b) Was the manner of driving such as to indicate a completely inadequate reaction to the danger ahead?

If the answer to each of these queries is in the affirmative, then the basic elements of reckless driving are present.

(3) Defences

The fact that a vehicle 'behaved' dangerously on a road does not preclude a defence based on sudden loss of control of the vehicle through no fault of the

---

* Examples of evidence to support this are

a) prevailing weather conditions, particularly fog, ice or driving rain;

b) the presence of police or other warning signs specially, conspicuously and clearly placed as warnings of a danger ahead;

c) a danger ahead which must have been obvious, e.g. a crowded street;

d) the driver was a local person who must have known well the road concerned and its particular hazards.

driver by an involuntary loss of faculties (automatism) or unsuspected mechanical defect in the vehicle.

1) AUTOMATISM—This is sudden loss of control over mind or movement of limbs, or a sudden attack of illness producing limb movements which are involuntary and not consciously willed by the driver.

Hill v Baxter (1957)
See p. 14.

R v Sibbles (1959)
It is no defence to dangerous driving that it was caused by the sudden attack of a blackout or dizzy spell which the driver knew was likely to occur. The degree of probability that such illness or fit might occur is a question of fact for the court to decide when the driver knows of its liability to take place.

Watmore v Jenkins (1962)
A diabetic who drove for five miles in a state of confusion was convicted. The defence of automatism will avail only when the affliction is not connected with any deliberate act or conduct of the accused and arises from a cause which a reasonable person would not think likely to occur and which the accused did not think might happen. Evidence of continued driving movements tends to negative a defence of automatism.

R v Budd (1962)
When 'automatism' is put forward by the defence as an explanation no burden of proving it rests on the defence, but when evidence of it is put forward the onus lies on the prosecution to disprove it beyond reasonable doubt.

R v Arnold (1964)
See p. 13.

Stevenson v Beatson (1965)
Where the defendant suggested but failed to prove that he had been in a state of automatism he was convicted.

R v Isitt (1978)
In the absence of a defence of insanity or automatism a motorist has no defence to a charge of reckless driving on the ground that his mind was malfunctioning. Where his mind was working to the extent of purposely driving in order to get away from the scene of an accident he was driving even though his mind may have been shut to any moral inhibitions.

The following case goes even further than those above:

Simpson v Peat (1952)
Bad driving in the agony of collision is not sufficient to prove an offence under s. 2 or s. 3, providing the driver was driving properly and wisely before the collision took place.

II) MECHANICAL DEFECT

R v Spurge (1961)

A mechanical defect might be a defence if it causes a sudden total loss of control and was in no way due to any fault of the driver, but it is no defence where the defect was known to the driver or should have been discovered by him had he exercised reasonable prudence.

(4) Prosecutions

NOTE

It is common practice to link up, as an alternative, a charge of careless driving (triable summarily only) with that of the offence under s. 2, the main reason being that should the accused elect to go for trial on the more serious charge, the lesser one remains to be heard at the lower court should there be an acquittal on indictment.

The procedure varies according to whether the reckless driving charge is proceeded with summarily or not.

I) PROCEDURE WITH A VIEW TO COMMITTAL FOR TRIAL BY JURY

a) If there is a committal for trial by jury all other summary offences charged (including those of careless driving) are adjourned pending the result of the trial.

b) If there is a conviction on indictment further proceedings cannot be taken for offences based on facts considered by the jury, e.g. careless driving based on the same facts.

c) On acquittal the careless driving charge can be proceeded with summarily (provided NIP, if necessary, has been served and information laid within the period specified by law). This applies, too, to the case where a conviction for reckless driving is quashed on appeal.

d) If the magistrates find no prima facie case for trial by jury the charge is dismissed but the court can then deal with the careless driving charge if he has been served with a summons for this offence, or waives the summons, or the court decides to use its powers under RTA 1972, Sch. 4 (see p. 36).

II) PROCEDURE SUMMARILY

a) If the prosecutor wishes to apply for a summary trial, he should do so when the proceedings begin.

b) In a case where charges of reckless and of careless driving have been preferred, they cannot be heard together without the consent of the defendant.

c) When a defendant is convicted of careless driving and has also been summonsed for other summary offences arising out of the same incident, e.g. failing to conform to a traffic sign or to give precedence to a pedestrian at a crossing, the court may impose a substantial penalty for the careless driving and exercise leniency in respect of the others either by imposing a nominal sentence, or by deferring their adjudication after conviction by allowing the charges to remain on the file. This does not apply to other offences before the court on matters not arising out of the same facts, e.g. driving without licence, etc.

d) Where proceedings are taken against both parties involved in an accident, the cases cannot be heard at the same time unless both agree to this. If it is necessary to call either one of them, or both, to give evidence for the prosecution, the cases cannot be heard together, for a defendant cannot be called as a witness against himself.

(5) Evidence

Though the evidence of an eye witness is not needed, there must be some evidence of facts from which the court can infer the manner of driving. The mere fact of a collision by or between vehicles and their relative positions on a road or at a junction is not sufficient to secure a conviction, but evidence of tyre or skid marks, damage caused, condition of the vehicle together with the relevant positions of the vehicles may be sufficient.

R v Pomeroy (1935)
A charge of driving while disqualified should not be heard along with other charges under the Road Traffic Acts because this would prejudice the defendant (i.e. reveal a previous conviction).

Harris v Adair (1947)
An offence of driving or attempting to drive under the influence of drink can be tried along with one of reckless driving with the defendant's consent.

R v Ashbourne JJ (1950)
Cases against different defendants or several charges against the same defendant, if the facts are substantially the same, may be heard together provided all parties consent.

R v Taylor (1927)
Evidence of reckless driving five miles away was held to be admissible.

Hallett v Warren (1929)
Evidence of dangerous driving a few minutes earlier and two miles from the accident was admissible. The case suggests that where it is intended to adduce evidence of previous bad driving (or carelessness if careless driving is charged) the roads concerned must be within the court's jurisdiction and should be included in the information and in the notice of intended prosecution (see *R v Budd* (1961) below). Insufficient proof of such driving at one named road would not be a bar to conviction if proved at another named road.

R v Budd (1961)
The road upon which the reckless driving is alleged must be named in the notice of intended prosecution.

R v Chambers (1939)

When two defendants are tried before the same court (separately or together) on charges arising out of the same set of facts (e.g. an accident in which both were involved) the magistrates should announce their finding in the first case before starting to hear the second.

R v Ward (1954)

Evidence that the driver was under the influence of drink so as to be incapable of having proper control is not necessarily of itself evidence of dangerous driving, though admissible as a factor to be considered (see *R v McBride* below).

R v McBride (1961)

Providing the parties consent, a charge of driving while unfit through drink or drugs may be tried with one under ss. 2 or 3. Evidence of drinking is also admissible where a charge under s. 2 or s. 3 only is preferred but the court has an absolute discretion to allow this only when there is substantial proof that the drink taken adversely affected the driver and does not merely prejudice the case against him.

3. Road Traffic Act 1972, s. 17—pedal cycles

Section 17 provides the same offence in respect of riding a pedal cycle (recklessly) as does s. 2 in respect of motor vehicles, and the same principles apply. The offence, though, is triable summarily only. The section covers any cycle, not being a MV, whether it is a bicycle, tricycle or has four wheels or more (RTA 1972, s. 191).

4. Road Traffic Act 1972, s. 164—offenders: name and address: arrest

I) APPLICATION—The section applies only in respect of drivers of MV or riders of pedal cycles and offences under RTA 1972, ss. 2, 3, 17 and 18, i.e. reckless, careless or inconsiderate driving or riding.

II) NAME OR* ADDRESS—A driver or rider alleged to have committed any of these offences commits a summary offence if he refuses, on being requested *by any person* having reasonable ground for making the request, to give his name or* address, or gives a false name or* address.

---

* Note the 'or'—this is to avoid difficulty, e.g. if falsity is in one but not the other, or name is given but address refused.

III) POWER OF ARREST—The power to *arrest without warrant* is given to a constable who witnesses the offence, unless:

a) the offending MV driver either gives his name *and* address or produces his driving licence, or

b) the offending pedal cyclist gives his name *and* address.

NOTE
See also p. 314.

5. Road Traffic Act 1972, s. 1

OFFENCE

It is an offence to cause the death of another person by driving a motor vehicle on a road recklessly, i.e. by committing an offence against s. 2 (1–5 years).

I) COMPARISON WITH A MANSLAUGHTER CHARGE:

a) charge does not replace manslaughter which carries heavier liability (life imprisonment as against five years);

b) a manslaughter charge requires greater criminal culpability;

c) may be added as second count on indictment for manslaughter;

d) in both charges conviction may be of reckless driving under s. 2, although notice of intended prosecution has not been served;

e) manslaughter may be committed *anywhere* and with *any vehicle*.

II) EVIDENCE

R v Hennigan (1971)
The prosecution need only prove reckless driving and the fact that that driving was the cause of the death. There is no need to show that the reckless driving was the principal or a substantial cause of the accident. So long as it is more than a minimal cause the section applies.

It must be proved that the accused was guilty of reckless driving.

R v Thorpe (1972)
A blood/alcohol concentration above the prescribed limit tends to show that the amount of drink taken would adversely affect the driver, and evidence of this is admissible on a charge under s. 1.

III) PROCEDURE

a) When it is intended to prefer a charge of manslaughter or causing death by reckless driving, the coroner is informed so that the inquest may be formally opened (for the purpose of obtaining the coroner's order to dispose of the body) and adjourned until the prosecution is concluded.

b) If the intended charge is for a lesser offence (e.g. s. 2 or s. 3) the inquest should be concluded before the hearing.

R v Beresford (1952)
A charge of reckless or careless driving in which the circumstances involved the death of a person should not be tried by the court before the inquest upon such death is concluded.

IV) NOTES

a) The power to arrest for an offence under s. 1 is provided by the Criminal Law Act 1967, which makes it an 'arrestable' offence.

b) The provision of s. 179 re notices of intended prosecution does not apply.

6. Further references

As to:

a) disqualification and endorsements of driving licences—see pp. 159, 165;

b) notices of intended prosecution—see p. 284;

c) evidential value of breaches of Highway Code—see p. 52;

d) substitution of careless driving or cycling charge for one of reckless driving or cycling by a magistrates' court—see p. 36.

Chapter 4 Careless or inconsiderate driving or riding

1. Summary of offences

I: on indictment
S: summarily
P: provisional powers under s. 164 (see p. 29)

	OFFENCE	PLACE	TRIAL	AWW
a) Motor vehicles only	RTA 1972, s. 3: i) driving without due care and attention;	Road	S	P
	ii) driving without reasonable consideration	Road	S	P
b) All vehicles	Offences against the Person Act 1861*, ss. 35: Person in charge by wilful neglect cause bodily harm to any person	Any-where	I	See p. 3
c) Pedal cycles only	RTA 1972, s. 18: as for motor vehicles—see (a) above	Road	S	P

A-G v Joyce (1956)
Wilful neglect implies something of a negative nature. Failure to have a light at night on a horse-drawn vehicle can be wilful neglect.

NOTE
In any question dealing in general with offences of careless driving or riding, offences under the Highway Acts and Town Police Clauses Act are relevant—see pp. 1 and 3.

* This offence is not limited to injury caused by the driving or riding, nor to the driver or rider. Responsibility is on the person *in charge* of the vehicle. The injury can be to a passenger.

2. Road Traffic Act 1972, s. 3—motor vehicles

NOTE
Students are advised to read first the introduction relating to s. 2 on p. 24.

(1) Offences

It is an offence to drive a MV on a road:

a) without due care, or

b) without reasonable consideration for other road users.

R v Surrey JJ ex parte Witherick (1932)
A charge of driving 'without due care and attention or without reasonable consideration for other persons using the road' is bad for duplicity.

As to AWW, see p. 29.

(2) 'Without due care'

Simpson v Peat (1952)
If a driver did not exercise that degree of care and attention which a reasonably prudent man would have exercised in the circumstances, he is guilty even though it might be an error of judgment. In particular, it is a question of fact whether the defendant was driving carelessly.

McCrone v Riding (1938)
A learner driver cannot plead his inexperience as a defence to a charge of careless driving. The law requires the same standard from a learner as from an experienced driver.

Liddon v Stringer (1967)
A bus driver, reversing on the signal of his conductor, knocked down and killed a pedestrian and was convicted of careless driving. An appeal on ground of not being vicariously liable for negligence of conductor was dismissed as conductor was driver's 'eyes'; the driver had a duty to see that his 'eyes' were in a position to see what they should see.

NOTES

a) Because carelessness often creates danger, consideration of a charge under s. 2 (reckless driving) is generally necessary.

b) For this reason, this charge is generally regarded as being an alternative to s. 2, i.e. as the sole charge where the evidence does not justify a charge of reckless driving, or as a second 'count' to a charge of reckless driving (see p. 27).

c) Advantages of adding this charge to one under s. 2 are:
i) accused has opportunity to plead guilty to lesser charge, and this may be acceptable in the circumstances;
ii) if there is a committal for trial on s. 2, the s. 3 charge remains to be prosecuted in the lower court if the s. 2 charge fails on indictment.

d) If both charges are preferred, prosecution has to elect which one it wishes to proceed with.

e) Section covers trolley vehicles but not tramcars.

RES IPSA LOQUITUR

The civil law rule of evidence known as 'res ipsa loquitur' (facts can speak for themselves), which properly pertains to civil actions for damages based on negligence, seems to be intruding itself into criminal proceedings for careless driving arising out of accidents. The rule provides that where an accident is such as would not happen in the ordinary course of events with proper care, this itself affords reasonable evidence, in the absence of an explanation by the defendant, that the accident arose from want of care. The following cases illustrate it.

Wright v Wenlock (1971) No explanation
Car left the road and collided with a telegraph pole. Prosecution proved car and tyres to be in good condition. W was unable to give any explanation. Justices accepted submission that there was no case to answer for res ipsa loquitur does not apply on its own. *Held*, on appeal: though res ipsa loquitur has no application to criminal cases, the facts of a case may be such that in the absence of some explanation by the defendant, the only proper inference is careless driving. The prosecution does not have to negative every possible explanation, where none is offered by the defendant.

Rabjohns v Burgar (1971) No explanation
B's car collided with a wall. Road was dry and day fine. B could offer no explanation. There were skid marks behind the car. Justices found there was insufficient evidence on which to convict. *Held*, on appeal: the facts in such a case may be so strong that the only inference is that there has been careless driving.

Butty v Davey (1971) Explanation acceptable
Lorry negotiated one sharp bend but failed the next which was 130 yards further on and collided head-on with another lorry. Speed found not to be excessive. Defendant contended that the cause was a slippery road and the case was dismissed. *Held*, on appeal: res ipsa loquitur applies but the defence explanation was not fanciful and the justices were entitled to accept it.

Bensley v Smith (1972) No explanation

Car crossed central white line, went over to its offside and collided with car coming in opposite direction. No fault in the car and defendant could offer no explanation. Justices thought the cause could have been momentary illness and dismissed the case. *Held*, on appeal: as the defence of mechanical defect or illness was not put forward by the defence, the justices were wrong to speculate on potential defences. The crossing of the white line was itself evidence of careless driving in the absence of an explanation by the defence.

(3) 'Without reasonable consideration'

This offence is not generally regarded as an alternative to a 'reckless driving' charge for it does not necessarily include evidence of lack of care or of danger to others. It is applied to cases of 'bad manners' in driving, e.g. deliberately choosing to drive through a pool of water to splash pedestrians.

Pawley v Wharldall (1965)

Passengers on a bus alarmed at the speed it was being driven by the defendant are other persons using the road.

NOTE

As to power of a summary court to allow a charge under this section to be 'substituted' for one of reckless driving which has been heard but not proved, see **4** below.

3. Road Traffic Act 1972, s. 18—pedal cycles

The two offences with regard to riding a cycle are the same as those for driving a MV under s. 3 (see above), i.e. riding:

a) without due care, or

b) without reasonable consideration for other road users.

NOTES

a) For power of court to substitute charge under this section where a charge of reckless riding is not proved, see **4** below.

b) Section covers any bicycle, tricycle or cycle with four or more wheels not being a MV (RTA 1972, s. 196).

c) As to AWW, see p. 29.

4. Power of summary court on a charge of reckless driving

A *magistrates' court* during or immediately after hearing a reckless driving (or cycling) charge it considers not proved, can direct or allow a charge of careless or inconsiderate driving or cycling to be preferred forthwith and proceed on it by informing the accused (or his representative) of this and giving him opportunity to answer the new charge (including cross-examination of witnesses already heard) but it must, if it considers a defendant prejudiced in his defence by this, adjourn the hearing.

A NIP need not have been served in respect of the lesser charges (RTA 1972, Sch. 4, Part IV, paras. 4 and 7).

5. Evidence and procedure

a) For the purposes of the above RTA offences:
   i) section 179 applies, i.e. notices of intended prosecution;
   ii) non-observance of Highway Code has evidential value—see p. 52.

b) The following apply to careless and inconsiderate driving and cycling offences as they do to offences of reckless driving and cycling:
   i) penalty for refusing name and address (see p. 29);
   ii) power to arrest without warrant (see p. 29);
   iii) the defences of automatism and mechanical defect (see p. 26);
   iv) the paragraphs on 'prosecutions' and 'evidence' (see pp. 27, 28).

Chapter 5 **Drink and drugs**

1. Offences relating to motor vehicles only

(RTA 1972)

(1) Introduction

a) Outline—The following broad outline of the subject should make it easier for the student who masters it to make his way through the rather complicated legal provisions which relate to the offences connected with 'drink and driving', which are of two kinds, as follows:

a) driving, etc. while unfit to drive through drink or drugs (the s. 5 offence), and

b) driving, etc. with alcohol in the body (as ascertained from a laboratory test of a specimen of blood or urine) above the prescribed limit (the s. 6 offence).

b) Arrest—

a) In respect of a suspected s. 6 offence the power to arrest depends on the outcome of the request made (in specified circumstances) by a constable *in uniform* for a breath test to be taken.

b) A constable, *whether in uniform or not*, can and should arrest and take to the police station any driver or person in charge of a MV found in such a condition through drink or drugs that he is unfit to drive. The breath test plays no part in this.

c) Breath tests at the police station—In the case of an arrest for either offence a breath test must be required at the police station. In the case of a s. 6 offence this will be for the second time—the first having provided the grounds for arrest.

I) ARREST FOR THE SUSPECTED S. 6 OFFENCE—A negative breath test is conclusive and is followed by release. If the test proves positive, or is refused, the person is subject to the procedure for obtaining a specimen of blood or urine for laboratory testing.

II) ARREST FOR A S. 5 OFFENCE—A positive test, or refusal, introduces the same procedure relating to obtaining a specimen for analysis as in (I) above. A negative test does not necessarily terminate proceedings for the charge alleges 'unfitness' through drink or drugs, and a person can still be unfit to drive though the alcohol in his body does not reach the prescribed limit, or through drugs alone, or a combination of drink and drugs. In the case of a negative breath test, if the s. 5 charge is being pursued (having regard to other evidence of condition, e.g. the evidence warranting arrest, medical test), the arrested person can still be required to furnish a specimen of blood or urine, the result of the analysis of which (or the refusal without reasonable cause to furnish a specimen) becomes of evidential value.

d) Result of laboratory test—If the result of the analysis reveals alcohol in the body above the prescribed limit, evidence to support the s. 6 charge is complete. The s. 6 offence can then also be preferred against a person arrested for the s. 5 offence, for the penalties for both offences are identical. Where the analysis does not reveal the presence of alcohol above the limit the s. 6 charge is not, of course, applicable but the report of the analyst as to proportion of alcohol (or drugs) found is of evidential value and may be introduced by the prosecution or the defence in the s. 5 charge.

e) Refusal to provide specimen—'Refusal' includes failure to provide.

f) Road and public place—Both the above offences relate to driving, etc. on a road (see p. 14) or other public place. The following cases refer to the meaning of 'public place' for the purpose of these offences.

R v Collinson (1931) Private field
A private field to which the public were temporarily invited to watch racing was held to be a public place, although it could be closed at any time and particular persons could be refused admission.

Elkins v Cartlidge (1947) Inn car park
A parking place at the side of an inn led through an open gateway into a further enclosure for parking. The enclosure was held to be a public place, as being a place to which the public had access in fact. Followed in *Sandy v Martin* (1974).

Pugh v Knipe (1972) Private car park of a club
The MV was on land owned by a private members' club outside the front entrance to the club premises and not separated from the members' car park. Access to it was from an unfenced public footpath giving access also to a public car park and swimming baths. There was no physical obstruction to prevent anyone from gaining access to the club car park at any time and no car park attendant was employed there. There was no evidence that the public actually used the club car park. *Held:* a car park for members only is not public. To turn this or other private land into a public place it is necessary to show that the public had access to it and actually went there and used it, and this was not done in the present case.

Williams v Boyle (1962) Dance hall car park
A car park at a dance hall is not necessarily a 'public place' if used by

private guests only. There must be evidence of use by the public who may be ticket holders.

R v Waters (1963)

A place may be a 'public place' notwithstanding that there is a right to exclude particular members or a particular class of the public. If only a restricted class of person is permitted or invited to have access, the place is a private place; if, on the other hand only a restricted class is excluded, it is a public place. Whether a place is a 'public place' is largely a question of degree and fact.

Before a public place may become a private place, there must be evidence to show that at a particular point of time there is some 'physical obstruction' to be overcome so that anybody going there does so in defiance of the prohibition.

(2) Unfit to drive through drink or drugs

(RTA 1972, s. 5)

a) Offences (triable summarily only)—Both relate to a MV on a road or public place. It is an offence:

a) *when driving or attempting to drive*, to be unfit* to drive through drink or drugs (s. 5 (1));

b) *when in charge*, to be unfit* to drive through drink or drug (s. 5 (2)).

Thomson v Knights (1947)

A charge covering 'drink or drugs' is not bad for duplicity.

Armstrong v Clarke (1957)

Insulin is a drug.

b) 'In charge'—Defendant to be deemed *not* in charge if he proves† that the circumstances were such (at material time) that there was no likelihood of his driving so long as he remained unfit through drink or drugs. If in any case evidence of driving (or attempt) is doubtful, the offence of being in charge can be used, for 'person in charge' includes driver.

Crichton v Burrell (1951)

'In charge' means being responsible for the control or driving and not necessarily that the person was actually driving or attempting to drive. The appellant was in possession of the ignition key and standing by the open door of the car when arrested. He had arranged for another person to drive him home and was waiting for the man at the time. *Held:* he was not in charge.

---

* A person is to be regarded as unfit to drive if his ability to drive is for the time being impaired.

† The onus is less than 'beyond reasonable doubt'—probability is sufficient.

Haines v Roberts (1953)
A person remains in charge until he has given the vehicle into another's charge.

John v Bentley (1961)
The court is entitled to find that the defendant had discharged the burden of proving that there was no likelihood of his driving whilst unfit by reason of his prior agreement with companions not to drive even though he was found in a drunken stupor on the floor of the vehicle.

Morton v Confer (1963)
The court must be satisfied on the balance of probabilities in all the circumstances of the case that there was no likelihood that the accused would depart from his intention not to drive while unfit to do so.

Woodage v Jones (1974)
A motorist cannot remove the responsibility of being in charge of a vehicle merely by turning his back on it and walking away. Once in charge of a vehicle on a road or in a public place he remains in charge until the vehicle is handed over to some other person's charge or he has arrived at the ultimate end of the journey. (In this case the motorist was half a mile away from his car.)

c) Procedure

I) AWW—*Any* constable can AWW any person committing an offence under this section.

R v Wilson (1975)
If facts justify the constable reasonably thinking the person is probably guilty, this is enough.

R v Roff (1976)
The arrest has to be contemporaneous with the offence, i.e. made while the offence is being committed or very shortly thereafter.

R v Estop (1976)
An arrest one hour after the offence, at another place, and by a police officer who had not seen the original offence, is not justified by the section.

II) BREATH TEST—A person arrested must be given an opportunity to provide a specimen of breath for test while at the police station (RTA 1972, s. 8). The offering of the breath test enables the provisions of s. 9 as to taking of specimens (and liabilities for failure to comply) to apply (see p. 49). If the test is accepted and proves negative then the procedure of s. 7 with regard to requesting a specimen of blood or urine (see next paragraph) applies, for the absence of positive test reaction does not rule out the presence in the body of alcohol to some degree or a drug, or a combination of both, which might have produced unfitness to drive.

III) EVIDENCE OF SPECIMEN ANALYSIS (s. 7)—

a) In any proceedings under s. 5 the court must have regard to any evidence given of the proportion or quantity of alcohol or drug in the body of the accused ascertained by analysis of a specimen of blood (taken by a doctor with consent of accused) or of urine provided by the accused.

b) The request for a specimen should be made by a constable for if this is done (but not otherwise) a failure or refusal to comply may (unless reasonable cause is shown) be treated by the court as supporting evidence given for prosecution, or rebutting any evidence for the defence as to the accused's condition at the relevant time—but note next paragraphs as to correct procedure.

c) The prisoner is not to be regarded as having failed (or having refused) to provide a laboratory specimen unless the constable:
i) *first* asks accused to provide a blood sample and this is refused;
ii) *then, secondly*, requests the provision of two urine samples within the next hour and there is a refusal or failure to comply; and
iii) *finally* again requests a blood sample, which is again refused.

The first specimen of urine is to be disregarded so far as analysis is concerned (s. 7 (3)) for it is of no value for that purpose. There is no need to preserve it (*R v Welsby* (1972)).

d) The constable requesting the specimen must offer to supply to the accused, in a suitable container, part of the specimen, or, in the case of a blood specimen which cannot be divided, another specimen which the accused consents to give.

Cases under the section indicate that the proper procedure is that the constable should tell the accused, when making the request:
i) the purpose—i.e. to determine the alcoholic content by analysis and thus secure evidence;
ii) that one sample (or part of it) will be provided for his own purposes if he wishes this;
iii) that he is entitled to refuse; and
iv) that his refusal might, by law, be regarded by the court as supporting the case for the prosecution unless he gives good reason for refusing.

e) If the accused asks for a specimen when it is being taken, evidence as to its analysis will not be admitted in evidence for the prosecution unless the specimen analysed is one of two taken (or part of a single specimen divided into two) *and* the other specimen or part was supplied to the accused.

Kidd v Kidd (1967)
The division of a specimen into three parts, instead of two, is not a failure to comply with this requirement. The intention is to give the defendant one part. Whether the other part is kept as one or divided into two is irrelevant.

R v Byers (1972)
It is best, to avoid confusion, for the constable, after the suspect has agreed to provide a specimen, to then ask: 'Do you want a part of the specimen?'

f) Proof of compliance with the above may be of such importance later that a complete record of the progress of the above procedure (including times) should be made in the notebook and included in any statement.

g) *Analysis of specimen* must be carried out by an authorised analyst. Analysts at the HO Forensic Science Laboratories and the MPD Laboratory have been authorised.

d) Evidence

I) ANALYSIS—On the question of unfitness to drive the court must have regard to evidence of analysis of the specimen—see (c) (III) above, and all the conditions which apply.

II) CONSENT—Refusal to give consent, on request of constable, to the taking of or to providing a specimen may be regarded as evidence for the prosecution or to rebut defence as to the condition of accused at the time, unless reasonable cause for refusal is given.

R v Lewis (1964)
The offer to supply part of the urine specimen must be made simultaneously with or shortly after or immediately preceding the request to provide the specimen. This section applies only to a request by a police constable, not to a specimen taken by a doctor.

R v Roberts (1964)
A man who has already urinated is deemed to have been 'requested to provide a sample' if he is asked to hand over the container to the police, but the fact that the defendant had himself asked to be allowed to urinate made no difference to the obligations placed upon the police to comply with the conditions which safeguard the admissibility of the analyst's certificate, i.e. explaining the purpose of the sample requested and offering to supply half of the specimen at the time of request.

R v Mitten (1965)
Failure to offer to supply a urine specimen either simultaneously or shortly after the request to supply does not render such evidence inadmissible as a matter of law, but the trial judge must exclude such evidence unless satisfied that the accused's case is not prejudiced as a result of the omission.

III) EVIDENCE BY CERTIFICATE—A certificate signed by an authorised analyst as to the proportion of alcohol or drug found in the blood, or if in urine the proportion in the blood which corresponds with that found in the specimen concerned, is evidence of these matters, but the prosecution cannot use a certificate:

a) unless a copy was served on accused not less than seven days before trial, and

b) if accused, not less than three days before the hearing, serves notice that he requires the analyst's attendance.

A certificate signed by a doctor that he took the blood sample with the person's consent is also evidence of such matters and of the doctor's qualifications.

e) Medical examination—The procedure under s. 7 (as to specimens of blood and urine) does not affect the long established practice of obtaining medical evidence based on physical examination.

(3) Alcohol in body being above the prescribed limit

PRIMARY OFFENCES (TRIABLE SUMMARILY ONLY)

These, applicable only to a MV on a road or other public place, are committed by:

a) *any person who drives or attempts to drive a MV* having consumed alcohol in such a quantity that the proportion thereof in his blood, as ascertained from a laboratory test for which he subsequently provides a specimen under this Act, exceeds the prescribed limit* (s. 6 (1));

b) *any person in charge of a MV* having consumed alcohol as aforesaid (s. 6 (2)).

It would be impossible to offer a breath test to a person while he is driving. 'Drive', therefore, has to be given its ordinary meaning by which a person may remain the driver though he is not in fact operating the controls, but the point at which he can be said to have ceased driving is a matter dependent on the circumstances of the particular case (*R v Price* (1968); *Campbell v Tormey* (1968); *Pinner v Everett* (1969)). Locking the car door is not, as such, to be regarded as the last act of driving (*R v Garforth* (1970)). A driver who has stopped the car and is conversing with passengers is not driving (*Stevens v Thornborrow* (1970)). Where the constable told the suspect that he was arresting him with a view to detaining him until the arrival of the breathalyser, which came within ten minutes, it was held that the lapse of ten minutes did not affect the issue (for he would be still be 'driving' for the purpose of the section)† but the arrest was fatal, for the fact of arrest made it impossible for him to be driving (*Erskine v Hollin* (1971)). That an arrest terminates driving has been endorsed by *Anthony v Jenkins* (1971) (suspected of having had drink *after* arrest in immediate pursuit for stealing a MV). A person who, being followed by a police car, tries to avoid liability under the section by driving home and getting out of the car before he can be approached by the police officer may still be held to be driving. 'Driving' is an act of duration and not of an instant, and 'at the time' must be given a broad interpretation as signifying the occasion rather than the moment of time when the request was made (*R v Sakhuja* (1971) (got out of car in the street outside his home) and *Brooks v Ellis* (1972) (got out in the driveway of his home)). Where, in a

---

* The limit prescribed is 80 milligrammes of alcohol in 100 millilitres of blood, or 107 milligrammes of alcohol in 100 millilitres of urine (RTA 1972, s. 12).

† Only because the constable had power to act under the section. Where a plain clothes officer suspected alcohol in body and sent for a uniformed constable to offer the breath test, it was held that it was not possible to extend 'driving' throughout the period it took the uniformed constable to arrive (*R v Masters* (1972)).

police check for stolen vehicles, M was still in the driving seat of his car in the queue of stopped vehicles when the police officer reached him, M was held to be still driving (*Mendham v Lawrence* (1971)).

Edkin v Knowles (1973)

An attempt was made by the court in this case to summarise the collective effect of decided cases but it did little more than to advise that:

a) driving does not necessarily cease when the vehicle is brought to a standstill, e.g. driving continues:
  i) until all operations connected with driving have been completed (switching off, brakes set, etc.);
  ii) while the vehicle is stopped temporarily to conform with a legal requirement (e.g. traffic lights or for a police check on stolen vehicles) or for any purpose connected with driving;

b) driving has ceased:
  i) when the driver has reached the end of his journey and has completed the final driving duties referred to in (a) (i) above;
  ii) when the motorist has been prevented (e.g. by having been arrested by a constable) or persuaded from driving.

Crampton v Fish (1969)

A supervisor can be guilty of aiding and abetting a learner driver having alcohol above the limit, if the condition of the learner driver was such that he must have known that the limit had been exceeded.

'In charge'—If the evidence supporting a charge of driving (or attempt) is weak the accused can be charged with being in charge, for 'person in charge' includes driver. A person will not be convicted for the offence under (b) on p. 43 if he proves that the circumstances were such (at the material time) that there was no likelihood of his driving whilst the blood-alcohol concentration remained in excess of the limit, but the court may disregard this defence if the defendant's likelihood of not driving the vehicle is based on the fact that he had been injured or the vehicle damaged (s. 6 (3)).

It will be noted later that the only application s. 6 has to a person 'in charge' (*not* the driver), so far as breath tests and specimens for analysis are concerned, is to a person in charge who has already been arrested under s. 5 for being unfit through drink or drug.

BREATH TESTS (S. 8)

a) General—It will have been noted that the above offences are related to amounts of alcohol in the body as determined by analysis of specimens of blood or urine. Specimens for analysis can be obtained only at a police station (if hospital cases are for the moment excluded) by following a set procedure there. The use of breath testing devices is simply a means of screening drivers in certain circumstances to find out whether there is prima facie evidence of alcohol in the body above the prescribed limit, so that further investigation of a suspected offence can be justified on this ground, for evidence of breath test results will not be given in court proceedings. The law provides, where the conditions precedent are fulfilled, for breath test devices to be used at the roadside, at a police station after arrest, and at a hospital.

b) At or near the roadside (s. 8 (1))

I) GENERALLY—The following may be required by a *constable in uniform* to undergo a breath test at or near the place where the request is made: a person driving or attempting to drive a MV on a road or other public place if the constable reasonably suspects him:

a) of having alcohol in his body, or

b) of having committed a traffic offence* while the MV was in motion, but in this case the request must be made as soon as reasonably practicable after the offence.

Williams v Jones (1971)
The onus of proof that the constable had reasonable grounds to suspect alcohol in the body is on the prosecution. Suspicion is not enough, it must be reasonable suspicion.

Cooper v Rowlands (1971)
Evidence should be given that the constable was in uniform, but the court can assume this in the case of a motor patrol officer, in response to whose signal the defendant had stopped.

R v Jones (1969)
The requirement for a breath test can be made off a road so long as it is made in the course of a chain of events following sufficiently closely on an observed driving on a road ('fresh pursuit').

PRACTICAL NOTE

The constable will require some indication of recent drinking to support 'reasonable cause to believe'. This does not apply to (b). It will be noted that the above provisions do not apply to a person in charge of a stationary vehicle, although the next paragraph (as to accidents) might.

II) AFTER ACCIDENTS—If a road accident involving a MV has occurred on a road or public place a *constable in uniform* may require to undergo the breath test any person he reasonably believes was driving or attempting to drive the vehicle at the time of the accident—either at or near the place where the request is made or (unless the person is in hospital) at a police station† specified by him (s. 8 (2)).

III) FAILURE TO COMPLY—If any such person without reasonable cause fails to take the test he commits a summary offence but no arrest can be made unless the constable has reason to believe (smell, conduct, etc.) that the person has

---

* *'Traffic offence'* means an offence under any provision of the RT Acts, the RTR Act 1967, or Regulations thereunder.

† This alternative is to cover a constable who is not carrying a breath tester. A refusal to go is equivalent to refusing the test.

alcohol in his body. The power to AWW does not extend to any person while he is in hospital as a patient. See *R v Kelly* (1972) on p. 47.

iv) TEST POSITIVE—If the test is positive (i.e. shows probable presence of alcohol above prescribed limit) the constable may AWW (except in case of a hospital patient).

v) TEST NEGATIVE—If the test is negative, *no* further steps are authorised under the Act, though the possible application of s. 5 (unfit to drive through drink or drug) may in special circumstances have to be considered.

vi) PRACTICAL POINTS RE TESTING DEVICES—

a) Discolouration of crystals may not be clearly seen in certain street lighting (e.g. sodium, mercury)—use torch, lamp on vehicle, etc.
b) The device is of no further use if test is negative and can be disposed of, but with care for crystals are corrosive. Immersion for a time in water in plastic container is recommended.
c) If test is positive take device to the station to support arrest action.
d) Used devices are of no use in court as discolouration spreads with time.

NOTES

The breathalyser must be assembled properly, otherwise it is not the device as approved. If failure to provide specimen is due to faulty device and not to refusal or fault of the driver an arrest is not justified (*Hoyle v Walsh* (1969)). The maker's instructions as to the use of Alcotest 80 have not the force of law. It is important that they should be followed as far as practicable but a departure from instructions does not necessarily vitiate a test if the constable has acted reasonably and in good faith on the knowledge of the facts he possesses (*DPP v Carey* (1969); *Gill v Forster* (1971); *R v Parsons* (1972)), and in the absence of any point made before the prosecution closes its case the constable will be presumed to have acted in good faith (*Rendell v Hooper* (1970)). With regard to the twenty minute interval direction a constable would be well advised to enquire when alcohol was last taken, but this is not a legal requirement (*DPP v Carey* (1969)). Formal proof of ministerial approval of Alcotest 80 is no longer necessary, and judicial notice can be taken of this fact (*R v Jones* (1969)). Where suspect refused to wait (after three minutes) for the arrival of the breathalyser it was held that there was a refusal to give a specimen and his arrest was justified (*R v Wagner* (1970)). An arrest is a necessary antecedent to later procedures, and for this reason the constable arresting should make it clear to the person (if practicable) that he is being arrested or taken into custody (*R v Wall* (1969)). The breath test must be offered by a constable who has the required suspicion, but this requirement is satisfied if the suspicion of constable A is passed on to constable B who requests the test (*Erskine v Hollin* (1971)). The offence relates to blood/alcohol concentration while driving: drink taken afterwards and before the laboratory specimen is obtained vitiates the analysis (*Rowlands v Hamilton* (1971)).

c) **At the police station**—Any person taken to the police station under the provisions of this Act (i.e. where roadside test is positive, on failure to comply at roadside where there is evidence of drinking, or refusal to go to a police station on request after an accident) or arrested under s. 5 as unfit to drive, must be given the opportunity to take a breath test at the police station.

Subsequent procedure depends on what results from the offer of the blood test:

I) POSITIVE TEST—Constable may proceed to request specimen for analysis (see later).

If an arrest is made under s. 5 and the station breath test is positive proceedings can be taken under s. 6 if there has been no abandonment of the intention to proceed under s. 5 at the time the breath test was offered (*Atkinson v Lumsden* (1970)). This applies even though medical evidence after examination does not support a s. 5 prosecution, if there has been no such abandonment of intention by the police (*Coneys v Nicholson* (1970)).

II) NEGATIVE TEST—Only procedure left is that under sections 5 and 7 (unfit to drive), if appropriate to the circumstances.

III) FAILURE TO COMPLY—No offence committed but proceed to request specimen for analysis (see below).

R v Kelly (1972)

'Fail' means not doing—whatever the reason, because in the subsection providing power to arrest on failure, and in the subsection enabling a laboratory specimen to be required on failure, the qualification 'without reasonable excuse' is omitted. In this case the defendant could not provide a specimen of breath because of a throat operation.

NOTE

Breath tests taken within a very short time after drinking alcohol give too 'high' a reading (due to alcohol still remaining in the mouth). After twenty minutes or so mouth alcohol disappears. It is to meet the possibility of the first reading being misleading that the second breath test is made compulsory at the police station—which would normally be more than twenty minutes after consumption of alcohol. It is, therefore, important that every precaution should be taken to ensure that a person in custody has no opportunity to take further drink (e.g. from a bottle in his possession) and also that at least twenty minutes transpire between first and second breath tests.

d) At a hospital—If in the case of **(b)** (II) above (accidents) the suspected driver is a patient in a hospital the breath test can be offered there by a *constable in uniform provided* the doctor concerned is notified and does not object on the ground that this would be prejudicial to proper care and treatment (see note (b) on p. 49).

I) TEST POSITIVE—Procedure for requesting laboratory specimen may be followed.

II) TEST NEGATIVE—Ends procedure under this Act, though proceedings may still be considered for s. 5 offence, if appropriate.

III) FAILURE TO TAKE TEST—Offence committed, if failure is without reasonable cause, but no power to AWW. Proceed to request specimen for analysis if presence of alcohol in body is reasonably suspected.

REQUESTS FOR SPECIMENS OF BLOOD OR URINE (s. 9)

a) The place—Requests for specimens for laboratory tests can be made only by a constable (not necessarily in uniform) and only:

I) AT A POLICE STATION—to which the person has been taken after arrest, or to which he goes at the request of a constable in uniform after an accident to be offered a breath test (see (2) above as to breath tests).

The conditions precedent are that the person has been offered a breath test *there* and *either*:

a) the test was positive, or

b) the person has failed (or refused) to provide the breath specimen (s. 8 (1)).

> **Butler v Easton (1969)**
> Breath test taken at one police station and prisoner taken to another station for provision of blood specimen. *Held:* invalid, for the request for the specimen of blood or urine has to be made at the police station at which the breath test was offered.

II) AT A HOSPITAL—at which the person is a patient after an accident.

The conditions precedent here are that a breath test had been offered previously (*whether on the roadside, at the specified police station, or at the hospital*) following an accident and either:

a) the test was positive, *or*

b) the person failed (or refused) to provide the specimen *and a constable has reasonable cause to suspect him of having alcohol in his body* (s. 9 (2)).

NOTE
The difference between conditions applicable to (I) and (II), which are italicised in (II) above, should be noted.

b) The request procedure (s. 9 (5))—*Before* making the request the constable *must* warn the person that failure to provide the specimen may make him liable to imprisonment, fine and disqualification of driving licence. If this is not done the consequences of failure to comply (see below) do not apply. The procedure (after the warning) is:

a) to request a specimen of blood;

b) if he refuses (a), to request two specimens of urine to be provided within one hour of the request;

c) if he refuses or fails to comply with (a) or (b) then he must be asked again to provide a specimen of blood.

If there is a refusal at stage (c) without reasonable cause an offence is committed (see below).

NOTES

a) A blood specimen can be taken only by a doctor.

b) In the case of a hospital patient the request for specimens cannot be made unless the doctor concerned has been notified and does not object. The doctor can legally object only on the grounds that the provision of the specimen, or the requirement to provide it, or the necessary warning as to liability, would be prejudicial to the proper care or treatment of the patient.

Baker v Foulkes (1975)
The police officer is not required to notify the doctor of his intention to warn the patient of the possible consequences of his failure to provide the specimen.

Oxford v Lowton (1978)
Provided that the doctor is told that it is proposed to require a specimen before the requirement is made, it does not matter that the patient overhears this being done. What matters is that the doctor should not be prevented from making an effective decision regarding the proper care of the patient.

OFFENCES OF FAILING TO UNDERGO BREATH TEST OR PROVIDE SPECIMEN (S. 8)

Note the two offences already referred to, i.e. without reasonable cause:

a) *in the case of a breath test*, failing to provide a specimen of breath when legally required to do so by a constable in uniform (s. 8 (3)) (refers to offers of tests 'on the spot' or at a hospital, but not at a police station unless after a road accident);

b) *in case of specimen for analysis*, failing without reasonable excuse to provide a specimen in pursuance of a requirement made under the Act, provided the procedure of s. 9 (5) and (7) has been followed (see the request procedure, p. 48) (s. 9 (3)).

The liability in (b) is to be proceeded against and punished as if the offence charged were the offence under s. 6 appropriate to the circumstances, i.e. according to whether the person had been driving, attempting to drive, or in charge of* the MV at the 'relevant time'.

'Relevant time'—This means in the case of a breath test taken as a result of an accident, the time of the accident; otherwise it means the time at which the

---

* This will only apply to an arrest under s. 5, for it will have been noted that s. 6 provides no powers as to breath tests or arrests in relation to persons not driving, or attempting to drive.

breath test was requested under s. 8 (1) (i.e. on or near a road because of traffic offence or on suspicion of having consumed alcohol).

NOTE

In the case of a refusal the excuse of a desire to have a solicitor present is not a reasonable one. A subsequent offer to supply does not undo a refusal (*Law v Stephens* (1971)). To lay down conditions for the supply of a specimen, e.g. that the doctor must take a blood specimen otherwise than in accordance with established practice, amounts to a refusal (*Rushton v Higgins* (1972)). A condition that the sample would be given to the defendant's own doctor rather than a police doctor, where both are present, is not a refusal where the defendant has shown that he is willing to do all that was required of him (*Bayliss v Thames Valley Police CC* (1978)). It is for the judge and not the jury to decide whether the excuse is reasonable (*R v Walters* (1971)).

RELEASE FROM CUSTODY

Any person who has been lawfully required to provide a laboratory specimen may be detained until he provides a breath test to a constable which has a negative result (s. 11).

CHARGE OR SUMMONS

As laboratory tests cannot be carried out without delay of several days the person in custody must be released to be proceeded against by summons if proceedings are dependent upon the result of an analysis (*R v McKenzie* (1970)).

EVIDENCE BY CERTIFICATE

The provisions concerning the admissibility in evidence of a certificate as to the result of the laboratory test are the same as for proceedings under s. 5 (see p. 49).

PREVIOUS CONVICTION

A conviction for driving or attempting to drive a MV on a road or public place:

a) while unfit to drive through drink or drug, or

b) with an excess proportion of alcohol in the blood, or

c) failing to provide a specimen for laboratory test in circumstances as will render him liable to be charged with and punished for the offence in (b)*,

is treated as a previous conviction on a subsequent conviction for any of those offences.

---

* See above as to effect of failure to comply (p. 49).

RECORDING OF PROCEDURES

The correctness of procedures, lapses of times, etc. may always be called to question in court proceedings. It is important, therefore, that every relevant aspect should be placed on record.

DISQUALIFICATION AND ENDORSEMENTS OF DRIVING LICENCES

See pp. 159, 165, respectively.

2. Offence relating to pedal cycles

RTA 1972, s. 19—pedal cycles

I) OFFENCE—It is an offence to ride a pedal cycle (not being a MV) on a road or public place being unfit to ride through drink or drug. Summary offence. .AWW if found committing offence. Section covers vehicles with four wheels or more.

II) 'UNFIT TO RIDE'—This means being under influence of drink or drug to such an extent as to be incapable of having proper control.

III) AUTO-CYCLES—A pedal cycle equipped with an auxiliary engine has, for other sections of the RT Acts, been held to be a motor vehicle, if the engine is not useless.

Floyd v Bush (1953)
If the engine is connected up an auto-cycle is a MV whether the engine is running or not.

IV) EVIDENCE—The provisions of the RTA 1972 (as to specimens of blood or urine) do not apply.

3. Offence relating to other carriages, horses and cattle

Licensing Act 1872, s. 12

I) OFFENCE—It is an offence to be drunk while in charge on any highway or other public place of any carriage, horse, cattle, or steam engine. Summary offence.

II) LIMITS—Does not apply to any case where there is also liability under the Road Traffic Act.

III) ARREST—Power to arrest without warrant is given for the above offence provided the person was *found committing* the offence.

Chapter 6 **Restrictions on use of highways, etc.**

1. Rules of the road

(1) The 'nearside rule'

What has been called the 'rule of the road' (i.e. that vehicles being driven or ridden on a road should be kept to the nearside) has existed from time immemorial, but until recently the law has gone no further than to require that a vehicle must be kept on the left or nearside when necessary to make way for an approaching or overtaking vehicle (Highway Act 1835, s. 78). The rule has been incorporated in the Highway Code which advises a 'road user on wheels' to keep to the left, except when road signs or markings indicate otherwise or when intending to overtake or turn right or to pass a stationary vehicle, pedestrians, etc. The code does not create offences, but failure to observe its provisions may be relied upon by parties to any proceedings (criminal or civil, and including offences under the RT Acts) to establish or negative any liability in question (RTA 1972, s. 37). There are also under the Road Traffic Acts some provisions compelling drivers to keep to the nearside in special circumstances, e.g. the unbroken white traffic lines, or when parking at night.

(2) The 'Highway Code'

This publication, for the guidance of all persons using roads, is issued by the Secretary of State. Failure on the part of a person to observe any provision of the code does not of itself amount to an offence, but may tend to establish or negative his liability in proceedings for any offence (RTA 1972, s. 37).

This booklet is readily available to police officers and no more should be needed for the purposes of this handbook than to recite the main headings of the Highway Code as a reminder of the range of subjects with which it deals, and to provide a basis upon which the student can test his knowledge of it.

ROAD USERS ON FOOT

Walking along	Crossing the road at junctions
Crossing the road	Crossings controlled by traffic
Zebra crossings	lights, police, wardens, or school
Pelican crossings	crossing patrols

Getting on and off public vehicles
Crossing one way streets, bus lanes,
  or where there is an island in the
  road, or any road at night

Guard rails
Emergency vehicles
Railway level crossings

ROAD USERS ON WHEELS
Vehicle, safe condition
Safety equipment
Signs and signals
Moving off
Driving along
Driving in fog
Safety of pedestrians
Animals
Lines and lanes
Single track roads
Overtaking
Road junctions, controlled and
  otherwise

Roundabouts
Reversing
Turning right
Turning left
Lamps
Use of horn
Flashing headlamps
Waiting and parking
Breakdown and accidents
Accidents involving dangerous
  goods

MOTORWAY DRIVING
General
Joining motorways
On the motorway
Overtaking
Stopping and parking
Lane discipline

Breakdowns
Obstructions
Warning signals
Leaving the motorway
Fog hazards

ADDITIONAL
Extra rules for cyclists
The road user and animals
The road user and railway level
  crossings:
  a) with gates and full barriers;
  b) open crossings;
  c) automatic half barrier
    crossings

Signals to other road users:
  a) direction indicators;
  b) stop lights;
  c) arm signals;
  d) police signals
Traffic signs and road markings
Stopping distances
Vehicle markings
First aid
Prevention of theft

2. Obstruction

(1) General

The basic right of any person to use a highway is nothing more than to have
free passage over it. Highways were and are provided to travel along and use
of a highway which is unreasonable, wilful, or negligent, and which thereby

prevents or is likely to prevent the right of another to free passage over it, is an obstruction, not only of the highway but of that right. Wilful or unnecessary obstructions of the highway (including footpaths and bridleways) are offences under a variety of statutes, some of them designed for traffic conditions of days long gone, but the most important of them are the Road Traffic Act 1972 and the Highways Act 1959.

(2) Summary of offences

ANY VEHICLE

Dangerous obstruction*: RTA 1972, s. 24
Cause or permit *any* vehicle or trailer to remain on a road so as to be likely to cause danger to others by reason of its condition, position, or other circumstances.

Procedure

Summons

MOTOR VEHICLES AND TRAILERS

a) **Obstruction: MV (C & U) Regulations 1978, r. 122**
   To cause or permit a MV or trailer to stand on a road so as to cause an unnecessary obstruction.

   Summons

b) **Obstruction by any person opening door: MV (C & U) Regulations 1978, r. 125**
   Open or cause or permit to be opened any door of a MV (or trailer) on a road so as to cause injury or danger to any person.

   Summons

BY ANY MEANS

Highways Act 1959, s. 121
Wilfully obstruct without lawful authority or excuse the free passage of any highway: see also Highways Act 1971, p. 74.

Summons generally but power to AWW if found committing

ROPES AND WIRES, ETC.

Highways Act 1959, s. 141
To place or cause to be placed across any highway any rope, wire or other apparatus likely to cause danger to other road users without giving adequate warning of the danger.

Summons

---

* Notice of intended prosecution needed.

Wall v Williams (1966)
Where a taxi driver executed a U-turn in a busy street and thereby held up traffic for about a minute it was held to be an unnecessary obstruction.

Arrowsmith v Jenkins (1963)
It is not necessary that the defendant should know that he was doing wrong if by his own free will he does something causing an obstruction (in this case by addressing a meeting on the highway).

Vanderpant v Mayfair Hotel Co (1930)
The right of the occupier of premises abutting a highway to make use of it for obtaining access to his premises and for loading and unloading goods is subject to the right of the public to use the highway.

Solomon v Durbridge (1956)
A motorist parked his car in a line of cars in a street and left it there for five hours. He argued that he was not causing an unnecessary obstruction because it was parked in a line of cars. *Held:* that he was guilty.

Worth v Brooks (1959)
The whole of the highway constitutes a road within the meaning of the regulation and a motor vehicle causes an obstruction by standing on the grass verge no less than if it was standing on the carriageway itself. (The obstruction might be held not to be unnecessary if the vehicle had broken down.)

Ellis v Smith (1962)
See p. 20.

Nagy v Weston (1965)
Under the Highways Act 1959, s. 121, an obstruction requires proof of unreasonable use and this is a question of fact and degree for the court to decide in all the circumstances including the place and length of time the obstruction took place, its purpose and other relevant factors and whether it was an actual as opposed to a potential obstruction.

Evans v Barker (1971)
Obstruction of a highway is not enough. The presence of a parked vehicle is to some degree an obstruction, but it must be proved to have been unnecessary, and this means unreasonable.

Langham v Crisp (1975)
A motorist parked on the side of the road when no vehicles were parked on the opposite side. He would not have been prosecuted for doing this and did not then cause an unnecessary obstruction. An obstruction did arise because vehicles later parked opposite his vehicle. The Crown Court decided that under these circumstances he had not caused unnecessary obstruction.

NOTES
a) The Highway Act 1835, ss. 72 and 78, and the Town Police Clauses Act 1847, s. 28, contain many obstruction offences which are now, save in

exceptional circumstances, of little more than academic interest: see chapter 1.

6) By s. 134 of the Highways Act 1959, a highway authority can require the owner or occupier of premises by notice to secure the removal of overhanging hedges, trees or shrubs endangering or obstructing pedestrians or vehicles, or interfering with the vision of drivers or lights from public lamps. Failure to comply within fourteen days enables the authority to remove the obstruction and recover costs.

3. Restrictions imposed on movement of traffic by local orders, etc.

Road Traffic Regulation Act 1967

MAKING OF ORDERS OR REGULATIONS FOR WALES

The functions of the S of S for the Environment can, as regards Wales, be carried out by the Secretary of State for Wales.

EXCEPTIONS—The making of orders or regulations re buses and bus stations, speed limits, traffic wardens, Crown vehicles, variation of specified maximum or minimum weights, hovercraft, or grass cutting or hedge trimming, and any case where joint action of both is required.

MAKING OF ORDERS BY LOCAL AUTHORITIES

'Local authority' means the county council (plus, in Scotland, the town council).

In respect of any orders made under this Act imposing restrictions on the movement of traffic (including pedestrians) the powers are exercised by the S of S for trunk roads and by local authorities (though in some cases the consent of the S of S is required) in respect of other roads within their areas. The procedures to be followed by a LA are provided by the Local Authorities' Traffic Orders (Procedure) Regulations 1969, with regard to:

a) traffic regulation orders, including prohibition on parking;

b) experimental traffic schemes;

c) orders relating to use of roads by PSVs, or to street playgrounds, or to parking places on or off the highway, and orders relating to speed limits.

The regulations in general provide for:

a) *consultations* beforehand with the COP, the highway authority (if the LA is not one), and any organisation representing persons likely to be affected;

b) *publication of proposals* in a local newspaper, the London Gazette, and by notices (giving information as to where plans, maps, etc. can be inspected) exhibited on each road concerned;

c) *consideration of objections* which have been made in writing within the specified period (twenty-eight days or twenty-one days according to the nature of the order); and

d) *public inquiry*—which may be held in any case, but must be held in circumstances specified by r. 7 of the regulations.

(1) Traffic regulation orders

RTR Act 1967 (ss. 1–5) as amended by Transport Act 1968

a) Nature—*Traffic regulation orders* may be made to prohibit, restrict or regulate the use of vehicles on roads for any of the following purposes, i.e. for the avoidance of danger or likelihood of danger, preventing damage to roads or buildings, easing flow of traffic, prohibiting unsuitable vehicles, preserving the character of a road (particularly for the benefit of persons on horseback or on foot or the amenities of the area through which the road passes).

The orders must be limited to one or more of the following:

a) requiring traffic to proceed in a specified direction or prohibiting it so proceeding, e.g. one way streets;

b) specifying the part of the carriageway to be used by traffic going in a certain direction, e.g. dual carriageways;

c) prohibiting or restricting waiting by vehicles or the loading or unloading of vehicles, e.g. 'no waiting' (but not to apply to bus services);

d) specifying, prohibiting, or restricting use of roads by heavy commercial vehicles;

e) prohibiting the use of roads by through traffic;

f) prohibiting or restricting overtaking;

g) regulating or restricting use of road (or any part of its width) by pedestrians.

NOTE

Traffic regulation orders for Greater London are governed by ss. 6–8 of the Act. An order may authorise the issue of means of identification (e.g. certificates) of vehicles exempted from the operation of the order. Regulations provide that after a TRO has been made the LA must forthwith take all steps reasonably practicable to cause to be erected, on or near the affected roads, traffic signs so placed as to afford adequate information being given to road users. The absence of such signs or their inadequacy might provide an adequate defence to proceedings for an offence.

OFFENCES—Contravention by a pedestrian or by using (or causing or permitting use) of a vehicle is an offence (RTR Act 1967, s. 1(8)).

b) General schemes of traffic control (s. 5)—An order can be made by councils for the stated purpose of a general scheme of traffic control, but they must be satisfied that the scheme—

a) is adequate as regards area of application;

b) takes adequate account of requirements for free traffic movement and need for ensuring reasonable access to premises;

c) takes adequate account of the effect of heavy commercial vehicles; and

d) provides for street parking places (using parking meters) which are suitable having regard to off-street parking places available or likely to be provided.

NOTE

Orders restricting waiting in specified streets generally permit (usually subject to conditions)—

a) loading or unloading of goods;

b) waiting long enough to allow a passenger to board or alight from a vehicle.

Whiteside v Watson (1952)
It was doubted whether selling to customers is 'unloading', e.g. selling fish and chips from the vehicle.

Sprake v Tester (1955)
It is not loading 'goods' to put a small parcel in a private car, but it might be if the object is not easily portable, e.g. a laundry basket or several chairs.

Funnel v Johnson (1962)
It is for the defendant to establish that the waiting was for a permitted purpose.

MacLeod v Hamilton (1965)
No offence is committed by parking if no signs are erected to show the existence of the order or if the signs do not conform to the Traffic Signs Regulations and General Directions 1975.

(2) Experimental traffic schemes (s. 9)

For the purposes of experiments in traffic control *temporary* orders can be made by the S of S (for trunk roads, n/e eighteen months) or by the local authority (not trunk roads, n/e six months) though the LA order can be extended by successive extensions n/e six months to a maximum total period of eighteen months. For definition of LA, see p. 56.

(3) Traffic regulation in special cases

The RTR Act 1967 (ss. 12–20) provides powers to regulate traffic flow (vehicles and pedestrians) in respect of particular places and special circumstances by the making of regulations or orders, or the issuing of notices. These should not be confused with traffic regulation orders, for this name is applied only to orders made under ss. 1–5. Limited powers are also available under the Town Police Clauses Act 1847. Local authorities are the same as for traffic regulation orders (see p. 56).

UNDER THE RTR ACT 1967

a) For road works, or to avoid danger or road damage (s. 12)

BY ORDER—An order can be made by the highway authority to prohibit or restrict use of the road (or part of it) by vehicles generally or by specified classes of vehicles or by pedestrians, except to gain access to premises. The order remains in force for three months, unless made by the Minister of Transport or approved for continuance by him. The order is to be notified in local newspapers seven days beforehand, and again within seven days after it has been made.

BY NOTICE—A more speedy control can be achieved by the issue of a notice, but the notice can operate for fourteen days only and this would provide time for the making of an order, if this were necessary.

OFFENCE—To contravene as a pedestrian or by using, or permitting use of, a vehicle is an offence.

b) For special roads—Section 13 prohibits use of any special road (motorway) by specified classes of vehicles, and authorises the Minister to make regulations controlling use and users of motorways. Use of such a road in contravention of this section or regulations made thereunder is a summary offence (see further on p. 64).

c) Trunk roads: one way traffic—Section 14 extends the power of the Minister (under the Trunk Roads Act 1946 and Highways Act 1959) to create trunk roads by enabling him to make such roads 'one-way' in parts, as may be required. To contravene such a 'one-way' provision (use, cause or permit) is a summary offence.

d) Restriction on vehicles on certain roads—The Minister may classify roads according to their character or the nature of traffic to which suited, and by order prohibit or restrict the use of roads (not being special roads) by vehicles generally or as to particular classes of vehicles. To drive a MV (or cause or permit) in contravention of such an order is a summary offence (s. 16).

e) Restriction: heavy vehicles on weak bridges (s. 17)—A bridge authority can by conspicuous notice (in prescribed form) at each end of such a bridge prohibit its use by any vehicle of which the weight (or weight of any axle), including load, exceeds the maximum specified in the notice. The specified weights are not to be less than five tons and three tons respectively. Warning notices may be erected at junctions of roads leading to the bridge. Driving, or causing or permitting driving, over a bridge in contravention of such a notice is a summary offence, without prejudice to civil action for damage caused.

f) Removal of vehicles from roads and parking places (s. 20)—The Minister may make regulations providing for the removal from roads, etc. of vehicles and loads contravening the law re position on the road, or causing obstruction or danger, or which appear to have been abandoned or broken down (see p. 310).

NOTE

As to powers of a local authority under s. 15 to regulate use of highways by PSVs, see p. 199.

UNDER THE TOWN POLICE CLAUSES ACT 1847

The local authority may make from time to time orders for the route to be observed by all vehicles and persons for the purpose of preventing street obstructions on the occasion of public processions, rejoicings, and any other such occasions where streets are thronged or liable to be obstructed. Breach of such an order is a summary offence.

(4) Street playgrounds

RTR Act 1967, ss. 26–27

A highway authority can make an order prohibiting or restricting the use of any road by vehicles so as to provide suitable *street playgrounds for children.* The order may apply to all vehicles or specified classes, and limit its application to particular days or periods of the day, but must provide for reasonable vehicular access to premises. Conspicuous signs at street entrances should indicate the conditions. The authority is authorised to make byelaws (subject to confirmation by the Minister or by the Greater London Council in respect of Greater London) relating to the use of a street playground and to safeguard the children from harm or injury.

Contravention of an order is a summary offence.

4. Parking places

Road Traffic Regulation Act 1967

(1) Parking places

1) GENERAL—Providing that access to premises will not be prevented by the parking place and no nuisance caused, certain local authorities can provide parking places by:

a) acquiring *land and/or buildings* for the purpose, and

b) authorising the use (by order) of any *part of a street* within their district for use as a *free parking place* (s. 28). It is an offence to ply for hire in such a parking place.

II) POWERS OF PARISH OR COMMUNITY COUNCILS (SS. 46–49A)—When thought necessary to provide and maintain parking places (free) in order to relieve or prevent congestion of traffic, such a council is empowered:

a) to buy and adapt any suitable land in its area, or

b) to appropriate not more than a prescribed proportion of certain defined council maintained property, i.e. a recreation ground, a playing field or other open space, or

c) by order, to authorise the use of any part of a road within the parish, but only with consent of the authority responsible for its maintenance, e.g. on a trunk road the Minister or the S of S, on roads other than a trunk road the county council, and on private roads the owner and occupier or other undertakings, e.g. railway, dock, harbour or other private owners.

(2) Payment for parking on highways

I) RTR ACT 1967, S. 35: 'DESIGNATION ORDERS'—The section breaks the rule that there can be no charge made for parking on a public highway. A LA may by order designate parking places on highways for which the authority may make charges. They have to consider:

a) need for maintaining free traffic flow;

b) preserving reasonable access to premises; and

c) adequacy of 'off street parking' in the district, and whether the order would encourage it.

'Local authority' means the council of a county, London borough, or of the City of London.

II) REGULATION OF DESIGNATED PARKING PLACES OUTSIDE LONDON—Where a designation order has been made, the LA must by order prescribe charges, being either the amount for an initial period and periods exceeding it or the amount payable regardless of any periods (see (v) below) or the charge for a permit (season ticket) instead of daily payment. The LA may by order also make provisions for regulating or restricting the use or operation of such parking places (e.g. methods of levying charges, use of approved meters); evidential value of indications of (or tickets issued by) parking meters; prohibiting misuse of such meters; exempting from payments, etc. (s. 36). If the designation order does not cover all hours, it will not apply during hours outside the order with regard to s. 36 (regulations) and s. 42 (offences), and any vehicle left on the parking place outside the hours will be deemed to have been just left there, if still there when a new period of the order commences. The LA can by order empower the LA itself, the chief officer of police, or any other person to cause removal of vehicles, in emergency, from the parking place, or to suspend the designation order in special circumstances, or to remove temporarily parking meters therefrom. The LA can buy or hire meters and must arrange for repairing and regular inspection, and testing of meters (s. 37).

III) OFFENCES (s. 42)—The following are offences:

a) *Driver* leaving vehicle in parking place otherwise than as authorised, or for longer (after excess charge incurred) than time authorised, or failing to pay any charge payable, or failing to comply with an order relating to manner of parking or driving in or out. If the offence is one of non-payment of the charge for a parking permit, acceptance of the charge due by the LA is a bar to prosecution.

b) *Driver or non-driver* contravening or failing to comply with any order relating to such parking places.

c) *With intent to defraud,* interfering with a parking meter or operating (or attempt) a meter by using other than appropriate coins.

NOTES

The section also provides that a meter is presumed to be of a type approved by the Minister until contrary is proved, and on charge of failing to pay excess charge, conviction may be for failing to pay initial charge if this is proved and it is not proved that excess charge had become due.

IV) PARKING METERS (DESCRIPTION AND TESTING) ORDER 1961—The order details the types of parking meters which can be used, the information which particular meters (according to the denomination(s) of the coin(s) to be used) must show, and the duties of the parking authority with regard to testing and maintaining meters, removal of faulty meters, and records of meters including inspections and repairs carried out. The most important provision from a police point of view is its last one which requires the authority to put notices on meters or near meter-parking places stating the periods during which meters operate under the order, the scale of charges, and information concerning offences relating to the parking place. The notice *may* include information as to the person (and telephone number) to be notified if a meter is found out of order.

V) PROVISIONS OF DESIGNATION ORDERS—Such an order generally requires:

a) *An initial payment* of the charge for *one hour*, or for *two hours,* to be paid into the meter immediately the vehicle has been parked. When the initial period has expired and the vehicle is driven away, it must not be returned to same parking place within less than one hour.

Strong v Dawtry (1961)
The legal obligation to make the initial payment immediately on parking is absolute, and there is no exemption for the driver who goes away for the short time necessary to obtain change for the meter.

b) *An excess charge* is payable for any period in excess of the time permitted by the initial payment as indicated on the meter. Entry into excess time is indicated by a yellow flag or colour on the meter face. Liability to this charge is normally brought to the attention of the offender by affixing to the vehicle the prescribed notice to this effect, which allows him seven days in which to pay the amount to the parking authority. Payment of this sum is a bar to proceeding for failing to pay the initial charge but a person who will not pay the excess charge and when summonsed pleads that his offence was failure to pay the initial charge only (i.e. by taking advantage of the unexpired time from a previous user of the parking place) may be convicted for the offence admitted. By s. 2 of the RTA 1974 the liability in respect of excess parking charges is extended to the owner of the vehicle. The procedure follows that for fixed penalties under s. 1 (see p. 292) and provides for action to be taken by the LA as well as the police.

c) *An offence* is committed by parking for an *excess period of more than two hours.* (This is indicated on the meter face by the appearance of a red flag or colour.) A motorist who stays longer than four hours at the same parking bay therefore necessarily commits an offence.

d) *Meter feeding*, i.e. putting more coins into the meter after the initial charge has been paid so as to extend the initial period and thus prevent the meter face showing that an excess charge had become due, is a summary offence.

5. Clearways

Under his powers to make traffic regulation orders (p. 57) the S of S has made the Various Trunk Roads (Prohibition of Waiting) (Clearways) Order 1963 which applies only to those sections of *trunk roads* which are referred to in Schedule 1 to the order.

It is a summary offence to cause or permit any vehicle, on such a section of road:

I) TO WAIT ON THE MAIN CARRIAGEWAY—(excluding any lay-by) except under direction or with permission of a uniformed constable. *Exceptions* relate to:

a) the following essential uses of vehicles, i.e. waiting in connection with:
   i) building operations, demolition, removal of any obstruction, road repairs or other works in, on, under or over the road, if to use the carriageway is necessary,
   ii) fire brigade, ambulance or police purposes,
   iii) delivery or collection of postal packets, or
   iv) collecting refuse or clearing cesspools by a local authority; and

b) necessary stopping, i.e.:
   i) to wait outside premises while a gate or barrier is being opened so as to permit access, or being closed after leaving the premises, or
   ii) stopping as required by law, or to avoid an accident, or for reason beyond control (e.g. breakdown), if it is not reasonably practicable to move vehicle off carriageway.

II) TO WAIT ON THE VERGE OR LAY-BY—to sell goods from the vehicle unless the goods are immediately delivered at or taken into premises adjacent to the vehicle.

6. Special roads (motorways)

(1) Highways Act 1959, s. 11

By s. 11 of the Highways Act 1959, the S of S or a highway authority can prepare a scheme to provide a special road (e.g. a motorway) for use only by the classes of traffic specified in the scheme. A scheme of a local authority has to be submitted to the S of S for confirmation. The proposals contained in any scheme must be published in a local newspaper and in the London Gazette. Copies of the draft scheme must be served on all local authorities and other interested parties. The S of S may cause a local enquiry to investigate the grounds of any objections received and may either confirm or modify the proposals after considering its findings. The S of S is also empowered to revoke a scheme or vary it by a subsequent scheme.

For the purpose of placing restrictions on the use by vehicles of special roads, the Highways Act 1959, Sch. 4 (as amended in 1971) creates eleven classes of vehicles. With regard to motorways, vehicles permitted to use them are limited (except in emergency) to the following classes:

Class 1—Heavy and light locomotives, MT, HMC, MC, motorcycles of 50 cc and over, and trailers drawn thereby, which comply with the regulations regarding construction and use, are wheeled vehicles with pneumatic tyres, and are not controlled by a pedestrian. The MV must be capable of 25 mph on the level under their own power when unladen and not drawing a trailer.

EXCEPTIONS: PCV, and agricultural machines for which a lesser rate of excise duty is chargeable.

Class 2—MV and trailers being used in accordance with an order made by the S of S in relation to:

a) conveyance of abnormal indivisible loads; or

b) special types, being vehicles:
   i) for moving excavated material, or
   ii) constructed for use outside UK, or
   iii) new types constructed for tests or trials, or
   iv) engineering plant;

   provided, in each case, that the MV is capable of 25 mph on the level under own power, when unladen and not drawing a trailer;

c) use for naval, military, air force or defence purposes.

(2) Motorways Traffic Regulations 1959

For the purposes of the regulations, a motorway is comprised of:

a) *the carriageway*, i.e. the part used by the traffic on each side of the central reservation, on each side being either a marginal strip or a raised kerb;

b) *the central reservation*, i.e. that part which separates the two carriageways;

c) *the marginal strip*, i.e. the continuous narrow strip of the nearside carriageway surface which is different in colour from the rest of the surface;

d) *the verge,* i.e. any part of a motorway which is not a carriageway or central reservation.

Wallwork v Roland (1971)
The hard shoulder is part of the verge and not of the carriageway.

No person, on a motorway, shall drive, move or stop a vehicle or cause or permit it to be driven, moved, stopped or to remain at rest in contravention of the following (RTR Act, s. 13, and 1959 regulations, reg. 3):

a) MV to be driven on carriageway only—except as is provided in these regulations (reg. 5).

b) One-way driving (reg. 6)—A driver must not:

a) fail to conform to traffic sign regulating entry into a motorway—'no entry', 'no left turn', 'no right turn';

b) drive or move otherwise than with central reservation (where there is one) on the right or off-side;

c) drive the 'wrong' way on the one-way entrances and exits;

d) make a U turn on any one-way stretch so as to be proceeding or facing in wrong direction.

c) Restrictions on stopping (reg. 7)—No vehicle is to stop or remain at rest on carriageway except when necessary because of breakdown, or lack of fuel, oil, water, accident, illness, emergency, to permit recovery or removal of object fallen on motorway, or to permit help to be given to any other person requiring it in above circumstances; but in all these cases the *vehicle must be moved to near-side verge* as soon as reasonably practicable, and not remain longer than necessary.

Regulation does not apply to vehicle which is prevented from proceeding by the presence of another vehicle, person or object on carriageway.

Higgins v Berhard (1972)
It is not an emergency where a driver, knowing that he is tired, enters a motorway and, overcome by fatigue, stops on the verge.

d) Reversing (reg. 8)—No vehicle is to be driven or moved backwards except when necessary to turn it to proceed forwards or to connect it to another vehicle.

e) Verges and central reservations (reg. 9)—No driving, moving, stopping or remaining at rest on a verge (except as permitted in reg. 7) or any central reservation.

f) Learner-drivers (reg. 11)—A provisional licence holder is not to drive, unless he has passed the driving test for the vehicle.

g) Off-side lane (reg. 11A)—Certain vehicles are not to be driven, moved, stopped or to remain at rest in this lane if there are three lanes all open to traffic moving in same direction.

Applies to all vehicles *except* motor cars (u/w n/e 3 tons), heavy motor car constructed and used solely to carry passengers, motor cycles, and MV drawing a trailer.

EXCEPTIONS—When necessary to overtake a vehicle with load of exceptional width.

h) Persons on foot (reg. 12)—No person on foot is to go or remain on any part of a motorway except when necessary to get to verge to comply with regulations, or to remove object or to give help as in reg. 7. Pedestrians are exempt when necessarily using motorway because of accident or emergency or of circumstances in reg. 7, or are carrying out public duties there (police, fire, ambulance) or responsibilities for care, maintenance, repairs, building, etc. with regard to the motorway (reg. 14).

i) Animals in vehicles (reg. 13)—The person in charge of it must ensure, so far as practicable, that:

a) an animal is not removed from or allowed to leave the vehicle on the motorway, and

b) if it escapes, or has to be removed from or allowed to leave a vehicle, it is confined to the verge, kept on a lead or under proper control.

j) Use by excluded vehicles (reg. 14)—Vehicles normally excluded can use a motorway to a very restricted degree, e.g. to clear, clean, maintain, repair and in other emergencies. The chief officer of police of the area (or superintendent or above on his behalf) in any emergency can authorise use of motorway by 'excluded' traffic for a period (and relax restrictions of these regulations if necessary) as an alternative route where another road (not a motorway) has become impassable.

k) Exemptions (reg. 15)—None of the above restrictions apply:

a) to anything done as directed or permitted by a constable in uniform, or as indicated by a traffic sign;

b) to anything necessarily done to avoid or prevent an accident, or give help in an accident or emergency, if as little danger and inconvenience as possible is caused to other road users;

c) to a constable, or member of fire or ambulance services in course of duty:

d) to anything necessary to test, repair, maintain, alter, inspect, survey or conduct an official census, or to remove works apparatus or structures.

l) Speed limits—See p. 83.

7. Footpaths, footways or bridleways

(1) Obstruction

See pp. 54–56.

(2) RTA 1972, s. 36

See p. 282.

(3) Vehicles (Conditions of Use on Footpaths) Regulations 1963

These regulations made under s. 49 of the Public Health Act 1961* provide that:

a) the weight (whether laden or not) of any vehicle or appliance when used on any footpath, footway or bridleway must not exceed:
i) one ton, or
ii) $12\frac{1}{2}$ cwts on any two foot wide strip of the footpath, etc. at right angles to the longitudinal axis of the appliance when at rest, or
iii) 8 cwts by any single wheel not in line with another except a roller n/e $12\frac{1}{2}$ cwts or $1\frac{1}{2}$ cwts for each inch of the width of the wheel in contact with the surface;

b) the speed must n/e 5 mph;

c) an authority must obtain the consent of any other person responsible for the maintenance of the footpath, etc. before using any appliance or vehicle thereon;

d) the area gas board must be consulted if there is a gas pipe under the footway, path or bridleway.

(4) Motor trials

See section **9** below.

(5) Parking on verges, footways, etc.

RTA 1972, s. 36B†

The section applies to vehicles other than heavy commercial vehicles, though regulations may exempt certain classes either completely or conditionally,

---

* Section 49 also provides the exemption from RTA 1972, s. 36 for LA vehicles (see (**2**) above).

† This section is not operative until s. 7 of the RTA 1974 is brought into force. As to heavy commercial vehicles see p. 76.

and a TRO may provide temporary relaxations. The offence is (and defences are) the same as for heavy commercial vehicles under s. 36A (see p. 76) except that s. 39B applies only on urban roads, i.e. roads to which a general speed limit of 30 mph or 40 mph applies.

8. Motor racing

Motor racing on any highway is illegal. Any person who promotes or takes part in a race or trial of speed between motor vehicles on a public highway commits a summary offence (RTA 1972, s. 14). Motor trials may be conducted if authorised under RTA 1972, s. 15—see below.

9. Motor trials

NOTE
The following does not apply to races or trials of speed between motor vehicles, which are illegal (RTA 1972, s. 14).

(1) RTA 1972, s. 15 and s. 35

It is an offence to promote or take part in a competition or trial involving the use of MVs on a public highway unless it has been authorised by regulations made under the Act, or by the RAC or the police (s. 15). If it takes place on a footpath or bridleway the trial has to be authorised by the LA concerned. Contravention of this section or failure to comply with any conditions of an authorisation by a LA is a summary offence. LA means county council or London borough council (s. 35).

(2) Motor Vehicles (Competitions and Trials) Regulations 1969

Any event conforming with any of the following descriptions is authorised by the regulations:

a) one involving not more than twelve competing vehicles, providing it is not within eight days of another such event (or part of it) organised by the same promoters or by persons belonging to the same 'promoting' club;

b) if no merit attaches to lowest mileage, and, on a public highway, there are no performance tests, no route, and competitors are not timed or required to visit the same places, except to finish at same place by a specified time;

c) if, on a public highway, merit is given only for good road behaviour and compliance with the Highway Code;

d) all competitors are members of HM forces and trial is part of service training (reg. 5).

AUTHORISATIONS BY RAC

An event not authorised by reg. 5 may be authorised by the RAC, which can vary or revoke its authorisation at any time before the event begins (reg. 6).

APPLICATIONS—To be made on prescribed form (obtainable from the RAC) to the RAC not less than two months beforehand and (except for a 'specified' event*) not more than six months beforehand (reg. 7).

CONDITIONS—(regs. 8 and 9) (amended 1974):

a) The payment of the fee is a condition of the authorisation.

b) The 'standard' conditions of an authorisation are set out in appendix 5 (see p. 350). The RAC can modify some of them, or impose additional conditions, in any particular case.

CONSULTATIONS BY RAC (REG. 10)—The following must be consulted:

a) the COP of any area in which a public highway route lies (to be informed at least six weeks before the event);

b) if route involves use of a road which is:
   i) designated a public path—the highway authority;
   ii) in a National Park—the planning authority.

DISTANCE—To be calculated by reference to most recent edition of the 1" Ordnance Map.

10. Cycle racing on highways

NOTE
This section (RTA 1972, s. 20) relates to pedal cycles only. Racing with motor cycles on roads is prohibited (see p. 68).

Cycle Racing on Highways Regulations 1960

It is an offence to promote or to take part in a *race* or *time trial* on a public highway unless it is authorised and conducted in accordance with the provisions of these regulations, which authorise races or trials of speed of certain kinds (subject to conditions) as follows:

I) TIME TRIALS—i.e. events the results of which depend on either:

Specified event means an event held not more than once a year and included in Schedule 4, e.g. Caravan Club International Road Rally, London Rally, International Rally, Veteran Car Run.

a) the *time taken* to cover the course, or

b) the *distance* covered by competitors in a given time,

provided individual competitors (or groups of not more than four forming a team and not competing against each other) start at intervals of not less than one minute.

II) CYCLE RACES CONDUCTED UNDER 'STANDARD' CONDITIONS—(not being time trials), as follows:

Competitors not to exceed 40; the race must take place in the daytime (half hour before sunrise to half hour after sunset); every competitor must travel at least 10 miles before repassing any point on the route (whether from the same or in a different direction) and not travel on roads subject to a speed limit of 40 mph or less for a distance exceeding $1\frac{1}{2}$ miles at one time, every such stretch of road being at least 3 miles apart (reg. 5).

III) CYCLE RACES AUTHORISED BY THE POLICE—Road races which do not fully comply with the 'standard' conditions (see (II) above) can be held provided the promoter obtains the authority of the COP by making written application and supplying the same particulars as must be provided in the case of a 'time trial' (see below) and provided also that the event is conducted in accordance with any conditions imposed by the COP for that area in addition to such 'standard' conditions as are not varied by police conditions. Police conditions, in particular, may relate to the times and days to be held; the places of start and finish of the race; the number of competitors; public highways (or parts) not to be used; and arrangements for marshalling and supervision (regulations 7 and 8).

CONDITIONS (REGULATIONS 3 AND 5)

The holding of a 'time trial' or a 'cycle race' as in (I) and (II) above is not properly authorised unless:

a) *at least 28 days written notice* is given to the COP for every police area concerned, and

b) *the following particulars are provided:* the times and day or days for the events; details of the routes to be followed; the starting and finishing points; the maximum number of competitors; arrangements for marshalling and supervision; and, if a 'time trial', the rules relating thereto.

If the requirements in (a) and (b) above have not been properly complied with or changes are proposed affecting the previous particulars supplied, the promoter may make application to the COP for authorisation to hold a 'time trial' or a 'bicycle race' which may be approved by him subject to such conditions in the latter case as he may think fit.

NOTES

a) A cycle race is not treated as being authorised unless held and conducted in accordance with the particulars provided and the conditions (if any) imposed.

b) The COP is empowered to close roads and re-direct traffic as required for road safety during a cycle race or trial, and the Minister is empowered to make regulations to vary the number of competitors taking part in particular events, or during specified periods, e.g. the Cycle Racing on Highways (Special Authorisation) Regulations (England and Wales) 1979 have increased the maximum number of riders who may take part in the 'Milk' cycle race and the 'Sealink International' to 84, and to 60 in the case of certain other events.

11. Control of dogs on roads

It is an offence (s. 31) to *cause* or *permit* to be on a 'designated road' any dog not held on a lead, unless it be proved that such dog:

a) was being kept for driving or tending sheep or cattle in the course of a trade or business, or

b) was at the time being used (and under proper control) for sporting purposes, or

c) was covered by an exception included in the terms of the order made by the LA in whose area the length of road is situated. A LA (i.e. the council of county in England and Wales, the common council of the City of London, a London borough in the MPD, or a regional or islands council in Scotland) may, after consultation with the COP, make an order specifying lengths of roads to be 'designated roads' for the above purpose. The procedure is regulated by the Control of Dogs on Roads Orders (Procedure) Regulations 1962. Public notice of the intention to make an order must be given in a local newspaper and displayed in a prominent position on the roads concerned, and such roads shown and marked on a map available for inspection at the council offices. Twenty-one days must be allowed for objections. The LA must consider the objections and may hold a public inquiry. Notice that an order has been made must be given in the same manner as above and also to objectors, and the LA must erect on or near the roads concerned signs considered by them adequate to notify road users of the effect of the order.

12. Vehicles plying for hire on highways

'Plying for hire' in its widest sense includes the use of highways by any vehicle for the purpose of the vehicle being hired as a whole for the conveyance of passengers and their effects, or being available to the general public for transport by payment of separate fares.

Until the introduction of the mechanically propelled vehicle, the law relating to the use of vehicles plying for hire in this way (cabs, brakes, stage coaches, etc.) was covered by the Town Police Clauses Acts 1847 and 1889, and similar statutes for the London area. The following, which would otherwise fall within the provisions of the TPC Acts, are controlled by other statutes:

a) *tramcars and trolley vehicles*—by either the Light Railways Act 1896 or a special Act of Parliament;

b) *public service vehicles* which are motor vehicles—by the RTA 1960 and regulations made thereunder (see chapter 14).

All other vehicles used on roads for the public service, either for hiring or carrying passengers at separate fares are termed hackney-carriages. A *hackney-carriage* may, therefore, be defined as any wheeled vehicle (except those named above):

a) used in standing or plying for hire *in any street*, or

b) standing *in any street* and having thereon the 'hackney-carriage plate'* required by the 1847 Act, or any plate resembling or intended to resemble it, or

c) being a horse-drawn omnibus, brake or other carriage plying or standing for hire to carry passengers at separate fares, *whether on a street or not.*

NOTE
The definition of PSV for the purposes of the RTA does not include a MV adapted to carry less than eight passengers and hired as a whole (a taxi) and these would be governed by the TPC Acts, where they are in force, or the special legislation for London. A taxi which does not stand or ply for hire on the street does not fall within the Acts, nor does a vehicle of the 'drive yourself' variety.

Application of the TPC Acts 1847 and 1889—The provisions of these Acts concerning hackney-carriages do not apply where the local council has not adopted the appropriate parts of Public Health Acts, and is not, therefore, a licensing authority.

Licensing of hackney-carriage (TPC Acts)—Every such carriage and every driver has to be licensed by the local authority. To give false information in an application for a licence is an offence. The carriage licence refers to the vehicle and is therefore transferable with it to a new owner. Convictions of a driver are to be endorsed on his licence.

Offences re licences—It is an offence:

a) to act as driver without current licence;

b) to lend or part with a driver's licence except to the proprietor;

---

* The plate, indicating the licence number and the authorised seating capacity, is issued by the local authority, and has to be affixed to the vehicle.

c) to permit use of carriage as hackney-carriage without a licence or while the licence is suspended;

d) to stand or ply for hire with an unlicensed carriage, or not have the licence number openly displayed on the carriage.

Byelaws—The local authority may make byelaws concerning the operation of hackney-carriages within its district, and this will apply to hackney-carriages operating in or from railway stations, belonging to or being used by the railway company. The byelaws may relate to conduct of proprietors and drivers, taxi stands, rates of fares, property lost or found in carriages, etc.

General offences

BY DRIVER OR PROPRIETOR—The following are offences: driver refusing to carry number of persons covered by the licence; or when at a stand refusing without reasonable excuse to drive to any place within the licensing district at request of hirer; demanding higher fare than that agreed upon, or exacting more than proper fare; taking greater fare than that authorised by byelaws; not driving the agreed distance; refusing to wait after receiving a deposit to cover this, or failing to account for the deposit; permitting a person to be carried without consent of hirer; driver permitting another person to drive without consent of proprietor; driver being intoxicated while driving, or endangering anyone in life, limb or property by wanton or furious driving, or other wilful misconduct; driver leaving carriage in public place without someone proper to take care of it; doing hurt or damage to person or property; suffering carriage to stand across any street, or refusing to give way to another carriage, or obstructing or hindering driver of another carriage in picking up or setting down any person; wrongfully trying to prevent driver of another carriage from being hired.

BY HIRERS—The following are offences: refusing to pay on demand the proper fare; wilfully damaging the carriage; breach of any byelaw.

Notifiable diseases—(Public Health Act 1936, ss. 159 and 160):

a) It is an offence for any person suffering from a notifiable disease, or person in charge of such patient, to enter a public conveyance carrying passengers at separate fare, or any other public conveyance without previously notifying the owner or driver.

b) In any case in which a person suffering from such a disease is to be conveyed in a public conveyance, the fact must be notified to the MOH of the district and the vehicle disinfected before again used.

References—For road restrictions re:

a) speed limits—see chapter 7;

b) traffic signs (including pedestrian crossings)—see chapters 8 and 9;

c) conformity with C and U Regulations—see chapter 18.

13. Charity walks

The booklet entitled *Safety on Charity Walks* recommends consideration of alternative ways of collecting money, involving less personal risk. If a charity walk is to be organised the booklet advises:

a) choice of route to avoid traffic as much as possible:

b) avoidance of night walks (particularly dangerous); and

c) observance of following code and notification of code to walkers.

The Code

I) PRELIMINARY—Inform police early, give full information and follow police advice.

II) ROUTE—Use open spaces, footpaths rather than roads or lanes. Avoid a heavy traffic road unless it has adequate continuous verge or pavement. If start or finish is at night use for this a road with good lighting with actual start and finish *off* a road.

III) TIME—Avoid night, and in particular 10 pm to midnight.

IV) ORGANISATION—No mass start, but in groups at intervals. Adequate number of marshals at start, along route and at finish. Refreshment stops to be off road. Care to be arranged for those dropping out through fatigue or injury (lameness, blisters). No litter. No disturbance caused. No cars to accompany walkers at walking pace.

V) PEOPLE ON WALKS—Should not be under 15. Children should be accompanied by adults. If after dark—wear light or reflective clothing, and each group should have a torch. No obstruction, noise or litter. Obey Highway Code. Keep in small groups all the way. Use pavements, paths, verges; otherwise face oncoming traffic. Keep close to roadside, not more than two abreast. Extra care on bends and in narrow lanes.

14. Highways Act 1971

(1) Builders' skips

It is an offence to deposit on the highway, without permission of the highway authority, a builder's skip. Permission of the authority may be made subject to conditions specified in the permit. Where a permit is issued the owner must secure that the skip is:

a) properly lighted during the hours of darkness;

b) clearly and indelibly marked with his telephone number or name and address;

c) removed as soon as practicable after it has been filled.

It is defence to prove that default was due to the act of another person and that the owner had taken all reasonable precautions and exercised due diligence, but seven clear days notice of the defence must be given to the prosecutor, giving any information as to the identity (or to assist identification) that the owner has in his possession. The permit is a defence to an obstruction charge if conditions have been fulfilled, or the obstruction was caused by another person's act, etc. (s. 31). Though a permit has been granted the authority or a constable in uniform may require the owner to remove it and, if this fails, may remove it or reposition it (or cause this to be done), but must then notify the owner. If the owner cannot be traced, or after reasonable notice has not recovered the skip, the authority or the COP may dispose of the skip and its contents—recovering expenses from the owner as a civil debt. Proceeds of disposal must first be applied to meet reasonable expenses and the surplus given to the person entitled to them, if he can be traced: if not it can be retained by the authority or by the COP and paid into the Police Fund (s. 32).

NOTE

A skip is a container designed to be carried on a MV and placed on a road or other land for storage of builders' materials, rubble, waste, etc.

(2) Verge crossings

Where the occupier of premises adjoining or having access to a public highway habitually takes or permits to be taken a MV across a kerbed footpath or verge, the highway authority may serve notice on the owner and occupier of the premises that the authority proposes:

a) to execute works to provide a vehicle crossing over the footpath or verge, or

b) to impose such reasonable conditions as to the use of the footway or verge as are specified.

If any person knowingly uses a footway or verge as a crossing in contravention of any conditions imposed in (b) above, or permits this, an offence is committed (s. 40).

(3) Unauthorised interference with highway

I) APPARATUS—It is an offence to place in or under a highway or to break open a highway to place, maintain or repair, any apparatus without lawful authority or excuse (s. 41).

II) TREES, SHRUBS—The Highways Act 1959 (s. 59) prohibits the unauthorised planting of trees or shrubs near a made-up carriageway. The 1971 Act provides that an owner or occupier of neighbouring land can do this if a licence to this effect is granted by the highway authority (s. 43).

15. Heavy commercial vehicles

A heavy commercial vehicle (HCV) is any vehicle (whether a MV or not) constructed or adapted for carriage of goods and having an u/w exceeding 3 tons.

(1) Traffic regulation orders

A local authority may make such an order specifying through routes for, or prohibiting or restricting the use of specified roads or zones by, such vehicles.

(2) Parking on verges and footways

RTA 1972, s. 36A

I) OFFENCE—Parking a HCV partly or wholly on the verge of a road, or on a footway, or on any land between two carriageways which is not a footway*.

II) DEFENCES—There is to be no conviction if the defendant proves to the satisfaction of the court that the parking:

a) was in accordance with permission given by a constable in uniform, or

b) was to save life or extinguish fire or to meet any other like emergency, or

c) was in contravention but the following conditions were satisfied, i.e. the vehicle was on the verge or footway for purpose of loading or unloading, which could not have been satisfactorily performed otherwise, and it was not left unattended whilst so parked.

(3) Excessive weight

RTA 1972, s. 57

Where the use of a vehicle is prohibited by virtue of being overweight (see p. 220) and it is a HCV, there may also be given a direction in writing to remove it (and trailer(s) if any) to a place and under conditions specified. Refusal, neglect or other failure to comply is an offence.

---

* A LA may prosecute when para. 13 of Sch. 6 to the RTA 1974 is brought into force.

16. Road humps: experiments

Under s. 17 of the RTA 1974, experiments (for not more than one year in any one place) may be conducted by putting 'road humps' in the surface of roads as a means of controlling speeds of vehicles. The proposal to do this on any road must be published in local newspapers and advertised by notices on the road concerned. Objections have to be considered and a local enquiry may be held. A road hump must not raise the road surface by more than 5 in above, nor lower by more than 2 in below, the road surface on either side of it, and it must be of such shape that no damage is likely to be caused to tyres of a vehicle. If the hump is properly constructed and maintained, as well as indicated by the proper traffic sign, it cannot be deemed to constitute an obstruction.

Chapter 7 **Speed limits**

Road Traffic Regulation Act 1967

NOTE
Unless otherwise stated, references are to this Act.

(1) Introduction

By s. 78A a person convicted of exceeding a speed limit under any enactment of 1960 or later or the Parks Regulation (Amendment) Act 1926 is liable on summary conviction to a fine n/e £100 (£500 if on a motorway).

The maximum speed at which a MV can legally be driven on a road depends upon:

a) *the road concerned**, for many roads are subject to speed limits affecting all motor vehicles using them, and

b) *the type of vehicle*, for motor vehicles of particular classes or types are subject to a speed limit on any road, *viz.*:
   i) by s. 78 and Sch. 5 according to class (see para. (6) below) or
   ii) by being a special type of vehicle.

(2) Roads subject to speed limits

To be able to set out the standard principles in this respect the current fuel economy measures have been ignored. As to these see para. (8) below.

The basic provisions of law imposing speed limits on particular roads or roads in particular areas relate to the following:

a) *restricted roads*, where the 30 mph limit applies (see para. (3) below);

b) *motorways*—see para. (7) below;

---

* For the time being *all* roads have been made subject to speed limits as a result of special (and temporary) measures to secure economy in the use of motor fuel, but it has been thought best to preserve the general principles of the law concerning speed limits in this way, and to note this temporary departure from them. As to the effect of the economy speed limits, see para. (8) below.

(c) *roads or parts of roads made subject to special orders*, e.g.:
   i) under s. 74 to increase or decrease (from 30 mph) the limit on a road which would otherwise come under (a) above, or
   ii) under s. 77 for the purpose of public safety or to facilitate traffic movement, etc.;

d) *roads in certain public parks* under the Parks Regulation (Amendment) Act 1926.

NOTE

Traffic signs indicating the existence of a speed limit (and the limit) have to be placed on and along roads or parts of roads concerned (s. 75), but this does not apply in relation to a speed limit imposed under s. 77 if the order relates to *all* roads or classes of road (as do, for example, the current economy restrictions, which apply to all single carriageways and all dual carriageways), and where it applies only to a particular area speed traffic signs need be placed only at entry points to that area.

(3) 'Restricted roads'—30 mph (ss. 71–73)

A road is a '*restricted road*' if:

a) Street lamps on it are not more than 200 yards apart: lamps temporarily missing or out of action to be regarded as operational, and fractional variations as to 200 yards can be ignored (*Briere v Hailstone* (1968)), *but*:
   i) in the case of street lighting provided since July 1957 *on a trunk road or classified road* a special order made by the Minister has to be in force in respect of it;
   ii) where such lighting exists the appropriate authority* can by direction de-restrict it.

b) A direction of the appropriate authority* is in force that the road (not having the requisite lighting) is a restricted road.

Boyd-Gibbons v Skinner (1951)
The police need not call evidence to prove the direction unless the defence calls evidence that the road is not restricted. The presence of speed limit signs is prima facie evidence that the speed limit applied even without the requisite lamp posts.

NOTE

Where the speed limit on a restricted road (or part of it) is varied (e.g. raised to 40 mph) by an order under s. 74, the road (or that part of it) ceases to be a restricted road under s. 71 and a speeding offence on it has to be prosecuted under the order concerned, and not under s. 71.

---

* See para. (4) on p. 80.

EVIDENCE THAT A ROAD IS A 'RESTRICTED ROAD'

I) WHERE THERE IS THE APPROPRIATE LIGHTING SYSTEM—

a) on unclassified roads the presence of authorised 30 mph speed limit signs;

b) on trunk roads and classified roads the order concerning it or, where it is a pre 1 July 1957 lighting system, a certificate signed by an officer of the highway authority that this is so (s. 72): by the same section a certificate by an officer of the S of S is admissible to prove that a particular road is or is not a trunk road or a classified road;

c) evidence of absence of de-restriction signs is evidence that the road is restricted (s. 75 (4)).

II) WHERE THERE IS NO APPROPRIATE LIGHTING SYSTEM—There can be no conviction unless the limit is indicated by appropriate traffic signs (s. 75 (3)).

(4) Authorities for making speed limit orders

a) The only direct statutory speed limit is that of 30 mph on restricted roads by s. 71. All other speed limits are imposed by orders made under powers given by the Act.

b) Orders relating to trunk roads and special roads, or experimental speed limits, can be made only by the S of S.

c) Orders concerning other roads can be made by local authorities *with the consent of the* S of S. These authorities are:
i) in London—the Greater London Council;
ii) in all other cases—the county council.

d) All orders require prior public notice and (except those of the S of S) prior consultation with the chief officers of police.

(5) Offences

The following are offences:

a) driving a MV on a *restricted road* at a speed exceeding 30 mph (s. 71 and s. 78A);

b) driving a MV on *a road in a Royal Park* at a speed exceeding the maximum specified in regulations relating to the park (s. 78A and the regulation);

c) driving a MV *of any class* on a road at a speed greater than the speed specified in Schedule 5 to the Act as the maximum speed in relation to a vehicle of that class (s. 78 and s. 78A);

d) driving a MV on a road subject to an order made under s. 74 (not a 'restricted road') at a speed exceeding that specified in the order (the order and s. 78A);

e) driving a MV on a road in contravention of a *temporary* (*or experimental*) *order* made by the S of S (which may impose a minimum as well as a maximum speed limit) under s. 77 (the order and s. 77);

f) *on special roads* (e.g. motorways), driving a motor vehicle on a special road at a speed exceeding that applicable to the class of vehicle or the road by virtue of regulations (s. 13 and regulations).

(6) Speed limits according to type of vehicle other than on motorways

Section 78 and Schedule 5 (as amended by SI 1973 No. 747)

DEFINITIONS IN SCHEDULE 5

I) PASSENGER VEHICLE—one constructed *solely* for carriage of passengers and their effects, or a 'dual purpose vehicle'.

II) DUAL PURPOSE VEHICLE—constructed or adapted to carry both passengers and goods or burden, u/w n/e 2040 kg, and either:

a) having driving power capable of being transmitted to all wheels, *or*

b) constructed as follows:
   i) *roof*—permanently fitted, rigid, but may have sliding panel;
   ii) *seats*—fixed or folding, one row at least for two or more persons, sprung or cushioned, upholstered backrests attached to seat, or side or floor of vehicle; *position*—transverse, distance from rearmost part of steering wheel to backrests of the seats (or rearmost row if more than one) when ready for use to be not less than one-third of the distance from the same point to the rearmost part of the floor;
   iii) *windows*—of glass or transparent material on each side (not less than 2 sq. ft) and at rear (not less than 120 sq. ins).

III) LOAD-CARRYING TRAILER—one constructed or adapted to convey goods or burden, not being a living van.

IV) FOREIGN VEHICLE—

a) MV brought into GB and displaying a registration mark in accordance with the MV (International Circulation) Regulations 1971 (see p. 151), a period of 12 months not having elapsed since the MV was last brought into GB, or

b) MV in the service of a visiting force or of a headquarters.

V) RELEVANT CONDITIONS

a) *Appropriate weights to be legibly marked* in a conspicuous and readily accessible position as follows:

i) *on the drawing vehicle*—its kerbside weight* either inside the vehicle or outside it on its near side, and

ii) *on the trailer* being a living van, or being neither a living van nor a load-carrying trailer, its maximum gross weight* on the outside of the nearside.

b) *50 mph plate*, kept clean, unobscured, and plainly visible from behind the trailer, to be exhibited at the rear of the trailer in a conspicuous position. Plate must conform to specification and it is an offence to display the plate when the 50 mph limit does not apply. The plate must be circular (diameter not less than 4 in) or elliptical (not less than 3 in high and 4¼ in wide) the longer axis being horizontal. The rear facing surface must be black with the number 50 on it in white, silver or grey—each figure not less than 1¾ in high and 1¼ in total width.

c) *Certain weight ratios* must be observed.

VI) ARTICULATED VEHICLE—consisting of a MV drawing a trailer, the latter attached by superimposition on the MV so that when evenly loaded at least 20 per cent of weight of load is borne by the drawing MV.

VII) GOODS VEHICLE—constructed or adapted for conveyance of goods or burden, not including dual purpose vehicles.

PASSENGER VEHICLES (INCLUDING DPV)

	LIMIT (*mph*)
a) PSV (licensed) u/w exceeding 3 tons or adapted for more than seven passengers†	50
b) Not licensed as PSV—u/w n/e 30 cwt and for more than seven passengers†	50
c) Of u/w exceeding 3 tons or adapted for more than seven passengers but not in (a) or (b) above	40
d) Vehicles drawing one trailer‡:	
i) licensed PSV as in (a) above	40
ii) as in (a) but not licensed as a PSV	30
iii) car for not more than seven passengers†	40
iv) for more than seven passengers† and u/w n/e 30 cwt	40
e) Any vehicle drawing more than one trailer	20
f) Any vehicle not fitted with pneumatic tyres, or drawing a trailer not so fitted	20
g) An invalid carriage	20

---

* In kgs or imperial units, but must be the same medium for both the drawing vehicle and the trailer.

† Excluding driver.

‡ 50 mph if drawn by foreign vehicle or the relevant conditions are satisfied—see p. 81.

GOODS VEHICLES (NOT INCLUDING DPV)	LIMIT (*mph*)
The general speed limit	40

EXCEPTIONS

a) u/w n/e 30 cwt and not drawing trailer	50
b) Vehicle (not AV) drawing a trailer:	
i) being a motor car of u/w n/e 30 cwt if it is a foreign vehicle or the relevant conditions are satisfied— see p. 81	50
ii) being a HMC or motor cycle	30
iii) being a motor car of u/w exceeding 30 cwt *if* the trailer is a load-carrying type of u/w exceeding 5 cwt or (being neither a living van nor load carrying) has u/w exceeding 15 cwt	30
c) Vehicle drawing more than one trailer	20
d) Vehicle not fitted with pneumatic tyres if drawing a trailer or of u/w exceeding 1 ton, and any vehicle drawing trailer not so fitted	20
e) Vehicle not fitted with resilient tyres or drawing trailer not so fitted	5

LOCOMOTIVES AND TRACTORS

LIMIT

TYPE	WITHOUT TRAILER	ONE TRAILER	TWO OR MORE TRAILERS
a) *Locomotives* (heavy and light)			
i) Vehicle and any trailer drawn having pneumatic tyres, springs and wings, plus brakes of modern standard*	20	20	12
ii) Not conforming as in (i)	12	12	12
iii) Not fitted with resilient tyres, or drawing trailer not so fitted	5	5	5
b) *Tractors* as in (i) above	30	30	12
as in (ii) above	20	20	12
as in (iii) above	5	5	5

(7) Speed limits on motorways

The general speed limit is 70 mph. The limits placed on particular classes of MV by the MV (Speed Limits on Motorways) Regulations 1973 are as follows:

---

* Braking systems in the main have to be in accord with requirements of MV (C and U) Regulations (see Appendix 1). To come within (a) a locomotive and its trailer must not exceed certain weight limits.

	LIMIT *(mph)*
a) Goods vehicle u/w exceeding 3 tons, except when falling within (b) below	60
b) Any MV drawing a trailer (not an AV) if trailer has less than four wheels or is a close-coupled four-wheeled trailer, except when falling within (c) below	50
c) A MV of u/w n/e 30 cwt when drawing a trailer as in (b) above in circumstances where the speed limit for such a MV drawing such a trailer on a road not being a motorway (see para. (5) above) is 40 mph or less	40

(8) Fuel economy: speed limits variations

To deal with the fuel crisis, orders can from time to time vary general speed limits. An order made in June 1979 imposed a general limit of 70 mph on dual carriageways and 60 mph on single carriage roads. The order also specified limits on named roads throughout England, Wales and Scotland, but allowed the 70 mph on motorways to remain.

(9) Exemptions from speed limits (s. 79)

The following are exempt:

a) Vehicles being used for fire brigade, ambulance or police purposes, but only if observance of the limit would hinder the use of the vehicle for its official purpose on that occasion.

> **Aitken v Yarwood (1964)**
> A police officer exceeding the limit after his car had broken down in order to get to court in time to give evidence was held to be within the section. (It is suggested that the defence applies only because the circumstances were unforeseen but not in the case where the constable started the journey late.)

b) Vehicles of the armed forces used under official orders for combat, training, or other military purposes, or vehicles used for salvage purposes under the Merchant Shipping Act 1894.

c) Vehicles being used for experiments or trials under the Roads Improvement Act 1925.

(10) Speed limit signs

(Traffic Signs (Speed Limits) Regulations and General Directions 1969)

The prescribed signs (which must be illuminated at night by lighting or reflection unless the Minister has agreed otherwise) are provided by the local authority.

I) RESTRICTION SIGNS—These must be as follows:

a) The figures '30', '40', '50', or '70' in black on a white disc in a red ring, to indicate the commencement of the restriction.

b) Where a road not having the prescribed lighting system is by directions made a restricted road (30 mph) under s. 71 or by an order made subject to a higher limit (see p. 79) repeater signs, of the same pattern but smaller than the commencement sign, must be displayed on both sides of the road with not more than 400 metres (500 metres or more if the limit is more than 30 mph) between signs on the same side of the road and not more than 250 metres between signs on alternate sides of the road.

c) Where a temporary or experimental order made under s. 77 applies to all roads, no signs need be displayed. If it applies to all roads in a specified area, signs must be displayed at all entrance points to that area.

II) DE-RESTRICTION SIGNS—These must be as follows:

a) Transverse black bar across a white disc to indicate the point at which a speed limit ends, being a point where there is no other speed limit in force on the road, where the speed limit is a *maximum* one.

b) Transverse red bar across a blue disc, white numerals, to indicate where a speed limit ends, and no other speed limit is in force, where the speed limit in force is a *minimum* one.

(11) Evidence of speed

A driver cannot be convicted of speeding solely on the evidence of the opinion of one witness that he was exceeding the speed limit (s. 78A).

Brighty v Pearson (1938)
A court may convict on the evidence of two witnesses as to their opinion of the speed of a motor vehicle, but the corroborative witness must speak as to speeding at the *same moment of time* as the first witness and not some moments later at a place further along the same road.

Nicholas v Penny (1950)
There can be a conviction on the opinion of one policeman supported by evidence by him of the reading of a speedometer, stop watch or other mechanical means even though there was no evidence that the speedometer has been tested. Such evidence is of fact and not merely opinion.

Swain v Gillett (1974)
Two officers gave evidence of opinion of exceeding speed limit. Reference was made to speeds shown by speedometer but no evidence given of its accuracy. Information dismissed on this ground. *Held* (on appeal): the

evidence of the opinion of the two officers was sufficient. There is no statute which requires the speedometer to be tested. Justices may accept evidence of an untested speedometer and give the evidence such weight as they think fit.

(12) Procuring or inciting the offence (s. 78A)

If an employer publishes a timetable or schedule, or gives directions to conform with which his driver would have to exceed any speed limit, such time-table or directions may be produced as prima facie evidence of procuring or inciting the commission of the offence. A person aiding, abetting, counselling or procuring an offence is liable to same penalties as principal offender (Magistrates' Courts Act 1952, s. 35).

See also notices of intended prosecution on p. 284, and disqualification and endorsement of driving licences on pp. 159, 165.

Chapter 8 Traffic signs

Road Traffic Regulation Act 1967

1. A traffic sign

A traffic sign (s. 54) means any object or device (fixed or portable) and any line or mark on a road for the warning, direction, guidance or information of road users. Each sign must either:

a) *conform with regulations* made under the Road Traffic Regulation Act as to size, colour, type and character (including requirements as to the fixing or illumination thereof), or

b) *be specially authorised by the S of S* if not in accordance with the regulations.

Signs are of three broad classes, i.e.:

a) *Mandatory signs*, i.e. those which indicate a legal requirement, failure to conform with which constitutes either:
i) an offence in itself (e.g. traffic lights, double white lines on roads), or
ii) a breach of a particular regulation or order to which the sign is related (e.g. speed limit signs, 'no entry').
Such signs are *generally circular in shape, with either a red border or a blue background*. Exceptions—the inverted red bordered triangle of 'give way', and road markings.

b) *Hazard warning signs*, i.e. of road hazards ahead of which drivers should be made aware in the interests of road safety (e.g. 'road narrows', 'level crossing', 'road works', 'two-way traffic ahead').

c) *Informatory signs*—always square or rectangular, and with:
i) *green background, white border and letters*—direction signs (to places or numbered roads) on primary roads, or
ii) *white background, black border and letters*—direction signs on other roads, or
iii) *white background, blue border*—direction signs to local places.

2. Placing of traffic signs

(1) Except where a particular sign has been specially authorised by the S of S, a traffic sign *on or near a road* must be of the size, colour and type prescribed by regulations (s. 54).

(2) No traffic sign is to be placed *on or near* a road otherwise than in accordance with the provisions of the Act.

Exceptions—a notice relating to the use of a bridge, or a sign placed under a special Act of Parliament (e.g. re tramcars and trolley vehicles).

(3) The Act authorises the placing of traffic signs as follows:

a) *By the S of S* on trunk roads and special roads.

b) *By the highway authority* in accordance with general or special directions given by the Secretary of State, by statutory instrument, or in connection with a regulation of traffic order (see p. 56).

c) *By the police:* a constable, or other person directed to do so by a chief constable, can place on the highway any signs prescribed or authorised by regulations:
i) to give effect to police powers to regulate local traffic under the Town Police Clauses Act 1847 (see p. 60) or similar provisions under the 1839 Act relating to the Metropolitan and the City of London Police, or to regulate cycle racing on highways (see p. 69);
ii) to prevent or mitigate congestion or obstruction of traffic or danger to or from traffic in extraordinary circumstances—but this power extends for a period of 7 days only (s. 58);
iii) in London, for the purpose of police experimental traffic schemes.

d) *By anyone*, in the case of the prescribed red triangle sign placed on a roadway or footway to warn traffic of a temporary obstruction of the carriageway. The sign has to be placed on the same side of roadway as the obstruction and not less than 50 yards from it. The sign must be supported in an upright position, apex upwards, with no more than 300 mm between the lower side and the road surface (Traffic Signs (Temporary Obstruction) Regulations 1966, as amended by SI 1975 No. 49).

(4) *A highway authority* in England and Wales is, for the purpose of:

a) *trunk roads* and special roads—the Secretary of State;

b) *roads other than trunk roads*—the county council and, in London, the Common Council of the City, the Greater London Council or a London borough.

(5) The highway authority can by written notice require the owner or occupier of land to remove therefrom any object or device for the direction of road-users. On failure to comply the authority can itself effect the removal and recover costs, and (by s. 63) can enter land for this purpose (s. 61).

3. Offence: failing to conform

(1) It is an offence for a person driving or propelling a vehicle to fail to comply with the indication given by a traffic sign to which the section applies (RTA 1972, s. 22).

(2) To come within the section the sign must be lawfully placed on or near a road, be one of the prescribed size, colour and type, and either:

a) indicate a statutory prohibition, restriction or requirement, or

b) be one to which the Act or the RTR Act 1967 or regulation expressly makes subject to this section (s. 22).

(3) The signs expressly made subject to s. 22 (the offence, therefore, being 'failure to conform' under that section) are:

a) emergency signs placed by the police (see (3) (c) (ii) on p. 88);

b) 'stop' or 'give way' (at junction with major road);

c) 'stop' (at road works requiring one-way traffic);

d) signs at railway crossings, requiring drivers of large or slow vehicles to telephone for permission to cross;

e) the diagonal arrow (for keep left or keep right);

f) the red traffic light;

g) the double white lines;

h) 'no entry' (white bar on red circle background);

i) signs giving a direction for the purpose of a traffic survey.

(4) Although some other signs (e.g. 'no waiting', 'no entry') could be regarded as 'indicating a statutory prohibition' (see (2) (a) above) and thus covered by s. 22 it is generally preferred to take proceedings in all other cases for contraventions of the regulations or orders under which the signs were placed (and not for failing to conform to the sign) though the maximum penalty is generally less than that under s. 22.

(5) A traffic sign is deemed to be of prescribed size, etc. and authorised until the contrary is proved.

Rees v Taylor (1939)
It is no defence that the defendant did not see the sign. Mens rea is not essential.

Davies v Heatley (1971)
The sign must comply with regulations though its meaning may be clear.

Stubbs v Morgan (1972)
A requirement that a sign shall be lit during hours of darkness does not mean that during the day it must be capable of being lit at night.

4. Traffic Signs Regulations and General Directions 1975

The Schedules to these regulations specify the size, colour and type of the various traffic signs authorised for general use on roads, and are designed to bring our road signs into line with those used on the continent. The regulations provide for special significance to be given to the following signs—

(1) Traffic lights (reg. 34)

Drivers passing light signals are to proceed with due regard to other users of the road and subject to the direction of any uniformed constable or other duly authorised person engaged in regulating traffic.

The significance of the light signals are:

Red—Vehicles not to proceed beyond the stop line or, if line not visible, the signal.

EXCEPTION FOR FIRE BRIGADE, AMBULANCE AND POLICE VEHICLES—If observance would be likely to hinder the use of the vehicle for its purpose on that occasion the red light shall indicate that the vehicle shall not proceed in such a manner or at such a time:

a) as is likely to cause danger to the driver of another vehicle or as to necessitate such a driver to change its speed or course in order to avoid an accident, or

b) in the case of non-vehicular traffic, as is likely to cause danger to that traffic.

Amber with red—Denotes an impending change to green, but does not nullify the prohibition of the red light.

Green—Vehicles may pass the signals.

Amber—As for the red light, except that if when the amber light appears a vehicle is too close to the stop line or signals to stop safely it may proceed.

Green arrow—A vehicle may proceed in the direction shown whatever other lights may be showing as well.

R v Warren (1971)
A motorist who passed signals on which the primary red light was not working was held not to have committed an offence.

Radburn v Kemp (1971)

R, a cyclist, entered a junction when the light was green and was two-thirds across when struck by car driven by K who had started across junction when light changed to green. *Held:* K was wholly to blame, for a motorist who has the green light in his favour is under a duty not to enter the junction until it is clear of traffic already there.

(2) Signs at the approach to a major road

THE 'STOP' SIGN is used with the letters 'STOP' painted on the roadway, together with two white lines at the point at which vehicles must stop. A warning sign (an inverted red triangle) may be placed not more than 100 yards back. The 'stop' sign requires a driver to stop at the transverse lines (or, if not visible, at the major road) and not to enter the major road in such a manner or at such time as to cause a vehicle on the major road to change speed or its course to avoid danger or a collision.

THE 'GIVE WAY' SIGN is associated with two broken white lines at the road junction and an inverted white triangle on the road surface on the minor road at the junction. A driver must not pass the lines (if visible) or enter the major road in such a manner as to be likely to cause danger to or a collision with a vehicle on the major road or to cause it to change its speed or course.

Both the 'stop' and 'give way' signs must be illuminated (internally or externally) during darkness if within 50 metres of an electric street lamp, otherwise by reflecting material. The posts on which erected must be painted grey unless made of concrete.

(3) Arrow direction signs (white arrow on blue circle)

The sign has to be illuminated during the hours of darkness when mounted in a bollard, or if within 50 yards of an electric street lamp; otherwise it must be fitted with reflecting material.

Except when used on the central island of a roundabout or fitted with a 'dual carriageway' plate (in which case the offence is failing to conform under s. 22) the sign requiring a vehicle to proceed in direction indicated by the arrow indicates the effect of an order, regulation, byelaw or notice, and any contravention is an offence under that order or regulation, etc.

Brazier v Alabaster (1962)

A 'keep left' sign can only indicate that if a driver is going to pass it, he should keep to the left of it. It does not prevent a driver turning right before he reaches it.

(4) Carriageway markings (reg. 23)

The only road markings to which s. 22 applies (offence—failure to conform) are the *double white lines* (both continuous, or one continuous and the other broken). It is an offence—

a) *to stop* a vehicle on any length of road having these markings *except:*
   i) for a person to board or alight from it*;
   ii) to unload or load goods (see cases under 'no waiting streets', p. 58)*;
   iii) when *necessary* for road works or work on public utility services (gas, water, electricity, etc.) or for building operations or the removal of a road obstruction*;
   iv) for fire brigade, ambulance or police purposes;
   v) pedal cycles without sidecars (even if auto-assisted);
   vi) when required by law to stop, or necessary to avoid accident, or due to circumstances beyond control;
   vii) with permission of a uniformed constable or traffic warden;

b) for a vehicle *to cross or straddle* the continuous line when this line is to the left of the dotted line or another continuous line in the direction of travel, *except:*
   i) to turn right into a side road, or land or premises adjoining the road;
   ii) when unavoidable, or to pass a stationary vehicle, or to avoid an accident;
   iii) to comply with a direction of a police constable or traffic warden in uniform.

NOTE
It is not an offence in itself to cross or straddle the double white lines when the broken line is nearest to the vehicle, but doing so places a special responsibility on the driver to take care, so that the crossing of the double white line in such a case may be of evidential value in a case of reckless or careless driving. This also applies to the single white line on a road and to the transverse lines at the junction of a major road unless the latter are used in conjunction with the 'stop' or 'give way' traffic signs.

   Evans v Cross (1938)
   A white line on a bend or down the centre of a road is not a traffic sign if not as prescribed and authorised.

(5) Diagrams of traffic signs

Colour illustrations of the many traffic signs and carriageway markings approved for use on roads (to convey warnings, directions or some information to traffic), and other road and kerb markings (to show where waiting (except for loading or unloading) is prohibited or restricted) are contained in the schedules to the Traffic Signs Regulations and General Directions 1975 and HMSO publications *The Highway Code* and *The New Traffic Signs*.
   The illustrations also show diagrams of informatory 'plates' which may be used with certain of the traffic signs and road markings where relevant, e.g. 'one way', 'dual carriageway', 'single file traffic', 'school', 'reduce speed now',

---

* Exceptions do not apply if it is reasonably practicable to stop at a lay-by or on a road verge for these purposes.

'accident' and 'for 2 miles', etc. Road users (and students) must be conversant with the signs because many of them have no wording whatsoever and their significance is dependant upon recognition of the symbols they exhibit.

(6) Temporary signs (reg. 27)

Signs temporarily placed on or near a road:

a) to convey information or warning to traffic, or

b) to convey any prohibition, restriction or requirement for a temporary statutory provision, or

c) pending erection of a permanent sign

must be rectangular, though the corners may be rounded and one end may be pointed (as a direction indicator). Letters, numerals, and symbols must be of specified minimum dimensions and be black on a white or yellow background or white on a blue background. The sign may include an indication as to whether it is a highway authority, police, AA, RAC or RSAC sign.

(7) Traffic surveys

Failure to conform to a traffic sign used in conjunction with a traffic survey is an offence against the RTA 1972, s. 22—see p. 89.

Chapter 9 Pedestrian crossings and school crossings

The RTR Act 1967 empowers the following authorities to establish and maintain road crossings for foot passengers:

a) *the S of S for the Environment*—who has a duty to do so in respect of *trunk roads in England*;

b) *the S of S for the country concerned*—on *trunk roads in Scotland and Wales*, or

c) *the local authority**—in relation to any road of which it is the highway authority, though it has no direct authority because any proposal for a crossing has to be presented for approval as a scheme, after consultation with the COP and requisite public notice, to the appropriate S of S.

Section 23 authorises the making of regulations governing the movement of traffic (including foot passengers), prescribing the limits of, and the markings and traffic signs to be used at, road crossings. Such signs are authorised traffic signs under s. 54 (see p. 87).

1. Zebra crossings

'Zebra' Pedestrian Crossings Regulations 1971

NOTE
A crossing is deemed to comply with regulations until the contrary is proved.

(1) The crossing

I) MARKINGS—The limits of the crossing are indicated by the following road markings:

a) *studs*—two lines of them placed across the carriageway in accordance with the specifications provided by the regulations, and

---

* The council of a county in England and Wales, in London the GLC, a borough council or the court of Common Council, and in Scotland the local highway authority.

b) *stripes*—black and white alternately between and at right angles to the lines of studs.

NOTES

'Stud' means a mark or device on the roadway, whether projecting above the road surface or not. The stud marks may be white, silver or grey, but must not project more than 16 mm above the road surface. The road surface, if it affords sufficient contrast to the white stripes, may constitute the black stripes. Non-conformity to a slight degree (e.g. as to measurements, distances, studs missing, discolouration) is to be ignored if the general indication of the crossing is not impaired.

II) TRAFFIC SIGNS—The presence of a crossing is indicated to drivers by traffic signs consisting of yellow globes, mounted on posts (striped black and white, the lowest band being black) or on brackets, lit by a flashing light and placed at or near each end of the crossing.

NOTES

If there is a central reservation or street refuge on the crossing globes may be placed there as well. In the case of a particular crossing the S of S can authorise constant lights instead of flashing lights. Slight imperfections, or failure of lamps (so long as one globe at least is lit) do not affect the legality of the crossing.

(2) The Zebra controlled area

On each side of the crossing (or on one side only in the case of one-way traffic) an area known as the 'controlled area' is marked by a pattern of lines consisting of:

I) THE 'GIVE WAY LINE'—a white broken line transversely across the road one metre from and parallel to the nearer line of crossing studs.

II) THE 'ZIG-ZAG LINES'—two or more white broken lines extending along the carriageway in a zig-zag fashion away from the crossing, starting 150 mm from the 'give-way' line and ending 150 mm from the terminal line. Each line must contain not less than 8 (but this may be 2 where compliance is not practicable) and not more than 18 of the 'zig' and 'zags'. Each zig and each zag part of the line is to be 2,000 mm long, and the space between each of them to be 150 mm.

III) THE 'TERMINAL LINE'—the end of each zig-zag line must be marked by a stop mark (rectangular, 600×200 mm), thus:

$\bigvee\bigvee\bigwedge\bigwedge\bigg|$ ← the 'stop' or 'terminal' line.

NOTES

Lines may be of reflective material. Slight departures from the specifications provided by the regulations have no significance if the general indications are not materially impaired.

(3) Additional lighting

A lamp showing a white light may be provided at each end of a crossing (or a central reservation on the crossing) if the authority concerned is satisfied that the presence of a foot passenger there should be better indicated during hours of darkness. The lamp must not be less than 2 metres above the ground and the light must not be visible to approaching drivers.

(4) Use of Zebra crossings

Note that regulations 8 and 10 apply only to uncontrolled crossings, i.e. those not at the time being controlled by a police constable in uniform or by a traffic warden.

I) PRECEDENCE—A foot-passenger on an uncontrolled crossing has precedence over any vehicle, and the driver of the vehicle must accord such precedence if the foot-passenger is within the limits of the crossing (as indicated by the markings described in para. **(1)** (i) above) before any part of the vehicle has come within those limits. Parts of a crossing on each side of a street refuge or central reservation are to be regarded as separate crossings (reg. 8).

II) STOPPING ON A CROSSING—

a) The *driver* of a vehicle (any vehicle) must not cause the vehicle or any part of it to stop within the crossing limits unless this is due to circumstances beyond his control or necessary to avoid an accident.

b) No *foot-passenger* shall remain within the crossing limits longer than necessary for passing over the crossing with reasonable despatch (reg. 9).

III) OVERTAKING IN THE 'CONTROLLED AREA'—When any part of a vehicle enters the controlled area the driver shall not:

a) pass ahead of another moving vehicle* on the approach side of the crossing and proceeding in the same direction, or

b) pass ahead of any vehicle stationary† in order to comply with reg. 8 above (reg. 10).

IV) STOPPING IN A ZEBRA CONTROLLED AREA—The driver of a vehicle shall not cause any part of his vehicle to stop in a Zebra controlled area (i.e. that part, or those parts, of it marked by zig-zag lines) (reg. 12).

---

* In the case of there being more than one such vehicle the regulation refers to the vehicle nearest the crossing (reg. 10).

† If on a crossing in a one-way street there is a central reservation or refuge, the parts on each side are separate crossings, and where a vehicle stops on one side of the reservation to give precedence to a foot-passenger on that side reg. 10 does not prohibit a vehicle proceeding along the other side from passing ahead of it (reg. 11).

v) EXCEPTIONS—The following are excepted:

a) reg. 12 does not apply to a pedal bicycle without a sidecar, whether having means of mechanical power or not (reg. 12);

b) stopping to comply with reg. 8 or reg. 10, or to avoid an accident or from circumstances beyond control;

c) stopping necessary for the purposes of a fire brigade, ambulance, police, building operations, or essential services;

d) stopping to make a left or right turn;

e) a PSV not on excursion or tour, stopping after passing the crossing to allow persons to board or alight (reg. 14 and reg. 15).

> **Moulder v Neville (1973)**
> Driver must stop if pedestrian is on the striped area, even though the vehicle is already within the zig-zag lines.

2. Pelican crossings

'Pelican' Pedestrian Crossings Regulations and General Directions 1969

This type of road crossing allows a foot-passenger to operate light signals by pushing a button in order to give himself precedence over traffic on the carriageway by bringing traffic to a stop at the crossing.

(1) Markings

Markings are as for Zebra crossings.

(2) The approach

The approach has three features:

a) the usual *double line of studs* to the centre of the road*;

b) a *white stop line* between 1·7 and 2 m from the crossing and extending from the near side to the centre of the road*;

c) a *white line* (100 mm wide) along the centre of the road starting at (a) and finishing at the stop line.

NOTES

a) On a road where the speed limit exceeds 30 mph the distance between the approach studs and the crossing must be not less than 23·5 m nor more

---

* All across the road in a one-way street.

than 26·5 m (instead of the normal 14–16 m) and where it exceeds 40 mph the 'stop line' must be 300 mm wide.

b) Imperfections in the pattern of the studs or white lines do not nullify the legality of the approach mark if the general pattern is not materially impaired.

(3) The light signals

These consist of a combination of traffic light signals, pedestrian light signals and indicators for pedestrians which normally show a green light signal to drivers and a red 'standing man' signal to pedestrians, but when operated by the push button are synchronised to show a sequence of light signals as follows:

TO TRAFFIC		TO PEDESTRIANS	
SIGNAL	MEANING	SIGNAL	MEANING
a) Green	Drivers may proceed	Red—standing man	Don't cross
b) Amber	Stop, unless unsafe to do so	As above, but on pressing push button the word 'WAIT' on control box is illuminated	Wait for the green signal, drivers have priority
c) Red*	Stop, pedestrians are crossing	Green—walking man, steady light	Cross—vehicles are stopped
d) Amber— flashing	Proceed if clear: give precedence to those on crossing	Green—walking man, flashing light	Precedence to those on crossing: others should not start to cross.
e) Green	As in (a)	Red—standing man	As in (a)

(4) The apparatus

The mechanism controlling the light signals must be approved (in writing) by or on behalf of the Secretary of State, and may be designed so as to be operated by remote control or their operation suspended if necessary. The container of the light signals must be coloured black, and any post upon which

---

* For the benefit of blind pedestrians a continuous audible signal will operate only while vehicles are stopped by the red light.

mounted must be coloured grey and may have one white band the lower edge being not more than 1·7 m nor less than 1·5 m from the ground. The press button must be in a yellow container which bears a plaque explaining pedestrian signals.

The regulations require traffic light signals to be placed on each side of the carriageway at a crossing but adapted in the case of a one-way street crossing to show light signals to vehicles in one direction only. Two additional light signals for vehicles must be placed on the refuge or reservation of such a crossing whereas one only is required on the refuge or reservation of the crossing in a one-way street.

(5) Offences

It is an offence for:

a) *a pedestrian* to remain on the crossing longer than is necessary to cross with reasonable despatch (reg. 12);

b) *the driver of any vehicle:*
   i) to stop any part of it within the limits of (i.e. actually on) the crossing unless it is due to circumstances beyond his control or to avoid an accident (reg. 12);
   ii) when the steady amber light is showing, to proceed beyond the *stop line* (if any), or the light signals if the stop line is not then visible, unless the vehicle cannot safely be stopped because of its nearness to the line or signals when the amber is first shown (reg. 6);
   iii) when the red light is showing, to proceed beyond the stop line or the light signals (reg. 10);
   iv) whilst the flashing amber light is showing, to fail to accord precedence to a pedestrian within the limits of the crossing before any part of the vehicle enters those limits (reg. 11);
   v) to stop the vehicle (not being a pedal bicycle without a sidecar whether auto-assisted or not) between the crossing and the furthermost line of the approach studs from the crossing, but *exceptions* which apply are the same as for uncontrolled (Zebra) pedestrian crossings (see p. 96) (reg. 9);
   vi) passing the light signals not to proceed with due regard for the safety of other road users, and subject to the direction of a constable or traffic warden in uniform and on traffic duty (reg. 6).

McKerrell v Robertson (1956)
Precedence must be given to a woman pushing a perambulator as soon as the perambulator is on the crossing and before she herself has stepped onto it.

Rockie v Soppit (1956)
The driver of a police car must at all times give precedence like the driver of any other car.

Wishart v MacDonald (1962)
Precedence means 'go before' or 'in front of' and arises only where a collision between the vehicle and a pedestrian is likely, it not

being necessary for the pedestrian to complete the crossing before the vehicle proceeds if he is out of danger when continuing on normal course.

Police v Bedford (1965)

A motorist has an absolute duty to give precedence to pedestrians on a Zebra crossing—when a pedestrian halted to allow a car to pass over a Zebra crossing but was struck by the car following, he had not waived his right to precedence.

Burns v Bidder (1966)

The duty is not quite absolute where failure to accord precedence occurs solely because the driver's control is lost from him by an event outside his possible or reasonable control for which he was in no way to blame.

3. School crossing patrols

RTR Act 1967, ss. 24 and 25

County councils in England and Wales, the Commissioner of the Metropolitan Police and the Common Council of the City of London are authorised to appoint school crossing patrols (other than constables) for the control of children crossing or seeking to cross the road on their way to and from school between 8 am and 5.30 pm or on their way from one part of a school to another.

A patrol on duty must wear the approved uniform and may require vehicles of any type to stop by exhibiting the portable circular sign prescribed by the Traffic Signs Regulations and General Directions 1975 ('stop, children', in black letters and bar on a yellow fluorescent background with a red fluorescent border), or any other sign which may be prescribed by regulations. The sign may be illuminated by an internal or external constant light. If external the light must be fitted either on the sign or on the pole to which the sign is attached. In any proceedings it is to be presumed (unless the contrary is proved) that the children were on their way to or from school.

It is an offence for the driver or rider of a vehicle:

a) to fail to stop before reaching the place of crossing or where the children are waiting to cross, or

b) to start again, after stopping, in disobedience to the sign.

NOTES

a) The onus is on the defendant to prove that the uniform or sign is not of the prescribed size or type.

b) Traffic wardens may act as school crossing patrols.

Hoy v Smith (1964)
The sign must be exhibited so that traffic can read the words 'stop, children', but it need not be precisely at right angles to the kerb.

Franklin v Langdown (1971)
There is a duty not to pass the crossing place while the sign is exhibited, whether children are crossing or not.

Wall v Walwyn (1973)
Once a sign is properly exhibited by a school crossing patrol, a driver must stop and cannot continue until the sign is removed.

Chapter 10 **Lights on vehicles**

1. Road Traffic Act 1972 (as amended)

NOTE
References are to the Road Vehicle Lighting Regulations 1971. The Act and regulations do not apply to certain invalid carriages: see p. 302.

(1) Definitions

a) Vehicle—means a vehicle of any description and includes a machine or implement of any kind drawn or propelled along roads whether by animal or mechanical power. (The Act and regulations do not apply to tramcars or to vehicles used on railway lines nor to certain invalid carriages—see p. 302.)

b) Road—means any highway or other road to which the public has access.

c) Hours of darkness—means the time between half an hour after sunset and half an hour before sunrise.

> **Gordon v Cann (1899)**
> *Held:* 'sunset' means sunset according to local, not Greenwich, time.

d) Obligatory lamps—are those rear and front lamps (side lamps or the pilot bulbs of the headlamps where combined head and side lamps are fitted) which the law requires to be fitted to every vehicle and illuminated whilst the vehicle is used or parked on a road by night and, in bad visibility, by day (see p. 131). As to headlamps, see p. 128.

(2) Obligatory lights and reflectors

THE GENERAL RULE (SS. 68, 69)

During the hours of darkness every vehicle on a road must carry:

a) *at front—two lamps* each showing to the front a light which is white or, if each is incorporated in a headlamp which emits a yellow light, yellow;

b) *at rear—two lamps*, each showing a red light to the rear, and *two reflectors*, red, unobscured, efficient.

NOTES
The above lights have to be visible from a reasonable distance. The absence of any one or of all constitutes one offence only. It is the duty of the person who causes or permits the vehicle to be on the road during the hours of darkness to provide the reflectors. When being used as such an obligatory lamp must be clean and efficient. As to exemption while parked see p. 124.

VARIATIONS

I) SOLO BICYCLES AND PEDAL TRICYCLES (S. 74)—are required to have one of each, i.e. one front lamp, one rear lamp, and one rear reflector.

Exemption—No lights need be shown (but rear reflector is necessary) on:

a) a solo bicycle (MPV or not), or a pedal tricycle wheeled by a person on foot as near as possible to the left hand side of the road, or

b) a bicycle or tricycle (*not* being a MPV) when stationary owing to exigencies of traffic or stopping to comply with a traffic sign or direction, if it is as near as possible to the left hand side of the road.

II) INVALID CARRIAGES (S. 74)—unless exempt (see p. 302) require one front lamp, two rear lamps and two rear reflectors.

III) ANIMAL DRAWN AGRICULTURAL VEHICLES (S. 75)—

a) if carrying inflammable agricultural produce on internal operations of farm—no lights needed;

b) if an agricultural implement or any vehicle used by person engaged in agriculture to carry *his own* produce or articles required *by him* for agriculture—only one front light (lamp to be carried on offside) needed, and no rear light, unless latter needed by virtue of a projecting load (see p. 105).

NOTE
'Agriculture' includes the use of land as meadow land, pasture, orchard land or for market gardens or allotments, but *does not* include use of land as woodlands.

IV) VEHICLES DRAWN OR PROPELLED BY HAND—

a) No light or reflector is required if the vehicle (hand-cart, truck, etc.) is kept as near as possible to left hand side of carriageway *and* its measurements (including load) do not exceed 2½ ft wide, 6 ft long and 4½ ft high.

b) If any of above measurements is exceeded the following applies:
i) if *not more* than 4 ft wide—one front lamp *and* a rear lamp or reflector are required;

ii) if exceeding 4 ft in width—two front lamps *and* one rear lamp *or* reflector are needed.

v) MULTI-PURPOSE LAMPS—separate lamps need not be carried if one lamp fulfils all requirements of the Act and regulations applicable to separate lamps (e.g. a lamp showing a white light to front and red to rear).

vi) COMBINED LAMPS AND REFLECTORS—if a tail lamp is such that it is an efficient red reflector when not lit, it is to be regarded as an adequate reflector when lit or otherwise.

(3) Restrictions on colour of lights (s. 70)

No vehicle shall show:

a) a red light to the front, or

b) to the rear any light other than a red light or a white light for, and when, reversing.

Material designed primarily to reflect a white light as light of that or another colour (reflectors, fluorescent materials) is, when reflecting light, showing a light for the purposes of the Act, whereas material merely capable of reflecting the image of light but not designed for that purpose (chromium plating, driving mirror) does not show a light (s. 80). Reflection from amber reflectors fitted on cycle or tricycle pedals are excluded from the prohibition.

The following are exceptions:

a) internal illumination;

b) illumination of the number plate, taxi meter or any device for giving signals to overtaking traffic, but the last named (direction indicators) must conform to legal requirements;

c) illumination of boards, plates or route or destination indicators;

d) lights required by regulations to be shown on vehicles or combinations of vehicles of excessive length (see p. 114);

e) *lamps showing a blue light* on vehicles of the following services: police, fire brigade, ambulance, salvage corps, Forestry Commission Fire Dept., Blood Transfusion, HM Coastguard and its Auxiliary Service, National Coal Board Mine Rescue, S of S for Defence bomb disposal units, dealing with nuclear accident or incident involving radio-activity, RAF Mountain Rescue, and RNLI vehicles for launching lifeboats;

f) *lamps showing amber light* on road clearance (dealing with frost, ice, or snow) or breakdown vehicles at the scene of an accident or breakdown or towing a BDV; vehicles used for maintaining, cleansing or watering roads, or for installation, maintenance or repair of any apparatus which is in, on, over or under a road (e.g. electricity, gas, water, telephones, etc.); a 'special type' if the order authorising it also exempts it from s. 70.

NOTES

The excepted lamps (in (e) and (f)) must be *rotating flashing beacons* used only when necessary to indicate the urgency of the purpose for which the vehicle is being used or to warn others of its presence on the road. Breakdown vehicles may use the amber light only when in the immediate vicinity of an accident or breakdown, but may then also use white lights (to illuminate the scene) which may be deflected or swivelled as required, but not so as to dazzle other drivers. Flashing beacons must be at least 5 ft above the ground, and rotate horizontally at a constant flash rate of between 60–150 per minute. More than one lamp can be used but the maximum wattage of lamps fitted must not be exceeded, i.e. 36 for an amber light, and 55 for a blue light. It is an offence for any vehicle not authorised as above to carry a blue lamp of the types described above (or a similar lamp).

(4) Restriction of movement of lamps (s. 71)

No front light shall be moved by swivelling, deflecting or in any other manner while the vehicle is in motion, but this does not apply to:

a) n/e two lights (other than obligatory lamps) which are deflected on turning of the front wheels of the vehicle, provided that in the case of a dipped beam lamp the highest part of the illuminated surface of the lamp is not more than 1200 mm from the ground (reg. 10);

b) amber reflectors on pedals of cycles;

c) special lamps carried on breakdown vehicles when used in the immediate vicinity of an accident or breakdown (reg. 65).

(5) Overhanging or projecting loads (s. 76)

I) LATERAL OVERHANG AND FRONT LIGHTS—If a load overhangs more than 12 in laterally from the centre of the front sidelight on that side the vehicle must carry a sidelamp within that distance in substitution for (or in addition to) that lamp, but this does not apply to a vehicle fitted with moveable platform for overhead working.

II) LATERAL OVERHANG AND REAR LIGHTS—If the load overhangs more than 12 in laterally from the outermost part of *the vehicle* (or its rearmost trailer) a rear lamp must be carried on the vehicle (or trailer) as near as practicable to the edge of the overhang and in any case within 12 in of it, but this does not apply to any vehicle carrying loose agricultural produce not baled or crated (reg. 37).

III) REAR PROJECTION AND REAR LIGHTS—If a load projects rearwards more than $3\frac{1}{2}$ ft behind its tail lamp(s) or reflector(s) then the vehicle shall carry a rear lamp so that no part of the load projects more than $3\frac{1}{2}$ ft behind that rear lamp but in respect of the following a 6 ft projection instead of $3\frac{1}{2}$ ft is allowed (reg. 36):

a) vehicle carrying a fire escape;

b) a MPV being a LT or an Ag Tlr on which is mounted an agricultural implement, whether a vehicle or not.

If rear lamps or reflectors are *not* visible from a reasonable distance because of the load, then the lamps and reflectors must be fitted to the rear of the load as if it were the rear of the vehicle (reg. 62).

(6) Vehicles towing and being towed (s. 77)

a) Front lights need not be shown on a towed vehicle.

b) Rear lights need only be shown on the rearmost vehicle.

c) Reflectors need only be carried on the rearmost vehicle.

Provided that—

a) if the distance between any two vehicles exceeds 5 ft then the foremost vehicle must show rear lamps, and the rearmost front lamps unless its width does n/e 1600 mm;

b) if any part of a towed vehicle or its load projects more than 12 in laterally from the centre of the front light on the drawing vehicle, the towed vehicle must have a white light showing to the front so that no part of it or its load projects more than 12 in.

(7) Offences (s. 81)

a) Cause or permit vehicle to be on a road in contravention of ss. 68 to 79 of the Act or regulations made under it, or fail to comply with these provisions.

DEFENCE—for driver or person in charge to prove to satisfaction of court that offence arose through negligence or default of another whose duty it was to provide the vehicle with any lamp or reflector.

b) Sell or expose for sale an appliance for use as reflector or tail lamp to conform with this Act (or regulations), not being one which complies with the Act (or regulations).

2. Road Vehicles Lighting Regulations 1971

NOTE
Most measurements relating to positioning of lamps are to be taken from the 'illuminating surface of the lamp' and in this summary 'IS' is used to denote this phrase. In tackling the regulations it is best to master first the basic principles and to ignore the exceptions to them until this has been done.

(1) Abbreviations used

Ag Imp	agricultural implement or machine, not horse drawn
Ag Imp (H)	as above, horse drawn
Ag T	agricultural tractor (as to meaning of 'agricultural' see p. 46)
EP	engineering plant
Excavator	vehicle constructed for moving excavated material and fitted with tipping or other device for discharging load
HD	horse drawn vehicle, not agricultural implement
IS	illuminating surface, i.e. the surface of a lamp through which light is emitted when lit, or the area of a reflector designed to reflect light
Ind T	industrial tractor (see p. 11)
LPV	large passenger vehicle for eight or more passengers
Post 1954	supplied by manufacturer or, if registered, first registered on or after 1st October 1954
Pre 1954	as above, before 1st October 1954
RT	vehicle designed and constructed to carry round timber
ST	special trailer, i.e. authorised as a special type
WT	works truck
W Tr	works trailer
Group A	locomotives, heavy tractors (u/w exceeding 50 cwts), goods vehicles, and goods carrying trailers other than a ST or EP
Group B	land, agricultural or industrial tractors, fire fighting appliances, vehicles belonging to a LA, or gritting machines
Group C	trailers of the type referred to in Group B excluding the tractors

(2) Obligatory front lamps (sidelights)

(As to obligatory headlamps see p. 128)

I) HEIGHT FROM GROUND—to highest part of IS must not exceed:

a) HD—100 mm

b) LT, Ag T, Ind T, Ag Imp, EP—2100 mm

c) any other vehicle—1700 mm or, if shape of body makes this not possible, 2100 mm.

Exception—The regulation does not apply to a LPV or MV propelling a snow plough.

II) DISTANCE FROM OUTER EDGE OF VEHICLE—(to outside edge of IS) is not to exceed 400 mm, but this does not apply to a tower wagon or a bicycle, whether a MV or not.

III) POSITION—

a) *HD*—not more than 460 mm behind the axle (or the front axle if more than one axle) measured to centre of IS;

b) *where one lamp is carried* (except bicycle, whether MV or not)—on offside;

c) *if two lamps*—to be fixed on opposite sides of the vehicle and at the same height from the ground (exception: if vehicle is asymmetric compliance may be as far as reasonably practicable having regard to the shape of the vehicle);

d) *dual purpose lamp* (combined front and rear lamp)—if used on a motor cycle sidecar, LT, or a horse- or hand-drawn vehicle, must be fixed so that no part of the vehicle or its equipment extends laterally on the same side as the lamp more than 410 mm from outer edge of IS of the obligatory front lamp contained in the lamp.

NOTES

If electric, the wattage of the bulb (or total wattage if more than one bulb supplies the light) must n/e 7 watts. The wattage must be indelibly marked on the metal cap or glass of each bulb, readily legible. Light must be diffused by frosted glass or its equivalent, and the lens be white.

(3) Obligatory rear lights

CHARACTER

I) SIZE—If circular the lit area must not be less than 2 in in diameter. If not circular the lit area must not be less than the area of a 2 in diameter circle and be so shaped that a 1 in diameter circle could be inscribed in it.

Exceptions—In the case of the following substitute 1½ in for 2 in above:

a) a pedal cycle (except a four-wheel cycle), a motor cycle n/e 250 cc or its sidecar, a horse-drawn or handpropelled vehicle, a trailer fire pump, or an Ag Imp.

b) a motor cycle exceeding 250 cc or its sidecar.

II) WATTAGE—Every electric bulb to be not less than 5 watts, with wattage indelibly marked on the glass or metal cap, readily legible. Exceptions as in (I) (a) above.

III) SHAPE AND WIRING—Where two lamps are needed both must have the same appearance when lit, the same lit area, and the wiring such that the failure of a bulb in one lamp does not affect the operation of the other lamp.

NOTE

The regulations governing character of rear lamps do not apply to such lamps carried on a MV or a trailer manufactured in Italy if bearing two separate groups of letters consisting of 'IGM' and 'LP'.

POSITION

The regulations provide two sets of requirements, one under reg. 23 and Sch. 1 and the other under reg. 23A and Sch. 1A. If the obligatory rear lights conform fully with the requirements of the latter the provisions of reg. 23 and Sch. 1 do not apply to the vehicle.

Requirements of reg. 23A and Sch. 1A—(applicable to any MV and any trailer but not a motor cycle):

a) two obligatory rear lamps are carried at all times;

b) they are symmetrically positioned and at the same height from the ground;

c) the extreme outer edge of the vehicle is not more than 400 mm from the furthest part of the IS on that side;

d) distance between inner edges of the IS of the lamps is not less than 600 mm (or 400 mm if the overall width of the vehicle is less than 1300 mm);

e) with regard to the IS of each lamp:
   i) the lowest part is not less than 350 mm from ground, and
   ii) the highest part is not more than 1500 mm from ground or, if the body shape makes this impracticable, 2000 mm;

f) specified vertical and horizontal angles of visibility have to be complied with.

Requirements of reg. 23 and Sch. 1 (which apply if the above conditions are not met):

a) *Where one light only is required* it is to be on the centre or offside, not more than 20 in from the rear, and not higher than 3 ft 6 in nor less than 15 in from the ground. *Exceptions:*
   i) a pre 1954 LPV: up to 30 in from rear and no limit as to height;
   ii) pedal cycle with no wheel exceeding 18 in in diameter (tyre inflated): up to 12 in from the ground;
   iii) hand propelled vehicle: within 3 ft 6 in from rear, and an additional requirement that the lamp must be within 16 in of offside.

b) *Where two rear lights are needed* the requirements given below apply.

NOTE

In view of the complications of the exceptions it is suggested that, so far as the examination student is concerned, the general requirements (given first under each heading below) and the exceptions relating to Group A are all that is needed.

I) DISTANCE FROM THE SIDE—One lamp on each side, no part of the vehicle or its equipment to extend beyond nearest part of lit area of the lamp on that side more than 16 in (or, in the case of a pre 1954 vehicle—24 in).

Exceptions—24 in for a post 1954 LPV and any hand drawn vehicle; 30 in for Group A and ST.

II) DISTANCE FROM REAR OF VEHICLE*—30 in maximum.

Exceptions—20 in for four-wheel pedal cycle, a motor cycle which has a sidecar attached (30 in for the sidecar); 3 ft 6 in for HD, ST and Group A; 4 ft 6 in for EP and Ag Imp; 9 ft for RT if an additional rear light is carried not less than 12 in from the rear.

III) MAXIMUM HEIGHT FROM GROUND (TO HIGHEST PART OF LIT AREA)—3 ft 6 in.

Exceptions—Excavator—4 ft 6 in; ST, WT, pre 1954 W Tr—5 ft; EP, Ag Imp, Group B—6 ft 3 in; lamp on near side of LPV being double decked and with doorless opening at rear—8 ft.

IV) MINIMUM HEIGHT FROM GROUND (TO LOWEST PART OF LIT AREA)—15 in, or if pre 1954, no limit.

Exceptions—No limit in the case of Group A, ST, EP, HD.

V) BOTH LAMPS TO BE AT SAME HEIGHT FROM GROUND.

Exceptions—Motor cycle with sidecar, LPV, EP, Ag Imp.

VI) DISTANCE APART—i.e. from any part of the lit area of one lamp to any part of the lit area of the other: no restriction.

Exceptions—21 in in the case of LPV, ST, or Group A (other than a WT or W Tr).

(4) Obligatory reflectors

GENERAL REQUIREMENTS

Two reflectors (*one* in the case of cycles with or without a sidecar and solo motor cycles) must:

a) be *mounted* on a vertical plane, facing squarely to the rear on opposite sides of the vehicle, kept clean and plainly visible from the rear;

b) if *circular*, have a minimum reflecting surface of at least 1½ in diameter, or, if not circular, of not less than that area and be able to contain a 1 in diameter circle;

c) be of shape capable of lying wholly within a 6 in diameter circle;

d) not reflect any letter, number or other marking;

e) be positioned as in (a) above, also as shown below (the abbreviations on p. 107 applying).

NOTE
(a) and (b) do not apply to:
i) vehicle made in Italy (not brought in temporarily by a visitor to GB) if reflectors have marking 'IGM', plus 'C.1' or 'C.2';

---

* In the case of a goods MV or trailer carrying a projecting load the distance is to be measured from the rear of the load.

ii) reflector bearing numeral mark I, II, or AU40 followed by LI, LIA, LIII or LIIIA.

REQUIREMENTS AS TO POSITION

As with rear lamps there are two sets of requirements—one under reg. 30 and Sch. 2, and the other under reg. 30A and Sch. 2A. If the reflectors conform fully with the latter the provisions of the former do not apply.

Requirements of reg. 30A and Sch. 2A (applicable to any MV except a motor cycle and to any trailer). These are the same as for rear lamps under reg. 23A (see p. 109) with the additional requirement that no reflector on a MV shall be triangular, and every reflector on a trailer shall be triangular.

Requirements of reg. 30 and Sch. 2 (which apply if the above requirements are not met):

Where one reflector only is required

The same provisions apply as for vehicles requiring one rear light (see p. 109).

Where two reflectors are required

Mainly the same as for rear lights, though the exceptions differ:

I) DISTANCE FROM SIDE—not more than 16 in.

Exceptions—Pre 1954 LPV—36 in on near side, 24 in on off side; RT—30 in†; post 1954 LPV, HD—24 in; Ag Imp (H)—no limit.

II) DISTANCE FROM REAR—not more than 30 in.

Exceptions—four-wheel cycle—20 in; motor cycle which has sidecar—20 in (but sidecar 30 in); all horse-drawn vehicles—3 ft 6 in; EP and Ag Imp—4 ft 6 ins*.

III) MAXIMUM HEIGHT FROM GROUND TO HIGHEST PART OF REFLECTING AREA—3 ft 6 in.

Exceptions—5 ft in the case of ST, EP, Ag Imp and Ag Imp (H), Group B, Group C, post 1954 WT and W Tr; 4 ft 6 in for Group A; 9 ft for RT†.

IV) MINIMUM HEIGHT FROM GROUND TO LOWEST PART OF REFLECTING AREA—15 in.

Exceptions—No limit for ST, EP, Ag Imp, WT and W Tr, Groups B and C.

V) BOTH THE SAME HEIGHT FROM GROUND.

Exceptions—EP, Ag Imp and Ag Imp (H).

VI) DISTANCE APART—21 in.

---

* 9 ft if an additional rear light is carried within 12 in from the rear of the vehicle, and not more than 5 ft from the ground.

† If an additional rear light is carried within 12 in of rear of the vehicle.

Exceptions—Motor cycle and sidecar, WT and W Tr—no limit; HD and post 1954 LPV—24 in; pre 1954 LPV—36 in; non goods carrying trailer n/e 4 ft wide—14 in.

(5) Front (non-obligatory) lamps

I) POSITION—Such a lamp shall be fixed so that with regard to its IS:

a) the highest part is not more than 1200 mm from the ground, except on a snow plough, aerodrome fire tender or runway sweeper, LT, Ind T, Ag T, Ag Imp, or EP;

b) the lowest part is not less than 500 mm from the ground unless the lamp is used only in fog or falling snow.

Exceptions—The regulation does not apply to lamps n/e 7 watts fitted with frosted glass or other diffusing material; a vehicle first used before 1st January 1952; a vehicle constructed or adapted for use for combative purposes or engineering operations in combat areas if its construction or nature is such as to render compliance impracticable; any other vehicle of the armed services supplied before 1st January 1956.

II) ANTI-DAZZLE: DIPPED BEAMS—A dipped beam is a beam (from a headlamp) which is deflected downwards, or both downwards and to the left, so that at all times it is incapable of dazzling any person on the same horizontal plane as the vehicle at a greater distance than 7·7 metres from the lamp and whose eye level is not less than 1·1 metre above that plane. No lamp showing a light to the front shall be used (except on a motor cycle) unless the beam of light therefrom:

a) is at all times a dipped beam*, or

b) can be deflected at will of the driver so as to become a dipped beam, or

c) can be extinguished by a device which at the same time either causes the lamp to emit a dipped beam or causes another lamp to emit a mixed beam.

Exceptions—The regulation does not apply to direction indicators, lamps with electric bulbs not emitting more than 7 watts in total, a lamp on a four-wheeled pedal cycle, or to distinctive or special lamps (i.e. as to colour: see p. 104).

III) SIDE-DEFLECTION—The beam of light from not more than two lamps (other than obligatory lamps) may be deflected to either side by the movement of the front wheels when being turned for steering purposes, but in the case of any lamp complying with (I) (a) and (b) above the highest part of the IS must not be more than 1200 mm from the ground.

---

* In this case the lowest part of the IS must not be less than 500 mm from ground, unless it is used only in fog or falling snow.

IV) WATTAGE MARKING—Every electric bulb used in a front lamp and every sealed beam lamp on a MV must be indelibly and legibly marked with its wattage.

(6) Lights on stationary vehicles

A vehicle stationary on a road must *not* show a light to the front exceeding 7 watts from any lamp or sealed beam lamp with a rated wattage exceeding 7 watts. (Where two or more bulbs are fitted to the same lamp and can be illuminated together the total wattage must n/e 7 watts, and where a lamp performs the dual function of headlamp and sidelamp, only the pilot bulb may be lit when the vehicle is stationary.) This regulation does not apply:

a) during an enforced stoppage of a vehicle;

b) to PSVs (including trolley vehicles) stopping to pick up or set down passengers;

c) to interior illumination of vehicle;

d) to a lamp on a tower wagon being used for its special purpose;

e) to direction indicators;

f) to blue and amber lights permitted to be used by special services (see p. 104);

g) to search-lights or other special lights fitted to vehicles used for naval, military, air force, fire service or police purposes;

h) or fitted to vehicles for carrying out emergency repairs to the utility services (gas, electricity, water, sewers or telegraph lines) whilst repairs are actually being carried out; or

i) to special lamps fitted to a breakdown vehicle used for illuminating the scene of an accident or breakdown, provided that the amber warning lamp is also being shown.

(7) Reversing lights

Not more than two to be carried (reg. 26), each lamp to be electric and not to exceed 24 watts (anti-dazzle rules apply). To be used only for reversing (reg. 29), and switched on only by:

a) selection (automatic) of reverse gear, or

b) driver operating a switch. (If the vehicle is first used after 1st July 1954, the switch must serve no other purpose and have a device readily visible to the driver in his seat to show that lights are on.)

ANTI-DAZZLE—Each lamp must be incapable of dazzling a person standing on the same horizontal plane as the vehicle at a distance greater than 7·7 metres from the lamp, and whose eye level is not less than 1·1 metre above that plane.

(8) Long vehicles and trailers: additional lamps

The following lamps are to be carried when on a road during hours of darkness:

SIDE MARKER LAMPS

Where the overall length of a vehicle or two or more vehicles (including any load) exceeds 60 ft there must be (during hours of darkness) on each side one such lamp not more than 30 ft from the front extremity, one not more than 10 ft from the rearmost extremity and others between, as necessary, so that there is not more than 10 ft between one lamp and another. *Exceptions* are:

a) any combination of vehicles which includes a broken-down vehicle;

b) vehicles with special appliances or apparatus, or carrying abnormal loads as specified in the C & U Regulations 1978 if provided with the required projection markers.

Where on a road during hours of darkness a load is supported by a MV and one or more trailers (not being an AV) the overall length of all exceeding 40 ft but not 60 ft, one side marker lamp must be carried on each side at the rear extremity or not more than 5 ft behind the rear extremity of the MV and if the load extends more than 30 ft to the rear, an additional side marker lamp not more than 5 ft behind the centre point of the overall length of that load.

FRONT MARKER LAMPS

Every trailer towed by a MV (on a road during hours of darkness) and not part of any combination referred to above:

a) *if exceeding 2300 mm in length*, must carry a front corner lamp on each side, and

b) *if exceeding 9·15 m in length* (excluding drawbar and fitting), a side marker lamp not more than 1530 mm behind the centre of the overall length of the trailer.

Exceptions—The requirement in (a) above does not apply to a trailer:

a) drawn by a passenger vehicle (for not more than seven passengers or their effects) or a DPV if the combined overall length in each case does not exceed 12·7 m;

b) displaying obligatory front lights within 12 in of extremities of side projections in compliance with s. 77 (3) of the 1972 Act (see proviso (b) to para. (6) on p. 106;

c) being a BDV being towed;

d) of width n/e 1600 mm.

CHARACTER AND POSITION OF SIDE AND FRONT CORNER MARKER LAMPS

a) If powered by electricity the lamps must be connected to the vehicle's electric supply, the wattage of the bulb (or total of the bulbs) must n/e 7 watts (which has to be indelibly marked on the glass or cap) and each lamp must be fitted with light diffusing frosted glass or other such material. Note in the case of a vehicle constructed to carry round timber the electric supply may be from a battery of at least 3 volts.

b) The illuminated area of the white front corner marker lamp and of both the white and red sections of the side marker lamp must be not less than the area of a 25 mm diameter circle.

c) Every lamp must be kept properly lighted, clean and in efficient condition, and also visible from a reasonable distance to a person facing the lamp. (Vehicles and combinations of vehicles which are required to fit these lamps during the hours of darkness need not fit them during the daytime.)

d) The highest part of IS of each lamp must be within 1530 mm from the ground, but side marker lamps are permitted up to 7½ ft in the case of an AIL authorised under the Road Transport Act, s. 4, e.g. special developments, prototypes, etc.

e) Front corner marker lamps must be carried within 1530 mm of the foremost part of the trailer (this may be extended to 3660 mm if by virtue of such extension no part of the trailer to the front of either lamp has an overall width of more than half of the maximum overall width of the trailer) and may be fitted to the front end if not obscured by the trailer, no part of which must protrude laterally more than 910 mm beyond the lamp.

f) If the IS of a front corner lamp on a trailer is more than 910 mm but not more than 1530 mm behind the foremost part of the trailer and no part of the trailer on the same side (being less than 1530 mm from the ground and in front of the lamp) projects outwards more than 510 mm from the nearest part of the IS, then the position of the lamp may be such that any other part of the trailer may project outwards by not more than 510 mm beyond it.

(9) Long vehicles and trailers—side reflectors

There are two sets of requirements concerning side reflectors, one by regs. 50–56, and the other by reg. 56A and Sch. 2A. If the requirements of Sch. 2A are fully complied with, then the provisions of regs. 50–56 do not apply to the vehicle.

A side-facing reflector is one which is not an obligatory reflector, is amber in colour, and bears the appropriate approval mark.

Provisions of reg. 56A and Sch. 2A

a) At least one side-facing reflector must be fitted to the middle third of the vehicle.

b) The lowest part of the IS of each reflector must not be less than 350 mm from the ground, and the highest part not more than 900 mm unless the structure of the vehicle makes this not possible, in which case the maximum is 1500 mm.

c) The foremost part of the IS of the foremost reflector must not be more than 3 metres from the front of the vehicle.

d) The distance between the IS of two reflectors must not be more than 3 metres.

e) The rearmost part of the IS of the rearmost reflector must not be more than 1 metre from rear of vehicle.

f) Each reflector is to be so fitted that its IS is vertical and at right-angles to the lengthwise axis of the vehicle.

g) No reflector is to be triangular, and every reflector is to be kept clean and plainly visible.

If the above requirements are not fulfilled, the provisions of regs. 50–56 apply.

Provisions of regs. 50–56

Two side-facing reflectors on each side have to be carried during the hours of darkness by every MV and every trailer the length of which exceeds 8 metres and 5 metres respectively.

The regulation does not apply to: PSV; BDV being towed if length does n/e 8 metres; mobile crane; engineering plant; material excavator; vehicle brought temporarily into GB by person resident abroad; a vehicle in unfinished condition proceeding to works for completion; VPE (regs. 50–56).

POSITION:

a) One on each side shall be not more than 500 mm from the extreme rear of the vehicle, and the other not less than one-third or more than two-thirds of the length of the vehicle from the extreme rear;

b) none to be less than 400 mm from the ground;

c) none to be higher from the ground than:
   i) 1200 mm on a post 1st October 1970 vehicle, or
   ii) 1500 mm on a pre 1st October 1970 vehicle;

d) each to be vertical, face squarely to the side; and

e) be kept clean and plainly visible from the side of the vehicle.

(10) Obligatory headlamps

See pages 128.

(11) Direction indicators

NOTE

The names used below to indicate the various types of indicators have no legal significance, but have been introduced to assist the student and to facilitate reference.

a) Vehicles to which indicators must be fitted

GENERAL RULE—Every MV (post 1936) and every trailer (made post 1st July 1955) is required to be fitted with indicators.

EXCEPTIONS—The regulation does not apply to:

a) *motor vehicles:* Ind T; a two-wheeled motor cycle (with sidecar or not); one for which obligatory lamps are not required or are non-electric; one which cannot by construction (own power and on level) or by law exceed 15 mph; L Loco; LT; WT; PCV.

b) *trailers:* LI; W Tr; Ag Tlr; BDV; part of AV and made pre 1st September 1965 drawn by MV not required to be fitted with indicators; drawing another trailer behind it; or which has no electric lamps or whose dimensions permit both rear or both side indicators of the drawing MV to be visible at a point 6 metres to the rear of the trailer (loaded or not), when the MV and the trailer are in a straight line.

b) Types of indicators for motor vehicles—The following provides a short description of each type and the name (of no legal significance) given to it for ready reference and to provide an aide-memoire. All have to emit a flashing light, except (I) which, instead, may be steady.

I) 'RISING BAR'—An arm (on each side of the vehicle) with transparent sides and which, in the 'off' position, rests in a recess or a receptacle on the side of the vehicle not more than 6 ft behind the windscreen. When switched on the arm becomes illuminated and rises to a horizontal position so as to become visible from front and rear of the vehicle from a reasonable distance.

II) 'SIDE-FLASHER'—A fixed lamp replaces the rising arm in (I) above. When in use the lamp must emit a flashing light visible from front and from rear from a reasonable distance.

III) 'FRONT AND BACK'—One indicator on each side at front, facing front, and at rear, facing the rear, flashing when in use.

IV) '1965 TYPE'—The system which became generally compulsory for MV first used on or after 1st September 1965 but which could be fitted before then—dealt with in para. **(i)** below.

v) '1977 TYPE'—Introduced by an amendment to the 1971 Regulations by SI 1977 No. 1560. Three indicators required on each side, i.e. at front and at rear with one indicator on the side between them. Each must conform to specifications as to position and angles of visibility. Dealt with in para. **(j)** below.

The type or system of indicators to be fitted to a motor vehicle, if not the 1977 type indicators, depends on the date of first use of the vehicle as follows:

a) first used pre 1965—any of the types (I) to (IV) above;

b) otherwise—'1965 type'*

---

* If first used post 1st January 1974 each indicator must have the appropriate approval mark on it, and if the rear indicators can be operated on either of two levels of illumination the wiring for them must be as for stop lamps: see p. 122.

c) **Types of indicators for trailers**—Trailers manufactured post 1st January 1975 must have on each side at the rear one indicator visible from a reasonable distance from the rear. If it is not of the '1977 type' for a trailer it must be either:

a)   a '1965' type'*, or

b)   'Part VI' type, as to which see below.

A 'PART VI' TYPE INDICATOR—may be either:

a)   *an illuminated sign* of 6 in minimum length, breadth n/e one-quarter of length, steady or flashing light; or

b)   *a flashing light* (15–36 watts)—illuminated area not less than 3½ sq in if two-wheeled (or four-wheeled close coupled) trailer, otherwise 12 sq in. Centre of lit area not more than 16 in nearer to centre than the outermost part of the body.

d) **Rear indicators: exemptions**—A MV needs no rear indicators if its trailer has one indicator on each side at the rear and the MV is part of an AV or is owned by a government department, and used for naval, military, or air force purposes, but if the overall length of the MV exceeds 19 ft 8 in flank indicators are needed within one-third of the length from the front. A flank indicator is one which can be seen when flashing from the front and from the rear of the vehicle on the side in which the indicator is placed. A BDV is not required to have indicators required by a trailer while being towed in consequence of the breakdown.

e) **Maintenance of indicators**—Every indicator fitted to a MV or trailer (whether obligatorily so or not) shall at all times when the vehicle is used on a road be maintained clean, and in good and efficient working order (reg. 76).

f) **Indicators fitted to exempted vehicles**—Though indicators are not required to be fitted to vehicles to which reg. 70 does not apply (see para. (a) above), if indicators are fitted to them they must comply with the following standards:

I) A TWO-WHEELED MOTOR CYCLE† (WITH OR WITHOUT SIDECAR)—with any one of the following: 'bar'; 'side-flasher'; 'back and front' or, if no electric lighting equipment, the non-electric 'hand' signal (see below).

II) OTHER MOTOR VEHICLES†

a)   *If no electric lamp and first used pre-* 1st September 1965, any indicator fitted must be of the 'hand' type, i.e. in the form of a hand 6 in or more long (on each side of the vehicle) presenting white surface to front and rear, positioned not more than 6 ft behind base of windscreen, so that when operated it projects at least 6 in beyond widest part of the body and remains 'steady'.

---

    * See note relating to motor vehicles (para. (**b**)). This type is described in para. (**i**) below. If the MV has '1965 type', then the trailer has to have the same type, and this includes an AV.
    † The regulation does not apply to pre 1936 vehicles.

b) *If with electric lighting* and the '1977 type' is not used—depends on date first used, i.e.:
i) if pre 1965—any one of the types described in para. (**b**) (I)–(IV) above.
ii) is post 1965—'1965 type'*

III) TRAILERS—If an exempted trailer does have indicators these must comply with para. (**c**) above.

g) Additional indicators—No indicator additional to the basic requirements can be fitted unless it is permitted by, and conforms with, the provisions relating to each type of indicator.

h) General requirements: electrically operated indicators—The following requirements, with the slight variations shown, are common to all types of indicators:

a) right hand turn indicators to be on the offside, and left hand turn indicators on the near side;

b) colour of light emitted to be amber†;

c) light to be diffused by frosted glass or other adequate means;

d) flashing light to be emitted at the rate of 60–120 per minute‡; duration of flash to be enough to permit full brightness to be achieved; to be fully observable at a reasonable distance;

e) one indicator on each side to be so fitted that driver can readily be aware when it is operating, unless there is a device which gives warning (audible or visible) to driver in his seat that indicators on that side (of MV and any trailer being drawn) are operating;

f) no indicator may be so fitted that when not in operation it is likely to mislead the driver of another vehicle or anyone controlling traffic;

g) every indicator on each side (including trailer when drawn) to be operated by one and the same switch;

h) total wattage of bulb(s) in an indicator not to be less than 15 watts or more than 36 watts, but this does not apply to the '1977 type' or the 'rising bar'.

NOTE
The most important types from the point of view of a student are the '1965' and '1977' types, which are dealt with below, and he should bear in mind the application of the above requirements to them.

i) '1965 type' indicators—This type became generally compulsory for all vehicles first used on or after 1st September 1965, but could be fitted to

---

* See note at foot of p. 117.

† The regulations which permitted 'red to rear and white to front' relate to types of indicators now rarely used.

‡ If one indicator fails (other than by short circuit) the others on the same side may continue to flash at a slower or faster rate than this.

vehicles used before that date. Five kinds of indicators, each with its own specification, were approved for use and named according to the position(s) from which the light emitted could be seen. The specifications cover the angles of light to be emitted by each of the five kinds of indicators, and the positioning of each one on the vehicle according to its type. These legal requirements are observed in the manufacture and production of vehicles (and indicators) and for this reason have been excluded from this summary.

KIND OF INDICATOR	TO BE VISIBLE FROM
Front	In front of vehicle
Shoulder	In front and alongside vehicle
Side	In front, alongside and rear of the vehicle
Flank	Alongside and rear of vehicle
Rear	The rear of the vehicle

REQUIREMENTS FOR MOTOR VEHICLES—On each side of a MV there must be fitted either:

a) *one rear indicator and one front indicator,* in which case at least one flank indicator is needed as well if the distance between front and rear indicators exceeds 19 ft 8 in or, if the MV is the traction part of an AV, one such indicator at a distance from the foremost part of the MV not greater than one-third of its overall length*; or

b) *one rear indicator and at least one shoulder indicator**; or

c) *at least one side indicator.*

NOTE

(b) and (c) provide visibility from front, rear and sides, but no visibility alongside is needed in (a) unless the distance of 19 ft 8 in between front and rear indicators is exceeded.

PARTICULAR POINTS

a) A MV needs no rear indicators if its trailer has one indicator on each side at the rear *and* the MV is part of an AV or is owned and used by the armed services for naval, military, or air force purposes, but if the overall length of the MV exceeds 19 ft 8 in at least one flank indicator is needed within one-third of the overall length measured from the front.

b) One or more additional indicators may be fitted on the side of a MV or trailer, but not on the front or rear.

c) Wattage requirements do not apply to an additional indicator.

d) Every indicator (except flank or additional) must have a lit area showing to front or rear of $3\frac{1}{2}$ sq in in the case of:
   i) MV of u/w n/e 2 tons†, or
   ii) a passenger vehicle for not more than twelve passengers (ex. driver)†, or

---

* In any case where more than one type of indicator is required on each side, one indicator which satisfies (or two or more which satisfy) the full requirements as to visibility (front side and rear) can be fixed on each side instead.

† If not drawing (except in an emergency) a trailer of kind described in (iii).

iii) a trailer with less than four wheels, or a four-wheel trailer having two close coupled wheels on each side,
and 12 sq in in any other case.

e) An indicator must be optically separated from any other lamp carried by a vehicle.

f) Where more than one indicator is fitted on the side of a MV, AV, or combination of vehicles (MV drawing one or more trailers), they must all flash at the same time.

g) Refer to para. (**h**) above for the general requirements which relate (with exceptions) to all indicators.

REQUIREMENTS FOR TRAILERS—See p. 122 and the general rules in para. (**h**) above.

j) '1977 type' indicators—This system will almost certainly be fitted to new models, but there is no legal compulsion about this, for the relevant regulation (70A) simply provides that the regulations concerning the fitting and specifications of the other types of indicators do not apply to a vehicle which has indicators complying fully with Sch. 5A of the regulations, the practical effect of which is summarised below.

CHANGES FROM THE 1965 TYPE SYSTEM—In connection with motor vehicles the main differences are:

a) instead of the five types of indicators, there are three, namely:
i) *front*—fixed on and showing to the front;
ii) *side*—fixed on the side between the front and rear at a distance from the front of the vehicle n/e 1800 mm and emitting light visible only from alongside and from the rear;
iii) *rear*—fixed on and showing to the rear;

b) all three types of indicators have to be fitted on each side of the vehicle;

c) the exemption relating to rear indicators on the MV part of an AV and on service vehicles does not apply.

d) a requirement is introduced requiring that each pair of indicators (i.e. the pair at the front, or on the side, or at the rear) must symmetrically match as to position and be at the same height from the ground, except that in the case of an asymmetrical vehicle (not symmetric in shape) these requirements are to be complied with so far as is possible having regard to the shape of the vehicle;

e) restrictions on wattage do not apply.

FEATURES COMMON TO THE '1965' AND THE '1977' SYSTEMS

a) The provisions concerning emission of light, angles of visibility and position on the vehicle are so closely proximate as to be regarded, for practical purposes, as identical.

b) The regulations concerning additional indicators, levels of brightness, and use as hazard warnings apply.

c) For other common features see para. (**h**) above, items (a)–(g).

TRAILERS—One rear indicator has to be fitted on each side at the rear of the trailer. The specification for it is the same as that for the rear indicator of a MV, and the common requirements set out in para. (**h**) (a)–(g) apply.

k) Two levels of brightness: rear indicators—Where, in the case of a post 1st January 1974 vehicle, the illumination from its rear indicators can be operated at two levels, the wiring of them must be as for stop lamps having two levels of illumination (see p. 123). A 'post 1st January 1974' vehicle is a vehicle required by law to be fitted with indicators and:

a) in the case of a MV was first used on or after that date and was manufactured post 1st August 1973;

b) in the case of a trailer was manufactured post 1st January 1974.

The indicators on such vehicles also have to bear the appropriate approval marks.

If any post 1st January 1974 vehicle not required by law to fit indicators does in fact fit them then this regulation applies to such indicators.

Exceptions—a non-electric vehicle and a two-wheeled motor cycle, with or without sidecar (reg. 71).

l) Use of indicators as a hazard warning—An 'appropriate device' may be fitted to a MV to operate simultaneously one or more of the direction indicators on both sides of the vehicle, plus one or more on both sides of any trailer being drawn, provided the device includes a warning light which indicates to the driver that the device is being operated, and is operated by a switch solely controlling the device. No device other than an 'appropriate device', as defined above, can be used for operating indicators in this way. The device may only be used when the MV is stationary on a road for the purpose of warning other road users, by the simultaneous illumination of the indicators, of a temporary obstruction of the carriageway of a road (reg. 77). As to emergency use of indicators on PSVs see p. 201.

(12) Stop lamps

DEFINITION—A lamp for the purpose of warning other road users, when lamp is lit, that the brakes of the MV (or the drawing vehicle, or the combination of vehicles) are being applied.

Every MV and trailer (with the exceptions given below) must be fitted with a stop lamp, provisions relating to which depend on the date on which the MV was first used (or, in case of trailer, was made) as follows:

a) Pre 1st January 1971—One is obligatory to be placed at rear, not left of centre, showing a red light. Another *one* may be fitted on the rear nearside if it comes into operation at the same time as the obligatory one, except when the offside stop light is operating as a flashing direction indicator. The light emitted must be steady and diffused by frosted glass or other adequate means (regs. 72 and 73).

b) Post 1st January 1971—Two stop lamps to be fitted each one to comply with the conditions of Sch. 6. (Exceptions: two-wheeled motor cycle (with sidecar or not) and IC—one lamp only required). The scheduled conditions are:

a) steady red light to be shown when the operating brake (not the parking brake) is applied;

b) filament wattage not less than 15 nor more than 36, durably and legibly marked on glass or metal cap of bulb, or, instead, (except in case of a motor cycle) having the appropriate approval mark on it (see p. 298).

c) Post 1st January 1974—The same as for post 1st January 1971 vehicles, plus the following requirements:

I) BRIGHTNESS—Wiring to be such that each stop lamp can be operated at two levels of illumination so that:

a) when the obligatory lights are switched off, the lamp, when used, is lit at the higher level;

b) when the obligatory lights are on, the lamp is lit, when used, at the lower level, except that when a fog lamp is lit as well a stop lamp may show brightness at the higher level.

II) APPROVAL MARKS—Each lamp is to bear the appropriate mark and number (see p. 298).

III) FAILURE OF BULB—Failure of one bulb in one lamp must not extinguish the other lamp(s).

IV) POSITION—To face squarely to the rear. (If an imaginary line is drawn to the rear through the centre of the lit area parallel with the chassis length, the light should be visible at least to a point 15 degrees above and below that line, and throughout an angle of at least 45 degrees on each side of it.)

No part of lit area to be less than 400 mm nor more than 1500 mm above ground when vehicle is unladen (but may be 2100 mm if construction of vehicle makes compliance impracticable). If one lamp only is required (motor cycle and IC) at centre or to offside of centre. If two or more are fitted, two must operate together, be evenly spaced from centre one on each side, at same height, with no part of lit area of one within 600 mm of that of the other.

EXEMPTIONS—Stop lamps are not required on:

Ag Tlr; L Loco; LI; LT; Ind T; PCV; W Tr; WT; BDV being towed; moped n/e 50 cc; MV limited to 15 mph by construction or by law; vehicles without electric lamps or not requiring obligatory lamps; trailer drawn by MV not required to be fitted with stop lamps; every vehicle except rearmost in a combination of vehicles; trailer drawn by a MV fitted with two stop lamps, both of which are visible from 6 m to the rear of the trailer; MV first used pre 1st January 1936.

NOTE
If a stop lamp is fitted to any vehicle though not required by the regulations, then it must comply with the requirement of Sch. 6—see (**b**) above. Every stop lamp must be maintained in clean condition and in good, efficient working order.

3. Standing without lights

By the Road Vehicles (Standing Vehicles) (Exemption) (General) Regulations 1975 the following exemptions with regard to showing 'obligatory' lights apply to vehicles standing or parked on a road to which a speed limit of not more than 30 mph applies, if the conditions specified are fulfilled, as follows:

I) IN A RECOGNISED PARKING PLACE—*if* the manner of standing or parking does not contravene any enactment or instrument relating to the parking place.

II) ELSEWHERE THAN AS IN (I)—*if:*

a) on a road not being a one-way street the near side of the vehicle is as close as may be and parallel to the edge of the carriageway, and in a one-way street as close, etc. either with the near side of the vehicle to the near side of the road, or its off side to the off side of the road; *and*

b) no part of the vehicle is within 15 yards of a junction of that road with another, whether the junction is on the same side as the vehicle or not.

The vehicles covered by these regulations are:

a) passenger vehicles (constructed to carry not more than seven passengers, excluding the driver);

b) goods vehicles n/e 30 cwt. u/w;

c) invalid carriages;

d) motor cycles and pedal cycles, with sidecar or not.

A '*recognised*' parking place is one which:

a) is established under a RTR Order or by a LA in exercise of its powers to provide parking places; or

b) has its limits indicated by the appropriate road marking traffic sign (i.e. by the longitudinal broken line that is also used to indicate the edge of a carriageway at a road junction or lay-by); or

c) has a surface of a colour or texture different from that of the road used primarily by through traffic; or

d) has its limits indicated by a continuous strip of surface of a colour and texture different from that of the remainder of the road.

NOTE
Any vehicle which has an overhanging projecting load (on which additional lighting is required by law) or with a trailer attached is excluded from the regulations. The regulations do not authorise standing or parking which is not lawful. The index plate is also exempt from illumination.

4. Motor Vehicles (Construction and Use) Regulations 1978

(1) Lighting equipment

a) *If provided with any front or rear lamp,* a MV must be equipped with such lighting equipment and reflectors that it can comply with the law relating to obligatory lamps or reflectors, i.e. the provisions of the RTA 1972 and any regulations made thereunder.

b) If a MV has a *headlamp* (i.e. any lamp exceeding 7 watts) this must be so constructed and fitted that its use would not contravene the anti-dazzle regulations (reg. 71).

Exceptions—The above does *not* apply to any such lamp carried if it cannot be readily used because it has been painted over or fitted with a mask or, if electric, because there is no system of wiring permitting ready use. A 'lamp' does not include a direction indicator; a lamp used for stop signals; a reversing light; internal illumination; or lamps for providing working illumination at night for land machines, works vehicles, or engineering plant otherwise than on a road. The special lamps required on overhanging loads, trailers and towing vehicles are also excluded.

(2) Maintenance

Every obligatory lamp, reflector, and headlamp, *if fitted,* shall *at all times* be maintained in such condition as to enable the vehicle to comply with law regarding obligatory lights, reflectors, and anti-dazzle when the vehicle is being driven on a road during the hours of darkness (reg. 105).

It is a *defence* to a charge (of failing to maintain in proper condition by day so that the vehicle can be driven at night) to prove:

a) that the defect arose during that journey, *or*

b) that it was due to a defect in the lighting equipment or a reflector of the vehicle and that steps had previously been taken to have it remedied with reasonable expedition.

5. Application of Act and regulations

The Act and regulations apply to Crown vehicles. The person deemed to be causing or permitting the vehicle to be on a road is the person named by the department concerned as being responsible. The Act and regulations do not apply to railway locomotives, carriages and trucks, or to tramcars, but do apply to trolley vehicles.

6. General exemptions

The following exemptions are provided by the 1971 Regulations.

(1) Vehicles brought temporarily into GB

Under regulation 63, vehicles brought temporarily into GB by persons resident outside the UK are exempt from the requirements of law regarding lights on vehicles provided the lighting equipment complies with the provisions of either of the following conventions:

I) THE PARIS CONVENTION 1926—This requires the visitor to have an international certificate in respect of any vehicle and trailer. There is no need for reflectors and it is sufficient for the vehicle to have:

a) *generally*—two front white lights and one red rear light (on trailer if so drawn);

b) *on solo motor cycles*—one front white light and one red rear light.

II) THE GENEVA CONVENTION 1949—This requires:

a) *generally*—two front white or yellow driving lights and two other similar type passing lights (i.e. anti-dazzle) of the prescribed standards of lighting and two white side lights: one rear light and two rear red reflectors.

b) *motor cycles*—with or without sidecar require one front white or yellow driving or passing light, one red rear light and a reflector.

The law respecting lights on overhanging and projecting loads must be complied with.

(2) Vehicles of the home forces and of the visiting forces of Canada, USA, Belgium and West Germany

Regulations 57 to 61 make provision that the above vehicles may be:

a) *totally exempt* when:
   i) used in connection with authorised training or exercises, if not less than

48 hours notice is given to chief officer of police in every area concerned;
ii) on manoeuvres specified by Order in Council;

b) *partially exempt:*
i) during tactical or driving exercises (notified to chief of police as above): if not less than 6 or more than 12 vehicles are proceeding in convoy at intervals of not more than 20 yards apart, the leading vehicle must have front obligatory lights; the front lights on the remainder need not be visible from a reasonable distance; the rearmost vehicle must have rear obligatory lights, but any other vehicle in the convoy requires only sufficient light under the vehicle so that its presence may be detected from the rear; such vehicles are also permitted to carry searchlights which might be moved or deflected while in motion (reg. 58);
ii) combat vehicles are exempt in relation to *size and position* of rear lamps and reflectors if they satisfy modified requirements (reg. 59).

(3) Vehicles of other visiting forces

Under reg. 60, these are exempt from the regulations relating to obligatory front and rear lights and reflectors if complying with the provisions of the Geneva Convention as in (1) (II) above.

7. Registration marks: illumination

Illumination of rear registration marks

Road Vehicles (Registration and Licensing) Regulations 1971, reg. 19

During hours of darkness the rear plate on a motor vehicle or its rearmost trailer on a road must be so illuminated that, in the absence of fog, every letter and figure is easily distinguishable and, if registered after September 1938, visible from within every part of a square the diagonal of which extends 60 ft directly behind it (or 50 ft for cycles, invalid carriages and pedestrian controlled vehicles which may also display the registration mark so as to be clearly legible from both sides of the vehicle). This does not apply to any vehicle while it is exempted from showing normal obligatory lights to front and rear.

8. Regulations governing headlamps

NOTE
A reference to a speed limit in relation to a MV means that it cannot by construction exceed that limit on the level.

(1) Application

The 1971 Regulations apply to any MV on a road which has electric obligatory sidelamps. They do not apply to a pre 1931 MV; PCV; Ag Imp; L Loco; LT; WT; RR; 6 mph MV; vehicle brought in by visitor if lighting conforms to Geneva Convention; vehicles of HM and visiting forces; vehicle purchased by person only temporarily in GB and who is about to be resident abroad—for n/e one year.

(2) Definitions

'Sealed beam lamp'—a lighting unit sealed by manufacturer which cannot be dismantled without rendering the unit unusable.

'Matched pair of headlamps'—one on each side of centre line of vehicle (ignoring any sidecar), at the same height, and at same distance from centre line (a variation of 25 mm being allowed).

'Moped'—motor bicycle n/e 50 cc equipped with pedals by which it is capable of being propelled.

'Headlamp'—lamp designed to illuminate road in front, not being a front fog lamp.

(3) Obligatory headlamps—for two- (and some three-) wheeled vehicles (reg. 15)

The regulation applies to (a) any two-wheeled vehicle and (b) a three-wheeled vehicle first used pre 1st January 1972 or, if first used post 1st January 1972 (except motor cycle) it has an u/w n/e 400 kg and overall width n/e 1·3 metres.

Nature—Each such MV shall carry either:

a) one headlamp on the centre line (excluding any sidecar to determine this) so wired that driver can cause either a main beam or dipped beam to be emitted (*exception:* on a pre 1st January 1972 moped with or without a sidecar or a MV not capable of more than 25 mph the light emitted must be dipped beam only); or

b) a matched pair of headlamps, wired to enable driver to cause both lamps at same time to emit either main beams or dipped beams (*exception:* a 25 mph MV to emit dipped beams only).

Wattage—The rating of the filaments (or at least one of them) in any lamp is not to be less than as follows (dates given are those of first use):

I) MOPEDS (WITH OR WITHOUT SIDECAR)

a) *incapable of exceeding 25 mph on the level:*
   i) pre 1st January 1972—10 watts;
   ii) post 1st January 1972—15 watts;

b) *capable of exceeding 25 mph:*
   i) pre 1st January 1972—15 watts;
   ii) post 1st January 1972—18 watts.

II) MOTOR CYCLES (WITH OR WITHOUT SIDECAR) N/E 250 CC

a) pre 1st January 1972—15 watts;
b) post 1st January 1972—18 watts.

III) ANY OTHER VEHICLE

a) dipped beam—24 watts;
b) main beam—30 watts.

NOTE
On vehicles subject to this regulation each lamp in a matched pair shall be placed so that no part of its lit area is less than 300 mm from the lit area of the other in the pair (*exceptions:* Ind T; engineering plant; motor bicycle).

(4) Obligatory headlamps—four- (and some three-) wheeled vehicles (reg. 16)

The regulation applies to any three-wheeled MV (not a motor cycle with sidecar) first used post 1st January 1972 of u/w exceeding 400 kg or overall width exceeding 1·30 metres, and to all vehicles with four (or more) wheels. Every MV shall carry either:

a) *a matched pair of headlamps* (as in (**3**) (b) above, including exception), or

b) *two or more matched pairs of headlamps,* so arranged that
   i) they form two groups, one group on each side;
   ii) the lamps in one matched pair* can be dipped leaving the others to emit main beams;
   iii) the main beams in all lamps can be extinguished at the same time by the driver and cause the dipped beams in (b) above to be (or continue to be) emitted.

EXCEPTION—In the case of a pre 1st October 1969 PSV with a matched pair of headlights it is sufficient if one lamp can emit a dipped beam, without a main beam being emitted from either lamp.

WATTAGE—Not to be less than 30 watts.

DIPPED BEAMS: POSITION—Every lamp emitting a dipped beam must be so placed on one side of the vehicle that no part of its lit area is less than 600 mm (350 mm for a pre 1st January 1969 vehicle) from the lit area of any other such lamp on the other side, and in the case of a post 1st January 1972 vehicle the outermost part of the lit area is not more than 400 mm from the outermost part of the vehicle on that side.

---

* The pair which is not nearer to the centre than any other pair.

(5) Single side/headlight units (reg. 17)

Where only one obligatory side lamp and one obligatory headlamp is carried, both can be in same unit. On a motor cycle with sidecar requiring two side lamps and one headlamp, one side lamp can be in same unit as the headlamp. On a vehicle carrying two obligatory sidelamps they may be combined:

a) if the vehicle has only two obligatory headlamps, with such lamps, or

b) with the two obligatory headlamps in the matched pair which are at least as far away from the centre of the vehicle as any other obligatory headlamp in another matched pair of obligatory lamps,

so as, in each case, to form two single units each comprising an obligatory headlamp and an obligatory side lamp.

(6) Obligatory headlamps: requirements (reg. 18)

Every such lamp shall:

a) be securely fixed to the vehicle;

b) be such that the direction of the beam from it can be adjusted (whilst the vehicle is stationary) to conform with the regulations;

c) be kept in a clean and efficient condition.

(7) Requirement for matched pairs (reg. 19)

Every pair (i.e. one lamp on one side and that on the other side which matches it to form the pair) shall comply as follows:

a) both of same shape and area when lit;

b) both be wired so that:
   i) beams from each at one time are the same (either dipped or main) and can only be switched on or off together;
   ii) if they emit supplementary main beams, these can only be switched on or off together with the main beams from another pair of obligatory headlamps;

c) both emit beams of same colour (white or yellow).

NOTE
A 'supplementary beam' is a main beam which can also emit a dipped beam and can only be used in conjunction with a main beam from another obligatory headlamp on the same side of the vehicle. The regulation does not apply to a pre 1st October 1969 PSV.

(8) Front fog lamps

May be beam of white or yellow only.

(9) Requirements as to use of headlamps

I) FOUR-WHEELED VEHICLES—A MV which has four or more wheels must, if moving on a road during the hours of darkness, keep lit a matched pair of obligatory headlights (reg. 21).

II) TWO/THREE-WHEELED VEHICLES—In the case of a MV with two or three wheels the same applies as in (I) above in relation to its obligatory lamp, or as the case may be, to its matched pair of obligatory headlights (reg. 22).

The regulations do not apply to:

a) PSV first used pre 1st October 1969 if one headlamp is kept lit, or, in fog or snow, one front fog lamp is kept lit;

b) a vehicle being towed by another;

c) a vehicle propelling in its front a snow plough;

d) a vehicle on a road actually lit by street lighting of lamps not more than 200 yards apart.

The regulations do not apply in fog or when snow is falling if the following conditions are fulfilled:

a) in the case of (I) above the vehicle carries two lit 'permitted lamps' (pl).

b) in the case of (II) if the following applies:
   i) *vehicle with one obligatory headlamp:*
   if a front fog lamp is carried, that lamp is kept lit, or
   if a three-wheeler, it carries two pl which are kept lit, or
   if a two-wheeler, it carries two pl, one only of which is kept lit;
   ii) *vehicle with matched pair of headlights and two pl:*
   if a three-wheeler—both pl are kept lit, or
   if a two-wheeler—one pl only is kept lit.

'Two permitted lamps' mean two front fog lamps, or one front fog lamp and one headlamp (not being an obligatory headlamp) complying as follows:

a) one lamp to be fitted on each side of centre line;

b) both same height above ground;

c) same distance from centre line;

d) no part of illuminated area of one lamp to be less than 350 mm from any such part of the other (or if first used post 1st January 1971, 400 mm). Under reg. 22 these measurements are varied to 300 mm for a three-wheeler under reg. 15 and 400 mm for three-wheeler under reg. 16 (see p. 128).

(10) RV (Use of Lights during Daytime) Regulations 1975

A vehicle in motion on a road during daytime hours must display lit its obligatory lamps* during any period when poor visibility conditions† prevail on that road, but where one headlamp or one front fog lamp or one or both of two 'permitted lamps' is permitted in fog or falling snow (see para. (9) above) the same will be sufficient compliance with this regulation (reg. 2).

---

* Front lamps, headlamps, and rear lamps.
† Adversely affecting visibility so as seriously to reduce the ability of the driver (after use of any screen wiper and washer) to see other vehicles or persons on the road or the ability of other road users to see the vehicle.

Chapter 11 **Registration and licensing of motor vehicles**

Vehicles (Excise) Act 1971 *and* Road Vehicles (Registration and Licensing) Regulations 1971

1. Introduction

The Secretary of State for the Environment is the registration and licensing authority.

An excise duty is levied in respect of the *use or keeping of motor vehicles on public roads. A 'public road' means a 'road repairable at public expense'.* This is achieved by the requirement that all such motor vehicles must be registered with and licensed by the licensing authority, i.e. the S of S. The law can be summarised under the following headings:

a) registration;

b) excise motor licences;

c) trade licences;

d) taxation.

For the purpose of the Act the owner, in relation to a vehicle, means the person by whom it is kept.

2. Registration

(1) The registration book

(referred to as RB)

When the vehicle is registered for the first time the S of S issues a RB to the owner or person keeping the vehicle. The RB contains prescribed particulars of the vehicle.

(2) Change of ownership (reg. 12)

a) *The former owner* must deliver the RB to the new owner and notify forthwith, in writing, the S of S stating the particulars of the vehicle and the name and address of the new owner.

b) *The new owner* (except as in (c) and (d)) must forthwith enter his name and address in the RB and send it to the S of S.

c) If he does not intend to use it on a road repairable at public expense, the new owner is required to do no more than to notify in writing the S of S of his acquisition of the MV, but if he subsequently wishes to use it on such a road he must first fill in and send the RB to the S of S.

d) If he intends to use it only under a trade licence he need not notify his acquisition until he either disposes of the vehicle or has had the vehicle for 3 months, whichever is the sooner.

e) Destruction or permanent export of the vehicle must be notified forthwith and the RB returned to the S of S (reg. 14).

NOTE

The S of S has approved an arrangement by which insurers who take posses-sion of a MV in settlement of a claim (on the basis of total loss) forward the RB to him to be overstamped as a 'write-off' with the words 'seriously damaged vehicle—insurance total loss payment'. This is designed as a safeguard against a not uncommon practice by which a dealer who has acquired such a MV as scrap from the insurers causes it to be repaired and sold without revealing the fact that the MV had been so seriously damaged as to have been considered beyond worthwhile repair.

(3) Change of address (reg. 13)

The owner must enter the new address in the RB and send it forthwith to the S of S to be noted and returned.

(4) Alteration to vehicle (regs. 10 and 11)

The owner must notify forthwith in writing any change affecting the particu-lars recorded, and send the RB and licence (if necessary) for amendment. If the alteration renders a higher rate of duty payable, the owner must send a new declaration with the RB and licence, for amendment and return.

(5) Alteration to registration book

It is an offence to deface or mutilate a RB or to alter or obliterate any entry, or to make any entry or addition to it except such as the law requires on change of ownership (reg. 8). A *duplicate* of the licence or the RB may be supplied if the original is lost, destroyed, mutilated, or accidentally defaced. If subsequently found the original must be returned to the S of S (reg. 6).

(6) Offences

It is an offence:

a) to supply false information for registration or respecting any change in recorded particulars, or

b) to forge, or to fraudulently alter, use, lend, or allow to be used, any licence, trade plate, identification mark or RB (s. 26).

NOTE

The registration book must be produced by the owner for inspection at any reasonable time on request of a police constable or a person authorised by the S of S (reg. 8).

The S of S must supply free of charge to the police or a local authority full particulars of registration, and to any person showing reasonable cause, for a fee of £2, the name and address of the owner of the vehicle and particulars of its last licence (reg. 15).

(7) The registration mark (RM) (reg. 9)

a) Allocation—On registration, an index mark (i.e. a registration number) is assigned to and has to be fixed on the MV in the prescribed manner.

The mark is attached to the vehicle until it is broken up, destroyed, permanently exported.

b) Offences—It is an offence to drive a MV on a public road (s. 22):

a) *without a RM* unless the MV is being taken to be registered and there had been no reasonable opportunity of registration beforehand, or

b) with the *RM obscured or not easily distinguishable,* unless the driver proves that he had taken all reasonable steps to prevent this occurring.

c) Exhibition on a MV registered post 1st October 1938—the RM must be exhibited on the front and rear of the vehicle:

a) *On*
   i) *a flat rectangular plate,* or
   ii) *a flat rectangular surface,* forming part of the vehicle surface.

b) *Facing squarely to the front or rear (bicycle—to rear only),* except on:
   i) an IC or PCV in which cases the plate need not be rectangular and the front plate may have duplicate faces so as to be distinguishable from each side (but not from the front) or on both sides of the front mudguard, and
   ii) a works truck or agricultural machine, on which the RM may be on both sides or legible only from the back of the vehicle.

c) *Easily legible* in normal daylight:

i) up to 60 ft directly to the rear in the case of the rear mark of a bicycle, IC or PCV or

ii) up to 75 ft directly in front or to rear in all other cases, *and*

iii) from every part of an imaginary square of which the above distances form a diagonal, the diagonal extending directly to the front or rear as the case may be, but excluding any part of the square within 10 ft of the vehicle (reg. 18).

d) *Illumination of rear mark:* when the MV is used or kept on a public road during hours of darkness every letter and figure of the rear RM (on the MV or, if drawing others, the rearmost vehicle) must be so illuminated that the letters and figures are easily legible (in absence of fog), the relevant distances (and diagonals) being reduced to 50 ft and 60 ft respectively. These provisions do not apply where the vehicles are exempted from showing obligatory lights (reg. 19).

Where any vehicle is drawn by a MV, the RM of the drawing vehicle (or a duplicate of it) must be carried on the rear of the rearmost vehicle, but a trailer drawn by a restricted vehicle (see para. (VI) on p. 143) may exhibit the mark of any other restricted vehicle owned by the same person (reg. 22).

d) Exhibition—on a MV registered pre 1st October 1938—(reg. 20 and Sch. 3)

I) POSITION—Motor bicycle—on back of vehicle; any other vehicle—on front and back in vertical position (letters and figures easily distinguishable).

Exceptions—Motor cycle, IC or PCV may exhibit RM at the front on a flat plate having duplicate faces (to be seen from each side) or on both sides of the front mudguard.

II) ILLUMINATION—During hours of darkness on a road a lamp must illuminate (by reflection or otherwise) and render easily distinguishable any letter and figure exhibited at the rear of the MV or of the rearmost vehicle attached to it.

NOTE

These provisions do not apply to a WT or agricultural machine, on which the RM must be either on (and clearly visible from) both sides, or on the back and clearly legible to the rear, the letters and figures on the RM in each case being vertical (reg. 21).

e) Form and dimensions (Sch. 2, Part 2)

GENERAL REQUIREMENTS—These are that:

a) the RM shall be exhibited on a plate complying with British Standards specification and with 'B.S. AU 145a' legibly and permanently marked on it to indicate that it does comply;

b) the letters and figures must be black and not reflex reflective;

c) the background must be of reflex reflecting material and white (for front) or yellow (for the rear) kept clean and efficient.

3. Excise motor licences

(1) Offences

It is an offence to *keep* or *use* a MV on a public road without a current excise motor licence (s. 8), *except* when lawfully used:

a) under a trade licence, or

b) under an International Circulation Permit, or

c) when no duty is payable under the Act (s. 7).

By s. 38 a person keeps a vehicle on a public road if he causes it to be there for any period, however short.

By s. 8 (2) it is a defence to prove that while an expired licence for the vehicle was in force an application was made for its renewal which included the period in question, that the expired licence was being exhibited as legally required for a current licence, and that the period between the date of expiry of the expired licence and that of the alleged offence did not exceed 14 days.

In addition to the penalty for unlicensed use or keeping, the person responsible for licensing the vehicle (whether or not the registered owner) is also liable for payment of back duty calculated on the basis of one-twelfth of the annual duty for each month (or part) within the period from date or expiry of the last licence taken out for the vehicle or when the new owner notified the council of his acquisition to the date of the offence. The recovery of back duty is enforceable by the courts as a fine.

If the amount of back duty claimed is not admitted the onus of satisfying the court that the claim is unfounded rests with the defendant who must call witnesses or other evidence to the effect that during the relevant period (or part):

a) the vehicle was laid up, or

b) the vehicle was not used on a public road as in (c) above, or

c) the defendant was not the user or keeper of the vehicle (e.g. where no notice of acquiring it had been given).

Where proceedings are taken under the Magistrates' Courts Act 1957 (whereby a defendant might plead guilty by post) the amount of back duty payable will be notified with the summons under the same procedure (ss. 8 and 9).

(2) Duty to give information (s. 27)

Where an unlicensed MV has been used or kept on a road or a greater number of MV used at any one time than is authorised to be so used under a trade licence, it is an offence when so required by or on behalf of a COP or the S of S:

a) *for the owner of the MV* to fail to give such information as he can as to the identity of the keeper and/or user;

b) *for any other person* to fail to give such information as he can as to the identity of any of the persons concerned; and

c) *for the user of the MV* to fail to give such information as is in his power as to the identity of the person by whom the vehicle was kept at the time.

Osgerby v Walden (1967)
The prosecution must prove that the constable requiring information was acting on behalf of the COP.

DEFENCE—In the case of the keeper to prove that he did not know or could not with reasonable diligence have found out who the user or keeper was.

(3) Types of licences

The appropriate licence is to be exhibited on a MV at all times when it is being *kept or used* on a public road. Licences are of two kinds, i.e.:

I) A TRADE LICENCE—Issued to a trader (manufacturer, repairer, etc.) in motor vehicles or a vehicle tester, and may be used (subject to conditions) on any vehicle for the purpose of the holder's trade (see p. 146).

II) THE ORDINARY LICENCE—Issued to the registered keeper in respect of a particular vehicle. It cannot be used on any other vehicle, but may be transferred with the vehicle to which it refers.

Owner means the person by whom the vehicle is kept.

Abercromby v Morris (1932)
The owner who lends a car to a friend for a period on the undertaking that the friend will renew the licence is not liable for unauthorised use by the friend on expiry of the licence.

Carpenter v Campbell (1953)
Both lorry driver and company were convicted for *using* a vehicle without a licence. The LCJ said it was wrong to summons a driver who is in no way responsible for the renewal of the licence which is the owner's responsibility (*NB*: this does not of course preclude a charge of aiding and abetting by the driver).

The following particulars are shown on the licence:

a) the RM of the vehicle;

b) HP, cylinder capacity, seating capacity, or u/w;

c) the class (i.e. private, goods, hackney) make and colour of the vehicle;

d) the stamp of the licensing authority, date of issue and date of expiry;

e) amount of duty paid (or the word 'nil');

f) the period for which it is taken out. (The last month of expiry is shown as the centre bar of the licence.)

(4) Issue and renewal (regs. 4, 5 and 6)

A licence can be obtained on application on the prescribed form to the S of S not more than 14 days before the date on which it is to take effect. The application is to be accompanied by the duty payable, the RB, a current certificate of insurance or deposit and, where applicable, a test certificate or declaration of exemption or, in case of goods vehicles requiring them, certificates of type approval (see p. 214).

(5) Duration of licence

A licence may be taken out for any period of 12 months or, if annual rate of duty exceeds £8, for any period of 4 months. A 'seven day licence' can be taken out in respect of a goods vehicle authorised to be used on roads by order of the S of S under RTA 1972, s. 42, which relates to:

a) special vehicles or types of vehicles constructed for special purposes or for tests or trial;

b) vehicles (or types of vehicles) constructed for use outside the UK;

c) new or improved types of vehicles, or vehicles equipped with new or improved equipment; and

d) vehicles carrying loads of exceptional dimensions, provided in each case that the u/w of the vehicle exceeds 11 tons.

(6) Exhibition of licence (reg. 16)

The licence must be carried on the vehicle* in a *weather proof holder* and be clearly visible by daylight to a person at the nearside of the road in the following manner:

a) *bicycles, motor scooters, bicycles with trailers, tricycles*—on nearside in front of the driving seat;

b) *motor bicycles with sidecars*—on nearside of handlebars or nearside of sidecar in front of the driver's seat;

c) *other vehicles:*
   i) if windscreen fitted extends to nearside, on or adjacent to nearside of the screen, or
   ii) if vehicle has a driver's cab with a nearside window, on that window or on the nearside between $2\frac{1}{2}$ ft and 6 ft above ground and in front of the driver's seat.

OFFENCE—To use or keep on a public road any MV subject to duty under the Act without having fixed to and exhibited on it in the above prescribed

---

* Reg. 16 exempts display when the licence has been taken into a post office for the obtaining of a new licence.

manner a current excise licence for the vehicles (s. 12). The defence under s. 8 (see para. (1) above) applies here also.

Pilgrim v Dean (1974)
The offences of 'using' without an excise licence and failing to display the licence are not alternatives. Both are committed at the same time.

(7) Offences: misuse of licences

The licensing authority is careful not to issue licences on which erasure or alteration has been made, and while it is impossible to guarantee that a faulty licence will not be released for use, this fact should be borne in mind when an alteration or defect in a licence is evident.

The Vehicles (Excise) Act 1971 and the 1971 regulations also create a number of offences relating to licences, the following being of particular interest:

a) To forge, fraudulently alter or use, fraudulently lend or allow to be used by another person any identification mark, excise motor licence or RB (s. 26).

Taylor v Emerson (1962)
An unaltered licence, although expired, is still a licence for the purpose of this offence.

Cook v Lanyon (1972)
Where a MV on land not on a public road exhibited a current licence for another vehicle it was held there could be no conviction because fraudulent intent to avoid payment of duty had not been proved.

b) To alter, deface, or add anything to a licence or to exhibit any licence on a MV which has been altered, etc. or upon which the figures or particulars have become illegible or the colour has become altered by fading or otherwise.

c) To exhibit anything which is intended to be or could be mistaken for a licence (reg. 7).

Elias v Passmore (1934)
The seizure (although unauthorised) is excusable if the document is in fact used as evidence that a crime was committed.

4. Trade licences

Vehicles (Excise) Act 1971, s. 16

ABBREVIATIONS
TL—trade licence
LH—licence holder

(1) Introduction

A trade licence is an excise licence which enables a motor trader, or a vehicle tester, to use on a public road for the purposes of his trade or business a motor vehicle for which an ordinary excise licence is not in force. The licence covers, in respect of:

I) A MOTOR TRADER—All MV temporarily in his possession in the course of his business, and 'recovery vehicles' kept by him to deal with disabled vehicles.

II) A MOTOR MANUFACTURER—All MV kept and used by him *solely* for conducting research and developments in his business as manufacturer.

III) A VEHICLE TESTER—All MV submitted to him for testing in his business as a tester.

(2) Definitions

A MOTOR TRADER includes a manufacturer* or repairer of, or dealer in, MVs. The business of collecting and delivering is 'dealing' in MVs if it includes no other activity except as a motor trader.

A VEHICLE TESTER is one who, not being a motor trader, in the course of his business regularly tests MVs belonging to other persons.

A RECOVERY VEHICLE is a MV on which there is mounted, or which is drawing or carrying as part of its equipment, apparatus for raising a disabled vehicle partly or wholly or for drawing the vehicle when so raised, but is not used to convey goods except the disabled vehicle, and carries nothing else but articles necessary to operate the apparatus or deal with the disabled vehicle. A Land-Rover to which has been fitted a towing buoy is a recovery vehicle (*Sweeney v Dean* (1971)). Where a vehicle had lifting jacks fitted but could not carry out suspended towing it was held to be a recovery vehicle, for such a vehicle can be one of two kinds, i.e.

a) a vehicle for raising, and

b) one for drawing another when so raised (*Pearson & Son Ltd v Richardson* (1972)).

(3) Limitations on use

A TL does not entitle the holder:

a) to use more than one MV at any one time except where a recovery vehicle is drawing a BDV (*note:* more than one TL can be taken out by the same person: an AV counts as one vehicle);

b) to use a MV for a purpose other than a prescribed purpose (see p. 143);

c) to keep a MV on a road if it is not being used thereon.

---

* A TL held by a manufacturer covers, therefore, the vehicles referred to in both (1) (I) and (II) above.

(4) Issue and duration

Issued by the S of S, either for a calendar year, or for three months beginning on first day of January, April, July or October.

Exception—a TL for vehicles n/e 8 cwts u/w cannot be issued for less than a calendar year.

(5) Offences

The following are offences (S) (£50 or five times amount of duty, whichever is greater):

a) using greater number of vehicles at one time than authorised by licence(s);

b) using vehicle for purpose not prescribed;

c) using the TL to keep on a public road a MV not being used on that road.

(6) Road Vehicles (Registration and Licensing) Regulations 1971

I) FORM OF LICENCE—To contain following particulars:

a) name and business address of holder;

b) registration mark assigned to holder;

c) date of expiry and amount of duty paid;

d) serial no., and date stamp of office of issue.

II) CHANGE OF ADDRESS—Change of business name or address to be notified forthwith and licence returned for amendment (reg. 30).

III) ISSUE AND REPLACEMENT—Two plates (for front and rear) are issued in respect of each licence and appropriate to class of vehicles covered by the licence. Each bears registration number, and one will have the licence holder attached. If the trader handles Schedule 1 vehicles (bicycles, etc. under 8 cwts) as well as other vehicles he will be supplied with a second pair for use with Schedule 1 vehicles. The plates remain the property of the S of S and have to be returned when licence ceases to be in force or the business ceases. The holder must apply for replacements in case of loss, destruction, mutilation, defacement, illegibility, etc. If replacement is for loss of legibility or colour through no fault of holder, replacement can be free. If a lost trade plate is found after a replacement the holder must return it forthwith or, if not possessing it, take all reasonable steps to recover and return, or, if unsuccessful, notify the S of S of the facts (reg. 31).

IV) ALTERATION OF PLATES, ETC.—No person shall:

a) alter, deface, mutilate or add anything to a plate, or exhibit on any MV a plate altered or defaced, etc. or with figures or particulars illegible or colour altered by fading or otherwise, or

b) exhibit on any MV anything which could be mistaken for a trade plate (reg. 32).

V) EXHIBITION OF TRADE PLATES—No person shall use a vehicle on a public road under a TL except as follows:

a) with the trade plates fixed to it and displayed in same way as required for registration marks;

b) the front plate must be one with the licence holder, with the licence fixed to the plate and clearly visible by daylight (reg. 33).

VI) RESTRICTIONS ON USE—No person (other than LH) shall use on a public road a vehicle exhibiting a trade plate or a trade licence, but this is not to apply to a person *driving* with the consent of the LH if the vehicle is being *used* by the LH under the licence (reg. 34).

VII) PERMITTED PURPOSES—(reg. 35):

a) A motor trader shall not use a MV on a public road under a TL unless it is in his temporary possession in the course of his business as such, or for a purpose other than a business purpose and other than one of the following:
i) test or trial of vehicle (or equipment or accessories) in course of construction or repair, or after completion of either;
ii) proceeding to and from a public weighbridge (for u/w) to place of registration or inspection;
iii) test or trial for publicity purposes or for a prospective purchaser or proceeding to or from place of test or trial;
iv) delivery to place where the purchaser intends to keep it;
v) demonstrating the operation of the vehicle or its equipment or accessories when being handed over to a purchaser;
vi) delivery to parts of his own premises or premises of another manufacturer, dealer or repairer, and removing it directly back again to his own premises;
vii) going to and coming from a workshop refitting of body or special equipment or accessory, painting or repair;
viii) proceeding from premises of manufacturer, repairer or dealer, to railway station, aerodrome or wharf (for transport) or vice versa;
ix) journey to and from storage place, garage or salesroom where vehicle is to be or has been stored (or offered for sale);
x) to and from place of testing or where it is to be broken up or dismantled;
xi) in the case of a *recovery vehicle*, to and from place where its service is needed or it is being held available for rendering assistance to a disabled vehicle or (with trailer or not) carrying or towing a disabled vehicle from place of breaking down, or to a place for repair or storage or breaking-up;
xii) in the case of a *manufacturer's research vehicle*, this must only be used on a road by the manufacturer for research and development purposes (reg. 36).

'*Business purpose*'—purpose connected with his business as a manufacturer, repairer of or dealer in MV or of trailers, if the trailer business is carried on in conjunction with the motor trader business (reg. 35).

Use of trailer—where a MV used under a TL is drawing a trailer (except in the case of a recovery vehicle in (xi) above) the MV and trailer is to be deemed one vehicle.

b) *A vehicle tester* shall not use a MV under his TL on a public road for any purpose other than testing it or any trailer drawn thereby, or any accessories or equipment on the MV or trailer, in the course of his testing business (reg. 37).

VIII) CONVEYANCE OF BURDEN—(reg. 38)

Motor trader (excluding a manufacturer's research vehicle)—No goods or burden to be conveyed by a MV under a TL on a public road except:

a) a load carried solely for test/trial or demonstration of the vehicle or its accessories or equipment (as in permitted purposes (i), (iii) and (v) above), and returned to place of loading without removal from vehicle except for such purposes or in case of accident;

b) the load carried by a recovery vehicle necessary for its operation as such, or consisting of the BDV;

c) any load built in as part of the MV or permanently attached thereto;

d) a load of parts, accessories, etc. designed to be fitted to the vehicle when operating under permitted purposes (vi), (vii) or (viii) above;

e) load consisting of a trailer in the course of permitted purposes (iv), (vii) or (viii)—delivery, fitment, painting, repair, shipment.

Manufacturer's research vehicle—no load except:

a) one solely for testing vehicles or accessories or equipment and not removed except as part of the test or in case of accident; or

b) a load built into the vehicle or permanently attached thereto.

Vehicle tester—(reg. 39) no load other than one:

a) solely for test or demonstration and returned as in case (a) under motor traders, above;

b) built in as part of the MV or permanently attached thereto.

If trailer is partially superimposed on the MV, both are deemed one vehicle.

IX) CARRIAGE OF PASSENGERS—(reg. 40). No person to be carried on the MV or trailer drawn other than:

a) the driver being the licence holder, an employee of the LH or any other person driving with consent of LH while (unless the MV is for one person only) accompanied by the LH or an employee of his;

b) attendants required by the RT Acts;

c) person carrying out statutory duties of inspection of the MV or trailer;

d) a person in a BDV being towed;

e) an employee of the LH going to a place to drive vehicles on behalf of the LH in the course of his motor business;

f) the LH or an employee of his, if his presence (in either case) is necessary for the purpose for which the MV is being used;

g) a prospective purchaser or purchaser, or his servant or agent, or any person required to accompany him: in case of a purchaser the purpose of use must be to demonstrate operation of vehicle or equipment*;

h) a person testing or trying the vehicle for publicity purposes*.

5. Taxation†

(1) Taxation generally

A MV is taxed according to its classification and the amount of duty charge-able for a licence is set out in Schedules I to V to the Act. It is an offence to use a vehicle in an altered condition or in a manner or for a purpose for which a higher rate of duty is payable.

Proceedings for non-payment of duty (s. 8), under-payment of duty (s. 18) or using more vehicles under a trade licence than it allows (s. 16) may be brought only by or on behalf of the S of S or by a constable with the written approval of the S of S, which the S of S has already given to all constables. As to time limit on proceedings, see p. 299.

The class in respect of which duty has been paid is shown on the licence, but it may also fall into another class as well, by reason of its use, etc. though no offence will be committed unless this use makes payable a higher duty than that paid.

Vehicles which are taxed at a substantially reduced rate (provided the conditions applying are complied with), and in respect of which the offence of using for a purpose for which a higher rate of duty is payable is most likely to be encountered, are:

a) **Hackney carriages**—Taxed on seating capacity.

b) **Goods vehicle drawing trailer**—Additional tax is payable when a trailer is drawn, and the licence should specify that it is applicable to goods vehicles *and* trailer. Goods vehicles are taxed on unladen weight.

c) **Farmers' goods vehicles**—Such a vehicle is a goods vehicle registered in the name of a person engaged in agriculture and used on public roads solely by him for carrying produce of, or articles required for the purposes of, the agricultural land occupied by him and for no other purpose.

---

* Must be accompanied by the LH or an employee of his, except in case of vehicle made for one person.

† An IC conforming with certain requirements does not need an excise licence.

NOTE

The use of vehicle licensed at this reduced rate for a purpose for which a higher rate of duty is chargeable is an offence under s. 18, except that the owner of a goods vehicle or DPV so licensed may carry goods for another farmer, provided the carrying is:

a) occasional;

b) incidental to his own use of the vehicle and the goods form only part of the load carried; and

c) no payment is agreed or made.

Bruce v Odell (1939)

A supplier of fertilisers and agricultural goods is not engaged in the business of agriculture. The goods must be used for the business of agriculture of the person for whom they are carried to or from the carrier's farm or to or from the farm of another person engaged in the business of agriculture in the same locality.

Manley v Dabson (1949)

A marketing gardener taking vegetables to retail customers uses the vehicle in the business of agriculture.

Leach v Cooper (1950)

A wholesale greengrocer who buys crops growing in a field does not use in the business of agriculture a vehicle sent to collect them.

McBoyle v Hatton (1951)

A farm goods vehicle used to carry furniture from a sale room to a farmworker's cottage is not being used for the conveyance of articles required for the purpose of agricultural land.

J. M. Knowles Ltd v Rand (1962)

The term 'articles required for purposes of the agricultural land' can include livestock, eggs, seeds, fertilisers and tools.

MacMillan v Butter (1963)

The carriage of agricultural implements which have been sold by the farmer and are being taken to the purchaser are not articles required for the purposes of agricultural land which the farmer occupies.

Howard v Grass Products Ltd (1972)

A vehicle used for farm work by a person not in possession of farm land is not a farmer's goods vehicle.

d) Agricultural machines, etc.—taxed at specially low rate.

I) 'AGRICULTURAL MACHINE'—any Loco, tractor, or other agricultural engine not used on public roads for hauling, except for hauling:

a) own gear, farming appliances, living van, or water or fuel for the vehicle or for agricultural purposes;

b) articles or produce from one part of farm to another;

c) within 15 miles of the farm (or forestry estate) occupied by the registered owner, produce of the farm (or forestry estate) or land occupied with it, or fuel required on the farm (or forestry estate) or for domestic purposes of persons employed on it;

d) articles required for a farm by the registered owner of the vehicle who is the owner or occupier of the farm or a contractor engaged on agricultural work on the farm.

II) 'DIGGING MACHINE'—One designed, constructed and used only for trench digging or excavating or shovelling work, used on a public road only to get to or from place of use and then carrying nothing other than the necessaries for its propulsion or equipment.

III) MOBILE CRANE—Used only on roads in immediate vicinity of its working site, or going to or from that place.

IV) WORKS TRUCK—See p. 12.

London CC v Lee (1914)
A locomotive drawing trolleys laden with farm produce to market was employed by the farmer 'for the purposes of his farm'.

Cole Bros v Harrop (1915)
A locomotive being used for hauling manure to a farm is 'for purposes of the farm'.

Henderson v Roleson (1949)
Taking a pony to a show is not hauling agricultural produce.

Scarr v Wurzel (1951)
Unprocessed hides imported from abroad are 'agricultural produce'.

Brook v Friend (1954)
A tractor hauling a trailer loaded with bricks and a fireplace for installation at a farm worker's cottage on the farm is not hauling 'articles required for the farm'.

e) **Locomotives and tractors**—Taxed according to u/w.

f) **Showman's tractors**—Used by travelling showmen, taxed on u/w.

(2) Exemptions from duty

(Sections 4 to 7)

The following are exempt from duty, but in the case of any condition of exemption not being complied with the exemption is lost and the offence of using the vehicle without an excise licence may be committed.

I) REQUIRING RM AND RB BUT NO LICENCE

a) vehicles used on roads not repairable at public expense;

b) fire engines, ambulances and road rollers;

c) vehicles used on tramlines, not being tramcars;

d) vehicles used on public roads only to pass from land in owner's occupation to other land in his occupation and not for more than six miles in any week (sometimes referred to as 'restricted vehicles')—if exempted by the S of S.

II) REQUIRING RM AND RB AND TO EXHIBIT EXEMPTION DOCUMENT—In the case of the following application has to be made each year to the S of S as if for a licence, and a document (on the pattern of a licence but showing that no duty is payable) is issued. This document has to be exhibited in the same way as a licence, and the offences relating to alterations, etc. apply to it:

a) local authority vehicles solely used for fire brigade purposes, or as watering vehicles;

b) tower wagons used by a street lighting authority or a sub-contractor to that authority;

c) road construction vehicles used solely with permanently fixed machinery for construction or repair of public roads;

d) vehicles used solely for hauling lifeboats and gear, and lifesaving apparatus of HM Coastguard;

e) vehicles specially designed and used solely for snow clearance or for spreading grit, sand, etc. in icing conditions;

f) vehicles owned and used solely by invalids and disabled persons, namely:
   i) invalid carriages complying with the requirements set out on p. 302;
   ii) vehicles fitted with special controls to meet the physical disability of the owner/driver and for which fitting a government grant is available or has been paid;
   iii) vehicles owned by a person who has, on account of physical disability, to be driven and cared for by a full time attendant and who would be eligible for a Health Service invalid tricycle if he were able to drive it.

III) PARTICULAR USES—A vehicle does not become liable to duty by reason only that it is:

a) being driven to, from or during a previously arranged compulsory test (or for an examination for an approval certificate), or to a place for remedial work after refusal of certificate, or from such a place; or

b) owned by a LA and being used for snow clearance, road gritting, etc.; or

c) owned by the police or a LA being used for civil defence purposes; or

d) by virtue of the Representation of the People Act 1949, being used solely to convey voters, free of charge, to the poll at an election.

IV) CROWN VEHICLES—Such a vehicle carries a certificate of Crown ownership and bears a RM, but no licence or RB is issued in respect of it.

v) OTHER EXEMPTIONS

a) A British MV bought direct from the manufacturer here by an overseas resident may be exempted by the S of S if no VAT was payable or paid.

b) Vehicles in the service of visiting armed forces are exempt.

c) A vehicle being used under a current Northern Ireland excise licence is exempt.

(3) Goods vehicles

A goods vehicle (GV) is defined as any MPV (including tricycle of more than 8 cwts u/w):

a) *constructed for use* (i.e. originally), *or*

b) *adapted for use* (i.e. alteration of its original construction),

and *used* for the carriage of goods or burden, whether in the course of trade or otherwise.

NOTES

a) For the purpose of taxation GVs are classified as farmer's goods vehicles, showmen's goods vehicles, electrically propelled goods vehicles, tower wagons (whether electrically propelled or not) and *other goods vehicles.* The rates of duty (specified in Sch. 4) are based on their *unladen weight.*

b) *Adapted* means some alteration to the original construction of the vehicle and not merely some re-arrangement of equipment, e.g. the removal of a seat. This is a question of fact for the court to decide, e.g. where a drum of oil was placed on the back seat of a private car and a portion of the body was cut away at the rear to allow a tap to protrude outside, it was held to be a GV.

Flower Freight Co Ltd v Hammond (1962)
The addition of a reasonable sized luggage rack to a private car does not convert it into a GV (i.e. passengers' effects are not goods).

c) A private car (so licensed) may carry goods in the course of trade and is taxable at the private rate (not being constructed or adapted to carry goods).

d) A vehicle constructed or adapted to carry goods is not treated as a GV if *not used* for carrying goods or burden for hire or reward or for or in connection with a trade or business and must be licensed for private use.

e) A GV used to draw an empty trailer is liable to duty at the private rate if not itself carrying goods.

f) A motor cycle with a box sidecar may be a GV if so used.

g) Where a GV is used to carry goods for hire or reward or for or in connection with a trade or business and also to draw a trailer (laden or unladen) for any purpose, it is liable to additional duty according to the u/w of the drawing vehicle. If the drawing vehicle is not being so used to carry goods or burden, no additional trailer duty is payable if the trailer is unladen, or is laden for private purposes (i.e. not for profit or for any trade or business).

The following trailers are exempt—gritting machines, snow ploughs, road construction vehicles, and gas containers or plant.

h) Where a GV is used to carry goods in a trailer and the vehicle itself is empty, it is liable to goods and trailer duty only if the goods in the trailer are being carried for hire or reward, or for or in connection with a trade or business; otherwise it is liable to duty at the private rate.

i) A shooting brake land rover and utility vehicle, being constructed for carrying both goods and passengers, may be licensed as a GV.

(4) Hackney carriages

I) DEFINITION (S. 38)—A MPV which *stands or plies for hire* in any yard, premises or street, whether public or private. This includes 'private hire' and 'drive hire' vehicles.

II) EXCISE DUTY (SCH. 2)—The excise licence duty is calculated on seating capacity.

Where separate seats are provided one person must be counted for each seat. Where the vehicle is fitted with continuous seats, one person must be counted for each length of 16 in measured lengthwise, after allowing 18 in for the driver, left or right as the case may be, of the point of the seat directly behind the centre of the steering column (reg. 42).

III) HACKNEY CARRIAGE PLATES (S. 21)—Where a lower rate of duty has been paid than that for private use, the vehicle must carry a distinctive sign, i.e. a

Sign to be Exhibited by Hackney Carriages

Diagram

semi-circular sign or plate with the seating capacity (in white, silver or grey) on a black surface.

Exceptions—the following are exempt from this requirement:

a) tramcars;

b) vehicles which display the mark of the local authority indicating that they are licensed to ply for hire (see p. 71);

c) hackney carriages temporarily adapted for and used solely for conveyance of goods in the course of trade;

d) vehicles with seating for twenty persons or more (reg. 41).

IV) OFFENCES—

a) Using the vehicle for a purpose for which a higher rate of duty is payable.

b) Driving (or, where not being driven, keeping) the vehicle—
i) without the hackney-carriage mark or sign being exhibited, or
ii) with the mark or sign obscured or rendered or allowed to become not easily distinguishable.

It is a defence to (b) (ii) to prove all reasonable steps were taken to prevent this happening.

(5) Foreign-owned vehicles

A person *resident* outside the UK who brings a MV *temporarily* into GB must supply particulars of the vehicle to the registration authority (i.e. AA, RAC, RSAC or GLC) and may be exempt from excise duty for up to one year. No excise licence is required. The registration authority *may* allow the vehicle to retain the identification mark of its own country; otherwise a mark consisting of a number and the letters QA, QB, etc. will be assigned and a registration card issued. A 'nationality sign' must be exhibited on the rear of the vehicle, except on vehicles registered by the British or United States authorities in Germany, or by the US in France. The display of foreign registration marks or temporary British 'Q' marks must be considered prima facie evidence that the vehicle is on a temporary visit and is entitled to vehicle excise duty exemption. Date of arrival can be verified by reference to the date-stamped customs document in possession of the owner, or by reference to the Greater London Council, to which all convictions relating to driving of these vehicles must be reported and where a central register of foreign-owned vehicles and their drivers is kept.

(6) Documentary evidence

See p. 286.

As to evidential value of official registration and licensing records—see p. 289.

Chapter 12 Driving licences

Road Traffic Act 1972 (as amended by RTA 1974)

NOTE
References to regulations are to the Motor Vehicles (Driving Licences) Regulations 1976. The S of S for the Environment is now the licensing authority for the whole country.

1. Offences

No person shall:

a) *drive* a MV (including trolley vehicle but not tramcar) on a road unless he is the holder of a current licence covering the class or description of the MV concerned (this does not apply to the steersman of a ,locomotive limited to 5 mph acting under orders of the licensed driver);

b) *cause or permit* any person to drive without such a licence (s. 84).

NOTE
It is not an offence to drive without a licence (or to cause or permit this) if the driver has held and is entitled to obtain a licence for the class of vehicle concerned and his application for a licence has been received by the S of S, or the S of S has temporarily withdrawn the licence for correction. An added requirement is that if the licence concerned is a provisional licence the appropriate conditions must still be complied with. The exemption does not apply beyond the date on which:

a) the date on which the new licence is granted or issued, or

b) where a new licence is not issued, the expiration of the period of one year from the date of the application or of the surrender for correction.

2. Types of licences

The range of driving licences or authorities to drive is as follows:

a) *The driving licence* for a qualified driver, i.e. a full licence.

b) *The provisional driving licence* for an unqualified driver, in respect of which the holder must observe certain conditions while driving until he/she has qualified for a full licence by passing the driving test.

NOTE
A licence issued in Northern Ireland is valid in GB.

c) *Permits issued under the MV (International Circulation) Order 1975,* namely:
i) *convention driving permit*—issued under the authority of a country outside the UK in the form prescribed by the Order and headed 'International Driving Permit', or
ii) *domestic driving permit*—issued under the law of a foreign country authorising driving in that country, including driving permits issued to members of the armed forces of that country for driving outside that country, or
iii) *British forces (BFG) driving licence*—issued in Germany to members of British forces (including civilian components) or their dependants in that country.

NOTES
The above authorise a person resident outside the UK but temporarily in GB to drive, and (except BFG) to be employed in driving, any MV to which the permit relates, and (except BFG) extends to driving a PSV without a PSV driver's licence, but only for 12 months from date of last entry to this country and subject to currency of the permit. The age limits on driving apply, except that in the case of a HGV or PSV brought temporarily into GB the age of 21 years is reduced to 18 years. If the holder becomes resident in GB the permit is, for 12 months afterwards, deemed to be a driving licence under the 1972 Act.

Urey v Lummis (1962)
Permits issued by visiting forces are authorities only for the purpose of allowing the holder to drive but not to supervise a learner as the qualified driver.

d) *Additional drivers' licences* for PSV and HGV—see p. 166.

3. Full licences

A full licence, i.e. a licence which is not a provisional licence, is issued by the S of S. The licence cannot be issued unless the applicant during the preceding 10 years:

a) has held such a licence, or one issued in Northern Ireland, the Isle of Man or the Channel Islands, or

b) has passed the official driving test in respect of the MV concerned or the group of vehicles to which it belongs (s. 85).

NOTES
See special provisions relating to temporary visitors from abroad, above.

Motor vehicles are placed in 'groups' by the MV (Driving Licences) Regulations 1976, so that the authority given by a licence to drive may be limited to vehicles of a particular group or groups. The groups appear in the licence which is also given a code reference (e.g. DL 4A) that identifies the groups and age of the holder to which it relates. A full licence (with exceptions) may be used as a provisional licence for driving vehicles in groups it does not cover, in which case the conditions applying to the use of a provisional licence apply. The exceptions are:

a) any vehicle the person is barred from driving by reason of age;

b) a motor cycle exceeding 250 cc unless the driving test for such a motor cycle has been passed;

c) where the licence is one limited to vehicles of particular construction or design, or authorises the driving of a mowing machine or a PCV only.

4. Provisional licences

(1) Conditions

This licence is issued for a period of 12 months and subject to conditions that, until the holder has passed the test, he shall not drive the MV concerned:

a) unless he is under the supervision of a 'qualified driver' (i.e. one who holds a current ordinary driving licence for that same class of vehicle), who is present with him in or on the vehicle: this condition does not apply:
i) when undergoing a test or a test of competency to drive a HGV, or
ii) where the vehicle (not being a motor car, i.e. n/e 8 cwts or exceeding 3 tons) is constructed to carry only one person and is not adapted to carry more than one, e.g., a 'bubble car' or an Ag T, or
iii) to an electrically propelled goods or load carrying vehicle (even though classed as a 'motor car') not constructed or adapted to carry more than one person and not exceeding 16 cwts unladen, or
iv) to a motor bicycle (with or without a sidecar), or
v) to a road roller not exceeding 3 tons u/w and constructed or adapted to carry a load;

b) unless there is displayed on the vehicle so as to be clearly visible to other road users from within a reasonable distance front and back of the vehicle a letter 'L' in red (4 in high, 3½ in wide, 1½ in thick) on a white background (7 in × 7 in);

c) when the vehicle is drawing a trailer (does not apply if the learner driver is driving an Ag T or an AV);

d) if carrying a passenger (pillion rider) who is not a qualified driver in the case of a solo motor bicycle (but not an auto-assisted tandem type pedal cycle) (reg. 8).

NOTES

a) A motor car must be constructed to carry more than one, otherwise it cannot be driven by a learner driver.

b) Where a MV which is not a motor car is constructed or adapted to carry more than one, the learner driver must be accompanied by a qualified driver.

c) If using a solo motor bicycle (other than a tandem type pedal cycle with auxiliary engine) any pillion passenger carried by the learner driver must be a 'qualified driver'.

d) A passenger who is not a qualified driver may be carried (either as pillion or in sidecar) on a motor cycle combination.

A provisional licence may be limited to certain classes of vehicles in the same way as ordinary licences but does *not* authorise the driving of a *solo* motor bicycle exceeding 250 cc until the holder has passed a test (s. 88). As to use of full licence as provisional licence, see note at end of section on full licences, above.

(2) Driving tests

A successful examinee is given a certificate for the purpose of obtaining a full licence. An examinee who fails cannot undergo another test for the same vehicle group for at least one month. Reg. 13 provides that tests for persons in the service of the Crown may be conducted by examiners appointed by the S of S for Defence, chief constables and chief officers of fire brigades. The Commissioner of the MPD is given similar authority for the testing of drivers of PSVs and hackney carriages residing in the Metropolitan Traffic Area. An employer of more than 250 drivers (e.g. a bus company) is authorised to appoint suitable examiners to conduct tests of competence, if approved by the S of S and subject to such special conditions as he may impose in addition to making proper arrangements for the conduct of the tests in accordance with the regulations and the keeping of suitable records.

5. Licences generally

a) **Applications**—The application must be in the prescribed form and provide the prescribed particulars. Further evidence of any particulars given may be required (e.g. a birth certificate). An applicant is required to surrender at the time any previous licence held by him.

b) Duration—Unless revoked or surrendered a driving licence remains in force until the holder's 70th birthday or for three years, whichever period is the longer.

Exceptions:

a) A licence granted to a person having a disability can be for a period of not less than one nor more than three years.

b) A provisional licence is for one year.

c) Change of particulars—If the name or address of a licence holder ceases to be correct, he must surrender the licence to the S of S forthwith and furnish the new particulars. Failure to comply is an offence (s. 89).

d) Court powers as to date of birth and sex—A court on conviction of an offence, for endorsement and disqualification purposes, may order convicted person to state date of birth in writing. Particulars of birth and sex will have to be given by a person replying to the court in accordance with s. 1 of the Magistrates' Courts Act 1957 ('guilty pleas'). If he does not do this the court, on conviction involving disqualification or endorsement, can order him to furnish the information to the court. Knowingly to fail to comply with an order under this section is a summary offence (s. 104).

e) Duplicate licence—A duplicate licence, issued to replace a licence which has been lost or defaced (fee £2), is a complete duplicate of the original and its endorsements, and has the same effect as the original. If original is found during currency, the person to whom it was issued must return it to the S of S or, if not possessing it, take reasonable steps to secure it and return it (reg. 12).

f) Signature—Every person to whom a licence is granted shall forthwith sign it in ink with his usual signature (reg. 11).

g) Appeals—Any person aggrieved by refusal to grant, or revocation of, or a limitation placed upon, a driving licence, may, after giving notice to the S of S, appeal to a magistrates' court of the area in which he resides. The decision of the court is binding (s. 90).

h) Revocation—Where a licence has to be endorsed or has been issued in error or needs to be amended the S of S can by notice in writing to the holder revoke the licence and require the holder to deliver up the licence forthwith.

6. Physical fitness

Section 87

An applicant for a licence has to make a declaration as to whether he is suffering (or has suffered) from:

a) a *'relevant disability'*, i.e. a prescribed disability or any other disability likely to cause his driving to be a source of public danger, or

b) a *'prospective liability'*, i.e. not a relevant disability but one which, being of intermittent or progressive nature or otherwise, may become a relevant disability in course of time.

If it appears from the declaration (or from enquiry) that there is a relevant disability the licence must be refused unless:

a) the applicant has passed a test and disability has not arisen or got worse since that test or

b) the disability appears to be appropriately controlled, or

c) in the case of a provisional licence, the disability is not one of those prescribed.

If a disability of *any kind* likely to cause public danger is discovered during a driving test, notice of this is to be served on the applicant and:

a) if the danger extends to driving any MV, no licence can be granted;

b) if it does not apply to particular vehicles it may be granted with driving limited to such vehicles.

If the licensing authority is satisfied at any time of the existence of a relevant disability in the holder of a licence, it can by service of a notice revoke the licence with effect from a date specified in the notice, not being earlier than the date of service, it then being the duty of the holder to surrender the licence forthwith.

In the case of a prospective disability the same power (and duty) with regard to revocation applies, but on an application for it a new licence may be issued for a specified period, not less than one nor more than three years.

By s. 87A a licence holder who becomes aware that he is suffering from a relevant or a prospective disability not previously disclosed, or that one previously disclosed has become more acute, must notify the licensing authority forthwith*, but this does not apply if the disability has not arisen before and he reasonably believes that the disability will not extend beyond three months after he first becomes aware of it. The remainder of s. 87A relates to the procedure to be followed by the licensing authority on reasonable belief that an applicant or a licence holder† suffers from a disability, mainly that the licensing authority may require the applicant or licence holder to authorise the authority to obtain from his doctor a medical report, or to submit to a medical examination, or, in the case of a provisional licence, to take a driving test.

The relevant disabilities are: epilepsy; mental disorders of serious nature, e.g. being an in-patient or liable to detention in a mental hospital, or subject to guardianship or under care of local authority; sudden attacks of giddiness‡ or

---

* The offence cannot be prosecuted in England or Wales except by the S of S or a constable acting with the approval of the S of S (s. 170A).

† At present in force only in relation to applicants.

‡ Where this is due to a heart condition and a 'pacemaker' has been surgically inserted, the applicant must satisfy the authority that his driving would not be likely to be a source of public danger and that adequate arrangements have been made for medical supervision.

fainting; inability to read in good daylight (with glasses, if worn) the registration mark of a motor car with 3½ in symbols at 75 ft or 3⅛ in symbols at 67 ft. (*NB*—for a PCV driving licence the distances are 45 ft and 40 ft respectively.)

If on a claimed test of fitness to drive the applicant is successful, the licence must be granted, but may be limited to those vehicles in respect of which fitness was proved by the test.

NOTE

It is an offence for a person to drive a MV on a road while his eyesight is defective, unless it is *at that time* sufficiently corrected to enable him to read a registration mark (as above).

A constable may, on reasonable suspicion, require a person driving to submit to a test of his ability to read the said mark from the required distance with no means of correction other than that used at the time of driving, i.e. to do the test without spectacles if spectacles were not being worn at the time. It is an offence to refuse to submit to such a test (1972, s. 91).

DUTIES OF COURTS AND INSURERS—Where an accused in any proceedings for an offence committed in respect of a MV appears to the court to be suffering from a relevant or a prospective disability the court must notify the licensing authority. An authorised insurer must give similar notification where there is a refusal to issue to a person insurance cover for a MV on (or including) the ground of the state of health of that person.

7. Production of driving licence

Section 161

a) **Production for examination**—The following persons must produce for examination to a police constable, on request, his driving licence* to enable the constable to ascertain the name and address of holder, date of issue and by which authority issued—

a) a person *driving* a MV on a road;

b) the person supervising (not being the driving test examiner present as such) a learner driving a MV on a road;

c) a person† who the constable reasonably believes:
   i) was the driver of a MV when an accident occurred owing to its presence on a road, or
   ii) has committed an offence regarding the use of a MV on a road.

---

* This section applies also to the production of driving permits issued under the MV (International Circulation) Order 1975, and to driving licences issued in N. Ireland.

† Where the person concerned is a 'learner driver' the duty to produce extends to the person reasonably believed to have been the supervising driver at the time.

b) Statement of date of birth—Any such person as is described in **(a)** above shall state his/her date of birth on request of a constable:

a) on failure to produce licence as above forthwith, or

b) where a licence granted by a LA* is produced, or it is one which the constable reasonably suspects was not issued to him, or was granted in error, or contains an alteration to particulars made with intent to deceive (RTA 1972, s. 162, and reg. 24).

c) Revoked licence—If a licence has been revoked by the licensing authority and the holder has failed to deliver it to that authority a constable may require him to produce the licence and, on production, may seize it and deliver it for cancellation to the licensing authority.

d) Obtained on false statement—If a constable has reasonable cause to believe that the holder of a licence (or any other person) has *knowingly* made a false statement to obtain the licence, he may require the holder to produce it, and take possession of it as evidence.

e) Penalty—Failure to produce licence in any of the above cases is a summary offence, but there cannot be a conviction if the licence was produced in person by the holder at such police station as he may have specified (at time of request for production) within five days (not including the day of request).

8. Disqualifications

(1) Duplication

A person is disqualified for obtaining a licence to drive a MV of any class if he is the holder of a current licence to drive a MV of that class, whether the licence is suspended or not (s. 97).

The purpose is to avoid duplication of licences, i.e. anyone having more than one licence in force at the same time in respect of the same class of vehicle. This does not apply to the renewal of a licence before its expiry if the date of commencement follows on or is subsequent to the date of expiry of the current licence. A licence can be issued within two months before the date on which it is to take effect.

NOTE
The holder of a licence to drive a particular group of motor vehicles can be granted a provisional licence to enable him to learn to drive other vehicles. If he passes the test and applies for an ordinary driving licence, he should surrender the first licence to the licensing authority and obtain a licence covering all the vehicles he is qualified to drive, but this is not a legal requirement and it is possible for a person to hold separate licences for

---

* Licences issued by the S of S will contain information as to date of birth.

different groups of vehicles. In practice, the fact that the holder has a licence is evidence that he made a declaration when applying for it that he was not disqualified for obtaining it.

(2) Disqualification due to age or conviction

A person may be disqualified for obtaining or holding a licence:

a) by reason of age, or

b) by order of the court on conviction of certain offences.

DISQUALIFICATION BY REASON OF AGE (s. 96)

A person is disqualified for holding or obtaining a licence to drive a MV of a class specified below if he is under the age specified in relation to it.

a) Invalid carriage	16 years
b) Motor cycle	17 years
Exceptions—for a motor cycle which is a PCV or a mowing machine, or is a moped as defined below	16 years
c) Small passenger or small goods vehicle	17 years
d) Agricultural tractor	17 years
Exception—if tractor is wheeled, overall width n/e 8 ft, is exempt from or subject to low rate of duty, and draws no trailer other than one with overall width n/e 8 ft, being either a two-wheeled or a close-coupled trailer*	16 years
e) Medium sized goods vehicle	18 years
f) Other motor vehicles	21 years

Exceptions—
Road roller not steam propelled, unladen weight n/e 11½ tons, not constructed or adapted for carrying load, no wheel having a pneumatic, soft or elastic tyre   17 years
Heavy goods vehicle being lawfully driven under a training agreement†   18 years

DEFINITIONS—

'*medium-sized GV*'—constructed to haul or carry goods and not adapted to carry more than nine persons including driver, its permissible maximum weight exceeding 3·5 but n/e 7·5 tonnes.

'*small GV*'—as above, but the permitted maximum weight n/e 3·5 tonnes.

---

* An implement attached is part of the tractor and not a trailer.
† I.e. under an approved scheme for training drivers of HGVs.

'small passenger vehicle'—constructed solely to carry passengers and effects and adapted to carry not more than nine persons including the driver.

'moped' (for driving licence purposes) means—

a) if first used post 1st August 1977, a motor cycle (not being a mowing machine or PCV) with maximum design speed n/e 30 mph, kerbside weight n/e 250 kg, engine capacity n/e 50 cc;

b) if first used pre 1st August 1977, a motor cycle with engine n/e 50 cc, and equipped with pedals by which it is capable of being propelled.

(*NB:* many small motor cycles first used pre 1st August 1977 are under 50 cc but do not have pedals and are, therefore, motor cycles and not mopeds for driving licence purposes.)

NOTE
The RT (Drivers' Ages and Hours of Work) Act 1976 provides 'saving' provisions relating to persons who held driving licences immediately before 1st January 1976.

DISQUALIFICATION ON CONVICTION

A person must (obligatory) or may (discretionary) be disqualified by the court for holding or obtaining a driving licence *on conviction** of any of the *offences* listed in Sch. 4 to the RTA 1972, as follows:

Obligatory disqualification

a) Unless the court for *special reasons* thinks fit not to disqualify, or to disqualify for a shorter period, it must disqualify for:
i) *not less than 12 months* on conviction of an offence in *Part I* of the Schedule, namely: motor manslaughter; causing death by reckless driving; reckless driving within 3 years of conviction for 'reckless driving' or 'causing death by reckless driving'; driving or attempting to drive while unfit through drink or drug, or with a proportion of alcohol in the blood above the prescribed limit, or failing to provide a specimen for laboratory test where the original basis was driving or attempting to drive; motor racing or speed trials on highway;
ii) *not less than 3 years* on a second conviction within 10 years of driving or attempting to drive while unfit through drink or drugs, or with excess alcohol, or failing to supply blood or urine sample.

b) Unless the court is satisfied having regard to all the circumstances that there are grounds for mitigation and thinks fit to disqualify for a shorter period or not at all, it must disqualify for *not less than 6 months* on conviction of an offence involving 'obligatory' or 'discretionary' disqualification after two or more endorsements for similar convictions within the three years preceding the date of offence.

---

* This includes cases dealt with by probation or absolute or conditional discharge (CJA 1967, s. 51).

NOTES

a) The wording in (b) above does not restrict the court's discretion not to disqualify for 'special reasons' as in (a).

b) The period of disqualification imposed under (b) above must be in addition to any other period of disqualification imposed either previously or on the same occasion.

Discretionary disqualification—The court *may* disqualify for such period as it thinks fit for any offence against Part III of the Schedule and those offences indicated in Part I as 'discretionary', namely: reckless or careless driving; speeding; driving while disqualified; driving (or causing or permitting driving) under age; in charge while unfit to drive through drink or drug, or with a proportion of alcohol in the blood above the prescribed limit, or failing to provide a specimen for laboratory test where proceedings were based on being in charge (not driving); driving while disqualified; an offence concerning the carriage of passengers on motor cycles; failing to conform with direction of PC regulating traffic or with stop sign, traffic lights, or double white lines; parking in a dangerous position; certain offences on special roads; offences relating to pedestrian crossings, school crossings, or street playgrounds; C and U Regulations offences* concerning dangerous condition or load, brakes, steering or tyres; failing to stop after accident; no driving licence in a case where a licence could not be granted, or where only a provisional licence could be granted and the conditions applicable to it were not being observed; provisional driving licence offences; no insurance, defective eyesight or refusing to submit to eyesight test; stealing or taking without consent a MV (or attempting these offences) or possessing an article for use for purpose of committing these offences.

Powers of Criminal Courts Act 1973, s. 44—The Crown Court may for an IO punishable with not less than two years imprisonment, disqualify for any period it thinks fit, if satisfied that a MV was used to commit the crime. Such a disqualification is not to be endorsed on licence, nor does it count for 'totting up' purposes.

NOTES

a) A disqualification extends to the driving of all types of motor vehicles on a road. The licensing authority is notified by the magistrates' clerk of every order for disqualification made by the court. A licence obtained by a disqualified person is of no effect.

b) A disqualification may be ordered to operate until a driving test is passed, whether or not such a test has been previously passed. In such a case the person disqualified can drive with a provisional licence but, if he contravenes the conditions of that licence, he is driving while disqualified (*Scott v Jelf* (1974)).

c) Appeal against an order for disqualification can be made in the same manner as against a conviction, pending the result of which the order may be suspended by the court to which the appeal is being made.

---

* Not to apply if defendant proves he did not know or have reasonable cause to suspect that facts were such that an offence would be committed.

d) If the court does not disqualify at all or does so for a shorter period, the grounds for such special reasons must be stated in open court and entered in the court register.

e) A court may impose a longer period of disqualification than the compulsory limit provided.

f) CJA 1967, s. 26—a magistrates' court cannot impose disqualification in the absence of the defendant except at a resumed hearing following an adjournment to enable him to be present. A notice of adjournment (stating reason) must be served on defendant. If there is no appearance at the adjournment the court can decide not to disqualify in his absence (though it can then do so) and can issue process to compel appearance.

g) A court may impose disqualification or endorsement in addition to an order for probation or absolute or conditional discharge.

h) A person who is convicted of *'aiding and abetting or inciting the commission of a Schedule offence'* is as liable to disqualification for holding or obtaining a driving licence as the principal offender and the same conditions apply except that the power of the court to disqualify is always a discretionary one. A conviction as an aider and abetter will count as a previous conviction if so endorsed on the defendant's licence.

i) Where a court convicts and commits for sentence to the Crown Court it can order disqualification until the Crown Court has dealt with the case.

Special reasons—Any special reasons put forward must relate to the offence as distinct from the offender. Both the police (against refusal to disqualify) and the defendant (against refusal to recognise special reasons) can appeal on the issue of special reasons as a matter of law.

I) HELD TO BE 'SPECIAL REASONS'—

a) The offender had reason to believe that a misleading cover note issued by the insurers properly covered the use.

b) A servant driver was ordered by his master to use an uninsured vehicle unknown to him, it *not* being unreasonable for him to obey without question.

c) The owner of a repaired vehicle requested the garage proprietor to return it to his address after repair: it was reasonable for him to expect that it would be covered by insurance under the garage proprietor's trade requirements.

II) HELD NOT TO BE 'SPECIAL REASONS'—

a) The offender had held a clean licence for twenty-eight years.

b) Disqualification is considered a severe penalty in the circumstances.

c) The offender had an honest belief that his own or his friend's policy covered the use of his vehicle when driven by his friend without making certain of the fact.

d) A drunken driver stopped his car as soon as he began to feel incapable of controlling it and fell asleep.

e) The defendant allowed his unlicensed wife to drive very slowly along a lonely moorland road for 150 yards with no risk of accident.

Taylor v Kenyon (1952)

From the moment it is ordered in open court, a disqualification is effective. Knowledge of disqualification need not be proved.

Removal of disqualification—A person disqualified may, by way of complaint, summon the superintendent of the district or chief officer of police concerned (or other officer designated by him) to show cause why the disqualification should not be removed. It is the general practice for the applicant to give evidence and to call witnesses, all of whom are subject to cross examination. After objections (if any) have been put forward on behalf of the police the court of conviction (not necessarily the same judge or justices) will decide to grant or refuse the application having regard to the applicant's character, his conduct subsequent to order for disqualification, the nature of the original offence, his reasons for making the application and other relevant factors. If the applicant fails further application cannot be considered until three months have lapsed.

An application for removal of a disqualification will *not* be considered by a court unless:

a) *not less than two years* have elapsed since the disqualification order was made, if it was imposed for *less than four years;*

b) *half the period of disqualification has expired* in the case of an order for *not less than four years but less than ten years;*

c) *not less than five years* have expired *in any other cases.*

NOTES

a) The period of suspension after conviction (e.g. pending an appeal) and before the order for disqualification was made is not to be counted within any period which must expire before removal of the order is applied for.

b) A court cannot consider an application for removal of a disqualification which was imposed for two years or less or which required the defendant to pass a test (because the disqualification can only be removed by passing the test).

9. Offences by person disqualified

If a person disqualified for holding or obtaining a driving licence while so disqualified:

a) obtains a licence, or

b) drives on a road a MV, or (if limited disqualification) a MV of the class for which disqualified,

he commits an offence (RTA 1972, s. 99).

AWW—*A constable in uniform* may AWW any person driving or attempting to drive a MV on a road whom he reasonably suspects of being disqualified for holding or obtaining a driving licence (RTA 1972, s. 100).

10. Endorsement

Section 101

NOTE
The subject of endorsement is not listed in the syllabuses for promotion examination, but is included here for general information.

Where the court orders disqualification for an offence in Schedule 4 it must order endorsement of current licence as well. If there is no disqualification it need not order endorsement when for 'special reasons' it thinks fit not to do so, and cannot do so for the C and U offences in Schedule 4 where the specified conditions apply—see p. 162. The endorsement is entered on every licence subsequently obtained by offender until he is entitled to have a licence free from endorsement.

NOTES
a) It is an offence for the person accused of any of the Schedule offences not to deliver or send his driving licence (by registered post or recorded delivery) to the clerk of the court not later than the day before the hearing, or to have it with him at the hearing. In practice a notice to this effect is attached to the summons served on the defendant.

b) Endorsement may not be ordered for an offence not in the Schedule. If the defendant does not produce his licence for inspection on conviction he commits an offence and the licence becomes suspended until it is produced (so that the erring defendant is not licensed to drive in the meantime).

c) Endorsements still operative are entered on any new licence issued, and it is an offence to apply for or obtain a licence without giving particulars of a current endorsement when the application for it is made.

d) An applicant is entitled to a licence free from any endorsement which was ordered not less than four years previously, except that an endorsement for 'driving or attempting to drive while unfit through drink or drugs' cannot be removed for a period of eleven years (the periods include the length of time disqualified).

e) Special reasons for not endorsing should be stated in open court and entered in the court register.

f) If endorsement is ordered the court must notify the licensing authority which issued the licence and of the area in which the defendant lives. If an appeal court upholds an appeal against endorsement or a relevant conviction it must notify this to the same authorities.

g) Appeal lies by way of case stated against an endorsement ordered by the court and against its refusal to endorse, whether or not special reasons have been considered.

11. Summary of driving licence offences

It is an offence:

a) to drive without a driving licence;

b) to cause or permit any person to drive without a licence;

c) to fail to produce driving licence on request;

d) to fail to sign a driving licence forthwith in ink (*NB*—this is not a continuing offence) (reg. 11, 1976 Regulations);

e) to fail to comply with the conditions of a provisional driving licence;

f) to drive, or to apply for or obtain a driving licence, whilst disqualified;

g) to forge, alter, use, lend or allow a person to use his licence;

h) to make or possess a document so resembling a licence as to be calculated to deceive;

i) to knowingly make a false statement to obtain a driving licence or variation of driving licence;

j) to fail to produce driving licence to court when summonsed for a Schedule offence.

12. Drivers' licences for PSVs and heavy goods vehicles*

The ordinary driving licence is issued under the provisions of Part III of the 1972 Act. An additional licence is needed to drive a PSV (under Part III of the 1960 Act, see p. 191) or a HGV (under Part IV of the 1972 Act—see below).

---

* 'Heavy goods vehicle' means

a) an articulated GV, or

b) a large GV, i.e. a MV (not an AV) which is constructed or adapted to carry or to haul goods and exceeds 7·5 tonnes in permissible max. weight.

Under s. 112 of the 1972 Act it is an offence to drive a HGV of any class on a road unless licensed under this Part of the Act to drive a HGV of that class, or to cause or permit another person to drive a HGV unless that person is properly licensed, but the section does not apply to an employee acting solely as steersman of a vehicle limited to 5 mph or less and under the orders of a licensed driver, nor of a vehicle being properly used under a vehicle excise licence granted at the reduced rate for agricultural or forestry purposes.

A provisional HGVDL is issued subject to prescribed conditions (see 1977 Regulations) and it is an offence for a person to fail to comply with any such conditions, or to cause or permit another person *under 21 years* of age to drive a HGV in contravention of any such conditions to which that person's licence is subject (s. 114).

HGV (Drivers' Licences) Regulations 1977

NOTE
The licensing authority is as for PSV drivers' licences.
HGVDL: heavy goods vehicle driver's licence.

a) The regulations provide for the issue of licences to drive HGVs (including provisional licences) and for driving tests.

b) The conditions relating to the use of provisional HGVDL (or a full licence used as such) are:
i) supervision by person who holds either a full HGVDL or an ordinary licence to drive a HGV of the class concerned, except when undergoing test;
ii) exhibition on front and rear of the vehicle of the appropriate 'L' plates;
iii) no trailer is drawn except as part of an AV.

c) The 'L' plate (15 in high × 12 in) has 'HGV' (2 in high) in red letters on white rectangular strip at the top, and, below, a red 'L' (6 in high with 5 in base) of 1½ in thickness within a white circle in the centre of a light orange 12 in square.

d) It is an offence (under reg. 28 and the regs. cited) to:
i) apply for HGVDL if already holding one, or if disqualified for such a licence or a Part II licence, or if HGVDL has been suspended (reg. 3);
ii) fail to sign licence in ink forthwith (reg. 7);
iii) fail to observe conditions of provisional licence (reg. 9);
iv) fail to deliver forthwith to licensing authority, on receipt of notice to do so, HGVDL which has been suspended or revoked (reg. 11);
v) fail to notify licensing authority and deliver up the HGVDL on disqualification, revocation, or refusal to grant in respect of a Part II licence (reg. 13);
vi) if duplicate is in force and original licence found (to knowledge of holder), fail to notify licensing authority and, if not possessing it, to take reasonable steps to obtain possession of it, or possessing the found original, fail to return it to appropriate licensing authority (reg. 14);
vii) fail to produce driving licence on request (reg. 15).

e) The duty to produce an HGVDL to a constable is the same as that in respect of an ordinary licence (see p. 158), and the five days period for production at a police station applies. The licence must also be produced to a GV examiner on request but in this case the grounds of being involved in an accident or suspected of a traffic offence do not apply and the period of grace is one of ten days for production of the licence at the examiner's office (reg. 14).

f) The regulations do not apply to a vehicle which is: tracklaying; propelled by steam; RR; L Loco; LT; WT; PSV; engineering plant; special road construction vehicle; industrial tractor (unladen weight n/e $3\frac{1}{2}$ tons) designed for work off roads or on road construction and incapable of more than 20 mph; digging machine; exempt from excise duty on minimal road mileage; traction part of AV being a motor car, if no trailer is drawn; used only for haulage of lifeboats; manufactured pre 1st January 1940, used unladen and not drawing trailer; armoured or in service of visiting force; driven by constable to remove road obstruction or public danger or to safeguard vehicle, or its load or property; AV if MV part does n/e unladen weight of 15 cwt; a MV (not AV) of unladen weight n/e 10 tons owned by (or on loan or hire to) the holder of a PSV licence and driven by a person having a PSV driver's licence, being used as a breakdown vehicle in respect of a PSV (including towing); a MV fitted with a crane as a permanent fixture and used solely for dealing with disabled vehicles, of unladen weight n/e 3 tons and not constructed or adapted for carrying a load except loose tools and equipment; a fire fighting or fire salvage vehicle owned and controlled by S of S for Defence; a 'play bus'.

A 'play bus' is a passenger vehicle adapted to carry any goods or burden and owned by someone or somebody concerned in providing play equipment for children by conveying it from place to place for or after such use. The exemption applies only if the vehicle is being driven for the person or body referred to above for carriage of such equipment for use by children to or from a place where it is to be or has been made available for such use, but no account is to be taken of any journey to or from a place for repairs, or in any case where its use would not make it liable for payment of excise duty under the Vehicles (Excise) Act 1971.

13. Documentary evidence

See page 286.

Chapter 13 **Insurance of vehicles**
Road Traffic Act 1972

1. Offences

Section 143

No person shall use, or cause or permit another person to use, a MV on a road without there being in force a policy of insurance or a security covering the use of the vehicle by that person (or other person) in respect of third party risks. (For exceptions see **3** below.)

See *Hill & Sons Ltd v CC of Hampshire* (1972) and *Sheldon Deliveries Ltd v Willis* (1972) on page 21.

Lloyd v Singleton (1953)
Any person besides the owner who has control on the owner's behalf can permit its use, e.g., a chauffeur or manager of a company (permit uninsured person to drive).

Brown v Roberts (1963)
For the insurance offence there must be an element of controlling, managing or operating the vehicle in order to prove 'using', so that a person who is merely a passenger in the vehicle does not, on that account only, use it.

Cobb v Williams (1973)
An owner riding as a passenger in his own car was 'using' without insurance where the insurance did not cover the driver.

Newbury v Davis (1974)
A lending of a MV on the condition that the borrower insured it before use is not 'permitting use without insurance' by the lender.

The MV must be intended or adapted for use on roads, not, for example, a dumper (see p. 9).

Milstead v Sexton (1964)
The use of a towed MV on a road must be covered by insurance in respect of third party risks because it still remains a MV.

Elliot v Grey (1960)
A vehicle is in use on a road even when it is stationary and unattended, and must be insured.

2. Defence

It is a defence for a person to prove that he did not own the vehicle, that he did not possess it under a hire or loan contract, that he was using it in the course of his employment, and that he had no reason to believe that it was uninsured.

A-G v Downes (1959)
The special defence afforded an employee, who did not know that the vehicle was not insured, does not preclude convictions of the master for causing or permitting the offence.

3. Vehicles exempted

The following are exempted:

a) A vehicle owned by a person who has deposited and keeps deposited with the Supreme Court the sum of £15,000. This exemption is provided by the production of a valid certificate of deposit (see p. 171).

b) Invalid carriages.

c) Crown vehicles.

Salt v MacKnight (1947)
The exemption does not extend to the use of a Crown vehicle by a government-official for private purposes.

d) Vehicles owned by a local authority or a joint board or joint committee on which are representatives of a local authority, or a police authority (or Receiver of MPD), or a specified body, i.e. a Passenger (or London) Transport Executive, or subsidiary*.

e) Vehicles driven for police purposes by or under direction of a constable or a person employed by the police authority.

f) Vehicles used for salvage purposes under the Merchant Shipping Act 1894.

---

* With regard to the foregoing, only when being driven under the owner's control.

g) Vehicles requisitioned by the Army or RAF in the public service of the Crown.

h) Tramcars and trolley vehicles authorised by special Act.

i) Vehicles of visiting armed forces. Such vehicles are exempt in the same way as Crown vehicles, but members of these forces are not exempt when using their own private vehicles or when not using vehicles in the course of duty (RTA 1972, s. 144).

j) National Health Service vehicles being used in accordance with the terms on which they were made available to the person, body or authority concerned.

NOTE
It is an offence to use in the territory of a member state of the EEC (except GB or Gibraltar) a motor vehicle registered in GB or a trailer (coupled or not) kept by a person permanently resident in GB, if that MV or trailer is exempt from insurance by s. 144, unless there is in force *in relation to the person* using it a policy of insurance covering civil liabilities according to the law of the state concerned. The offence may be treated as having been committed in any place in this country so far as proceedings, time limit, and evidence by certificate are concerned (RTA 1972, s. 145 (3) (*aa*)).

4. Requirements as to policies

Section 145

a) Every policy must insure against any liability incurred:
i) by the death of or bodily injury caused to a person arising out of the use of the vehicle on any road in GB (*NB:* the policy is not by law required to cover any employee of the insured as to death or injury in the course of his employment, or any contractual liability);
ii) in respect of the use of the vehicle (or any trailer) in the territory of each member state of the EEC;
iii) for payment of the cost of any emergency medical or hospital treatment (see p. 180).

b) The policy must be issued by an authorised insurer, i.e. one carrying on MV insurance business in GB and a member of the Motor Insurers' Bureau at time of issue.*

c) The policy or security is of *no effect unless a certificate* has been issued in respect of it (s. 147).

---

* Does not apply to certain foreign vehicles—see p. 327.

5. Requirements as to securities

The security (which is an alternative to the normal form of insurance) must be given by an authorised insurer, or by some body of persons which carries on in the UK the business of issuing securities, and has deposited (and keeps deposited) with the Supreme Court the sum of £15,000 in respect of the business. The security is to consist of an undertaking to make good (up to at least £25,000 in the case of PSVs and £5,000 in any other case) the failure of the secured person to discharge any liability which would have to be met under a policy of insurance, subject to the conditions specified in the security (s. 146).

6. Conditions which do not affect validity of insurance

If delivery of the certificate (of insurance or security) has been made so as to put the policy or security into effect the insurers cannot avoid their liability to meet claims made by third parties by including conditions in the policy or security relating to:

a) the age, physical or mental condition of a person to drive,

b) the condition of the vehicle;

c) the number of persons that the vehicle carries;

d) the weight or physical characteristics of the goods carried;

e) times when or areas in which the vehicle is used;

f) horsepower or cylinder capacity or value of the vehicle;

g) carrying of particular apparatus;

h) carrying of particular identification marks other than the identification plates; or

i) passengers not being carried.

> **Bright v Ashford (1932)**
> A policy with a condition that pillion passengers should not be carried is valid and not made void by this section.

> **Jones v Welsh Insurance Corpn (1937)**
> A policy with a condition authorising the goods to be carried for the assured's business only is valid.

NOTE

A breach of any such conditions does not prevent the insurers recovering from the insured any sum they might have had to pay in discharge of their liability to a third party.

7. Types of certificates

The forms of certificates are prescribed by the MV (Third Party Risks) Regulations 1972, as follows.

(1) A certificate of insurance

Form A—relating to a specified vehicle or vehicles.
Form B—not specifying any particular vehicle.
Form C—*the cover note* issued as a temporary measure until the policy and form A or B (above) are issued. The note is normally issued for periods of 14 or 28 days and may be renewed.

> **Cartwright v MacCormack (1962)**
> A cover note expires at midnight on the specified date, irrespective of the time of commencement.

(2) A certificate of security (form D)

Issued in respect of a security which has been effected. Where the certificate covers the use of more than ten vehicles (e.g. a taxi company) duplicates may be issued for display on the vehicles in a holder similar to (and to be displayed alongside) that for excise licence.

(3) A certificate of deposit (form E)

Is proof that the vehicle specified is exempt from the need for insurance cover by virtue of the owner of the vehicle having deposited with the Supreme Court the sum of £15,000 as a guarantee to discharge any liability which might have to be discharged in respect of third party risks. Deposits are generally made by owners of large fleets of vehicles. The certificate must be signed by the depositor and duplicates may be issued for display on and in respect of each vehicle as in the case of a certificate of security.

(4) A certificate of ownership (form F)

Issued in respect of vehicles owned by a local or police authority or a 'specified body' which is exempt from the need for insurance cover. The certificate must be signed by some authorised person of the authority concerned.

(5) A certificate of foreign insurance

Motor Vehicles (International Motor Insurance Card) Regulations 1971

An International Motor Insurance (Green) Card is provided by the British

Motor Insurance Bureau (or foreign bureau) on application being made by a visiting driver through his insurers (foreign or British).

NOTE
Insurance policies, certificates, and securities of insurance issued in Northern Ireland are valid in the United Kingdom. As to vehicles from EEC and certain other countries, see p. 326.

8. Production of certificates

Section 162

(1) Production to constable

Every person mentioned in the next paragraphs *must* on demand of a police constable:

a) give his name and address *and* that of the owner of vehicle;

b) produce the relevant certificate of insurance or of security (certificate of foreign insurance, deposit or ownership) or other evidence of compliance with s. 143*, and

c) produce any 'test certificate' issued in relation to the vehicle or, being a GV, its plating certificate where this is required in respect of the vehicle.

NOTE
Proceedings for failure to produce any certificate referred to in (b) and (c) above cannot be sustained if it is produced within five days at any police station specified by the person concerned.

(2) Drivers

The persons required to give the information and/or produce the documents required in the preceding paragraph are any person:

a) driving a MV on a road, or

b) reasonably believed by the constable:
   i) to have been the driver of a MV concerned in a road accident, or
   ii) to have committed an offence relating to the use of a MV† on a road.

---

* As to certain foreign vehicles, see p. 326.
† Invalid carriages are excluded from the operation of this section.

(3) Those accompanying learner drivers

This section also requires the 'competent driver' who accompanies a 'learner driver' on a road (or is reasonably believed by a police constable to have been doing so) at the time when the MV was concerned in a road accident, or when an offence is believed to have been committed by the 'learner driver' in relation to the use of the MV, to give to the constable on request his name and address and that of the owner of the MV.

(4) Accidents

As to the duty to produce evidence of insurance in cases of road accidents, see p. 242.

By s. 166 the driver of a MV (other than IC) involved in a road accident causing personal injury to another person *must* (unless the appropriate certificate was produced at the time of the accident to a police constable or other person having reasonable grounds for requiring it):

a) *report the accident* at a police station or to a police constable as soon as practicable and in any case within 24 hours; and thereupon

b) *produce the certificate* relating to insurance cover, but no proceedings for failure to produce can be taken if the document is produced within five days at a specified police station.

Lee v Knapp (1966)
The defendant, after accident, left his van and instructed an employee to wait in the van to give the necessary information; convicted of failing to stop and give particulars. Appeal against conviction dismissed. The obligation to give particulars is a personal one and cannot be transferred to an agent.

(5) Owners

By s. 167, the *owner* of a MV must give such information as may be required by or on behalf of a chief officer of police to determine whether or not there was any contravention of s. 143 (insurance) on any occasion when the driver was required to produce evidence of insurance cover under the above sections (162 and 167).

Tremelling v Martin (1971)
M called at the police station within the five days but left with the required documents before the police officer (called to the telephone) could examine them. *Held:* production must be for a reasonable time to allow examination to take place, whether at the time the driver is stopped or at the police station.

9. Examination of certificates, etc.

The purpose of examining a certificate relating to insurance cover is to determine whether or not an offence under s. 143 is being committed. The exercise is, in the main, one of finding answers to questions posed to test the position, having regard to the circumstances in which the MV is being used on a road, e.g.:

a) Is the vehicle exempt from the provisions as to insurance (see p. 170)?

b) If exempt, in what cases are certificates required as evidence of this (i.e. of deposit or ownership)?

c) If certificates of deposit or ownership are produced, is the certificate current and does it relate to the vehicle in question?

d) With regard to certificates of insurance or security:
   i) does the certificate relate to the vehicle?
   ii) does it relate to the driver?
   iii) is it in force?
   iv) do the circumstances of user conflict in any way with the limitations or conditions imposed by the policy (as evidenced by the certificate)?

The following cases have a bearing on the application and interpretations of forms and limitations commonly found in insurance certificates.

I) DRIVER WHO IS DISQUALIFIED

Edwards v Griffiths (1933)
Where a policy excludes a driver who is disqualified for holding or obtaining a licence, these words must be construed as meaning a disqualification by a court or by virtue of age, and not disqualifications on medical grounds, e.g. mental incapacity.

Mumford v Hardy (1956)
The phrase 'a person disqualified for holding or obtaining a licence' in a third party policy of insurance includes a person who has obtained a driving licence by falsely stating his age.

II) 'SOCIAL, DOMESTIC AND PLEASURE PURPOSES'

McCarthy v British Oak Insurance Co (1938)
A car lent to a friend for a pleasure trip, the friend paying the owner for the petrol in it, is being used for social and domestic purposes and is not hired.

Wood v General Etc. Assurance Co (1949)
Held: that a motor car was not being used for 'social, domestic and pleasure purposes' where the owner was being driven by an employee to an interview in London to negotiate a contract in connection with his garage business.

Lee v Poole (1954)
Carrying furniture, without payment, for a friend is use for 'social, domestic and pleasure purposes'.

Whitehead v Unwins (York) Ltd (1962)

Insurance to cover 'domestic purpose' does *not* cover the carriage of cattle food by a farmer.

III) 'HOLDER MAY DRIVE ANY OTHER VEHICLE NOT BELONGING TO HIM'

Boss v Kingston (1963)

A policy in respect of a named vehicle may authorise the holder to drive any other vehicle not belonging to or hired by him. The insurance cover lapses on sale of the vehicle to which it applies unless the policy provides for a continued user of the named vehicle after sale.

Rogerson v Scottish Etc. Insurance Co (1931)

A policy covering the assured's car or any car being used instead of the insured's car does not cover him when he has got rid of the insured car and is using another car.

IV) EMPLOYMENT OF DRIVERS

Bryan v Forrow (1950)

A policy covering the policy holder or 'his paid driver' covers a paid driver who is paid as a driver not necessarily by the policy holder or in the general employment of the policy holder.

Lyons v May (1948)

A garage proprietor who drove the owner's lorry from the garage to the owner's premises after effecting repairs to it was not in the owner's employment.

Marsh v Moores (1949)

The MV was driven on a particular journey by a servant acting within the scope of his employment, but in an unauthorised and improper way (allowing an unlicensed girl friend to steer the car whilst he sat beside her to operate the handbrake). The justices dismissed the charges of using and permitting the use without insurance. *Held, on appeal:* if a policy covers employees, driving by one in an unauthorised manner but within the scope of his employment will normally be covered and the insurance offence was not committed. (If the journey was not authorised or not within the scope of the servant's employment the position would be different.)

V) ACCEPTANCE OF LIABILITY BY INSURANCE COMPANY IN DOUBTFUL CASE

Carnill v Rowland (1953)

A cover note limited the driving of a motor cycle only if its sidecar was permanently attached. The driver removed the body of the sidecar leaving only the chassis and wheel. The insurers considered themselves on risk and the respondent was held to be insured against third party risks. *Held, on appeal:* where the policy clearly excludes liability the test of insurance is not whether an insurance company considers itself 'on risk', but where the interpretation of the conditions is doubtful justices may have regard to the fact that the company accepts liability.

VI) AGRICULTURAL PURPOSES

Agnew v Robertson (1956)
A policy covering use 'solely for agricultural or forestry purposes includ-ing the haulage of agricultural produce or articles required for agricul-ture' does not cover use of a tractor to convey household furniture of a newly engaged farm servant to the farm.

VII) TRAILERS

Rogerson v Stephens (1950)
A motor car and trailer are not a single entity and a summons charging the use of a 'motor car and trailer' without insurance is bad.

Kerridge v Rush (1952)
If a policy excludes the drawing of more trailers than the law allows, doing this renders the policy void and an offence against s. 143 is committed.

VIII) SUPERIORITY OF POLICY

Biddle v Johnson (1965)
A policy over-rides the certificate when an inconsistency exists between them.

IX) EVIDENCE

Williams v Russell (1933)
The onus of proving that he holds a valid insurance policy is on the defendant. The contents of the certificate can be proved by the constable to whom it was produced without a notice to produce.

Egan v Bower (1939)
A letter from insurers is not admissible as evidence to prove terms of a policy. An offence may be evident although the insurers may be willing to accept liability (see *Carnill v Rowland* (1953), p. 177).

10. Motor Vehicles (Third Party Risks) Regulations 1972

These regulations deal with the various forms of certificates (which must be printed in black on white paper and not bear any advertising matter on back or front) and the conditions and requirements which relate to them, as follows:

a) a certificate must be issued within four days of the issue or renewal of an insurance policy or security (reg. 6);

b) the owner of a MV to which a certificate of deposit or ownership applies must destroy the certificate before selling or otherwise disposing of the MV (reg. 8);

c) the applicant for a vehicle excise licence (other than a trade licence) must produce the appropriate certificate (of insurance, security, deposit, ownership, etc.) for the vehicle: persons who let on hire vehicles intended to be used solely for that purpose and to be driven by or on behalf of the hirer are exempt from compliance (reg. 9);

d) every company, local authority or person depositing £15,000 with the Supreme Court must keep records for one year of the particulars prescribed in relation to every certificate issued, and these must be supplied free of charge (on request) to the S of S or to any chief officer of police (reg. 10);

e) the S of S must be informed by the company concerned where a policy or security has ceased to become effective without the consent of the assured, otherwise than by his death or by effluxion of time (reg. 11);

f) no policy or security is to be transferred with consent of the holder to another person, until the relevant certificate has been returned to the company, and if the policy ceases to be effective otherwise than by expiry of time the relevant certificate must be returned within seven days (reg. 12);

g) the insurers must issue a new certificate on request by the insured where the original has been lost or destroyed: if defaced the certificate must be returned before the replacement is issued (reg. 13).

Failure to comply with any regulation is an offence.

11. Duty of vehicle owner to give information to police

Section 167

In respect of any occasion when the driver of a MV has been required to produce insurance documents, *the owner* of the vehicle must give such information as is requested by or on behalf of a chief officer of police to determine whether or not an insurance offence had been committed. ('Owner' includes each party to any hiring agreement.)

Failure to comply is an offence.

Foster v Farrell (1963) (Scottish case)
'By or on behalf of a chief officer of police' means by the chief officer or by a constable authorised by him to require the information. If the information is required by a constable not so authorised no obligation to give the information is imposed and any statement obtained may be held to be inadmissible.

'Chief officer of police' means the Commissioner of the City or MPD and any chief constable.

12. Duty to give information on an insurance claim

Section 151, as amended

A person against whom a claim is made in respect of any liability required to be covered by insurance under s. 145 must, on demand by or for the claimant:

a) state whether or not he was insured or had a security, or would have had if the insurer had not avoided or cancelled the policy or the security; and

b) if he was or would have been covered as above, give such particulars with respect to the policy or security as were specified in any certificate of insurance or security delivered, and, where no such certificate was delivered, the following particulars: the RM or other identification particulars of the vehicle concerned, the number or other identifying particulars of the insurance policy, the name of the insurer, and the period of insurance cover. To refuse or to give false information is an offence.

13. Payments for treatment of road accident casualties

By s. 145, a policy of insurance or other security is required to cover liability relating to third party risks for the payment of emergency medical treatment given in respect of bodily injury (fatal or otherwise) to any person caused by or arising out of the use of a MV on a road. The sections of the 1972 Act dealing with such payments are as follows:

a) Section 154—If a payment is made (except under **(b)** below) under insurance cover (whether or not liability is admitted) in respect of death or bodily injury, the insurer or owner, as the case may be, if he knows hospital treatment was given, must also pay reasonable hospital expenses, but not exceeding £200 per in-patient, or £20 per out-patient.

b) Section 155—Where medical or surgical treatment is immediately required for bodily injury arising out of the use of a MV on a road, and given by a qualified practitioner or at a hospital, the person who was using the MV must pay, if claim is made, to the practitioner or hospital (as case may be) a fee of £1.25 for each person treated, and, in case of treatment otherwise than at hospital, a sum to the practitioner to cover travelling (if over two miles to the scene) at the rate of 2½p per complete mile and additional part of a mile.

c) Section 156—The claim for payment under the above sections may be made orally at the time or in writing within seven days (personal delivery or by registered post) and may be recovered as a civil debt. On request of such a claimant, the police must supply any information available as to the identification marks of vehicle concerned and the name and address of its user at the time of the accident.

14. Compensation for victims of uninsured drivers

In 1946 an agreement was made between the Minister of Transport and the representative body of insurance companies called the *Motor Insurers' Bureau* by which the bureau undertook to consider payment of compensation to third party victims of any road accident in circumstances where insurance claims could not legally be made because the vehicles involved were not insured or not effectively insured. An injured party able to establish negligence against the driver of a vehicle may be awarded the same compensation from the bureau as he would have received if the driver had been properly insured. The address of the bureau is 60 Watling Street, London EC4, and it is a condition precedent to recovery of the whole or part of the judgment debt and costs awarded against an uninsured person that notice of the proceedings must be given to the bureau either before or within 21 days after they commence. Solicitors have been recommended to immediately notify the bureau on behalf of a client in any case where a doubt arises that the defendant driver is properly insured in respect of third party risks. Coroners have also been advised by the Home Office to notify the bureau in fatal accident cases so that it may arrange for representation at the inquest.

Although it is under no obligation where an offending driver cannot be traced, the bureau is prepared to consider sympathetically the making of ex-gratia payments in such cases.

By the RTA 1974, s. 20, an insurance policy issued in the UK (including N Ireland) for the purpose of the RTA 1972, s. 143, is not valid unless issued by an authorised insurer who is a member of the bureau, but a policy issued by such a member is not invalidated by the insurer later ceasing to be a member.

Chapter 14 **Public service vehicles**

Road Traffic Act 1960 (as amended by the Transport Act 1978)

1. Definitions

Section 117

a) A PSV—is a MV (not a tramcar or trolley vehicle) used for *carrying passengers for hire or reward*, either:

a) *at separate fares*, in which case the definition applies to *all* motor vehicles, or

b) *not at separate fares* (i.e. the vehicle is hired) in which case (to exclude hackney carriages or taxis) the definition applies only to a MV constructed to carry eight or more passengers.

NOTE
A trailer shall not be used to carry passengers for hire or reward (C & U Regulations, reg. 133).

b) Hire or reward—means that payment is made to the operator either by each passenger separately, or as a fixed sum in relation to the hiring of the vehicle (s. 118). The following cases are not to be regarded as carrying passengers for hire or reward (so that the vehicles are not PSVs while so used): motor vehicles:

a) when belonging to an education authority for the purpose of school buses and while being so used;

b) used for certain National Health Service purposes, e.g. regular collection and delivery of outdoor patients to and from hospitals or clinics for treatment;

c) used to carry agricultural workers to and from work during the six months starting 1st June.

c) A separate fare—means a payment made individually by a passenger whether in respect of the journey only or inclusive of other charges, e.g. hotel accommodation, making part of the journey by other means (e.g. train) or admission to a special function or event. A separate payment made in respect of the journey to any person (i.e. to owner or any other person whether an agent or employee of the owner or not, e.g. a club secretary or organiser) is a separate fare. Where a PSV does not belong to an education authority and is being used as a school bus it shall not be treated as carrying passengers at separate fares.

2. Types of PSVs

There are three kinds:

SEPARATE FARES

a) Stage carriage—passengers carried at separate fares, not being an express carriage.

b) Express carriage—where no separate fare is less than 21p*.

NOT SEPARATE FARES

c) Contract carriage—where the MV is hired as a whole and separate fares are not paid.

> **Aitken v Hamilton (1964)**
> Separate fares means payment by individual passengers, whether or not under a firm arrangement for fixed payments, or according to a tariff of payments.

NOTE

The term 'PSV' brings to mind a bus. It is important to remember that where separate fares are charged *any* MV (e.g. taxi, private motor car, or motor cycle combination) becomes a PSV, i.e. a stage carriage or, if fare charged is 21p or more, an express carriage—but note the statutory exceptions under s. 118 referred to in (**d**) below.

> **Hawthorn v Knight (1962)**
> Bus hired by club to take members to work, each member paying the treasurer a weekly sum, was held to be used under a contract of hire as an express carriage.

> **Wurzal v Addison (1965)**
> A private hire car (licensed private) to carry n/e seven passengers was engaged by one of several employees to carry them from the factory to

---

* Excluding specially reduced rates for children, students, workmen's season or period tickets, etc. Regulations can raise minimum fare and introduce different minima for different purposes (TA 1968, s. 145).

the housing estate where they lived for a daily fare. Each passenger contributed his share to the hirer. *Held:* the vehicle was being used to carry passengers at separate fares; it mattered not that a passenger paid a fare to someone other than the driver or owner of the vehicle.

Wurzal v Wilson (1965)
Bus hired by firm to take employees from work to their respective homes, the employees paying a weekly contribution to the firm amounting to half the cost. *Held:* the hirer was using the vehicle as an express carriage without a road service licence because he had means of knowing (actual knowledge is not necessary) that he could not lawfully carry them if they were in fact contributing to the sum paid by the firm.

Albert v Motor Insurers' Bureau (1971)
A car owner who was regularly carrying his workmates to work, expecting to be paid in cigarettes or money, was held to be carrying passengers for hire or reward.

Payment by one person only is sufficient to constitute use at separate fares, if the person is carried for hire or reward other than in the course of a business for carrying passengers, and this applies where payment is made to reserve a seat (e.g. booking in advance with deposit), whether the right to travel is exercised or not.

d) Exceptions—The following exceptions are made by s. 118 and Sch. 12 and *apply only to vehicles in which seating is provided for not more than seven passengers*, i.e. the acceptance of separate payments in them does not make the vehicle a PSV in the following circumstances:

a) *On special occasions*, i.e. the occasion of a race meeting, public gathering, or other like *special* occasion.

b) *Car sharing on certain journeys* if the following conditions are fulfilled:
   i) not more than seven passengers (taxi*—four);
   ii) if a taxi* the agreement for separate fares has not been initiated by the driver or owner of the vehicle, or by a person from whom the vehicle has been hired or hire-purchased or who receives remuneration in respect of arrangements made for the journey;
   iii) there must have been no previous advertisement as to separate fares†;
   iv) previous advertisement can be made if the facilities are being provided

---

* The word 'taxi' is used to denote a vehicle in which 'passengers are carried in the course of a business of carrying passengers'.

† No account is to be taken of a notice displayed or an announcement made in or at:

a) a place of work re journeys to be made from that place by people who work there;

b) a place of worship for the information of persons attending; or

c) the premises of a club or other voluntary association re journeys arranged incidentally in connection with its activities.

In (b) and (c) the exemption extends to notices contained in a periodical issued by the place of worship, club or association to its members.

under a social car scheme and the consent of the LA and commissioners concerned has been obtained and not withdrawn, and the advertisement states that these consents have been given (a social car scheme is one in which facilities are provided to meet the social and welfare needs of a community and are not made for any commercial purpose or with a view to profit);

v) the journey must not be made in connection with or as an extension of any bus service in which the vehicle owner has a financial interest.

c) *Parties of overseas visitors*, provided that each passenger must have been outside GB when his arrangements for the journey were concluded.

d) *On any occasion other than the above* provided the following conditions are fulfilled:

i) the organiser of the party must not be the holder of the PSV licence (if any) for the vehicle, or (if no PSV licence in force) the owner, driver or hirer or anyone receiving a reward for doing so;

ii) there must be no previous advertising to the public of the arrangements (the exceptions detailed in the footnote to para. (b) above apply);

iii) no differentiation of fares is to be made on the basis of time or distance;

iv) in the case of a journey to a particular destination all passengers must be carried to it, or near to it, or for the greater part of the journey, and no passenger should be one regularly using the route at about the same time of day to or near the same destination from a place from or through which the journey is made.

3. Contract carriages

These are PSVs not carrying passengers paying separate fares and constructed for eight or more passengers. Exceptions apply with regard to 'separate fares' in the following cases:

a) *parties of overseas visitors*, and

b) *other occasions*,

as described in **(2)(d)** (c) and (d) above, if the conditions specified are fulfilled and the following, in addition, are complied with:

a) *The driver* must carry a *'work ticket'*, which must be produced to a constable *in uniform* on demand, showing:

i) the name and address of the PSV licence holder and the registration mark;

ii) the driver's name and address;

iii) the route, destination and times of starting and finishing the journey.

b) *The holder of the licence* must within 72 hours after completion of the journey make a record (to be kept for six months), showing the above particulars and the name and address of the organiser.

NOTES
a) If the above conditions are not complied with the exceptions do not apply
   and the contract carriage is being used as a stage carriage or an express
   carriage, and a road service licence (dealt with later) is needed.

b) Whenever advertisements are seen regarding tours at separate fares, the
   vehicle must be a stage or (more likely) an express carriage operating
   under a special road service licence.

Birmingham Bus Co v Nelson (1932)

A railway company ran excursions to a certain station, where the defendants' buses met the passengers and conveyed them to a chocolate factory.
The railway company received an inclusive fare from each excursionist,
and paid the defendants a sum for each passenger carried in the buses. It
was held that the buses were express carriages, it being immaterial that
nothing was paid to the defendants by the passengers. (Note that if the
sum paid for each passenger had been less it would have been a stage
carriage.)

Drew v Dingle (1934)

A lorry owner regularly used his lorry to carry other people's goods to
market and also carried some of the people with their goods. *Held:* it was
an express carriage although the driver contended that the payments
were for the carriage of the goods only.

4. Licensing

England and Wales is divided into 'traffic areas', each of them being under the
control of *three* traffic commissioners appointed by an order under the general
direction of the S of S for dealing with the issue of licences for, and regulating
the use of, PSVs. There is a right of appeal to the S of S (whose decision is
final):

a) against the decision of the traffic commissioners to refuse the grant of a
   PSV licence or RSL, and against the suspension, or revocation of any such
   licence, or of any conditions attached to them;

b) against the revocation or limitation of duration of a certificate of fitness.

All the above licences, etc. are dealt with later in this chapter. The traffic
commissioners of each area are required by s. 156 to keep a record of all
licences granted or backed by them, and a police constable or any person
authorised by a LA is empowered to inspect and take copies of or extracts
from the records without payment. Other persons having reasonable grounds
may do so on payment of the prescribed fee. A copy of any such entry, duly
certified by or on behalf of the commissioners to be a true copy, is admissible
in evidence without proof of the signature.

5. PSV licences

Section 127 and PSVs (Licences and Certificates) Regulations 1952, as amended

It is an offence to cause or permit the use of a MV as a PSV without the appropriate PSV licence (obtainable from the traffic commissioners of the area in which the vehicle will ordinarily be operated).

PSV licences are of three kinds corresponding with the classes of PSVs, i.e.:

a) Stage carriage licence—which authorises use of the vehicle as stage or contract carriage and subject to any conditions in road service licence as an express carriage.

b) Express carriage licence—which authorises use of the vehicle as express or contract carriage and in special circumstances, with written consent of commissioner, as a stage carriage.

c) Contract carriage licence—which authorises use of the vehicle as a contract carriage only.

> **Carpenter v Campbell (1953)**
> Where it is the employer's duty to get any licence and he has failed to do so, the driver should not be prosecuted.

> **MacLean v Fearn (1954)**
> The driver of a bus on hire as a contract carriage carrying children to school allowed several adults to travel in it and accepted small unsolicited tips from them. *Held:* the bus was not being used as a stage carriage.

Each licence is in force for one year from date of issue and is valid in all traffic areas. It must be exhibited in a weatherproof holder in the same manner as the excise licence (usually alongside it); loss, destruction or defacement must be notified forthwith. The licence holder must notify change of address within seven days. The commissioners may refuse, suspend or revoke the licence if it appears to them that the person is not a fit person to hold such a licence.

6. Certificates of fitness

Section 129 and PSVs (Licences and Certificates) Regulations 1952, as amended

(1) Issue

a) A PSV licence cannot be granted for a vehicle *adapted to carry eight or more passengers* unless a certificate of fitness is issued in respect of the vehicle by a *certifying officer* of the traffic area (or a certificate of type conformity (see p. 214)).

b) A certificate may be issued for seven years, or such shorter period (not less than one year) as is specified in writing by the certifying officer.

c) The certificate will not be issued unless the MV complies not only with the C and U Regulations, but also with the requirements of the PSVs (Conditions of Fitness, Equipment and Use) Regulations 1972.

d) Change of ownership does not invalidate the certificate but a certifying officer may revoke or suspend, and a PSV examiner appointed by the S of S may suspend, a certificate if a PSV is found to be (or likely to become) unfit for service, by serving a notice of suspension or withdrawal. Suspension may be delayed for 48 hours to enable defects to be remedied.

e) *If a certificate of fitness is revoked, the PSV licence is rendered void* until a new certificate is obtained. Manufacturers of PSVs may, after satisfying the S of S and paying the prescribed fee, issue a declaration that a new vehicle conforms to a type currently approved by the S of S. Upon production of this, a certifying officer may, with or without examination of the vehicle, issue a *certificate of conformity* and this shall have the same effect as a certificate of fitness. The S of S may withdraw his approval of a type vehicle at any time and thus render ineffective any certificate relating to vehicles of that type (s. 130).

(2) Duty of a licence holder (s. 132)

A licence holder must notify the traffic commissioners of the area:

a) *where it happens*, of any failure of, or damage to, the vehicle likely to affect the safety of passengers or road users, and

b) *where the licence was issued*, of any alteration to the structure or fixed equipment of the vehicle (except replacement of parts).

(3) Power to inspect vehicles

A certifying officer or PSV examiner (s. 128) may, on production of his authority if required, in respect of a PSV:

a) require it to be stopped, e.g. by a uniformed constable on his behalf if so requested;

b) enter and inspect it; and

c) at any reasonable time enter premises where he has reason to believe a PSV is kept.

NOTES

a) It is an offence to obstruct the officer or examiner, or to fail to stop on being so required under this section.

b) Police officers may be appointed by the S of S to act as PSV examiners.

c) For duty placed on holder to produce the certificate of fitness when so required, see **(5)**(d) on p. 190.

d) The holder of a PSV licence can request a certificate of 'freedom from defects' from the examiner (s. 133A).

7. Road service licence (RSL)

Sections 134–143

(1) Offences

It is an offence to *use, cause* or *permit* to be used a *stage* or *express* carriage except under the authority of a RSL or a permit issued under s. 30 of the Transport Act 1968 (see p. 191). It is also an offence for the holder to fail to comply with the conditions of such a licence.

(2) Issue

The RSL is granted by the traffic commissioners of the area in or through which a proposed bus service is intended to operate, and authorises a service to be provided on a specified route (s. 135).

> **Hamilton v Blair and Meechan (1962)**
> In the case of a hiring of a vehicle it is the driver of the vehicle who 'uses' it within the section, and not the owner or hirer (even though a passenger).

> **G. Newton Ltd v Smith (1962): W. C. Standerwich Ltd v Smith (1962)**
> *Held:* the holder of a RSL is responsible for any wilful or negligent act of his employee in leaving the specified route, as the offence is one of absolute liability.

The commissioners hear in public applications for, and objections to, the grant of RSL. Particulars of applications, grants and conditions which apply, revocations and suspensions are published regularly in *Notices and Proceedings*, the official record of proceedings before the commissioners.

The licence is not valid in any other area until it is backed (i.e. confirmed) by the commissioners of that area, who may vary or add conditions with regard to the use of vehicles under the licence in the extended area (s. 137).

Licences for '*corridor areas*' (i.e. where passengers are not taken up or set down but are carried through from one traffic area to another, no vehicle being permitted to halt for more than 15 minutes) need not be so backed, but the commissioners of that area may prescribe the route and attach conditions (s. 138).

(3) Conditions

The grant of a RSL may be made subject to conditions relating to—

a) limitation of fares;

b) regulation of stopping places;

c) time tables;

d) setting down of passengers;

e) the safety and convenience of the public.

If any of the conditions are broken the licence may be revoked, suspended or varied. Particulars of the grant of a licence are sent by the traffic commissioners to every chief constable and LA in whose district the service is operated, as is every subsequent amendment, revocation or suspension (s. 136).

(4) Duration

This is normally for approximately three years, but by s. 139A a short-term licence may be granted for a period of six months or less.

NOTE

Grant, revocation, or suspension of a RSL must be notified to the LA and the police concerned.

(5) The PSVs (Licences and Certificates) Regulations 1952 (as amended)

These regulations deal with the procedure relating to PSV and RS licences and certificates of fitness. The main requirements relating to RS licences are:

a) *Applications* are to be made in a specified form (reg. 37).

b) *The licence holder* is under a duty to surrender the RSL (or backing) when he has ceased to operate vehicles under it (reg. 48); to return it within five days of receipt of a written request from the commissioners notifying suspension or revocation (reg. 11), or within seven days for amendment re change of particulars (reg. 8); and to report forthwith any loss, defacement or illegibility of a licence or certificate so that replacement can be made (reg. 10).

c) *The death of the licence holder* must be notified forthwith. Application by new owner or legal representative to ensure continuance of licence must be made within 14 days (reg. 12).

d) The holder of a RSL, backing or certificate of fitness must *produce it for examination* at his principal place of business when so required by a police officer, a certifying officer, a PSV or goods vehicle examiner or any person authorised (in writing) by the traffic commissioners for that area (reg. 9).

8. Road service permits

Transport Act 1968, s. 30

a) A RSL is not required if the use of a vehicle as a stage carriage is authorised by a permit under s. 30 issued by the Traffic Commissioners, who have to be satisfied that the permit is required to enable a bus service to be provided on a route on which no other transport facilities are available to meet the reasonable needs of the route and, if it is to be a school bus, that the education authority concerned has consented to the use of that vehicle for the purpose.

b) A school bus permit may authorise the use of the vehicle as an express carriage but, in any case, is subject to the condition that non-pupil passengers cannot be picked up except to the extent of space not required by pupils, and other conditions may be added.

c) The law relating to notification of the police (of grant, variation, suspension, revocation), keeping of records, forgery, and fraudulent applications applies to a permit as it does to a RSL.

d) The exemption under s. 30 applies only to the need for a RSL, and the remainder of the law relating to PSVs applies. A greater relaxation of the law applies to minibuses providing community bus services or operating under the Minibus Act 1977, subjects which are dealt with on pp. 202, 203.

9. PSV (Drivers' and Conductors' Licences) Regulations 1934

and 1960 Act ss. 144, 145

(1) Offences (s. 144)

It is an offence:

a) for any person to act as a driver or conductor of a PSV, not being the holder of the appropriate licence to act as such;

b) to employ as driver or conductor of a PSV a person who is not the holder of such a licence.

NOTE

A licence is obtained from the commissioners of the area in which applicant resides.

(2) Licences

I) DRIVER—Lowest age: 21 years; must be the holder of an ordinary driving licence and pass a test for the driving of PSVs. The licence may be limited to special types, e.g. single deckers.

II) CONDUCTOR—Lowest age: 18 years.

III) APPLICATIONS—To be made on prescribed forms, accompanied by two certificates of character, and signed by two ratepayers who have known applicant for past three years and one from employer, and evidence that he can read and write and is conversant with the Highway Code. The applicant may also have to prove that since the age of three years he has not had an epileptic attack, and is not suffering from any relevant disease or disability. It is the practice of the police to check character and references on request from commissioners.

IV) GRANT—Issued by the traffic commissioners of the area in which resident, valid for three years and in other traffic areas. Appeal lies to magistrates' court against refusal to grant, revocation or suspension (for misconduct or on account of physical disability).

V) LICENCE—To be signed by holder on receipt, and, if revoked or suspended, returned to commissioners within three days after notice to do so. Loss or destruction to be notified forthwith, and defaced licence returned, for replacement.

VI) PRODUCTION—On request of *any constable*, certifying officer, PSV or goods vehicle examiner or other *authorised person*, a licence holder must produce his licence or *state the address at which it will be available for inspection at any reasonable time during the next five days*. (*NB:* It shall not be demanded at that address until he has had reasonable time to make it available (reg. 11).)

(3) Badges

A badge is issued with the licence, and the driver or conductor (when acting as such) must wear the badge which is evidence of the licence being in force and a means of identification by the public (by the letter and number shown on it). The letter indicates the traffic area, followed by the serial number. A driver's badge normally has a red background, and a conductor's badge a green background. Particulars of the badge must be given when reporting a driver or conductor for an offence.

Similar provisions as apply to the licence relate to loss, destruction, deface-ment of badges, and surrender of badges on revocation or suspension.

10. PSV (Conditions of Fitness, Equipment and Use) Regulations 1972

The following provisions apply when a PSV is being used to carry passengers.

(1) Conductors (reg. 49)

The general rule is that a conductor must be carried on a *stage carriage* if the seating capacity exceeds 20 passengers.

EXCEPTIONS—No conductor is required on a single decker vehicle if:

a) seating does not exceed 32 and the entrance and emergency exits are at the front of the vehicle easily seen by driver from his seat and means are provided for him to become aware of any person outside the vehicle being trapped by the closure of the entrance door;

b) this has been authorised by a certificate of the traffic commissioners for that particular service or in the particular circumstances.

(2) Equipment

a) *All PSVs* must carry an approved *fire extinguisher* in a readily available position. Such apparatus must be one of the types specified and must be clearly marked with the appropriate BSI number, with the name and address of manufacturer or vendor. It must be maintained in good and efficient order (reg. 41).

b) *Express and contract carriages must carry first aid equipment* (as specified) in a suitable container.

(3) 'Use'

a) Every *exit, entrance and gangway* must be kept clear of any unnecessary obstruction (reg. 43).

b) No person shall cause or permit unnecessary obstruction of the driver (reg. 44).

c) The body (external and internal), all windows, fittings and seats must be kept in *good and clean condition* (reg. 45).

d) The *internal lamps* must be lit during the hours of darkness when passengers are carried, except on the top deck of a double decker bus if passengers are stopped using it by an effective barrier at the bottom of the staircase (reg. 46).

e) The *petrol tank* must be closed and not be filled when the engine is running (reg. 48).

f) No highly *inflammable* or other dangerous substance must be carried unless safely packed so as not to cause damage or injury, even in the event of accident to the vehicle (reg. 50).

g) The name and address of the firm, company or its representative to whom the PSV licence was issued must be conspicuously painted on the nearside in characters at least 1 in high in colours contrasting with their background (reg. 40). By the PSVs (Licences and Certificates) Regulations, when a vehicle is *hired out*, a notice must be exhibited showing to the front or nearside as follows: 'ON HIRE TO'—(name and address of holder of RSL under which used).

11. Trailers: MV (C and U) Regulations 1978, reg. 135

No *trailer* must be drawn by a PSV except one which is:

a) a gas producer unit; or

b) an *empty bus* being towed by an *empty bus* in an emergency; or

c) used only for the carriage of the effects of passengers travelling on that or any other PSV operated by the same person or as part of a joint service.

(Authority to use trailer must be included in the RSL; the trailer and the means of attachment must be approved by a certifying officer.)

12. PSVs and Trolley Vehicles (Carrying Capacity) Regulations 1954

NOTE

This subject is not included in examination syllabuses, but is included for general information purposes.

These regulations provide that PSVs are to be licensed for excise purposes on their seating capacity, i.e. as for hackney carriages (see p. 150), and also regulate the carrying of standing passengers.

(1) Capacity markings

The seating capacity of every PSV must be clearly marked in letters at least 1 in high, inside and visible from outside or on the rear or nearside of the vehicle. On a double decker the capacity must be shown in respect of each deck.

Vehicles specially constructed or adapted for carrying standing passengers must be marked with the standing capacity in addition to the seating capacity (reg. 8).

(2) Exceeding capacity: offence

It is an offence to carry seated passengers exceeding in number the seating capacity of the PSV (as calculated for excise purposes and marked on vehicle) and also, subject to the following exceptions, to carry standing passengers.

EXCEPTIONS

Regulation 4

a) In the case of a *stage carriage* (or trolley vehicle), standing passengers up to *one-third* of the seating capacity of the vehicle (or of lower deck if double decked) or *eight* (whichever is the less) may be carried (but no standing passengers are allowed on the upper deck of a double decker):
   i) during the hours of *peak traffic*, or
   ii) to *avoid undue hardship* (e.g. on last buses at night).

b) The *traffic commissioners* may authorise standing passengers to be carried (within the limits described above) subject to such conditions as they think fit:
   i) in *express* carriages;
   ii) in *specially constructed single decked* vehicles on specified services or in specified areas;
   iii) on the lower deck of *double decked PSVs and trolley vehicles* specially constructed or adapted for the purpose;
   iv) on the lower deck of certain double decked vehicles certified by the commissioners as not requiring a conductor,

provided that standing passengers must not be carried:

   i) on the *upper deck* of a *double decked vehicle*;
   ii) on a *half-decked* PSV;
   iii) to the front of the rear of the driver's seat;
   iv) unless a *conductor is carried**;
   v) on a PSV with seating capacity not exceeding twelve if the first certificate of fitness was issued after 11th April 1958, unless specially constructed or adapted to carry standing passengers.

c) When the only passengers are persons under the age of 19 years (excluding necessary attendants if not more than six are carried), then *three children* (not over 15 years of age or having attained 15 during the current school term) *count as two passengers*. If the PSV has twelve seats or less (see (v) above) a maximum of nine children may be so counted, and no standing passengers are allowed except as permitted in (a) above, i.e. limited to n/e one-third of seating capacity (reg. 3).

NOTE

When dealing with cases of overloading, it is normal practice to count the number of passengers in the presence of the conductor and to note the number of children being carried for the information of the court in evidence later.

Spires v Smith (1956)

The offence of 'carrying' excess passengers is committed by the operator, not by the driver or conductor; the latter might be liable for aiding and

---

* Does not apply if operating under certificate of commissioners that a conductor is not needed.

abetting the operator, but it is wrong to charge the conductor with 'permitting' overcrowding.

13. PSVs (Conduct of Drivers, Conductors and Passengers) Regulations 1936

(1) Drivers and conductors

Drivers and conductors of all PSVs must:

a) behave in a civil and orderly manner;

b) take reasonable precautions to ensure safety of passengers *in, on, entering* or *alighting* from the vehicles;

c) not smoke in or on the bus during a journey *or* when it has passengers aboard;

d) *not wilfully deceive* or refuse to inform a passenger or intending passenger re *destination, route* or *fare of any journey*;

e) correctly give particulars re *name, address, employer* and *particulars of licences* to a constable when requested, or to other person having reasonable cause to ask for them; and

f) *not obstruct* or neglect to give information and assistance to an authorised examiner of the vehicle (reg. 4).

> **Reid v MacNicol (1958)**
> *Held:* the regulations impose a duty on the driver to take precautions for the safety of passengers entering the bus and this includes persons entitled to enter the bus, but no person is entitled to enter a moving bus.

> **Marshall v Clark (1958)**
> *Held:* it was immaterial that the regulations do not define 'reasonable precautions', which is a question of fact for the court to decide.

> **Ellis v Smith (1962)**
> A driver who has left his vehicle at the end of a duty period is still responsible until his relief takes over.

(2) The driver

The driver:

a) *of any PSV must not* speak to the conductor or any other person when the vehicle is in motion unless necessary for safety reasons (reg. 5), but SI

1975 No. 461 permits use of radio communication for operational or emergency purpose;

b) *of a stage or express carriage must:*
i) stop the vehicle close to the nearside when picking up or setting down passengers on a road, and
ii) *not* cause the bus to stop longer than necessary on a road (reg. 7).

(3) The conductor

The conductor:

a) *of any PSV must:*
i) *not* speak to the driver or distract his attention when the PSV is in motion unless to stop the vehicle or for good reason;
ii) ensure that the destination, route and fares are clearly and correctly displayed where means for this are provided; and
iii) enforce the regulations relating to conduct of passengers (reg. 6);

b) *of a stage or express carriage must not* delay unreasonably long the signal to the driver to start, except at place where the PSV is permitted to remain (reg. 8).

(4) Passengers

Regulations apply not only when a PSV is carrying passengers but also while it is waiting to pick up passengers, and extend not only to passengers but also those who intend to become passengers.

The following are offences under the regulations.

I) ON ANY PSV—It is an offence (reg. 9):

a) to use obscene or offensive language or be disorderly;

b) to enter or alight except by the door provided;

c) to wilfully obstruct passengers entering or alighting;

d) to enter or remain on board when told not to do so because the bus is full or not allowed to pick up at that point;

e) to travel on top deck unless seated, or in any part not for passengers;

f) to wilfully interfere with any part of the PSV or its equipment in a manner calculated to interfere with the working of the vehicle, or to cause injury or discomfort to any person;

g) to distract the driver's attention, save to stop the vehicle;

h) to signal the vehicle to start;

i) to spit upon, damage, soil or defile any part of the vehicle;

j) to distribute any written or printed matter or advertise any printed article;

k) to wilfully remove, deface, displace or alter any notice-board, etc.;

l) to annoy other persons by using noisy instruments, singing or shouting, on the vehicle;

m) to throw money from a vehicle to be scrambled for, or throw bottles, litter or liquid likely to annoy or cause danger or injury;

n) to throw any article, streamer, balloon, flag, etc. or attach or trail such things from the vehicle in a manner so as to overhang the road or

o) to obstruct or impede any authorised person* in the execution of his duty.

II) ON ANY STAGE OR EXPRESS CARRIAGE—It is an offence (regs. 9, 10 and 11):

a) to smoke or to *carry* a lighted cigar, cigarette, or pipe in or on any part of a vehicle where smoking is prohibited;

b) to beg, sell or offer for sale any article in the vehicle;

c) if passenger's condition or clothing is offensive (to the vehicle, or passengers), to enter or remain in the vehicle after an authorised person* has requested him to do otherwise, and has *returned his fare, if previously paid*;

d) to have a loaded firearm, or any dangerous or offensive article (a passenger requires the consent of an authorised person* to carry with him any bulky or cumbersome article which must be placed on the vehicle as directed);

e) to bring into the vehicle any animal without consent of an authorised person*, or to keep it there after request to remove it or to place it on the vehicle as directed;

f) to use or attempt to use an altered or defaced ticket or an expired season or period ticket with intent to avoid payment, or a non-transferable ticket issued to another person;

g) on request (unless holding a ticket) refuse to declare his journey, pay his fare, take ticket, or refuse to show ticket—unless fare is offered instead; SI 1975 No. 461 adds failure to pay driver on entry (if no conductor) or to use coin equipment;

h) to leave or attempt to leave the vehicle without paying and with intent to avoid payment;

i) at the end of a journey to refuse to surrender ticket on request, or to leave the vehicle on request;

j) being a season ticket holder, refuse to give up ticket at the expiry of the period, if so required.

(5) Police powers (reg. 12)

a) Any passenger 'in' or 'on' a PSV who is reasonably suspected by the driver or conductor of committing any of the above offences, must give his name

---

* An employee of the licensee (reg. 2).

and address on demand to the driver or conductor. Failure to do so is an offence (1960, s. 147, and reg. 12).

b) Any passenger committing an offence may be *ejected* by the *driver or conductor* or by a *constable on request* of either of them.

c) By the PSV (Arrest of Offenders) Act 1975, which does not apply to Scotland or N Ireland, if a constable reasonably suspects that a person has contravened or failed to comply with any regulation relating to conduct of passengers he may require that person to give his name and address, and if that person:
i) refuses to give this information to the constable, or
ii) gives a name and address but does not answer to the satisfaction of the constable questions put to him by the constable for the purpose of ascertaining whether the name and address are correct,

the constable may without warrant arrest him.

NOTE
The S of S can by Order extend this power to apply to passengers offending against byelaws under the Tramways Act 1870.

(6) Prosecution of offences

The 1960 Act, s. 161 provides that proceedings in England and Wales for any offence under Part 3 of the Act (relating to the licensing of PSVs) and any regulation made thereunder (other than as to the conduct of passengers or carrying excess passengers) can be instituted only:

a) by or on behalf of the DPP, or

b) by a person authorised by:
i) the commissioners of a traffic area, or
ii) the council of a county or country district, or
iii) a chief constable.

Price v Humphries (1958)
A magistrates' clerk should satisfy himself that the authority to prosecute is in existence before issuing the summons. Objection on this point by the defence at court must be taken before the case for the prosecution is closed to enable the authorisation to be pronounced.

Proceedings for an offence by a passenger (see p. 197) or for carrying excess passengers (see p. 197) may be instituted by any person.

(7) Powers of local authorities

I) TO REGULATE BUS ROUTES, ETC—A county council can by order regulate the use of highways by PSVs, either generally or by specified classes of PSVs during limited periods of the year. The section does not apply to Greater London (RTR Act 1967, s. 15).

II) TO RUN PSVS—The only remaining provisions of the RTA 1930 authorise councils of districts (but not county councils) to run bus services (but not contract carriages).

14. PSVs (Lost Property) Regulations 1978

Property found in a PSV must be handed immediately by the finder to the conductor in the state it is found, or, if not practicable, delivered to lost property office of the operator. The conductor (or driver if no conductor) must search his vehicle before or at the end of each journey for left property, which is to be handed to the operator within 24 hours. If claimed before he hands it over the conductor shall, if satisfied that the claimant is the owner, hand it back without charge. The claimant shall give his name and address to the conductor who must report it to the operator. Property claimed while in custody of the operator shall be returned to the owner on proof of ownership and on payment of the appropriate charge (as specified by the regulations).

The operator may dispose of objectionable property at any time, and destroy or dispose of perishable property after 48 hours. A record must be kept by the operator and be available for inspection by a police officer or other authorised person. The operator (or his representative) is authorised to open packets, bags and other receptacles for purpose of identifying owner or ascertaining the nature or the value of the property.

15. Hours of driving

The provisions of Part VI of the Transport Act 1968 apply to drivers of PSVs or any other MV constructed or adapted to carry more than twelve passengers as they do to goods vehicles—see p. 223.

16. Carriage of persons suffering from notifiable diseases

For the provisions of the Public Health Act 1936, see p. 73.

17. International bus services and coach tours

Road Transport (International Passenger Services) Regulations 1973

The regulations apply to a PSV for nine or more passengers (including driver) used for the international carriage of passengers. They do not apply to N Ireland. The enforcement of the regulations is primarily the responsibility of PSV examiners appointed under the RTA 1960. Obstruction of an examiner in the execution of his duty is an offence. The general effect of the regulations is that the provisions relating to PSV licences, road service licences, licensing of drivers and conductors, and the condition, fitness and equipment of PSVs do not apply to international passenger services. For police purposes the regulations may be summarised as follows.

I) INTERNATIONAL BUS SERVICES—

a) The regulations apply to vehicles registered in EEC member states.

b) Every vehicle used requires an EEC authorisation appropriate to the service being operated. In the case of a vehicle registered in this country authorisations are issued by or through the S of S.

c) It is an offence to operate an international bus service except under and in accordance with the authorisation referred to in (b) above.

d) If the PSV is registered in the UK the exemptions do not relate to PSV licences and road service licences.

II) INTERNATIONAL COACH TOURS—the coach not remaining in GB longer than three months. The exemptions apply:

a) *to a PSV registered in any member state (other than UK) or in N Ireland* when used only to carry passengers who are travelling to GB from a place in a member state (other than UK) or in N Ireland, or are travelling from GB to any such place;

b) *to a PSV registered in any other place abroad* when used only while carrying passengers making a temporary stay in GB.

18. Emergency signals

Regulation 118 of the C & U Regulations 1978 allows the audible warning instrument of a PSV to be sounded at any time to summon assistance for its crew. In addition the device for operating traffic indicators as a hazard warning (see p. 122) may also activate the horn to call for assistance.

19. Minibus Act 1977

a) The Act provides for the use of vehicles to carry more than seven but not more than sixteen passengers by bodies concerned with education, with religion, with social welfare or with other activities for the benefit of the community.

b) Such a vehicle is not to be treated as a PSV if:
   i) it is specified under a permit issued under the Act, and
   ii) it is not being used to carry members of the public at large or for profit, and
   iii) it is being used by the body holding the permit and the conditions of the permit are being fully observed.

c) Permits are granted by the traffic commissioners of the area in which the vehicle is ordinarily kept, and any other body designated by an order under the Act.

d) An order has been made designating every county council (and its equivalent in London and Scotland) as well as over fifty bodies concerned with matters described in (a) above. Every such body has within one month of the grant of the permit to send a copy of it to the Secretary of State, and within one month after 31st December each year to send to the Secretary of State a return giving details of each permit granted, varied or revoked during the year ended 31st December.

Minibus Regulations 1977—*Documents to be displayed* in a minibus operating under permit are (i) the driver's notice and (ii) the permit disc.

I) DRIVER'S NOTICE—To be affixed on the inside of the bus so as to be easily readable by the driver without interfering with his control of the vehicle. It specifies the conditions attached to the permit and a warning to the driver (see below).

II) THE DISC—It is circular in shape, and gives the following information: the disc number (DOE plus number); by whom, to whom and date issued; and registration mark of the vehicle to which it relates. It has to be affixed inside the bus so as to be easily readable from outside the bus and not interfere with the driver's control of the vehicle.

CONDITIONS OF USE:

a) Notice and disc to be properly displayed; the driver to be over 21 and hold a driver's licence (not provisional).

b) Children not be carried between home and school without the consent of the local commissioners and education authority.

c) Only passengers of the classes described in the notice to be carried.

WARNING—This informs the driver that failure to comply with the above conditions may result in a prosecution for causing the vehicle to be used without a PSV licence, and of the driver if he does not hold a PSV driver's licence.

20. Community bus services

Transport Act 1978, s. 5 and s. 6

a) The provisions of the Act are designed to facilitate the provision of more adequate bus facilities in rural areas, and relate to vehicles constructed or adapted for at least eight but not more than sixteen passengers.

b) Traffic commissioners may grant a RSL authorising the use of such a vehicle as a stage, express, or contract carriage* so as to provide a community bus service, using volunteer drivers.

c) The commissioners must be satisfied that the applicants are a body of persons (corporate or not) who are concerned for the social and welfare needs of one or more communities, and propose to provide the bus service without profit to themselves or any other person. In the case of a permit they must also be satisfied that no other transport facilities are available to meet the reasonable needs on the proposed route.

d) A PSV licence is not needed, nor need the driver hold a PSV driver's licence, but:
   i) the driver must be a volunteer, and if not holding a PSV driver's licence must fulfil any conditions which may be prescribed, and
   ii) the vehicle (unless a PSV licence applies to it) must fulfil conditions prescribed by regulations as to its fitness, equipment and use†, and
   iii) the vehicle must display such disc or other document as may be prescribed for a community bus.

e) The three conditions in the above paragraph constitute conditions applicable to the RSL or the permit.

f) 'Volunteer' means unpaid, disregarding reasonable expenses incurred in making himself available to drive and payment for earnings lost by making himself available to drive in exceptional circumstances.

g) A PSV is exempt from MOT test, but a community bus is not.

---

* If the requirement is only for a stage carriage authorisation, this can be met by the grant of a permit under s. 30 of the Transport Act 1968 (see p. 191).

† Some regulations have been made, and as to equipment and use follow closely the regulations relating to PSVs, as on p. 192, excluding (3) (g).

Chapter 15 **Goods vehicles**

1. Operators' licences

Transport Act 1968, Part V

NOTE

The Transport Act 1968 introduced the general requirement that any person using a goods vehicle for commercial purposes has to do so under the authority of an 'operator's licence'. Small goods vehicles (SGV) are excluded from such licensing, while large goods vehicles (LGV), in addition to authorisation by operators' licences, may require special authorisations for certain road journeys.

(1) Goods vehicle

A goods vehicle (GV) is a MV (not a tramcar or trolley vehicle) constructed or adapted for use for the carriage or haulage of goods, or a trailer so constructed or adapted (s. 92).

(2) Large and small goods vehicles

These are differentiated as follows:

NATURE OF VEHICLE	IS A SGV IF N/E	IS A LGV† IF EXCEEDING
a) Not forming part of a vehicle combination:		
i) having a relevant plated weight (rpw), or	3·5 tonnes	16 tons
ii) if no rpw an unladen weight	1525 kg	5 tons

† A LGV does not include a *hauling* vehicle.

NATURE OF VEHICLE	IS A SGV IF N/E	IS A LGV† IF EXCEEDING
b) forming part of vehicle combination, but not articulated		
i) if all vehicles* in the combination have rpw, the aggregate rpw	3·5 tonnes	16 tons
ii) in any other case, the aggregate unladen weight of all vehicles*	1525 kg	5 tons
c) forming part of an articulated combination		
i) if trailer part has an rpw, that rpw plus unladen weight of the MV	3·5 tonnes	16 tons
ii) in any other case, aggregate unladen weight	1525 kg	5 tons

NOTE

Relevant plated weight means the maximum gross weight not to be exceeded, as specified in the Ministry plate or the manufacturer's plate (see p. 255) where not yet Ministry plated.

(3) Need for licence

Subject to the exceptions given below it is an offence for any person to use a GV on a road for the carriage (or haulage) of goods:

a) for hire or reward, or

b) for or in connection with any trade or business carried on by him,

except under the authority of an operator's licence (OL) (s. 60).

NOTES

The licensing authority is the chairman of the traffic commissioners of the area in which the centre from which the vehicles operate is situated, or his deputy. By s. 92 the 'user' is

a) the driver if the MV belongs to him or he possesses it under an agreement for hire, purchase or loan;

b) in any other case, the person whose servant or agent the driver is.

The functions of a local authority is a business (s. 60).

Exceptions—An OL is not required in the case of:

a) small goods vehicles (SGV), or

b) vehicles exempted by regulations (s. 60).

The GV (OL) Regulations 1977 exempt the following vehicles:

I) PUBLIC SERVICES—i.e. vehicles:

a) used for police, fire and ambulance purposes;

---

* Any small trailer (unladen weight n/e one ton) to be excluded.

b) discharging local authorities' responsibilities re civil defence, sanitation, food and drugs, weights and measures, weighing vehicles, clearing, salting or gritting, etc. roads in snow or ice conditions;

c) licensed as PSVs (and trailers) or hackney carriages;

d) used for funeral purposes.

II) RESCUE SERVICES—for firefighting or rescues from mines, to carry lifeboat or life-saving apparatus, or crew on behalf of HM Coastguard or RNLI.

III) ARMED FORCES (INCLUDING VISITING FORCES)—their own and hired vehicles used for services purposes, including mobilisation, manoeuvres, exercises and training.

IV) PARTICULAR KINDS OF VEHICLES

a) *DPV*, RR*, PPV*, or any electrically propelled vehicle or a showman's vehicle*;

b) *passenger vehicle for n/e fifteen passengers*, exclusive of driver and effects* when adapted to draw or drawing a trailer;

c) *agricultural machine** liable to reduced excise duty being used solely to haul such objects as are specified in the Act;

d) *incomplete vehicle*, i.e. without permanent body but carrying goods for test or trial, or articles for its own construction;

e) *tower wagon** if the only goods carried are those required for its work as such;

f) *vehicle fitted with apparatus, machine, etc.* as a permanent fixture if only goods carried are those required for use with the fixture or the running of the vehicle;

g) *gross weight n/e 3½ tons*—a vehicle first used pre 1st January 1977 of unladen weight n/e 1525 kg, if maximum gross weight shown on its plate exceeds 3·5 tonnes but not 3½ tons.

V) LIMITED USE

a) Used under a *trade licence*;

b) trailer not constructed primarily to carry goods but used incidentally for that purpose in connection with *road construction maintenance or repair*;

c) used for carrying goods within an aerodrome.

The GV (OL) (Temporary Use in GB) Regulations 1975 (as amended) exempt goods vehicles from almost all European countries which are brought into GB temporarily (n/e three months) carrying goods by road from a place abroad, and not used for collection and delivery of goods within this country. Limitations are placed on the nature of goods carried.

---

* Exemption covers a trailer drawn by this MV.

(4) Authorised vehicles (s. 61)

Vehicles authorised to be used under an OL are:

a) *motor vehicles* owned by the holder (or possessed by him under agreement for purchase, hire or loan) and specified in the licence;

b) *trailers* similarly owned or possessed but not exceeding at one time the maximum number specified in the licence.

NOTE

The OL may authorise up to a specified maximum an additional number of MVs to be acquired, but any such subsequent acquisition within this maximum will be covered by the OL for one month only unless within that time it has been notified to the licensing authority.

NOTE

The licence does not cover a vehicle transferred to operate from a centre outside the area of the authority which issued the licence for a period longer than three months. Within this period the vehicle must return to its original centre or the OL for the other centre be varied to include the vehicle. Two or more successive periods not separated by three months or more is regarded as a single period of a duration equal to the aggregate of those periods. A vehicle cannot be included in more than one OL, nor can an operator have more than one OL in any one licensing area. The connection of a MV with its OL is evidenced by the exhibition of an identity disc in the same way as the excise licence—see p. 139.

(5) Objections

Objection to the grant of an OL can be made by any prescribed union or association (members of which are persons holding operator's licences or employees of such persons); a COP; or a local authority.

NOTICE OF OBJECTIONS—To be in the form prescribed by the regulations, sent to the licensing authority within three weeks of the notice of application appearing in *Applications and Decisions*, and a copy sent to the applicant at the same time, giving the grounds of objection (s. 63).

(6) Transport managers

Section 65*

In respect of each operating centre (OC) covered by the OL there must be specified in the OL a person† (the licence holder, if an individual, or an employee of his) who is to be responsible for the maintenance and operation‡

---

* Not operative at date of publication.

† Two or more persons may be specified and thus share the responsibilities.

‡ Includes securing proper licensing of drivers and compliance with drivers' hours.

of authorised vehicles normally operating from that centre. It is a condition of the licence that the specified person(s) shall hold the appropriate manager's licence and that, if an employee of the licence holder, he holds the position of responsibility specified in the OL.

NOTE

If a new operating centre is subsequently opened this condition does not apply for a period of three months from date of opening. If a specified person ceases to hold 'office' (death, resignation, etc.) the condition is deemed not to be contravened for a period of three months, plus, if variation of OL is applied for in that time, the period required for appeal by applicant.

OFFENCE—If, as regards an OC, a condition of an OL under this section is being contravened, or during the time when matters required to be specified as above are not so specified an authorised vehicle is used under the licence from the OC concerned, the licence holder commits a summary offence.

(7) Conditions attached to OL

a) *Automatic*—see s. 65 (above).

b) *Imposed on grant*—the OL may be granted subject to any of the following conditions, requiring the licensing authority to be informed by the holder:
   i) of specified changes in organisation, management, or ownership of the carriers' business;
   ii) if a company, of any change in persons holding shares;
   iii) of any other event specified affecting the licence holder (s. 66).

Contravention of condition under s. 65 or s. 66 is an offence.

(8) Interim licence

This is a temporary licence which may be granted to an applicant pending the determination of the application, and any appeal from it. It is not regarded as an OL as far as the requirements as to transport managers are concerned (s. 67).

(9) Duration of OL

An OL normally continues in force until the specified date (24th March or the last day of any other month) next before the expiry of five years from the commencement of licence. This period can, however, be shorter, e.g. on request of applicant, or shorter or longer if desirable to arrange a suitable and convenient programme of work for the licensing authority (s. 67).

(10) Variation of OL

An OL can only be varied on an application by the licence holder to the licensing authority, e.g. to include additional vehicles, to increase or reduce maximum numbers, to remove specified vehicles, to alter particulars of transport manager or to change or remove a condition (s. 68).

(11) Revocation, etc. of OL

The licensing authority can revoke, suspend or curtail an OL, or attach special conditions instead, on any of the following grounds:

a) contravention of condition;

b) conviction (during preceding five years) of certain offences;

c) false statement, or a statement of expectation not fulfilled, made in any application for OL or variation of it;

d) bankruptcy or liquidation (not being a voluntary one for reconstruction);

e) material change of circumstances relevant to grant or variation of OL;

f) a person disqualified for holding an OL has become a director or partner (or holds a controlling interest) in a company operating under an OL, contrary to a direction made by the licensing authority which imposed the disqualification (see below).

(12) Disqualification

When a licence is revoked the licensing authority can order disqualification indefinitely or for a specified period and, in addition, direct that if the person disqualified becomes connected with the control of a transport undertaking at any time, or within a specified period, the OL of the company may become liable to revocation, suspension or curtailment (s. 69). To apply for an OL while disqualified is an offence and any OL obtained is of no effect. A disqualification may be limited to the holding of an OL in specified areas. No action is to be taken under this section by the licensing authority without first holding an enquiry, if the person requests this (s. 69). Appeal lies to the Transport Tribunal (s. 70).

(13) Goods Vehicles (Operators' Licences) Regulations 1977

INSPECTION OF DOCUMENTS—Copies of the following documents are to be kept available for inspection at the offices of the licensing authority:

a) *Applications and Decisions*—which is a statement of application received, dates and places of enquiries, and decisions of the licensing authority as to grants, revocations, suspensions, etc. of licences. Any person may not only inspect, but also obtain copies on paying the prescribed fee.

b) *Applications Made*—open to inspection by any persons authorised in writing by any of the authorities which can object to grants.

c) *Licences Issued*—during currency of licence, by any person having grounds for inspection (regs. 6 and 7).

IDENTIFICATION OF SPECIFIED VEHICLES—In respect of every vehicle specified in an OL the licensing authority issues to the licence holder an identity disc. The LH must cause a valid identity disc appropriate to the vehicle to be affixed to the vehicle during such time as is specified in the OL (whether being used under the OL or not). It must be in a waterproof container:

a) if the vehicle has an excise licence properly exhibited, adjacent to that licence;

b) otherwise, in or adjacent to the place where an excise licence would be required to be affixed.

When the disc is affixed the person for the time being in control of the vehicle must keep it readily legible (reg. 11).

TEMPORARY VARIATIONS—If the holder of an OL wishes to make a temporary substitution for a GV (specified in the OL) which has been withdrawn from, or becomes unfit for, service, the licensing authority can vary the OL without the normal requirements for applications for variations being complied with. When this is done (or the temporarily added GV is withdrawn) the relevant identity disc must be returned to the licensing authority (reg. 12).

RETURN OF LICENCES AND DISCS

a) If a specified GV ceases to be used under the OL the licence holder must within three weeks notify the licensing authority, and return the OL (for variation) and the relevant disc.

b) If an OL is varied the licence holder must, on request, return the OL for variation, and return discs relating to any GV removed from the OL.

c) If the OL is revoked, ceases to have effect (other than by expiry), or is suspended or curtailed, or a condition is to be added to it, the licence holder must within five days after a notice to that effect has been delivered to him, or sent to him by recorded delivery, send or deliver to the licensing authority the licence and also the discs relating to such GV as the licensing authority specifies—for cancellation, retention or alteration, as the case may be (reg. 16).

NOTE
As to powers under Part V and evidence by certificate, see pp. 213 and 289.

2. Special authorisations for large goods vehicles

Transport Act 1968, ss. 71–84

NOTE
These sections had not been brought into force at date of publication. Students should check on this. Remember that GV includes trailers.

(1) Definitions

LARGE GOODS VEHICLE (LGV)—see p. 204.

CONTROLLED JOURNEY—a journey between places in GB separated by a distance exceeding 100 miles, being a journey for the whole of which goods are carried if:

a) *in a container* (volume not less than 600 cu ft by external measurement), or on a *pallet* (surface area not less than 50 sq ft) without being taken out of the container or off the pallet (whether one vehicle or successive vehicles are used), or

b) *otherwise*, the goods are carried on the same LGV without being taken off it.

(2) Special authorisation (s. 71)

It is an *offence* to use a LGV on a road:

a) to carry goods on, or on part of, a controlled journey, or

b) to carry more than 11 tons of prescribed goods other than on a controlled journey,

except under a special authorisation under Part V of the Act.

NOTE
If the vehicle is itself carried on a vessel, aircraft, or other means of transport it is still deemed to carry the goods, but the distance to be calculated is the aggregate of miles covered by the vehicle when not so carried. An authorisation for a controlled journey held by one person who uses a vehicle to carry the goods part of the way may expressly authorise other persons to carry the goods on that journey without each having a separate authorisation. The limit of 11 tons applies to the carriage of goods on a combination of vehicles as it does to a single vehicle.

(3) Applications for grant

Applications for grant, etc. are to be made to licensing authority of area in which the relevant OC is situated. The licensing authority has in most cases to send copies to Railways Board and the Freight Corporation, who may within 14 days serve notice of objection on the licensing authority and the applicant (ss. 72 and 73). In urgent cases the licensing authority if it considers there is no reasonable objection, can grant an authorisation which remains in force for three months unless the licensing authority directs a shorter period (s. 75).

(4) Conditions (s. 76)

The licensing authority can attach conditions, which may:

a) relate to the vehicles which can be used under the special authorisation;

b) require the making and preservation of records of the transport services operated;

c) require copy of any conditions defining the transport service authorised to be carried by drivers.

Contravention of a condition is an offence.

NOTE
Falsification of any record reported under this section or s. 81 is an offence (s. 83).

(5) Duration

Duration is as for an OL (see p. 208).

(6) Variation

Applications for variation in the kind of transport service authorised, or of conditions attached, can be made to the licensing authority (s. 78).

(7) Revocation, suspension, curtailment and disqualification

These can be directed by the licensing authority on grounds and with consequences similar to those applying to an OL (s. 79). Appeals lie to Transport Tribunal.

(8) Consignment notes

a) The goods shall not be carried on a LGV unless a consignment note (prescribed as to form and particulars) has been completed and signed as prescribed and is carried by the driver (s. 81).

b) This does not apply:
i) if a particular exemption (given by regulations) applies;
ii) if carriage of goods is lawful without an OL;
iii) to any case in which a dispensation, granted by the licensing authority applies.

c) The consignment note is to be preserved after the journey for a period prescribed by regulations by the person who used the vehicle (or if a controlled journey—the last vehicle) for carrying goods on that journey.

OFFENCE—using or driving a vehicle in contravention of (a) above, or failing to comply with (c) above.

(9) Power to enter and inspect (s. 82)

By a GV examiner, etc.

An officer (as defined below) may:

a) ask for production of records or documents (re special authorisation and consignment notes) required to be carried by a driver or to be preserved, and inspect and copy them;

b) by notice in writing require production of documents in (a) at the office of the licensing authority within such period as is specified in the notice (not to be less than ten days);

c) at any time enter a LGV to inspect it or goods carried;

d) at any time reasonable in the circumstances enter premises where LGV is reasonably believed to be, or any records as in (a) are to be found, and inspect the LGV or inspect and copy such records found there;

e) at any time reasonable in the circumstances enter the premises of an applicant for or holder of an OL to inspect facilities for maintaining authorised vehicles.

NOTES

In all except (e) the officer must produce his authority if so required. Officer is a GV examiner or any person specially authorised under the section by the licensing authority. To exercise powers a vehicle may be detained during such time as is required. If an offence under 1968, s. 83 and 1972, ss. 169 or 170 (forgery, false entries) is suspected the article or document can be seized, and in such a case, if no charge is preferred within six months, an application can be made to a magistrates' court for an order as to disposal in same way as under the Police Property Act 1897. Failure to comply with (a) or (b) or obstructing exercise of powers is an offence.

By a police officer

By sub-s. (9) all the above powers can be exercised by a police constable, who shall not, if wearing uniform, be required to produce his authority.

(10) Evidence by certificate (s. 84)

In any proceedings for an offence under Part V a certificate signed* by or on behalf of the licensing authority relating to an OL, special authorisation or traffic manager's licence is evidence of the facts stated, as to grant, duration, suspension, terms and conditions, disqualifications, and whether or not a person holds an OL on any date.

---

* Signature is to be deemed authentic until contrary is proved.

3. Plating and testing

RTA 1972: GV (Plating and Testing) Regulations 1971 (as amended)

(1) Applications of regulations

The regulations apply to goods vehicles which are:

a) HMC and motor cars constructed or adapted to form part of an AV; other HMC and other motor cars of unladen weight n/e 1525 kg;

b) semi-trailers; other trailers of unladen weight exceeding 1020 kg; trailers being converter dollies of unladen weight n/e 1020 kg manufactured post 1st January 1979.

Exceptions (vehicles which can be described generally as not being load-carrying in the ordinary sense of the term) are given in (5), on p. 218.

(2) Plating

This means marking on a GV by means of a 'plate' the maximum weights applicable to that GV. Plating may be carried out:

a) by certificates of the manufacturer or of the Minister in respect of *new approved types;*

b) where (a) does not apply, at the *first examination* at which the GV passes its test for its goods vehicle test certificate.

Although a GV has to undergo a test for the goods vehicle test certificate each year there is no periodical test for plating, for weights once 'plated' remain the same unless the vehicle is altered.

I) APPROVAL OF NEW TYPES—(s. 47 and s. 48). When relevant regulations have been made prescribing 'type approval' requirements for motor vehicles of particular classes (as to design, construction, equipment and marking) a manufacturer may apply to and obtain from the S of S a type approval certificate. This will authorise him to issue in respect of each vehicle produced by him and conforming to the certificate a 'certificate of conformity' in which the 'design weights' (and, if a GV, the 'plated weights') are specified. Where no such certificate has been issued by the manufacturer the equivalent (called a 'minister's approval certificate') may be issued by the S of S (on application) in respect of a particular MV if he is satisfied that it complies with the relevant type approval requirements. In the case of both certificates the issuer will have to secure that 'plated weights' (in the case of a GV) are marked on the MV by means of a plate fixed to it. Both certificates will be the equivalent of plating certificates.

NOTE
The type approval scheme was first introduced in relation to goods vehicles, but it now extends to all vehicles and to vehicle parts.

II) PLATING ON FIRST EXAMINATION—A GV which has not been plated as above as an approved type is plated at the first occasion on which it is successfully tested for its goods vehicle test certificate (see below), in which case a plating certificate is issued and the 'plate' must be fixed to the vehicle.

NOTE

A new vehicle which does not have one of the certificates referred to in (I) above will not be plated by the Ministry until it is submitted for its first examination for a goods vehicle test certificate towards the end of the first year after registration. In this interval it will generally be subject to the weight restrictions specified in the manufacturer's plate which has to be affixed to a post 1st January 1968 goods vehicle in accordance with reg. 42 of the MV (C and U) Regulations 1978, for if a GV is not plated it is an offence to exceed the weight limits shown on a reg. 42 manufacturer's plate. If plated the offence is against reg. 147 of the MV (C and U) Regulations 1978.

III) THE PLATING CERTIFICATE—is the official documentary evidence of the applicable plated weights. It also sets out any restrictions on the use of the vehicle when fitted with particular tyres, and specifies the kinds of vehicle alterations which have to be notified to the Ministry. It need not be carried on the vehicle, but has to be produced in same way as an insurance certificate (see p. 174).

IV) THE PLATE—The plate (of paper) is enclosed in transparent plastic (approx. 6 in by 4 in) and must be securely fixed by the operator to the vehicle or trailer concerned and carried at all times. The plate must be conspicuous, readily accessible and kept legible. If the GV has a cab it must be in the cab. The particulars shown by a Ministry plate are similar to those shown on a manufacturer's plate (see p. 255).

V) NOTIFIABLE ALTERATIONS—Certain alterations to a plated GV have to be notified to the Ministry on a prescribed form before the altered vehicle is used on a road. The notifiable alterations are:

a) one to structure or fixed equipment which varies carrying capacity;

b) one affecting adversely any part of the braking system or its means of operation; or

c) any other alteration which materially renders the GV unsafe at any weight equal to any of its plated weights.

If a request to re-examine is made the necessary arrangements are made. If not, the Ministry decides whether there should be a re-examination and notifies the operator accordingly. Where any particular in a plating certificate becomes no longer applicable (not being a notifiable alteration) the operator *may* notify the Ministry accordingly in order to get the GV re-examined with a view to an amendment being made.

VI) LOSS OR DEFACEMENT—If a Ministry plate or plating certificate has been lost or defaced a replacement may be made on application in writing to the Ministry.

VII) OFFENCES—Any person who uses (or causes or permits to be used) on a road a GV:

a) with no plating certificate in force in respect of it, if such a certificate is required by the regulations*;

b) not complying with the requirements of the type approval certificate applicable to it;

c) drawing a trailer, where the plating certificate for the MV does not specify the maximum laden weight for the MV plus trailers (does not apply to a MV not constructed or adapted to form part of an AV);

d) which (or its equipment) has been altered so as to necessitate notification to the Ministry, this not having been done (it is a defence to prove that the alteration was not one specified in the relevant certificate as being notifiable) (s. 46);

e) marked, if plated, with any weight other than the plated weights or other weights authorised by regulations to be so marked (s. 172): in this case the offence is committed by the owner of the GV only.

NOTE
As to offences of false statements, entries or documents see (3) (IV), p. 217.

VIII) EVIDENCE—If the date of manufacture is marked on a GV under the 1967 Act or the regulations it is evidence of this date, and if any weight is so marked it is assumed to be the weight specified in the plating certificate unless the contrary is proved (s. 64).

IX) APPEALS—See (4), below.

(3) Testing

The standard MOT test (see p. 277) does not apply to GV subject to plating and testing. These have, instead, to be submitted for annual test at a vehicle testing station for the purpose of determining whether prescribed construction and use requirements are complied with. At the first of the tests the examination for the determination of 'plated weights' is also carried out. If the vehicle passes the test the goods vehicle test certificate is issued. If it fails, notification of refusal is issued and a re-test can be claimed. At any test of the GV the driver must (unless excused) be present and must drive and operate

---

* *Exemption from liability* for this offence extends to any case for which a certificate of temporary exemption is current (see (3) (III), p. 217) and use of a GV in going to, during and coming from an arranged test; or going to or from any place to get remedied defects on which a goods vehicle test certificate has been refused, or taking the GV by towing to be broken up; using it under a TL; taking an imported vehicle from place of arrival to place where it is to be kept (on occasion of first importation only); use of GV exempted from the C and U Regulations; removal or disposal of a GV under the Civic Amenities Act 1967; use of seized or detained GV by police or customs officers for purposes for which seized or detained. Exemptions also apply in islands other than the Isle of Wight, Lewis, Mainland (Orkney), Mainland (Shetland) and Skye.

controls as requested, contravention being an offence (reg. 8). A GV examiner has authority to drive any GV for the purpose of testing (reg. 7). An excise licence for a GV subject to tests cannot be taken out without production of the current goods vehicle test certificate or a declaration of exemption. In respect of a trailer a Ministry test date disc is issued as well as a goods vehicle test certificate.

I) THE GOODS VEHICLE TEST CERTIFICATE—contains a statement that the prescribed C and U requirements are complied with, the period of its validity, and the registration number of the vehicle (or if none the chassis or serial number; or if none, the examination serial number) (reg. 24). The certificate is valid until the last day of the period for its next periodic (i.e. annual) examination, which is stated in the current certificate.

NOTES
Appeal against a refusal lies to the area mechanical engineer and from him to the Minister. There are five kinds of tests, i.e.:

a) the first examination;

b) re-test after failure in (a);

c) the (annual) periodical test;

d) the re-test after failure in (c), and

e) the re-examination on appeal.

II) THE MINISTRY TEST DATE DISC—(for a trailer) is a plate which contains the following particulars—the identification mark allotted to the trailer; the date of expiry of validity; the number of the vehicle testing station shown in the goods vehicle test certificate. The trailer must carry the current disc in a legible condition, in a readily accessible position so that it is clearly visible by daylight from the nearside of the road (C and U Regulations, reg. 140). A disc is issued with each goods vehicle test certificate for a trailer, and is current for the same period as the goods vehicle test certificate to which it relates.

III) CERTIFICATE OF TEMPORARY EXEMPTION—Where a test cannot be carried out because of exceptional circumstances (e.g. severe weather, fire, failure of essential service, but not a breakdown of or a mechanical defect in the vehicle) a certificate of temporary exemption can be issued giving particulars identifying the vehicle (registration mark, chassis or serial number or test reference number), the date of issue and period of exemption (not to exceed three months).

IV) OFFENCES—It is an offence

a) to use (or cause or permit) on a road a GV (of the classes concerned) without a goods vehicle test certificate in force for it* (s. 46);

b) to fail to produce goods vehicle test certificate (or identity disc);

---

* The exemptions set out in the note at the foot of page 217 apply to this offence also.

c) in supplying information or producing documents for purposes connected with plating and testing, to knowingly or recklessly make a statement false in a material particular, or produce, send or otherwise use a document false in a material particular (s. 170).

NOTE
As to evidence from official records, see p. 289.

(4) Appeals

Appeals from unsuccessful tests may be made to the area mechanical engineer of the Ministry, against whose decision appeal lies to the Minister.

(5) Exemptions

The regulations do not apply to: PSV; LT; hackney carriages; DPV; WT; W Tlr; L Loco; LI; Ag Tlr drawn by LT; three-wheeled san v or a san v on an aerodrome; RR; road making vehicle or asphalt trailer; mobile crane; breakdown vehicle; engineering plant; tracklaying vehicle; steam or electric vehicle; tower wagon; straddle carrier; vehicles used solely for snow and ice clearance, firefighting or fire salvage, haulage of lifeboats, or funerals; vehicles fitted for testing new equipment of vehicle manufacturers; servicing or control vehicles at aerodrome; MV (under ICP) or trailer temporarily in GB (for first year); police vehicles maintained in approved workshops; vehicles exempt from excise licences and trailers drawn by them; vehicles for export or of visiting forces or licensed in N Ireland; *a living van; trailer with parking brake and over-run brakes only; vehicle used solely for carrying equipment for medical, dental, veterinary, health, education or clerical purposes;* the MV part of an AV drawing superimposed trailers and italicised above, or a trailer authorised to carry an AIL.

Greaves & Son v Peam (1971)
Where a W Tlr was taken to another part of works two miles away it was held not to be in immediate vicinity and thus not exempt as a W Tlr.

(6) Operators of goods vehicles: inspections and records (s. 59)

The S of S can make regulations requiring operators of goods vehicles to secure inspections of their vehicles by qualified persons to ascertain whether the C and U Regulations are complied with, and to keep (for n/e 15 months) records of such inspections and action taken to remedy defects found.

Contraventions of such regulations are summary offences, which can be put forward as grounds of objection to grant of an operator's licence, or for revocation or suspension of such a licence.

4. Inspection of fitness of goods vehicles

RTA 1972

a) Examiners (s. 56)—The S of S is empowered to appoint examiners to secure that GVs are maintained in fit and serviceable condition.

b) Powers to inspect

a) An examiner or certifying officer may at any time on production of authority if requested, enter and inspect any GV and for that purpose detain the GV for the time required for the inspection, and at any time that is reasonable enter any premises on which he reasonably believes a GV is kept. Obstruction is an offence.

b) An examiner or a *constable in uniform* may at any time require the person in charge of a GV stationary on a road to take the GV to a place (not more than a mile away) suitable for an inspection under s. 56. Refusal or neglecting to comply is an offence.

c) Powers re defective goods vehicles (1972 Act, s. 57)

a) After an authorised examination of a GV the examiner may prohibit the GV being driven on a road (either absolutely or for any specified purpose) if he finds it unfit, or likely to become unfit, for service, but must notify in writing the defects as well as the extent of the prohibition imposed. It is an *offence* to drive a GV on a road (or cause or permit this) in contravention of a prohibition under this section unless the GV is one expressly exempted by regulations made under the section*.

b) The notice must be given to the person in charge of the GV and include particulars of defects found, extent of restrictions on use of the GV, and state whether the prohibition applies immediately or at end of a specified period. It comes into force as soon as it is given if examiner regards defect as one creating immediate public risk; otherwise at a time not more than ten days later as examiner deems appropriate.

c) Contents of the notice must be also notified to the owner of the GV (if he was not in charge) and to the licensing authority if the GV is authorised under an operator's licence.

d) The examiner can in writing exempt from the prohibition certain uses of the GV subject to conditions, or by endorsement vary its terms or suspend it.

---

* By regulations the following do not contravene the prohibition:

a) submitting the MV for pre-arranged examination at testing station or other agreed place;

b) during course of inspection;

c) test or trial within three miles of place of repair with a view to removal of prohibition.

e) Unless removed as above the prohibition remains in force until removed by s. 58 (see below).

The prohibition may be made irremovable until vehicle has been inspected at an official testing station.

d) Removal of prohibition (s. 58)—A prohibition can be removed by *any* examiner or certifying officer if he is satisfied the vehicle is fit for service. On refusal to remove, application may be made to any licensing authority for re-examination by a certifying officer who can remove the prohibition. If there is again a refusal to remove, appeal lies to the Minister. Where an examiner or certifying officer withdraws a prohibition he must forthwith notify the owner and, if appropriate, the licensing authority accordingly.

e) Powers re over-weight vehicles (s. 57)

a) Where a GV is being weighed under s. 160 (see p. 315) and it appears to the GV examiner, or an appointed Ministry officer, *or to a constable authorised under the section by the COP* that the C and U Regulations weight limit is exceeded (or would be exceeded if used on a public road), he may by notice in writing to the person in charge prohibit the driving of the GV on a road until the weight has been reduced to the legal limit, and official notification has been given to the person in charge of the vehicle that he can proceed. He may also by a direction in writing require the person in charge to remove it (and any trailer) to such place and under such conditions as are specified in the direction.

b) Contents of notice to be sent to owner (if not in charge) and licensing authority if GV has an operator's licence. It is an *offence* to drive in contravention of prohibition. On any question that the weight has been reduced to the C and U limit, the burden of proof lies on the accused.

NOTE

As to driving licences for heavy goods vehicles, see p. 166.

5. Motor Vehicles (Rear Markings) Regulations 1970 (as amended 1972)

Every vehicle (except a passenger vehicle and the other vehicles listed as exceptions below) must carry at the rear of the vehicle (or at the rear of a load projecting to the rear if the load would otherwise obstruct the marking carried at the rear of the vehicle) a rear marking in accordance with the regulations, if

a) in the case of a MV it exceeds 3 tons u/w, or

b) in the case of a trailer it exceeds 1 ton u/w.

Motor Vehicles (Rear Markings) Regulations 1970 (as amended 1972) 221

The mark must conform with the regulations as to size, colour, and position, and be kept in a clean and efficient condition. 'Combination of vehicles' means the MV plus the trailer(s) drawn by it.

Type of markings—See appendix 3—slight variations (within limits set by the Schedule) are permitted.

VEHICLE	TYPE OF MARKING
a) MV of o/l n/e 13 metres, or trailer in a combination of vehicles of an o/l n/e 11 metres	1 or 2*
b) trailer in a combination of vehicles of an o/l exceeding 11 metres but n/e 13 metres	1, 2*, 4 or 5
c) if the o/l of the MV or the combination of vehicles exceeds 13 metres	4 or 5

Colours of markings

a) Letters—black.

b) Bars and the edging of 'long vehicle' plate—fluorescent material.

c) Background—Yellow reflex reflecting material.

Position—At the rear facing square to the rear, no part projecting beyond outermost part of vehicle, to be horizontal and within 400 to 1700 mm from the ground. In the case of a double mark (2, 3 or 5) both are to be at the same height from the ground, and each part to be as near as practicable to the outermost edge of the side on which fitted. A single plate (1 or 4) must have its centre coincident with the centre of the rear of the vehicle. Every part of each mark must be clearly visible from a reasonable distance to the rear at all times, except while loading or unloading if to make it visible during these operations would be impracticable on ground of undue expense or risk of damage to the marking.

Exceptions—The regulations do not apply to: passenger vehicles; living van of u/w n/e 2 tons; LT; L Loco; LI; LIC; Ag Imp; Ind T; WT; W Tlr; a pre 1st January 1940 vehicle; the MV part of an AV; BDV; EP; PSV trailer; vehicles designed for firefighting or fire salvage or for servicing aircraft, or designed and being used for transporting other vehicles; VPE; vehicle of home or visiting forces; vehicle brought temporarily into this country by an overseas visitor; a tar boiler; or an asphalt mixer.

As to foreign goods vehicles, see chapter 23.

---

* Where a 1 or 2 mark is applicable but is impracticable because of undue expense of fitment or risk of damage to these marks, rear marking 3 may be fitted instead.

6. International carriage of dangerous goods

The International Carriage of Dangerous Goods (Rear Marking of Motor Vehicles) Regulations 1975 permit but do not require the fitting of a plate at the rear of a vehicle engaged in carrying any dangerous goods on an international journey. If such a plate is carried it must comply with the requirements of the regulations, as follows:

Normally

a) *Size, etc.*—a rectangular plate constructed of orange reflecting material (except for a black border), 40 cm long by 30 cm high, border not more than 15 mm wide.

b) *Position*—at rear, perpendicular, clearly visible from a reasonable distance, securely attached, no part of it to project beyond outermost part of vehicle on either side.

In the case of a tanker carrying one kind of dangerous goods

a) *Size, etc.*—as in (a) above, but the plate to be divided by a black horizontal line across its middle, each rectangle thus formed bearing an identification number in black figures, i.e. in the upper section the code number (fixed by European agreement) of the kind of danger, and in the lower part that of the substance carried. If the letter X is displayed in the upper rectangle, this indicates that water must not be applied to the substance.

b) *Position*—as in (b) above.

Chapter 16 **Hours of driving and records**

1. Introduction

The aim of the EEC on the subject of driving of commercial vehicles and the keeping of records is to achieve by degrees EEC rules which will apply universally throughout the EEC countries. Since 1965 the relevant law in this country has been the subject of continual change for the purpose of bringing about this uniformity. The latest step in this direction is marked by two sets of regulations, namely the Drivers' Hours (Harmonisation with Community Rules) Regulations 1978 and the Community Road Transport Rules (Exemptions) Regulations 1978, with the result that all journeys by commercial vehicles, except journeys called 'domestic journeys', are covered by EEC rules. It is essential first to master the definitions of the vehicles which are affected by the EEC rules and by the British domestic rules, as follows:

BRITISH DOMESTIC RULES

a) *Passenger vehicles*—vehicles constructed or adapted to carry more than twelve passengers.

b) *Goods vehicles*—A Loco, MT, or any MV constructed for trailer articulation, or constructed or adapted to carry goods other than the effects of passengers, of not more than 3½ tonnes plated weight.

EEC RULES

a) *Passenger vehicles*—for more than nine passengers.

b) *Goods vehicles*—exceeding 3½ tonnes plated weight.

It is also important to bear in mind the following items.

a) The only driving completely exempt from all rules is that by:
   i) drivers of vehicles used by the police, fire services and the armed services (but not other Crown vehicles);
   ii) drivers whose driving is confined to places other than public roads;
   iii) a driver who is not driving in the course of his employment or for the purpose of a trade or business carried on by him.

b) Employers of drivers are responsible for ensuring that the law relating to hours of driving and keeping of records is complied with.

c) In connection with an offence relating to driving hours it is a defence to prove either:
i) that contravention was due to unavoidable delay in completing a journey arising from circumstances not reasonably foreseeable, or
ii) on a charge against a person not the driver, that it was due to the driver having been engaged in driving or on duty in someone else's employment (or under the orders of someone else), a fact of which he was not and could not reasonably have become aware.

d) The use of recording equipment (tachograph) fitted to the vehicle is required on journeys in EEC countries other than GB.

The rules relating to driving hours are dealt with in the following pages under headings related to the rules governing the type of journey being made, namely:

JOURNEY	SUBJECT TO
a) *National journey*, i.e. one within UK and not a domestic journey	EEC national rules
b) *Domestic journey*, i.e. one within UK and to which EEC rules do not apply	Transport Act 1968 and regulations under that Act
c) *International journey*, i.e. one made to or from an EEC country: it includes the part of the journey within this country	EEC international rules
d) *Mixed journey,* i.e. one affected by rules relating to more than one of the above	EEC mixed journey rules

2. Meaning of terms and abbreviations

(1) Terms used

DRIVER (DOMESTIC RULES)—One who drives in the course of his employment as such or drives for the purpose of a trade or business carried on by him (owner-driver).

DRIVER (EEC RULES)—Includes any person who drives, no matter for how short a time, and anyone who is carried on the vehicle to drive if necessary, though he may not have actually driven.

BREAK—The interval off duty which must be given for rest and refreshment after the maximum legal period on duty or continuous driving.

CONTINUOUS DRIVING—Unbroken period of actual driving time.

CONTINUOUS DUTY—Unbroken period of duty time, i.e. driving time and time spent on other work.

DAILY DRIVING—Time spent at the wheel actually driving between rest periods.

DAILY DUTY—Time spent in a day in driving plus other duties.

DAILY REST—The period of rest a driver must have had at any time he is at work during the 24 hours preceding that time.

DAILY SPREADOVER—The period during which the duty time can be spread.

FORTNIGHT—any period of fourteen consecutive days.

WEEK—any period of seven consecutive days.

(2) Abbreviations introduced

DRB—driver's record book;
B/Emp—the employer who issued the DRB;
E/dr—employee driver;
O/dr—owner-driver;
WD—working day;
WW—working week;
SGV—small goods vehicle;
OC—operating centre;
pw—plated weight.

3. Journeys made within the UK under EEC national rules.

(1) Application

The EEC national rules, with the exceptions given below, apply to drivers (EEC definition) of goods vehicles above $3\frac{1}{2}$ tonnes pw and of passenger vehicles which are *not* PSVs operating on a regular bus service where the route covered does not exceed 50 km (31 miles), i.e. a local and not a national bus service.

(2) Exemptions

In addition to the local bus service vehicles referred to above the following exemptions apply:

1) VEHICLES USED BY THE FOLLOWING AUTHORITIES OR SERVICES—civil defence; drainage or flood authorities; refuse collection by local authorities; water, gas and electricity services; highway authorities; refuse collection by local

authorities; telegraph or telephone services; carriage of mail by the PO; broadcasting services; vehicles used exclusively by other public authorities for public services; specialised medical services (e.g. ambulances, rescue vehicles).

II) *Certain types of vehicles*—i.e. tractors with legal speed limit of n/e 30 kph; local agriculture or forestry machines and tractors; vehicles used by circuses and fairs, specially constructed or adapted breakdown vehicles.

III) *Transport of certain things*—i.e. of live animals to and from local markets; of animal carcases; of organic waste not intended for human consumption; of milk between farm and dairy or distribution centre or vice versa.

IV) *Specialised vehicles*—used at local markets; or for worship; or for library purposes (books, records, cassettes); or for door-to-door selling involving multiple stops with the driver spending significant time in selling; or for cultural events or for mobile services connected with exhibitions; or for banking, exchange or savings transactions.

V) *Vehicles undergoing road tests*—for purposes of repair or maintenance.

(3) Hours limits

The limits given below are those applicable from 1st January 1981 with (when different) limits applying until that date shown in brackets.

Daily driving—8 (9)	Daily rest—11*
Weekly driving—48 (54)	Daily duty—11
Fortnightly driving—92 (106)	Daily spreadover—12½
Continuous driving—4 (4½)	Weekly duty—60
Weekly rest—29	Break—½
Continuous duty—5½	

NOTE
It would be an advantage to master the above limits so as to have a ready basis of comparison with limits for other journeys.

(4) Main points concerning hours limits

I) DAILY DRIVING—Can be 9 hours on 2 days in a week (except in the case of a non-rigid GV over 20 tonnes pw) but weekly limit must not be exceeded. If part of the driving is done off the road (e.g. on farm or quarry work) this need not count as driving but it counts as duty time.

II) CONTINUOUS DRIVING—If limit is reached a break must be taken. The limit does not apply to drivers who keep within 50 km (31 miles) of base.

III) WEEKLY REST—Has to be taken immediately before or immediately after a daily rest period in one uninterrupted stretch. The minimum is 24 hours. The additional 5 hours can, if preferred, be taken with daily rest periods elsewhere in the same week.

---

* For PSVs see para. **(4)** (IV) below.

IV) DAILY REST—

Goods vehicles—the 11 hours can be reduced twice a week to 9 hours (if rest is taken at base) or 8 hours (if away from base) provided the driver is compensated for lost time. Reduction may be made to 10 hours for up to 30 days for transport of harvest produce within a 50 km (31 miles) radius of base provided the reduction is added to the weekly rest period each week. Rest can be taken in a sleeper cab if the vehicle is stationary, but not on the vehicle otherwise. For two drivers with a sleeper cab the period can be 8 hours (for both) taken in every 30 (22 hours spreadover). If no sleeper cab it can be (for both) 10 hours in every 27 (17 hours spreadover).

PSVs—For crew members of PSVs on national journeys the daily rest period must be either:

a) 10 hours, or

b) 11 hours, which may be reduced twice a week to 10 hours and three times a week to 9 hours, provided the transport operation includes a scheduled break of not less than 4 hours (or two breaks of not less than 2 hours) and during these breaks the crew members to not do other work in a professional capacity.

V) DAILY DUTY—A driver who does not drive for more than 4 hours a day on each day of the week is exempt from duty and spreadover limits. He is also exempt from the limits on days on which he does not drive, but in respect of these days the first 11 hours of duty count towards the weekly duty limit.

VI) BREAKS—The half-hour break (except as stated below) can be replaced by two 20 minute, or three 15 minute, breaks spread over and immediately following the maximum duty, or continuous driving, period. A driver of a non-rigid vehicle over 20 tonnes pw cannot subdivide his break and if he reaches the limit on continuous driving (and only in this case) he must increase his break to one hour either immediately or by ensuring that the other half is taken sometime between starting and finishing driving for the day.

(5) Other relevant matters

I) DISTANCE LIMIT—A driver cannot drive non-rigid vehicles over 20 tonnes pw for more than 450 km (280 miles) in a day. He must then finish or be relieved by another driver. He can, however, drive other types of vehicles either before or afterwards to complete a day's work. The distance limit does not apply if the driver is accompanied by another driver from the start of the journey or if a driver on his own is using a calibrated EEC tachograph.

II) EMERGENCIES

a) A driver may in case of danger or circumstances outside his control, to render assistance, or as a result of a breakdown, and to the extent necessary to ensure safety of persons, of the vehicle or its load, and to enable him to reach a suitable stopping place or, according to circumstances, the end of his journey, break the distance limit, the daily and weekly driving limits, and the daily rest requirement, but reasons must be given in the DRB.

b) A driver is also exempt from the limits on daily duty, spreadover, continuous duty, breaks from duty, and weekly duty in specific cases of emergency, but the extent of these exemptions is limited in practice by the continued operation on continuous driving, breaks after continuous driving, and daily rest.

III) RECORDS

a) Operators of regular GV services (i.e. those operated at specified intervals along specified routes, goods being unloaded and loaded at predetermined stopping points) must draw up a service timetable and a duty roster. Each driver assigned to a regular service must carry an extract from the duty roster and a copy of the service timetable (see also p. 235).

b) With the exception of local traffic described below, all drivers not covered by (a) above must carry an EEC individual control book to record their work. The control book is not required by drivers who keep within 50 miles of base and do no more than 4 hours driving a day on public roads, but they must keep a specified simplified record instead (see p. 234).

4. Domestic journeys governed by British domestic rules

(1) Introduction

The Transport Act 1968, s. 96, and regulations made under the Act apply to vehicles not covered by the EEC national rules, i.e. journeys within the UK made by:

a) goods vehicles not exceeding $3\frac{1}{2}$ tonnes plated weight;

b) vehicles exempted from the EEC rules and listed on p. 225;

c) PSVs on a local regular bus service as defined on p. 225.

(2) Exemptions

The following vehicles are exempt from the British domestic rules except that in no case can a driver drive for more than 10 hours a day: goods vehicles and DPVs (e.g. Land-Rovers) used:

a) by doctors, dentists, nurses, midwives and veterinary surgeons;

b) for any service of inspection, cleaning, maintenance, repair, installation or fitting;

c) by the AA, RAC, or RSAC;

d) for cinematograph or radio or television broadcasting purposes.

(3) Hours limits

Transport Act 1968

The limits are the same as for journeys under EEC national rules with the following exceptions:

a) the daily limit is 10 hours and not 8;

b) the limits on hours relating to weekly and fortnightly driving, and to continuous driving, do not apply;

c) the weekly rest period is 24 hours instead of 29.

As to modifications applicable to drivers who for more than half their time drive passenger vehicles, see para. **(5) (a)** below.

(4) Main points concerning hours limits

I) DEFINITION OF 'WEEK'—*A week* is not the seven consecutive days of the EEC rules, but the fixed period between Saturday midnight and the following Saturday midnight. The fixed period can be changed, if necessary, on application to the local traffic area office.

II) DRIVING OFF ROAD—*Driving done off the road* for agriculture, quarrying, forestry, building work, or civil engineering is deemed duty time, but does not count towards the 10 hour driving limit, or towards the 4 hour driving limit referred to in (III) below. In the case of transport of milk between farm and dairy or distribution centre, and vice versa, there is, however, a maximum limit of 108 hours driving in a fortnight and an additional limit of 5 hours continuous driving at any one time.

III) DAILY DUTY AND SPREADOVER—A driver who does not drive for more than 4 hours on each day of the week is exempt from these limits for that week, and so is a driver exempt when he is at work but does not drive.

IV) BREAKS—A driver on days when he does not drive, or who does not drive for more than 4 hours each day of the week is exempt from taking breaks on those days or for that week respectively.

(5) Other relevant matters

(a) Drivers' Hours (Passenger and GV) (Modifications) Order 1971—The following modifications apply to a driver who spends all or the greater part of his time in driving a passenger vehicle or vehicles.

I) INTERVAL OF REST—The basic $\frac{1}{2}$ hour break does not apply to such a driver who has within a continuous period of $8\frac{1}{2}$ hours driven an aggregate of not more than $7\frac{3}{4}$ hours and had a period (or aggregate of periods) amounting to not less than 45 minutes when he has not been driving, provided the end of the last period of driving marks the end of his WD or he is then provided with the s. 96 interval.

II) WORKING DAY—The maximum of 14 hours becomes 16 hours if during the day all or the greater part of the time he has been driving vehicles subject to s. 96 has been spent driving one or more passenger vehicles.

III) DAILY REST—In respect of such a driver the interval is not to be less than 10 hours, except that on not more than three occasions in any WW the interval may be of less than 10 hours but not less than $8\frac{1}{2}$ hours.

IV) WEEKLY REST—Such a driver must have in every successive WW at least 24 hours off duty and this period must fall either wholly or in part within the two WWs concerned, or begin in the second WW and end on the first day of the succeeding 2-week period.

(b) Modifications in respect of emergencies—An emergency may be defined as an event requiring immediate action to avoid danger to life or health, serious interruption of essential public services or of telecommunications and postal services, or in the use of roads or airports, or damage to property. The modifications which apply are as follows:

I) TO GOODS VEHICLES—(see also appendix 6):

a) Daily driving, daily spreadover, continuous duty—no limits.

b) Daily duty—11 hours plus all emergency work.

c) Weekly duty—66 hours plus all emergency work.

d) Rest period—if the rest period of 10 hours is interrupted by the emergency, emergency work can be done provided that an aggregate of 10 hours rest is taken before normal duties start again.

e) Weekly rest—remains at 24 hours but can be postponed. If postponed the rest day must be taken within 28 days of the start of the week in which it was due in addition to the normal rest days due in that period.

II) TO PASSENGER VEHICLES—The definition of emergency is as stated above except that danger to animals is excluded and interruption of private or public transport is included.

Drivers' Hours (PV) (Exemptions) Regulations 1970: emergencies—The time spent by a driver in dealing with an emergency does not count as driving time and is to be regarded as time spent off duty. With regard to the weekly rest day for the week in which he spends time on emergency work the requirement for such a rest day is satisfied if he is off duty for a period of 24 hours less a period equal to the total time he spends on emergency work during that week.

Special needs—The driver of a PV who on any WD works:

a) in the carriage of physically or mentally disabled persons to or from a place where social or recreational facilities for them are specially provided, or

b) solely in the collection and delivery of blood for transfusion,

is exempt on that day from the limitation on hours of driving, provided:

a) he can obtain rest and refreshment for a period (or total of periods) not less than the time by which the WD exceeds *10 hours*, and

b) the WD does not exceed *14 hours*, and

c) this exemption has not applied to him on more than one previous WD in that WW.

c) Modifications on occasions of 'special needs'

I) GOODS VEHICLES—See appendix 6.

II) PASSENGER VEHICLES—See above as to the provisions of the Drivers' Hours (PV) (Exemptions) Regulations 1970.

d) Records—Subject to the exemptions given below all drivers must carry an individual control book to record their work.

EXEMPTIONS—Records of driving are not required to be kept by drivers of GV:

a) in respect of which an OL is not required;

b) on any day when they drive for 4 hours or less and keep within 25 miles of base.

5. International journeys

(1) Application

The exemptions given below excepted, EEC rules apply to all drivers (as defined by EEC rules) of passenger vehicles (for more than nine passengers) and all goods vehicles above 3½ tonnes pw if the driver or the vehicle or its trailer is going or has been outside the UK.

(2) Exemptions

As in paras. **3 (2)** (I) and (II) on p. 225.

(3) Hours limits

I) NON-APPLICABLE—Limits on continuous duty, daily duty, daily spreadover and weekly duty.

II) APPLICABLE

	Hours		*Hours*
Daily driving	8	Continuous driving	4
Weekly driving	48	Daily rest	11
Fortnightly driving	92	Weekly rest	29
		Breaks	½

(4) Main points about hours limits

I) DAILY DRIVING—9 hours is permitted twice a week, but not for driving non-rigid vehicles over 20 tonnes pw.

II) DAILY REST—As for national rules except for harvest reference—see para. **3(4)** (IV) on p. 227.

III) WEEKLY REST—As for national rules—see para. **3(4)** (III) on p. 226, with the addition that 5 of the 29 hours can be taken away and taken instead with daily rest periods in the same week.

IV) BREAKS—As for national rules—see para. **3(4)** (VI) on p. 227.

(5) Other relevant matters

I) DISTANCE LIMIT—As for national rules—see para. **3(5)** (I) on p. 227.

II) EMERGENCIES—As for national rules—see para. **3(5)** (II) on p. 227.

III) INDIVIDUAL CONTROL BOOK—As for national rules—see para **3(5)** (III) on p. 228.

6. Mixed journeys

EEC rules apply

(1) Introduction

A driver who is working under one kind of rules (EEC national or international, or British domestic) and then in the same day or week works under one of the other rules has to comply with the EEC mixed driving rules, which are summarised below.

(2) Drivers mixing only EEC international and national rules

The rule here is that for a period of 7 days immediately after completing international work the driver must keep to the international rules in connection with his national driving, though he can take advantage of the less restrictive EEC national rules on daily and weekly driving and weekly rest. The national rules as to duty, breaks after continuous duty and spreadover do not apply during this period.

(3) Drivers mixing EEC national and British domestic rules only

An example is the driving of vehicles subject to EEC national rules and also vehicles subject to domestic rules. The following limits apply for any day or week of this mixture of work and apply to all the mixed work added together. The driver will always be within the law if he keeps to the national rules all the time, but he can choose to use the higher domestic rules limits on driving time so long as he does not exceed the EEC driving limits when actually driving vehicles to which the EEC national rules apply.

HOURS LIMITS*

Daily driving	10	Daily rest	11
Weekly driving	60	Daily duty	11
Fortnightly driving	120	Daily spreadover	$12\frac{1}{2}$
Continuous driving	4	Weekly duty	60
Continuous duty	$5\frac{1}{2}$	Weekly rest	29†
Breaks	$\frac{1}{2}$		

(4) Driving mixing only EEC international with British domestic rules

The rule is that for a period of 7 days immediately after completing international work the driver must comply with the hours limits set out below, which apply to all the mixed work added together. The driver can continue to keep to the international rules if he wishes, or use the limits given below and take advantage of the higher domestic rules limits on driving time so long as he does not exceed international rules limits while actually driving vehicles to which the international rules apply.

HOURS LIMITS

Daily driving	10	Breaks	$\frac{1}{2}$
Continuous driving	4	Weekly driving‡	
Daily rest	11	Fortnightly driving‡	
Weekly rest	24		

The omitted headings do not apply.

(5) Drivers mixing EEC international with British domestic and EEC national rules

In these cases the rules set out in para. (4) above will apply during any period of 7 days at the beginning of which the driver has done international work.

---

* Note that with the exception of daily, weekly and fortnightly driving (which take account of the use of domestic limits when driving all vehicles) the limits are the same as for EEC national rules.

† The minimum is 24 hours. The additional 5 hours can, if preferred, be taken with daily rest periods elsewhere in the same week.

‡ There are no specific limits, but the amount of time that can be spent with vehicles subject to international rules in any day, week or fortnight is restricted to the limits imposed by international rules, see p. 231.

The only difference is that whenever during these 7 days the driver is driving a vehicle subject to national rules he can take advantage of the less restrictive EEC national rules.

7. Notes on EEC regulations concerning drivers' records

(1) Part-time drivers

The driver of a vehicle subject to the EEC Regulations, but who on no day drives for more than 4 hours or outside a radius of 50 km from the vehicle's operating centre, need only complete parts of his daily record sheet. However, he must record an estimate of his total driving time and the time of commencing and finishing duty. The part-time driver does not have to complete a weekly report.

As an alternative, a part-time EEC driver may keep a *simplified record book*, the form of which is set out in Sch. 3 to the 1976 Regulations (see p. 235). This simplified record book must contain a front sheet, instructions for use, weekly sheets, and duplicates, and a sheet of carbon or other means of copying.

(2) Crew members

A crew member of a vehicle within the scope of the EEC Regulations, on any day when such a vehicle is used, regardless of the length of the driving period, has to keep a record (an *individual control book*) as prescribed by regulations. There are special provisions however for some crew members: see under 'Part-time drivers', above.

A 'crew member' includes both drivers and mates. A driver's mate is anyone who accompanies the driver in order to assist him in manoeuvres and habitually takes an effective part in the transport operation, even though he does not drive.

NOTE

The Department of Transport classes persons as 'mates' only if they are on the vehicle because of a statutory requirement (e.g. attendants on abnormal indivisible loads). Mates whose primary function is only to assist with loading and unloading of, say, brewers' drays are not considered mates within the meaning of the EEC Regulations.

(3) Regular goods services

Special arrangements are made for crew members of goods vehicles within the scope of the EEC Regulations where these vehicles are used on a *'regular goods service'*.

A 'regular goods service' is one where a vehicle is used over a specified route according to a regular timetable and where goods are loaded and unloaded at predetermined stopping points.

Operators of such services must draw up a service timetable and a duty roster. The roster must indicate the name, date of birth and base of any crew member and details of duty and driving periods as would appear in a record book, for the current week and the weeks immediately preceding and following that week.

If these conditions are fulfilled and each crew member carries a copy of the service timetable and the relevant extract from the duty roster, the requirements for the keeping of records do not apply.

(4) Tachographs

EEC legislation requires tachographs to be used on goods vehicles but this has not yet been enforced in this country, although a programme has been drawn up for implementation of EEC policy. However, a driver using a vehicle fitted with an EEC approved tachograph is entitled to produce the tachograph sheet instead of drivers' records. The tachograph law applies to all crew members.

The crew member is required to enter on the sheet:

a) surname and first name;

b) date and place where record sheet begins and ends;

c) registration number of all vehicles used;

d) odometer reading;
   i) start of first journey;
   ii) end of last journey;
   iii) time of any change of vehicle.

The crew member must ensure the equipment is functioning properly and appropriate entries are made on the record sheet. Work carried out away from the vehicle must be recorded manually.

8. Drivers' Hours (Keeping of Records) Regulations 1976

NOTE
These regulations provide for the use of the EEC pattern of drivers' record book for both domestic and national journeys. The following is a summary of that part of the regulations which apply to 'domestic journeys' and to goods vehicles only. It is important to bear in mind that the requirement to keep records of driving, etc. does not apply to all drivers whose hours of driving are limited by law. So far as domestic journeys are concerned it does not apply

to vehicles exempted in circumstances described at the end of para. **(1)** below.

(1) Drivers' record books (DRB)*

MAIN REQUIREMENTS

a) The driver of a GV shall enter (and the employer shall cause an E/dr to enter) in a DRB, in accordance with the instructions for use† contained in the book, the information prescribed in the DRB as information required to be furnished by a crew member, and

b) the O/dr of a GV and the employer of an E/dr of a GV shall make, in accordance with the said instructions, such entries in the DRB as are required to be made therein by the undertaking, and the above applies to all the relevant instructions in the DRB relating to issue, use, preservation and return of the DRB (reg. 5).

NOTES

a) It is the duty of the employer to issue to an E/dr (and to keep him supplied with) a DRB. In the case of more than one employer the duty to issue a new DRB is that of the employer for whom the driver first acts.

b) When an E/dr ceases to be employed by his B/Emp he must return the DRB (and all duplicates and unused sheets) to the B/Emp. The issue of a new DRB is the responsibility of the first employer for whom he next acts as a GV driver.

c) If a driver drives GV and PV in any WW the entries in the DRB are to be in respect of both. If for different employers (one for GV and other for PV) it is the GV employer who is regarded as employer for the purposes of this regulation (regs. 5 and 6).

A driver shall have his current DRB (and all duplicates and unused record sheets) in his possession at all times when driving and on duty.

EXEMPTIONS—In the following circumstances the driver (and the employer, if any) is exempted from the regulations as regards entries in DRB and the driver from having possession of the DRB:

a) when during any day‡ the driver drives no GV other than one exempt from an OL, no records need to be kept concerning that day;

b) where during any day‡ the driving is for not more than 4 hours and not outside a radius of 25 miles from the OC of the vehicle; but in this case on

---

* EEC Regulation 543/69, as amended, prescribes the form of this book and it is set out in Sch. 1 to the 1976 Regulations where it is referred to as an 'Individual Control Book'. See appendix 7.

† See **(4)** below, and note that any failure to comply with these instructions comes within this reg., and is, therefore, an offence.

‡ Commencing at midnight.

the first day following during which this exemption ceases to apply, the driver must enter in his DRB the date and time his last WD ended, if this occurred during a period of exemption.

(2) Form of DRB

The book must conform to the model prescribed by the regulations (see appendix 7) and consist of:

a) a front sheet;

b) instructions concerning the use of the book;

c) daily sheets;

d) an example of a completed daily sheet, as a guide;

e) weekly reports.

The DRB is to be of standard format (105 × 148 mm) or larger, with its serial number shown by perforation or by stamping, a different serial number being given to each DRB. If the DRB contains more than fifteen daily sheets, each sheet must have its duplicate and one sheet of carbon paper (or other means) for making a simultaneous duplicate copy.

(3) Manner of keeping the DRB

I) ENTRIES

a) *The O/dr or employer* (before use) must enter or secure entry:
i) *on front sheet* the serial number of the OL covering the GV used, and of the DRB, as well as the number of daily sheets in the book, and
ii) *on each daily sheet*, the serial number of the OL.

b) *The driver* must, when making an entry in or signing a daily sheet in a book furnished with duplicates, ensure (by carbon paper or otherwise) that a simultaneous duplicate is produced.

II) DETACHING DAILY SHEETS FROM DRB FURNISHED WITH DUPLICATES—If the daily sheets have duplicates the duplicate of each sheet, on completion, must be detached by the driver and:

a) if an E/dr—within 7 days of completion deliver it to the B/Emp*, and

b) if an O/dr—within 7 days deliver it to the address shown on the front sheet of the DRB.

Defence—It is a defence to show that compliance was not reasonably practicable and that there was compliance as soon as reasonably practicable.

III) DRB WITHOUT DUPLICATE SHEETS—When completed by an E/dr it has to be returned by the driver to the employer, who has, within 7 days of the return, to

---

* It is the duty of the B/Emp to cause this to be done, and to examine and to sign the duplicate.

examine and sign each of the daily sheets used and which have not been previously examined and signed in the course of an inspection of the DRB.

A DRB is regarded as completed, in the case of a book with fifteen or less daily sheets and no duplicate sheets, when all daily sheets have been used or at end of 28 days from date the first sheet in the book was used, whichever is the earlier, and in the case of any other book, when all daily sheets have been used.

(4) The DRB instructions sheet

The instructions (which have to be included in the DRB and failure to comply with which may constitute an offence—see para. **(1)** above) are summarised below.

I) TO THE EMPLOYER

a) To complete the front sheet and to issue a DRB to each crew member.

b) To give instructions on correct use of the book.

c) To examine daily sheets and the weekly report every week, or if prevented from doing so, as soon as possible thereafter, and to sign the weekly report when this has been done.

d) To withdraw used books, allow inspection and to preserve them as required by law.

II) TO CREW MEMBERS

a) Book to be carried when on duty and produced to an authorised person on request. Book to be handed back to employer when his employment ceases.

b) Book to be produced to employer every week (or if impracticable, as soon as practicable afterwards) for him to check entries and to sign the weekly report.

c) After completion the book to be kept for 2 weeks for production if necessary, and then handed as soon as possible to the employer. Copy of weekly report to be kept.

d) *Front sheet*—to make sure information is correct, enter dates of first and last use of book.

e) *Daily sheet*—to fill in one for every day on duty as a crew member, and the registration number of any vehicle used during the day. Entries to be made at beginning and end of each period to which they relate. The daily sheet has to be signed.

f) *Symbols* for the daily sheet (see appendix 7) are as follows:
   i) bedstead—daily rest period;
   ii) bedstead with asterisk over it—total period of uninterrupted rest before going on duty;
   iii) chair—breaks;
   iv) steering wheel—driving periods;
   v) rectangle with diagonal inside—periods of attendance at work.

g) *Weekly report*—to be made out at end of every week in which one or more daily sheets have been made out.

h) *General*—no erasures, corrections or additions. Any mistake, even of form only, must be corrected under 'Remarks'. No sheet may be destroyed. All entries to be made in ink or with a ball point pen.

(5) Information to other employers

Where a driver has, as such, had in a period more than one employer:

a) each one, who is not B/Emp, must ask the driver to produce his current DRB and enter on the front sheet the information there required;

b) each one, when requested by the others, must supply information* in his possession relating to the current WW concerning any off-duty periods of not less than 24 hours required by s. 96, and the number of hours the driver has been on duty that week.

Where a driver changes employment his late employer shall, on request of the driver or his new employer, supply any information* possessed, as in (b) above.

(6) Production/return of DRB to employer

An E/dr must produce his current DRB on request for inspection by the B/Emp, or by any person by whom he is employed as a driver during the currency of the book, and shall return it to the B/Emp, at the end of any WW if so requested.

(7) Preservation of DRB

The DRB shall be preserved intact by an O/dr or by the employer of an E/dr (when returned to him) for a period of 6 months, reckoned, for O/dr, from date of completion or cessation of use, or, in case of B/Emp., the day of return to him. The same applies to the detached record sheets. If so required by a licensing authority or COP in a particular case the DRB (or sheet) shall be preserved for such further period(s) (not more than 6 months in aggregate) as the requirement specifies.

(8) Registers of DRBs

Registers are to be maintained, and appropriate entries made in them, by the:

a) O/dr—of all DRBs used by him;

---

* If requested the information must be given in writing.

b) employer—of all DRBs known by him to have been issued to or used by any E/dr of his*.

The register has to be preserved for 12 months from the last of the following dates to occur:

a) date on which he ceased to use a book, or on which the last book recorded in the register was returned, or

b) if any book recorded is not returned as required, the date when the reason for non-return is entered in the register.

All entries are to be made as soon as the required information is available and in ink, or with ball point pen. Provisions relating to erasures, etc. are the same as for DRBs.

Witchell v Abbot and another (1966)

Where a driver was given the option of staying to obtain rest at the place reached on the journey or returning to his home, the time spent on his return by car is not work in connection with the vehicle or its load.

Grays Haulage Co v Arnold (1966)

The employer is not to be found guilty of 'permitting' the offence merely by not taking steps which would have prevented the driver committing the offence.

Potter v Gorbould (1969)

Driver voluntarily spent rest period cutting up scrap metal for employer as overtime. Held that as he was working to the benefit of himself and employer he was working during his rest period.

Fox and another v Lawson (1973)

In calculating hours worked by a driver, regard is to be paid to hours worked (including driving) abroad.

9. Jurisdiction

By s. 103(7) of the Transport Act 1968, as amended by the Road Traffic (Drivers' Ages and Hours of Work) Act 1976, an offence in relation to drivers' hours can be dealt with by a court:

a) in the place where the first indication of the offence came to notice, or

b) in the place where the person proceeded against resides or is believed to reside when proceedings commence, or

c) in the place where the person has his employment.

---

* Where the employer operates GVs from more than one place he can maintain a separate register at each place but each must relate only to DRBs issued to his E/drs driving GV operated from that place.

Chapter 17 **Road accidents: duties of drivers**

Road Traffic Act 1972

1. To stop and give information

Section 25

When owing to the presence of a *motor vehicle* (including tramcars, trolley vehicles, and Crown vehicles) *on a road,* an accident occurs causing injury or damage to:

a) *any person* (other than the driver of that vehicle), or

b) *any vehicle** (other than that MV or a trailer drawn thereby), or

c) *any animal* (other than an animal in or on that MV or trailer drawn thereby)* or

d) *any other property* constructed on, fixed to, growing in or otherwise forming part of the land on which the road in question is situated or land adjacent thereto (RTA 1974, Sch. 6),

the driver commits an offence if he fails:

a) *to stop,* and

b) *to give,* on request of any person having reasonable grounds for so doing, *his name and address* and that of the *owner* of the vehicle, as well as its identification marks.

> **Ellis v Nott-Bower (1896)**
> A bicycle is a vehicle.

'Animal' means any horse, cattle, ass, mule, sheep, pig, goat or dog. The *'stop'* must be long enough to enable questions to be put to the driver if there is anyone in the vicinity who wishes to put them.

> **Jones v Prothero (1952)**
> The 'driver' who is in the MV while stationary is still the driver—driver

---

* Whether a MV or not.

convicted for not reporting accident to cyclist caused by the sudden opening of the car door.

Harding v Price (1948)
Held: 'mens rea' is an essential ingredient of the offence of failing to stop, so that there must be evidence that the driver was aware of the accident or the injury or had wilfully or negligently shut his eyes to it.

R v Miller (1954)
Injury has been held to include shock, and a hysterical and nervous condition can be actual bodily harm.

North v Gerrish (1959)
The section creates but one offence, but if there is a failure to comply with either of the requirements ((a) or (b)) the offence is committed.

Lee v Knapp (1966)
The driver committed an offence by going from the scene and leaving his employee to give the particulars.

2. To report the accident to the police

In the case of any accident as is defined above the driver must report it to a *constable* or at a *police station,* as soon as practicable, and in any case *within* 24 *hours if:*

a) in the case of any such accident he did not give his name and address at the time to a person having reasonable grounds for requiring it (s. 25); *or*

b) in an *accident causing personal injury* to another person he did not at the time produce the appropriate certificate or evidence required by the Act in relation to insurance (see p. 174) to a constable or person having reasonable grounds for requiring this (s. 166).

Dawson v Winter (1932)
If the driver refuses his name and address to a person reasonably requiring it at the time, he commits an offence although he reports to the police within 24 hours.

3. To produce insurance certificate

Section 166

In the case of an accident involving personal injury to another person where the driver of a MV involved (not an IC) did not at the time produce to a constable or some person having reasonable grounds for requiring it such certificate or evidence relating to insurance as is required by the Act, the driver commits an offence if he does not report the accident as soon as is practicable and in any case within 24 hours to a police constable or at a police station and, at the same time, produce the relevant insurance, etc. certificate but there can be no conviction for failure to produce if it is produced (by any person) within 5 days at a police station specified by him.

Peek v Towle (1945)
If the driver does not give his name and address, etc. because there was no one at the scene or no one asked for it or for any other reasons, he must report to the police within 24 hours.

Green v Dunn (1953)
Even though all particulars may have been supplied at the time, if there has been personal injury and the insurance certificate was not produced the driver must still report to the police.

Butler v Whittaker (1955)
Where, driving through a herd, all that driver heard was a 'slight knock' the prosecution should show not only that he knew there had been an accident, but also that he knew, or that the circumstances were such that it could be inferred that a reasonable man would know, that an injury had been caused to a cow.

Quelch v Phipps (1955)
The section is not limited to a collision, and applies e.g. where a person jumped off a moving bus, but there must be a direct cause or connection between the motor vehicle and the accident. An indirect connection is insufficient, e.g. a pedestrian injuring another by stepping back to avoid a car, etc.

Bulman v Bennett (1974)
The law does not say that a driver is entitled to wait up to 24 hours before reporting the accident. He must report it as soon as reasonably practicable.

Chapter 18 Motor Vehicles (Construction and Use) Regulations 1978

(as amended) (plus RTA 1972, s. 34 as to trailers and attendants)

1. Exemptions

(1) General exemption

The requirements of these regulations as regards *construction and weight* of any class of vehicle do not apply (except reg. 95 re weight restrictions and regulations concerning plating) for 5 years to any MV registered within 1 year after the date of the regulations provided that it complies with the Construction and Use Regulations 1973. As to the exemption of certain invalid carriages, see p. 302.

(2) Particular exemptions

I) ROAD ROLLERS (RR)—Regulations concerning wheel loads, weight, springs, mirrors, need for audible warning instrument, and tyres do not apply.

II) EXPORT VEHICLES—Vehicles proceeding to a port for export are exempted from requirements as to construction and equipment, except with regard to parking brakes, need for reverse gear, windscreen wipers, audible warning instrument. All the regulations regulating the use of vehicles on roads (80–144) apply except markings as to unladen weight and maintenance of speedometer.

III) FOREIGN VISITORS' VEHICLES—Vehicles temporarily brought in by a person resident abroad, provided they comply with requirements of the Geneva convention, or the 1926 International Convention, are exempt from all the regulations *relating to construction and equipment* except those dealing with overall length, overall width, and gas containers. All regulations regulating use of vehicles on roads apply.

IV) VEHICLES OF VISITING FORCES—These are not subject to the regulations relating to construction and equipment except as regards parking brakes, reverse gear, and emission of smoke and vapour, sparks or grit. Regulations concerning use of vehicles on roads, with the exception of u/w markings; trailer plates, and laden or unladen weights, do apply to them.

v) PRE-1906 MOTOR VEHICLES—(designed before 1st January 1905, constructed before 31st December 1905) certified as such by the Science Museum:

a) requirements as to speedometer, diameter of wheels, wings do not apply, nor does restriction on fitting and using gong, bell or siren;

b) brake requirements are in keeping with the original construction of the vehicles, and requirements briefly are:
   i) an efficient system;
   ii) on at least two wheels (one if three wheels or less); and
   iii) capable of bringing vehicle to rest within reasonable distance.

VI) TRAILERS—The following, i.e.:

a) a towing implement being drawn by a MV (and not attached to any other vehicle) otherwise than during hours of darkness and at speed n/e 20 mph, or

b) a vehicle being towed under statutory power or removal,

are exempt from all construction and equipment regulations concerning trailers, and also from the requirements to exhibit trailer plates and to have positioned on the drawing vehicle or trailer someone to apply brakes of the trailer.

VII) LAND TRACTORS—Land tractors which are HMCs or MCs and comply with certain conditions (e.g. hauling only a LI or LIC to or from a work site, or an Ag Tlr; carrying no load or certain specified loads; and speed n/e 20 mph) are exempt from regulations relating to springs, speedometer, warning instrument, and the requirements re width, overhang, brakes and tyres are the same as for a motor tractor.

VIII) VEHICLES BEING TESTED—The regulations do not apply to a vehicle being tested for a test certificate (see p. 277) so far as construction, equipment and maintenance of equipment is concerned, but the tester has to comply with the regulations which relate to duties of drivers of vehicles on a road (e.g. stopping engine, avoiding causing an obstruction, etc.).

IX) PEDESTRIAN CONTROLLED VEHICLES—PCVs are exempt from requirements re springs, overhang, tyres and wings.

X) BRITISH VEHICLES PURCHASED BY PERSONS TEMPORARILY IN GB—A vehicle made in GB purchased by a person temporarily in GB who is, or is about to be, resident abroad (if vehicle complies with Geneva and the 1926 International Convention) is exempt for a year from all construction and equipment regulations, except as regards gas containers. All the regulations relating to use apply. The vehicle must be subject to zero rating VAT.

XI) APPROVED TYPES AND EEC VEHICLES—Where a type approval certificate or a certificate of conformity has been issued in this country or in a member state of the EEC in relation to a MV or trailer because it conforms to a particular Community Directive (e.g. as to brakes) then relevant C & U Regulations do not apply to the vehicle, e.g. if the certificate relates to conformity with the relevant Community Directive then regulations relating to braking systems do not apply.

2. Offences

The Road Traffic Act 1972, s. 40(5) makes it a summary offence to contravene or fail to comply with any regulation or to use on a road a MV or trailer which does not comply with the regulations, or *to cause or permit* the vehicle to be so used.

As to 'using', or 'permitting' use—see chapter 2.

3. Attendants

(1) RTA 1972, s. 34

I) NOT DRAWING TRAILER—only requirement is for two persons to be employed in driving or attending a locomotive (heavy or light) on a *highway*.

II) DRAWING TRAILER(S)*—one attendant additional to the driver (or to the two persons required by (I) above) to be carried on vehicle or trailer at rate of one attendant for every trailer in excess of one.

III) 'CAUSE OR PERMIT'—This is an offence under the section.

(2) Exemptions

1978 Regulations, reg. 138

Section 34 does not apply to:

a) *AV or RR;*

b) *BDV* or a vehicle being statutorily removed (see p. 310), in each case being towed in such a way that it cannot be steered by its own steering gear;

c) *MT* drawing:
i) a closed trailer specially constructed to carry meat between docks and railway stations or between wholesale markets and docks or railways;
ii) a road repair, maintenance or cleansing machine;
iii) a San Tlr;

d) *L Loco* drawing a LI or LIC;

e) *LT* drawing a LI, LIC, or Ag Tlr;

---

* 'Trailer' does not include a water trailer or an agricultural vehicle not constructed to carry a load.

f) *MC or motor cycle* drawing two-wheeled trailer;

g) *MC* drawing four-wheeled trailer with two 'close-coupled' wheels on each side;

h) *WT* drawing W Tlr, neither vehicle exceeding 1525 kgs u/w;

i) *HMC or MC* drawing a gas trailer;

j) *any* MV drawing a trailer equipped with no other brakes than a parking brake and brakes which automatically come into operation on the overrun of the trailer;

k) *armed services'* vehicles if driver can apply brakes of trailer;

l) *towing implement* being drawn but attached only to drawing vehicle;

m) *locomotive,* if propelled by liquid fuel or electricity.

NOTE
If a trailer is equipped with power operated (or assisted) brakes which still operate when engine of drawing vehicle is not running—no attendant is needed if only one trailer, but one attendant is required for two or more trailers.

4. Audible warning instruments

Regulation 29

I) FITTING—*Every* MV (except WT or PCV) must be fitted with an instrument capable of giving audible warning of its approach or position, but not a gong, bell, siren (or similar sounding instrument) or a two-tone horn, for these can be fitted only on motor vehicles of the following services—police, fire, ambulance, Fire Salvage Corps, Forestry Commission or local authority fire dept., Blood Transfusion Service, HM Coastguard and its Auxiliary Service, NCB Mine Rescue, RAF Mountain Rescue Service, service bomb disposal units and RNLI vehicles for launching lifeboats.

NOTE
If the MV is one first used post 1st August 1973 the sound given must be continuous, uniform and not strident.

Exception: 'mobile shop'—A MV carrying goods for sale from the vehicle may have an *additional* instrument (which may be a gong, bell, siren or similar sounding instrument but *not* a two-tone horn) designed to indicate to the public that goods are on sale from the vehicle. (NB: *a two-tone horn* produces a sound alternating at regular intervals between two fixed notes. It is an offence to fit a musical or multi-tone horn to a vehicle first used on or after 1st August 1973.)

II) SOUNDING—Subject to the exceptions (and see p. 201 as to buses) it is an offence (reg. 118) to sound, cause or permit to be sounded, a warning instrument fitted to *or carried on any* vehicle:

a) *at any time* if:
  i) the vehicle is *stationary* on a road (other than at times of danger due to another moving vehicle on or near the road), or
  ii) the instrument is a gong, bell, siren (or similar sounding instrument), or a two-tone horn;

b) *between* 11.30 *pm and 7 am* on a MV in motion on a 'restricted road'.

Exceptions:

a) vehicles of the services referred to in (I) above being used for the functions of those services;

b) apparatus sounded to raise alarm of theft or attempted theft of or from the vehicle;

c) a 'mobile shop' (see (I) above) is exempt in respect of its additional instrument (not being a two-tone horn) but only if it is sounded for its exempted purpose and not between 11.30 pm and 7 am on a restricted road. This exemption does not extend to the provisions of the Control of Pollution Act 1974.

III) 'RESTRICTED ROAD'—This is one which has street lighting by lamps not more than 200 metres apart, or (where there is no such lighting system) which has been made subject to a 30 mph speed limit by a direction of the local authority.

5. Brakes

See appendix 1 and p. 274 (testing).

6. Closets, urinals, lavatory basins and sinks

No MV first used post 15th January 1931, or trailer, shall be equipped with any of the above unless the following are complied with:

a) a closet or urinal must be such that its contents cannot be discharged directly on to a road, but (except in a living-van) into tank on the vehicle, ventilated by a pipe to outside the vehicle;

b) such a tank (or closet or urinal if no tank) must contain chemicals (non-inflammable, non-irritant) suitable and sufficient to provide at all times an efficient deodorant and germicide;

c) no lavatory basin or sink shall drain into a closet or urinal or the tank into which either of the latter empties (reg. 39).

OFFENCE—It is an offence to cause or permit contents of closet, urinal, lavatory basin or sink carried on a MV or trailer, or of the tank to which they drain, to be discharged or to leak on to a road.

7. Cranes and lifting appliances

Regulation 134

Whatever is suspended from any lifting appliance (such as a crane) fitted to a vehicle to facilitate lifting (e.g. cable, chain, hook) must while the vehicle is in motion on a road, and the crane is not being used to support or lift, be secured to the crane or part of the vehicle so that no danger is caused, or likely to be caused, to any person on the vehicle or on the road.

8. Dangerous vehicles or loads

Regulation 97

a) A MV and every trailer drawn thereby, and all its parts and accessories, shall at all times be in such condition; and the number of passengers carried (and manner carried) in or on it; and the weight, distribution, packing and adjustment of its load shall at all times be such, that no danger is caused or likely to be caused to any person in or on the vehicle or trailer or on the road. (No offence is committed as to number of passengers carried by a PSV if the number allowed by law is not exceeded.)

Simmons v Fowler (1950)
An information charging failure to maintain vehicle in good condition must give particulars of the defective parts.

b) The load carried by a MV or trailer must at all times be so secured (if necessary by physical restraint other than own weight) and be in such a position that neither danger nor nuisance is likely to be caused to any person or property by reason of the load, or any part thereof, falling or being blown from the vehicle or by reason of any other movement of the load (or any part) in relation to the vehicle.

c) No MV or trailer shall be used for any purpose for which it is so unsuitable as to cause or be likely to cause danger or nuisance to any person in or on the vehicle or on a road.

9. Direction indicators

Covered by the RV (Lighting) Regulations 1971 (see. p. 116).

10. Doors

Regulation 125

No person shall open any door of a MV or trailer on a road (or cause or permit this) so as to cause injury or danger to any person.

11. Driver: position

Regulation 119

No person driving a MV on a road shall be in such a position that he cannot have proper control of it, or cannot retain full view of road and traffic ahead, and no person shall cause or permit another person to drive a MV on a road in such position.

12. Gas containers

If any MV (or its trailer) has fitted to it a container for storing gas as fuel for the MV, Sch. 3 has to be complied with (reg. 47). The Schedule provides rigid requirements as to the fitting and the construction of the container, pipe lines, unions, valves, gauges, etc., so as to afford the greatest protection from the risk of fire or explosion.

13. Glass

Regulations 25 and 26

(1) Definitions

a) *'Caravan'*—trailer constructed (not merely adapted) for human habitation.

b) *Safety glass*—when broken does not fly into fragments likely to cause severe cuts.

c) *Safety glazing*—material (not glass) such that when broken does not fly into fragments likely to cause severe cuts.

d) *Specified safety glass*—glass complying with relevant British Standard Specification No. and so marked.

e) *Windscreen*—includes windshield.

f) *Facing front*—at front and at an angle to a line drawn down the middle of the vehicle greater than 30°.

(2) MV first used prior to 1st January 1959

Windscreen and windows on outside facing front to be safety glass. *Exception:* upper deck of a double-decked vehicle.

(3) MV first used on or after 1st January 1959

(and not coming under heading (4) *below)*

Safety glass must be fitted as follows:

a) *passenger vehicle or DPV*—windscreen and all outside windows;
b) *goods vehicle, locomotive or MT*—screen and all windows in front and on either side of driver's seat.

(4) MV or trailer manufactured on or after 1st December 1977 and first used on or after 1st June 1978

(Caravan: first used on or after 1st September 1978)

a) Windscreen and all other windows wholly or partly in front of or on either side of any part of the driver's seat—specified safety glass, *with the following variations:*
   i) *motor cycles* without enclosed compartment for driver or passenger—windscreen of safety glazing;
   ii) *security vehicle*—can be safety glazing;
   iii) *temporary replacements* after breakage—safety glazing, and fitted only to complete journey or proceeding to get replacement;
   iv) *windows around driver*—can be safety glazing;
   v) *PSV*—interior door at side of driver's compartment can be safety glazing.
b) *Windows other than in (a)* above to be specified safety glass or safety glazing.

(5) All glass

Regulation 100

All glass and other transparent material fitted to a MV must be maintained in such condition that it does not obscure the vision of the driver while being driven on a road.

14. Lighting equipment

See p. 125.

15. Markings

The owner must cause the u/w to be painted or otherwise plainly marked on some conspicuous place on the nearside of *a locomotive, MT, or HMC* (reg. 80).

Exception—HMC not registered.

GOODS VEHICLES—Markings (in addition to any required by law, e.g. a Ministry plate) are permitted on the near side or offside, or on both sides, in respect of maximum weights under reg. 142 (plated weights) or regs. 85, 86, 89 or 90 (reg. 151). See also plating and testing, p. 214.

50 MPH SPEED LIMIT—Where a MV is drawing a trailer on a road in circumstances where the speed limit permitted is 50 mph the appropriate weights must be displayed as required by the 'relevant conditions' set out on p. 81 (reg. 96).

16. Mascots

Regulation 142

No mascot may be carried by a MV first used post 1st October 1937 in any position where it is likely to strike any person with whom it may collide unless not liable to cause injury by reason of any projection thereon.

17. Mirrors

Regulation 23

a) Passenger vehicles for more than seven passengers, and every goods vehicle (including DPV but not a locomotive or MT) must carry *at least two mirrors* (one external on the offside, and the other internally or on the nearside externally) so made and fitted as to assist the driver, if he so desires, to become aware of traffic to the rear and on both sides rearwards.

b) A LT must be fitted with such a mirror on the offside externally, *unless* the driver can easily obtain a clear view of traffic to the rear of the vehicle, and any trailer when drawn, without a mirror.

c) Every MV other than above must carry one mirror either internally or externally enabling the driver, if he so desires, to become aware of traffic to the rear.

d) In the case of a MV first used on or after 1st April 1969, the edges of an internally fitted mirror shall be surrounded by some material such as will render the edges and material unlikely to cause severe cuts if the mirror or material is struck by an occupant of the vehicle.

Exceptions—L Loco; WT; PCV; RR; motor cycle (two wheeled) with or without sidecar; MV drawing a trailer if a person on the trailer has a clear view to rear and has efficient means of communicating to the driver the nature of signals given by drivers of vehicles to the rear.

18. Motor cycles: passengers

Suitable supports or rests for the feet must be available for the use of any passenger (other than driver) who is being carried *astride* a motor cycle, whether it has a sidecar or not (reg. 129). See also p. 279 for RTA offences.

19. Noise: prevention of unnecessary

(1) Excessive noise offences

It is an offence:

a) to use, cause or permit to be used, on a road any MV or trailer which causes excessive noise, *unless*
i) noise was due to some temporary or accidental cause which could not have been prevented by due diligence and care on part of owner or driver, or

ii) in a charge against driver or person in charge (not the owner), noise arose from defect of design or construction, or through fault of some other person under a duty to ensure proper repair, adjustment, packing or loading and could not have been prevented by due diligence or care on part of driver or person in charge (reg. 114);

b) to use a MV on a road in *such a manner* as to cause excessive noise, which the driver could have avoided by reasonable care (reg. 115).

(2) Unnecessary noise while stationary

The driver of every MV when stationary (otherwise than through enforced stoppage for traffic reasons) must stop the engine or other machinery attached to or forming part of MV to prevent noise.

Exceptions —

a) when for the purpose of examination, the working of the engine or machinery is necessary to deal with a defect in it; or

b) when the working of the machinery on the MV is necessary for some ancillary purpose (e.g. winding winch gear); or

c) a MV propelled by gas produced by plant carried on it or on trailer being drawn by it (reg. 117).

(3) Control of noise by measurement

NOTE

The enforcement of these regulations (31 and 116) can be carried out only by using approved measuring devices for the use of which special training is required. It would seem, therefore, that no more is needed by police officers generally than an outline of the provisions concerned.

I) CONSTRUCTION—Every vehicle first used post 1st April 1970, with certain exceptions, must be so constructed that the noise emitted by it under 'specified conditions' does not exceed the maximum sound level prescribed by the regulations for the class of vehicle to which it belongs (reg. 31).

II) USE OFFENCES—To use (cause or permit) any vehicle on a road if at a time when the sound level of the noise emitted by it, as measured by prescribed apparatus under 'specified conditions', exceeds the maximum permitted for the vehicle (reg. 116). This regulation applies to trailers and to every MV first used post 1st January 1931, except road rollers and vehicles being taken by previous arrangement to or from a place for noise testing.

(4) Warning instruments and silencers

See p. 247 (warning instruments) and p. 260 (silencers).

20. Obstruction

Regulation 122

No person in charge of a MV or trailer shall cause or permit it to stand on a road so as to cause unnecessary obstruction thereof. See also p. 53.

21. Overall dimensions and overhang

As to overall dimensions (height, length, width), see appendix 4. As to overhang, see appendix 4 (for vehicles) and appendix 2 (for loads).

22. Petrol tanks

Every MV first used post 1st July 1973 and not manufactured pre 1st February 1973 shall be so constructed that:

a) any petrol tank attached to it shall be made of metal;

b) the tank is in a position to secure it against damage;

c) leakage is adequately prevented (reg. 19).

MAINTENANCE—A MV must at all times be maintained so to ensure compliance with (b) and (c), and this maintenance is required in respect of every MV irrespective of date of first use or manufacture (reg. 104).

23. Plates to be exhibited on vehicles

(1) Manufacturers' plates on goods vehicles

Regulation 42 and Sch. 2

Every goods vehicle to which this regulation applies has to have securely and conspicuously fixed to it in a readily accessible position an appropriate plate bearing the particulars referred to below. The regulation applies to:

a) *every HMC and MC first used post 1st January 1968—exceptions:* passenger vehicle; DPV; LT; WT; PCV;

b) *every trailer made on or after 1st January 1968* exceeding 1020 kgs u/w—*exceptions:* not constructed or adapted to carry a load, other than permanently fixed special plant or apparatus and n/e 2290 kgs total weight; living van n/e 2040 kgs u/w and having pneumatic tyres; trailer made and used outside GB before first used in GB; trailers exempted from regulation re trailer brakes (see p. 333); a W Tlr;

c) *every loco and MT first used post 1st April 1973—exceptions:* L Loco, LT, Ind T, WT, engineering plant, PCV, vehicle manufactured pre 1st October 1972.

d) trailer which is a converted dolly manufactured post 1st January 1979, not being a trailer in (b) above.

PARTICULARS REQUIRED ON PLATE

a) manufacturer's name;

b) chassis or serial number;

c) number of axles;

d) maximum axle weight for each axle (i.e. total for all wheels on the axle);

e) maximum gross weight (i.e. total for all wheels of vehicle);

f) year of manufacture, if a post 1st April 1970 trailer;

plus for motor vehicle

g) vehicle type;

h) engine type and power;

i) maximum train weight (i.e. weight transmitted to road by all wheels of MV and trailer) unless not constructed to draw trailer;

and for trailer

j) maximum load imposed on drawing vehicle.

NOTE

'Weight' means weight transmitted to road surface. Letters and figures to be not less than 6 mm high. If a GV has been plated under the Plating and Testing Regulations 1971, loading in excess of plated weights is an offence under C & U reg. 147. If the GV has not been so plated but has a manufacturer's plate the offence is under C & U reg. 95. When a reg. 42 GV is plated under the regulations the weights then plated supersede those contained in the reg. 42 plate.

(2) Trailer plates

See page 267.

50 MPH PLATE—As to the plate required to be displayed at the rear of a trailer when compliance with 'relevant conditions' raises the speed limit from 40 mph to 50 mph, see p. 81. Where a trailer is being drawn in circumstances requiring a speed limit of less than 50 mph, this plate shall not be displayed (reg. 96).

(3) Distinguishing plates for motor cycles

Regulation 46

I) REQUIREMENT—Every motor cycle first used post 1st August 1977 (exceptions below) must have a plate securely fixed in a conspicuous position stating whether the motor cycle is a standard motor cycle or a moped. The plate must conform to Sch. 2A and contain specified details (manufacturer's name, 'standard cycle' or 'moped', engine capacity, kerbside weight, maximum design speed, etc.).

II) EXCEPTIONS—The reg. does not apply to a motor cycle exceeding 150 cc or a mowing machine, or a PCV.

III) DEFINITIONS—

'Moped'—see p. 11.

'Kerbside weight' is that of the motor cycle with no person on it, with full supply of fuel in tank and an adequate supply of any other necessary liquid, and with no load other than loose tools or normal equipment.

'Maximum design speed' is the maximum speed the motor cycle is designed to achieve under own power on the level.

'Standard motor cycle' is a motor cycle which is not a moped.

24. Reversing

Every MV exceeding 410 kgs u/w must be capable of being so worked that it can travel either forwards or backwards (reg. 21). No person shall cause or permit a motor vehicle to travel backwards for a greater distance or time than requisite for the safety or reasonable convenience of its occupants or of other traffic on the road. Does not apply to RR or other road plant actually engaged in road work (reg. 120).

25. Seat belts and anchorage points

Regulation 17, as amended

A new reg. 17A will apply to vehicles manufactured post 1st June 1979 and first used post 1st April 1980. The main changes will be:

a) anchorage points must comply with EEC directives so as to secure uniformity within the EEC, and

b) seat belts must be fitted which restrain the upper and lower parts of the torso, include a lap belt, are anchored at no less than three points, and are designed for use by an adult for the driver's seat and the specified passenger's seat.

GENERAL RULE—Every motor car first registered post 1st January 1965 and every three wheeled motor cycle of u/w over 255 kgs first used post 1st September 1970 must be:

a) provided with anchorage points to which body-restraining seat belts may be securely fixed for:
   i) the driver's seat, and
   ii) the specified passenger's seat,
   provided that this paragraph shall not apply as so to require anchorage points to be provided for any seat which is a seat with integral seat belt anchorages;

b) provided with—
   i) a body-restraining seat belt designed for use by an adult for the driver's seat; and
   ii) a body-restraining seat belt for the specified passenger's seat.

EXCEPTIONS—MV used under trade licence, or being driven from premises of manufacturer, distributor or dealer to distributor, dealer, purchaser or hirer, and a MV specially constructed or adapted for a person suffering from some physical defect or disability, if a disabled person's seat belt is fitted.

Every seat belt* shall, if the seat for which it is provided is a seat with integral seat belt anchorages, be properly secured to the integral seat belt anchorage points forming part thereof, or, if the seat for which it is provided is not such a seat, be properly secured to the structure of the vehicle by the anchorage points provided for it under (a).

EXCEPTIONS—The reg. does not apply to: GV (unless made post 1st September 1966, registered post 1st April 1967, and u/w n/e 1525 kgs; passenger vehicle or DPV for more than twelve passengers; LT; WT; PCV; GV electrically propelled; MC constructed before 30th June 1964; a vehicle (used outside GB) imported here, while being driven from a place of arrival to residence of owner or driver, or from such residence to a place for the equipment to be provided; three-wheel motor cycle made pre 1st March 1970; two-wheel motor cycle with sidecar; MV manufactured post 1st October 1979 and first used post 1st April 1980.

Adjustments to seat belts

Regulation 17(6)

Applies to any motor car or motor cycle† manufactured post 1st October 1972.

---

* Except a disabled person's seat belt.
† In this case only if first used post 1st April 1973.

Does not apply to a seat belt comprising a lap belt and shoulder straps, or any restraining device for a young person, or a disabled person's seat belt.

The main requirements may be broadly summarised as follows:*

a) There must be a device, firmly fixed, into which the belt becomes stowed away when not in use. The device must be positioned on the rear side of the front door aperture, and at a sufficient height to ensure that no part of the belt which contacts the body of the wearer when in use lies on the floor, when the belt is in the stowed position.

b) The person wearing the belt must be able to remove the belt from the device and put the belt on either by using one hand or by taking the belt with one hand and transferring it from one hand to the other.

c) The belt fastenings (to secure the belt on the wearer) must be capable of being engaged and released with a single movement of one hand in one direction.

d) When put on by the wearer the belt must either adjust automatically to fit him, or be such that a manual device is convenient to use and can be operated by one hand.

DEFINITIONS

a) *Specified passenger seat* means:
   i) if only one forward facing seat alongside driver—that seat;
   ii) if more than one seat as in (i)—the furthest seat from the driver;
   iii) if no seat as in (i) or (ii)—the foremost forward facing seat furthest from the driver, unless there is a fixed partition separating the seat from the space in front of it alongside the driver.

b) *Seat belt*—a belt to be worn by a person in a vehicle to prevent or lessen any injury in an accident, including any special chair for a young person to which a belt is attached.

c) *Body restraining belt*—a seat belt providing restraint for upper and lower parts of the trunk in the event of an accident.

26. Seating capacity: half-decked vehicles

Regulation 40

Maximum seating capacity to be provided—for fifty passengers, calculated as is required for taxation purposes (see p. 150). 'Half decked' means not single nor double decked vehicle.

---

* They do not apply to a specified passenger seat as defined in definition (a) (iii), or to a GV exceeding 915 kg u/w having more than one seat beside the driver, the seats being joined together to form a single unit.

27. Silencer

a) Every vehicle propelled by an internal combustion engine must be fitted
with a silencer* suitable and sufficient to reduce the noise of exhaust gases
as far as reasonable (reg. 30).

b) While such a vehicle is being used on the road:
i) it is an offence to use, or cause or permit the use, so that exhaust gases
escape into the air without first passing through the silencer* required by
reg. 30;
ii) every such silencer* must at all times be maintained in good and
efficient working order and not altered for purpose of making greater the
noise of escaping exhaust gases (reg. 106).

28. Special types of vehicles

Regulations made under RTA 1972, s. 40, authorise the use (subject to
conditions) of special types of motor vehicles and trailers notwithstanding that
they do not comply in all respects with the requirements of the Construction
and Use Regulations as to overall dimensions or weight, e.g. abnormal indivisible loads, engineering plant and combine harvesters, but this subject is not
listed in the syllabus.

29. Speedometer

I) FITTING—Every MV first used post 1st October 1937 must be fitted with an
instrument (accurate to within 10 per cent) so constructed and placed as to
indicate readily to the driver at all times the speed of the MV, if and when he is
driving in excess of 10 mph.

Sellwood v Butt
Although the word 'speedometer' is not used, the regulation clearly
refers to an instrument which on its face discloses the speed of the vehicle.
A 'revolution counter' is not such an instrument.

Exceptions: WT; IC; motor cycle n/e 100 cc, or one neither constructed nor
adapted, nor used, to carry a driver or passenger; a MV always limited to
12 mph by law or by its incapability of exceeding this speed on the level under
its own power by reason of its construction (reg. 18).

---

* Or expansion chamber or other contrivance.

II) MAINTENANCE AND USE—Every such instrument must be kept:

a) in good working order and

b) free from any obstruction which might prevent it being easily read.

It is a defence to prove—

a) that the defect occurred on the journey during which the contravention was detected, or

b) that at the time of detection steps had already been taken to have the defect remedied with reasonable expedition (reg. 98).

30. Springs

Regulation 12

Every MV and every trailer drawn thereby shall be equipped with suitable and sufficient springs between each wheel and the frame of the vehicle.

Exceptions: MV registered pre 1st January 1932; motor cycle; WT; W Tlr; mobile crane; BDV being towed; PCV with pneumatic tyres; L Loco; LI; LIC; Ag Tlr; trailer used solely to haul felled trees; and the following if n/e 4070 kgs u/w:

a) MT if each unsprung wheel has pneumatic tyre;

b) MT used on railway shunting and not on road except to get from one railway track to another;

c) any vehicle specially designed and used on rough ground or unmade roads if tyres are pneumatic and speed n/e 20 mph;

d) any vehicle specially made and used solely for road sweeping if each wheel has a soft or elastic or pneumatic tyre and speed n/e 20 mph.

31. Smoke, vapour, ashes, sparks, etc.

(1) Construction, etc.

Every MV:

a) must be so constructed that no avoidable smoke or visible vapour is emitted therefrom (reg. 33);

b) *using solid fuel* must be fitted with:
i) an efficient appliance to prevent emission of sparks or grit, and
ii) a tray or shield to prevent ashes or cinders falling on to the road (reg. 38);

c) *driven by a compression ignition (e.g. diesel) engine* (except WT) and fitted with a device for supplying excess fuel for starting the engine, must have the device or its means of operation so fitted that it cannot readily be operated by a person carried on the vehicle, unless the device is such that it cannot cause supply of excess fuel while the engine is running or cause any increase in the emission of smoke or visible vapour (reg. 34);

d) *driven by a spark ignition engine* (not two-stroke)* first used on or after 1st January 1972 except
   i) a MV manufactured pre 1st July 1971, or
   ii) a two-wheeled motor cycle (with or without sidecar); or
   iii) a MV to which reg. 36 applies,
shall have the engine equipped with means to ensure that, while the engine is running, the vapours of gases in the crank case or other part of the engine must pass through the combustion chamber before escaping (reg. 35)†;

e) *driven by compression ignition engine*, first used post 1st April 1973 and manufactured post 1st October 1972—the engine shall be of the type for which there is issued a certificate in accordance with BS specification under number BS AU 141a: 1971 (reg. 37). The regulation does not apply to a MV with a Perkins 6.354 engine made pre 1st April 1973, or to a LT; L Loco; Ind T; WT; or engineering plant with a one- or two-cylinder engine.

OFFENCE—To use (cause or permit use) MV to which reg. 37 applies, if the engine (or any part) has been altered or adjusted so as to increase the emission of smoke from the vehicle (reg. 110).

(2) Maintenance and use

a) No person shall use (or cause or permit use of) on a road a MV from which any smoke, visible vapour, grit, sparks, ashes, cinders or oily substance is emitted so as to cause or be likely to cause damage to any property or injury (or likely to cause danger) to any person actually on or who may reasonably be expected to be on the road (reg. 109).

b) In the case of a diesel engine with a starting device supplying excess fuel to the engine:
   i) the device shall be maintained so that it does not supply excess fuel to the engine while the MV is in motion on a road, and
   ii) no person shall use (or cause or permit use of) the device to supply excess fuel to the engine while the MV is in motion on a road, but this does not apply where the device is designed so that it does not cause an increase in emission of smoke or vapour (reg. 111).

---

* For exceptions see p. 275.

† Most such vehicles first used post 10th November 1973 have to be legibly and indelibly marked in a conspicuous and easily accessible position with the approval mark showing compliance with the law relating to the emission of gaseous pollutants. In the course of time almost all such vehicles will have to be so marked (reg. 36).

c) In the case of a spark ignition engine, the means by which the gases in the engine crank case or other part of the engine are prevented from escaping into the atmosphere shall at all times when the MV is used on a road be maintained in good and efficient working order (reg. 112).

(3) Compliance approval mark

On every MV first used post 10th November 1973 there has to be legibly and indelibly marked in a conspicuous and readily accessible position an approved mark signifying that the vehicle meets requirements concerning the emission of gaseous pollutants by its engine. The approval mark required is changed from time to time to keep up with EEC agreements with regard to vehicles manufactured after specified dates. The newest of them applies to vehicles manufactured on or after 1st October 1976 and first used on or after 1st April 1977 (reg. 36 (7)).

The regulation does not apply to:

a) a vehicle manufactured before 20th September 1973; or

b) a MV with less than four wheels if:
   i) n/e 400 kgs in weight (laden or not), or
   ii) it is not constructed to exceed 30 mph on level ground and under own power; or

c) a vehicle exceeding 3,500 kgs (laden or not).

32. Standing vehicles

I) DARKNESS—It is an offence to cause or permit a MV to stand on a road during hours of darkness (except with permission of a police officer in uniform) otherwise than with its nearside as close as may be to edge of carriageway.

Exceptions: police/fire/ambulance; MV on road set aside as parking place or taxi stand, or PSV waiting place; MV picking up or setting down passengers according to directions given by COP; on one-way streets; vehicles used for building work, demolition, repairs to another vehicle, removal of traffic obstruction, road maintenance or repair, or for work in connection with gas, water, electricity or telephone services or electric transport undertaking (reg. 123).

II) ENGINE RUNNING—It is an offence to cause or permit a MV to be on a road unattended by a person licensed to drive it unless the engine is stopped and the relevant parking brake* effectively set. The requirement to stop the engine does not apply to a fire brigade MV being used for fire fighting; a gas-propelled MV carrying its own gas fuel; a MV being used for police or

---

* I.e. the parking brake to be provided under reg. 13 (see p. 332) or, if a MV to which reg. 5 applies, a parking brake according to EEC requirements.

ambulance purposes; a MV requiring its engine to drive special machinery which is part of it or mounted thereon, or to maintain electric power needed to drive the machinery, provided that the vehicle does not cause danger by its position, condition or other circumstances (reg. 124).

Butterworth v Shorthouse (1956)
Held: this offence did not require that both failures should be proved. Proof of one failure was sufficient for a conviction.

III) OBSTRUCTION AND NOISE—As to obstruction, see **20**, above, and as to stopping machinery to prevent noise, see p. 254.

33. Steam vehicle: furnace

Regulation 121

The driver of such a vehicle (other than a motor car) shall, unless two persons are carried on it to drive or attend to it, stop the vehicle whenever necessary to attend to the furnace.

34. Steering gear

Regulation 102

The steering gear of a MV must at all times when the MV is used on a road be maintained in good and efficient working order, and be properly adjusted.

35. Stop lamps

Covered by RV (Lighting) Regulations 1971 (see p. 122).

36. Television sets

No person shall:

a) use or install for use in a MV a TV set:
   i) if the screen (or part) is directly or by means of reflection visible to the driver in the driving seat, or

ii) if its controls (other than that for sound volume and main switch) are within reach of the driver in the driving seat;

b) use a TV set in a MV under circumstances or in a position such that it might cause distraction to the driver of any other vehicle on the road (reg. 143).

37. Towed vehicles

Regulation 128

This regulation applies where a MV is drawing a trailer or trailers:

a) where the connection between any of the vehicles is only a rope or chain, its length must be such that the distance between the trailer and the vehicle to which it is attached cannot *exceed* 4·5 metres;

b) if the distance between any of the vehicles exceeds 1·5 metres the means of attachment (*whatever it is*) must be made clearly visible to other persons using the road within reasonable distance on either side.

Measurement is between nearest points of vehicles concerned excluding parts or fittings designed as means of attaching one vehicle to another. See also trailers on p. 266.

38. Tracklaying vehicles

DEFINITION—A tracklaying vehicle is one so designed and constructed that its weight is transmitted to road by means of continuous tracks or a combination of wheels and such tracks so that at least half its weight is borne by tracks.

REGULATIONS—The MV (C & U) (Tracklaying Vehicles) Regulations 1955 apply, and these correspond in the main with the 1978 Regulations applying to wheeled vehicles. The following are the main variations:

a) *overall length*—n/e 30 ft;

b) *unladen weight*—in case of a heavy locomotive up to 15½ tons, but if tyres are soft or elastic and weight carrying rollers have resilient material between rims and road surface—17½ tons;

c) *trailers*—total laden weight n/e 13 tons; MV more than 26 ft long not to draw trailer except gas trailer or BDV;

d) *tracks*—flat; at least ½ in. wide, where they contact road surface, and so that total area of each track in such contact is at least 36 sq. in. for each ton of the total weight transmitted through tracks to the road surface or, in the case of a L Loco or LT registered pre 1st January 1936, for each ton of the u/w of the vehicle; tracks to be kept free from defect which might damage road or endanger any person on the MV or the road and maintained in good working order and properly adjusted;

e) *rollers*—resilient material to be between rims of weight carrying rollers and road, and in case of HMC, MC, and trailer drawn by them, springs to be between frame and weight carrying rollers.

EXEMPTIONS—*Resilient material:* RR, MV registered pre 2nd January 1932; L Loco; LI, Ag Tlr; round timber trailer; mobile crane; BDV being towed. *Springs:* WT; W Tlr.

39. Trailers: restrictions on use

(1) General

a) A two-wheeled motor cycle without a sidecar cannot draw any trailer. *Exception:* towing a broken-down motor cycle (reg. 130).

b) A motor cycle sidecar must be so attached that its wheel is not wholly forward or to the rear of the motor cycle (reg. 129).

c) A trailer drawn by a motor cycle must not exceed 254 kgs u/w or 1·5 metres overall width (reg. 131).

d) No trailer must be drawn by IC, straddle carrier or PSV. *Exceptions* re PSV: one PSV drawn by another (both empty) in emergency; gas trailer; trailer drawn under authority of the road service licence; trailer (and its means of attachment) approved by a certifying officer (regs. 132, 133 and 135).

e) No trailer is to be used for carrying passengers for hire or reward. *Exception:* BDV being drawn following the breakdown if:
i) speed n/e 30 mph, and
ii) in the case of a BDV for more than seven passengers, it (or the trailer on which it is carried) is attached to the drawing vehicle by a rigid draw bar (reg. 133).

f) For *overall lengths* when trailers are being drawn see appendix 4.

(2) As to number

Number to be drawn on a highway is not to exceed:

a) drawn by loco (heavy or light): **3**;

b) drawn by MT *if laden*: **1**; *if unladen*: **2**;

c) HMC or MC: **1***.

NOTES

a) A vehicle used solely to carry water for the drawing vehicle or an agricultural vehicle not constructed to carry a load is not a trailer under this regulation.

b) An articulated vehicle when being drawn by another MV because the AV has broken down shall, if the AV is unladen, be treated in relation to the drawing vehicle as one trailer.

c) The regulation does not apply to military vehicles.

d) Using (causing or permitting) trailer in contravention is an offence.

(3) As to overall length

See appendix 4.

(4) As to tow ropes, etc.

See p. 265.

(5) Trailer plates

Regulation 81

When being drawn on a road by a MV the trailer (or the rear-most trailer) must exhibit at its rear in a conspicuous position a trailer plate.

FORM—Equiangular triangle, white surface, with nine red reflex lenses (one in each corner and two between them on each side, each at least 19 mm diameter).

POSITION—Vertical; easily seen from behind; on centre or to offside: no part above 1·22 m from ground.

MAINTENANCE—Clean and unobscured.

EXEMPTIONS—Trailer of AV; BDV; round timber trailer; LI other than living van; LIC; Ag Tlr; water cart for and drawn by RR; drawn by motor cycle, or by motor car or DPV for not more than seven passengers; trailer carrying two obligatory reflectors required by Lighting Regulations 1971 and marked with an approval mark, either on a white background or within white border at least 12 mm wide.

---

* Two if one of them is a towing implement and the other is a vehicle part of which is secured to and either rests on, or is suspended from, the towing implement (reg. 137).

(6) Passengers

Regulation 134

No passenger to be carried in a living van (caravan) with less than four wheels or with four close-coupled wheels. The regulation does not apply during testing by a manufacturer, repairer, distributor or dealer.

40. Tyres

(1) Pneumatic tyre

A pneumatic tyre is one complying as follows—

a) inflated with air substantially above atmospheric pressure, and

b) can be inflated or deflated without removal from wheel or vehicle, and

c) when deflated, with normal load, sides collapse (reg. 3).

(2) Condition and maintenance

I) OFFENCES RELATING TO DEFECTS, ETC.—It is an offence to use (or cause or permit use) on road of any MV or trailer with a pneumatic tyre which:

a) is unsuitable regarding use to which vehicle is being put or types of tyres on other wheels;

b) is not so inflated as to make it fit for use to which vehicle is being put;

c) has a break in its fabric, or a cut exceeding 25 mm or 10 per cent of the section width of the tyre, whichever is greater, measured in any direction and deep enough to reach the body cords;

d) has any lump or bulge caused by separation or partial failure of structure;

e) has any portion of ply or cord structure exposed (reg. 107);

f) in case of a motor cycle n/e 50 cc has a tread which does not show through at least three-quarters of the tyre breadth, and round the entire circumference the tyre pattern is not clearly visible in relief;

g) in the case of any vehicle other than those mentioned in (f), the tread pattern (excluding any tiebar) does not have a depth of at least 1 mm throughout at least three-quarters of the tyre breadth and round the entire circumference. *Exceptions:* motor tricycle, u/w n/e 102 kgs incapable of exceeding 12 mph on level under own power; a PCV which is a WT.

Above does not apply to: L Loco; LT; LI; LIC; Ag Tlr being drawn by LT; BDV or a vehicle proceeding to place to be broken up, if in either case it is being drawn by a MV at a speed n/e 20 mph (reg. 107).

NOTE
No offence is committed by virtue only of defects (b) to (e) above, if the tyre is the type permitting safe use after puncture and collapse and if the wall of the tyre is so marked as to enable the tyre to be identified as one of this type.

II) OFFENCES RELATING TO RECUT TYRES—It is an offence to use (cause or permit use) on road MV or trailer if a wheel is fitted with a recut pneumatic tyre the fabric of which has been cut or exposed in the cutting process. *Exception:* BDV or vehicle to be broken up as above being towed by MV at not exceeding 20 mph.

III) OFFENCES RELATING TO MAINTENANCE—It is an offence to use a MV or trailer on a road any tyre of which has not been maintained in such condition as to be fit for use to which the vehicle is being put, or not free from a defect which might in any way cause damage to road surface or danger to persons on or in the vehicle or using the road.

IV) OFFENCES OF MIXING DIFFERENT TYPES OF PNEUMATIC TYRES

Two axled vehicles—It is an offence to use (or cause or permit use) on a road:

a) a vehicle* which has tyres of different types of structure fitted to the same axle, or

b) a MV having only two axles, each of which has one or two single wheels, if
   i) a diagonal ply tyre or a bias belted tyre is fitted on the rear axle, and a radial tyre is fitted on the front axle;
   ii) a diagonal ply tyre is fitted on the rear axle and a bias belted tyre is on the front axle.

The above does not apply if an axle is fitted with wide tyres which have not been specially constructed for an engineering plant.

More than two axles—It is an offence to use (or cause or permit use) on a road a MV if on one steerable axle tyres of one type of structure are fitted and on another steerable axle tyres of a different structure are fitted. The same offence applies to driven axles not being steering axles, all having to be fitted with tyres of the same type of structure (reg. 108).

(3) Testing tyres

See p. 274.

---

* Including trailer.

(4) Trailers

a) Post 1st January 1933, drawn by HMC or MC

a) To be fitted with pneumatic tyres.

b) Recut pneumatic tyres not to be used on trailer which does n/e 1020 kgs u/w; or is not constructed to carry any load other than a permanent fixture being plant or special appliance n/e 2290 kgs total weight; or is a living van n/e 2040 kgs u/w (reg. 78).

EXCEPTIONS—W Tlr; San V; water carrier for road roller; LI or Ag Tlr drawn by LT; BDV drawn by MV; drawn by HMC not requiring pneumatic tyres.

b) Otherwise—Must be pneumatic or of soft or elastic material.

EXCEPTIONS:

a) pre 15 January 1931, specially designed to convey:
i) horses and cattle and used for that or other agricultural purpose, or
ii) furniture and similar household effects and being so used;

b) LI or Ag Tlr, or a water carrier for road roller being used to construct or repair roads (reg. 77).

(5) Motor cycles

Must be pneumatic, but not a 'recut' (reg. 68).

Exceptions: WT or PCV if tyres are of soft or elastic material.

(6) Motor cars

Pneumatic only, except that the following may have soft or elastic tyres instead:

a) u/w n/e 1020 kgs;

b) WT;

c) first used pre 2nd January 1933;

d) San v*;

e) goods vehicle electrically propelled u/w n/e 1270 kgs.

Recut pneumatic tyres not permitted except on a GV of u/w 2540 kgs or more, rim diameter of wheel being 405 mm or more; or an electrically propelled GV (reg. 65).

(7) HMCs

Pneumatic tyres only, except that the following may have instead soft or elastic tyres:

---

* See note on next page.

a) first used pre 2nd January 1933;

b) exceeding 4070 kgs u/w and used mainly on rough ground or unmade roads;

c) San v*;

d) turntable fire escapes;

e) tower wagons;

f) WT (reg. 60).

(8) Motor tractors

Pneumatic or soft or elastic material. *Exception in case of land tractor if:*

a) each steering wheel tyre is smooth soled tyre contact with road is at least 60 mm wide, and

b) each driving wheel tyre (if u/w exceeds 3050 kgs) is at least 150 mm wide or (u/w n/e 3050 kgs) 76 mm wide *and* is either:
   i) smooth soled, or
   ii) properly shod with diagonal cross bars†.

NOTE
Recut pneumatic tyres not permitted if u/w is under 2540 kgs unless wheel rim diameter is 405 mm or more (reg. 56).

(9) Locomotives

Pneumatic or of soft or elastic material.
   If tyre is soft or elastic it must extend continuously around wheel rim, or be fitted in sections so that:

a) no gap between sections exceeds 20 mm, and

b) total of gap spaces on outer surface does n/e 150 mm.

EXCEPTION—L Loco if:

a) each steering wheel is smooth soled, and tyre contact with road is at least 125 mm wide, and

b) each driving wheel is at least 300 mm wide and is either:
   i) smooth soled, or
   ii) properly shod with diagonal cross bars† (reg. 52).

---

* I.e. one designed and used solely for street cleansing, collection of refuse or contents of cesspools, etc.

† If bars are soft or elastic they must be at least 60 mm wide, full breadth of tyre, not more than 76 mm apart. If not of soft or elastic material, same applies except that bars must be 76 mm wide and not more than 20 mm thick.

(10) Goods vehicles

Where a plating certificate is issued in respect of a GV each axle of the GV shall be equipped with tyres which, as regards strength, are designed and maintained adequately to support the axle weight for that axle as shown in the certificate (reg. 150).

41. Weights: laden and unladen

The S of S can authorise the use on roads of vehicles which do not comply in all respects with the provisions of the regulations. When provisions as to maximum weights are not complied with in respect of 'authorised' vehicles and/or their loads, conditions of use always include notification to and indemnification of the highway and bridge authorities concerned. Where a GV is 'plated' or bears a manufacturer's plate the relevant maximum weights in relation to it are shown on the plates.

42. Windscreen wipers and washers

a) One or more efficient and automatic wipers must be fitted to a MV so made that driver cannot (by opening windscreen or otherwise) get an adequate view to the front without looking through the screen.

b) The wipers must be capable of cleansing screen so that driver has adequate view to front, including front near and offside (reg. 27).

c) Wipers must be maintained in good and efficient order and properly adjusted (reg. 103).

d) Where wiper(s) are required as in (a) above the MV must have fitted a windscreen washer capable of clearing (with aid of wipers) the area swept by the wipers of mud or similar deposits. *Exceptions:* LT; vehicles incapable by construction of exceeding 20 mph on level under own power; vehicles being used for time being as stage carriages (reg. 28).

43. Wings

Unless adequate protection is afforded by the body, wings or other similar fittings to catch, as far as practicable, mud or water thrown up by wheels must be provided on the following vehicles:

a) *HMC or MC—Exceptions:* if part of AV the rear wheels, if trailer part is used solely for carrying round timber; unfinished vehicles on the way to a works for completion; WT (regs. 61 and 66).

b) *Trailers—Exceptions:* used for round timber; unfinished and going for completion; fire brigade pumps; where max. speed is 12 mph; water carts; LV; BDV; LI; LIC (reg. 79).

In the case of a motor cycle or IC wings are required for the proviso as to protection afforded by body does not apply (regs. 69 and 72).

44. View to the front

Every MV must be so constructed that the driver has a full view at all times of the road and traffic ahead (reg. 22). No person shall drive a MV on a road while in such a position that he cannot have proper control or retain full view of road and traffic ahead. To cause or permit this is also an offence (reg. 119).

45. Roadworthiness: testing, etc.

(1) Sale of unroadworthy vehicles

1972 Act, s. 60

OFFENCES: It is an offence:

a) *to sell, supply, offer to sell or supply, or expose for sale*, a MV or trailer for delivery in such condition that the use of it on a road would be unlawful by virtue of the C & U Regulations 1978, as regards brakes, steering gear, tyres, construction, weight, equipment; or maintenance of vehicle parts and accessories in such a condition that danger is or is likely to be caused; or lighting equipment and reflectors (the latter not complying with requirements re use on a road during hours of darkness);

b) *to alter a MV or trailer* so as to render its condition such that use of the vehicle on a road would be a breach of the C & U Regulations 1978 as to construction, weight or equipment.

LIABILITY—As above, or causing or permitting the offence—£200.

DEFENCES—Proof of any one of following:

a) sale, supply, offer, exposure for sale, or alteration was related to a vehicle for export, or

b) reasonable cause to believe vehicle would not be used on a road in GB in unroadworthy condition, or

c) (re lighting equipment) reasonable cause to believe vehicle would not be used during hours of darkness until put in a proper condition for this.

(2) Unsuitable or defective vehicle parts

1972 Act, s. 60A

This section creates the following offences:

a) *fitting a vehicle part to a vehicle* (or causing or permitting this) so that by this the use of the vehicle contravenes or fails to comply with any C & U regulation, and

b) *selling, supplying, or offering to sell or supply (or cause or permit any of these) a vehicle part*, having reasonable cause to believe it is to be fitted to a vehicle when such a fitting would cause the use of the vehicle on a road to contravene a C & U regulation.

The section does not apply to a vehicle for export, or where there was reasonable cause to believe the vehicle would not be used on a road in GB or would not be used until put into a condition not contravening the regulations. An authorised person is given power to enter places where such sales or fittings are made to test and inspect. Obstruction is an offence under the section.

(3) Testing vehicles

(As to special provisions re goods vehicles, see p. 219.)

a) Examination on premises by arrangement or after an accident.—The *MV (C & U) Regulations 1978, reg. 145*, provides that any constable *in uniform* or a certifying officer of the S of S or an authorised examiner of PSVs or goods vehicles (on production of his authority if requested) may test and inspect the *brakes, silencers, steering gear, tyres, lighting equipment and reflectors* of any motor vehicle or trailer *on any premises* subject to the consent of the *owner of the premises.* The power, however, must not be exercised unless the owner of the vehicle consents or there has been served on him a notice of the proposed examination, either:

a) personally or leaving it at his address *at least 48 hours*, or

b) sending it by recorded delivery to his address *at least 72 hours* before the time of the intended inspection.

When the vehicle has been involved in a road accident causing injury or damage, the serving of a notice is unnecessary if the examination takes place within 48 hours of the accident.

NB: for the purpose of this regulation the 'owner' is deemed to be registered owner, or the holder of a trade licence or international circulation order, and the 'address' (of a licence holder) to be that shown on the register of the registration authority or on the licence.

b) Spot checks on roads (1972, s. 53)

I) POWERS TO TEST—An authorised examiner* is empowered to test a MV on a road to ascertain whether legal requirements re brakes, silencers, steering gear, tyres, lighting equipment, reflectors, excessive noise, smoke, fumes or vapour are complied with, and to inform the driver of failures to comply. An examiner may drive a vehicle to test it but a vehicle shall not be required to stop for a test except by a constable in uniform. The driver may elect to have the test deferred to another time and place and must then supply the name and address of the owner, who will be given an opportunity to specify a period of 7 days within the next 30 days during which (and a convenient place at which) the test may be carried out on giving him at least 2 days notice (in writing).

NOTE
By para. 14 of Sch. 6 to the RTA 1974 an authorised person includes any person appointed by the police authority to act under this section under the direction of the COP.

Stoneley v Richardson (1974)
A handbrake defect was found by constable who was not an authorised examiner. Justices dismissed information. *Held:* the evidence of the constable was not inadmissible. The question of 'authorised examiner' did not arise until the driver refused to allow the examination.

When no period is specified at least 7 days' notice (in writing) of the test must be given. If the place has not been specified the notice will state a convenient place within any specified area. Where the driver is the owner, he may elect to defer the test and specify the period and place of test immediately.

Brown v McIndoe (1963)
The option to defer the test extends to the driver only (unless he is also the owner) and not the owner, nor need the examiner tell a driver of his option.

Where it appears to a *constable* that a test should be carried out forthwith because the vehicle:

---

* The following may act as authorised examiners—a certifying officer or PSV examiner appointed under RTA 1960; persons appointed as examiners under the RTA 1972 or by the S of S; a constable authorised under this section by the chief constable; and a person appointed by the police authority to act for purposes of the section under the directions of the chief constable. A person so appointed must produce his authority to act if required to do so.

a) has been involved *in an accident or*

b) is so defective that it ought not to be allowed to proceed,

the constable may require in (a) that it shall not be taken away until tested and in (b) that the test be *carried out* forthwith. It is an offence to obstruct an authorised examiner or to fail to comply with any of the above requirements.

NOTE
For testing of brakes on pedal cycles, see p. 281.

II) REMEDYING DEFECTS FOUND (1972, s. 54)*—During the road test the examiner under s. 53 can require person in charge to state whether he is the owner of the vehicle and, if not, the name and address of the owner. Failure to comply is an offence (£50). If defect found contravenes any C & U regulations the examiner can (irrespective of proceedings for the offence) give written notice to the vehicle owner specifying the defect and the C & U regulation requirement, and requesting him to give to the S of S within the 'permitted period' a certificate or a declaration under this Act.

a) *Certificate*—must contain two statements, one, signed by the person receiving the notice, that he has taken steps to get repairs done at a vehicle testing station or to get it examined at such a station to ascertain that the required repairs have been done, and the other by the authorised person at that station stating that he has carried out the repairs and certifying that on examination he found the repairs to have been done as required.

b) *Declaration*—signed by the person receiving the notice and stating that he has disposed of his interest in the vehicle and that he does not intend to use it again on a road in GB.

c) *Offences*—failure to give the notice or the declaration within the permitted period, or knowingly make false statement in certificate or declaration.

d) *Permitted period*—28 days from date of notice or such longer time as S of S, on application, may grant.

III) CHECKS ON CERTIFICATE (1972, s. 55*).—Within 30 days of the receipt of a certificate (see (II)) the S of S can require the owner to make the vehicle available for a further official test by an officer of the Minister. Para. (II) above then applies to such a test substituting Minister's officer for 'authorised examiner', and the general provisions re 'deferred tests' (see p. 275) also apply. Offences under s. 53 of obstruction and failure to comply apply to this section also.

c) **Tests at sale rooms, etc. (1972, s. 61)**—An authorised examiner can at any reasonable hour enter premises used for business of sale or supply or offer of used MV or trailers kept there, and test and inspect (including driving) any vehicle found there to check on its condition for sale in conformity with s. 60

---

* Not in force at time of going to press.

(see p. 273). Obstruction is an offence. 'Used' means that the vehicle has been previously sold or supplied by retail.

NOTE
By s. 61 (1A) of the RTA 1972 the power of an authorised person to enter, inspect and test is extended to doing so for purpose of ascertaining whether type approval requirements are complied with in relation to vehicles or vehicle parts.

d) Test certificates

I) GENERAL REQUIREMENTS—The MV (Tests) Regulations 1976 require:

a) the examination of certain motor vehicles annually after a specified period of time (now 3 years) following the date of their registration (or date of manufacture if used on any roads, in GB or elsewhere, before registration), but use before sale or supply by retail does not count, and

b) for the issue of:
i) *a test certificate* indicating that the vehicle has been found to comply with the relevant C & U and Lighting Regulations (valid for one year), or
ii) *a notification of refusal*, where there is non-compliance.

NOTE
Date of manufacture is the last day of the year in which finally assembled or, if modifications are made later before sale or supply by retail, the end of the year in which the modifications were made (1972, s. 44).

II) APPLICATION OF THE REGULATIONS—The Regulations apply to HMC, motor cars and motor cycles. The Regulations will also apply from 1st January 1978 to motor caravans (not being DPVs) of u/w exceeding 1525 kg and first registered (or manufactured) pre 1st January 1975. A 'motor caravan' is a MV constructed or adapted for carriage of passengers and their effects and which has, as permanent equipment, facilities reasonably necessary for the vehicle to provide mobile living accommodation for its users.

III) VEHICLE TESTING—The examination must be carried out at an approved vehicle testing station (outside which the prescribed sign must be exhibited) by an examiner authorised by the S of S. The requirements to be complied with relate to braking systems, steering gear, lighting equipment and reflectors, stop lamps, tyres*, road wheels*, seat belts and anchorages, direction indicators, windscreen wipers and washers, exhaust systems, warning instruments, bodywork and suspension†. Appeal against refusal lies to the S of S, who may require the vehicle to be submitted to a further test.

IV) THE OFFENCE (1972 ACT, S. 44 AND MY (TESTS) (EXTENSION) ORDER 1966)—It is an offence to use (or cause or permit this) on a road a MV (to which the regulations apply) without a current test certificate. *Exceptions:*

---

* So far as condition is likely to lead to rapid deflation of tyres.
† So far as condition may affect braking or steering.

a) *vehicles*—tracklaying vehicle; goods vehicle with u/w exceeding 1525 kg; PSV adapted to carry 8 or more passengers (but not a community bus service vehicle not having in force a PSV licence); an AV (tractor and trailer part); PCV; WT; IC n/e u/w 306 kg*; police vehicle maintained in workshop approved by S of S; locomotive; MT; vehicle to which the C & U Regulations do not apply; electrically propelled GV with u/w n/e 1525 kg; a hackney carriage in London (and certain provincial towns); a MV temporarily in GB under an ICP (during first year); a private hire MV licensed by a licensing authority on a certificate that grant of licence is subject to an annual test;

b) *uses of vehicles*, i.e. to go to or come from, or during, a pre-arranged test, or on failure of test to take it to place for remedying defects or by towing to be broken up; as an authorised 'special type'; being removed under statutory powers from road or car park; by police of seized vehicle for purposes connected with it, or by customs officers in relation to vehicle seized by them; vehicles used in certain remote parts of GB; use under trade licence.

NOTE
As to goods vehicle test certificates see p. 221.

(4) Dangerous condition

1972 Act, s. 24

It is an offence to *cause* or *permit* a *vehicle* (not necessarily a MV) or *trailer* to remain *on a road* so as to be likely to cause danger to others using the road by reason of its:

a) condition, or

b) position on the road, or

c) other circumstances.

(5) Goods vehicles and PSVs

Provisions relating to road-worthiness, inspections and tests of these vehicles are dealt with in the respective chapters (14 and 15) relating to them.

(6) Emission of gaseous pollutants

See p. 261.

---

* Up to 510 kilos if supplied and maintained by the DHSS.

Chapter 19 Motor cycles and pedal cycles

1. Motor cycles

(1) Review of law contained in previous chapters

For the benefit of students references to law already dealt with and relating particularly to motor cycles are framed below in the form of questions:

a) What is the definition of a motor cycle?

b) What is the minimum age for a driving licence?

c) What goods may a motor cycle (constructed to carry goods) carry without an operator's licence becoming necessary?

d) What are the provisions of the C & U Regulations relating to tyres and wings?

e) What is the law relating to:
   i) rear reflectors and rear lamps?
   ii) distinguishing plate?
   iii) exhibition of excise licence?
   iv) position and lighting of 'registration mark'?
   v) attachment of sidecars?

f) What restrictions apply to the drawing of trailers? When is a sidecar not a trailer?

(2) Brakes

See appendix 1 and (for testing) p. 274.

(3) Offences re carriage of passengers

It is an offence:

a) to carry more than one person in addition to the driver on a two-wheeled motor cycle (1972, s. 16);

b) to carry such an additional person otherwise than sitting astride, and on a proper seat securely fixed behind the driver's seat (1972, s. 16);

c) to carry a person (in addition to driver) on a two-wheeled motor cycle (with sidecar or not) with no suitable supports or rests for feet being available for him (C & U Regs. 1978, reg. 141).

(4) Protective helmets

The wearing of 'crash helmets' or protective head-dress of approved type is compulsory, and it is an offence for any person to sell, offer for sale, or let on hire (or offer to do this) any such helmet or head-dress as affording protection from injury in case of accident unless the helmet (head-dress) conforms to the type prescribed or authorised by regulation under 1972, s. 33.

MOTOR CYCLES (WEARING OF HELMETS) REGULATIONS 1973—Every person driving or riding on a motor bicycle (whether with sidecar or not) on a road shall wear protective headgear. *Exceptions:* a motor bicycle which is a mowing machine, or is being propelled by a person on foot, or driven or ridden by a follower of the Sikh religion whilst he is wearing a turban. Note that a person riding in a sidecar is not required to wear protective headgear. *'Protective headgear'* means a helmet manufactured for persons on motor cycles which, by its shape, material and construction could reasonably be expected to afford a degree of protection. If worn with a chin cup held in position by a strap or other fastening, the helmet must be provided with an additional strap or fastening (to be fastened under the wearer's jaw) for securing the helmet firmly to the head of the wearer. The helmet must be securely fastened to the head of the wearer. 'Motor bicycle' for the purpose of these Regulations means a two-wheeled motor cycle, and any wheels, if the distance between the centres of the areas of contact between such wheels and the road surface is less than 460 mm, shall be counted as one wheel.

2. Pedal cycles

(1) References to law contained in previous chapters

These are put in the form of questions to afford students opportunity to check knowledge:

a) To what extent, if any, do the offences of reckless and careless riding differ from similar offences committed by driving motor vehicles?

b) In connection with being unfit through drink or drug, compare the offences as regards:
   i) motor vehicles and
   ii) pedal cycles.

c) What restrictions are placed on the use of highways (including footpaths) for cycle racing or competitions?

d) What provisions apply with regard to 'obligatory lights', reflectors and night parking?

e) To what extent do general statutes relating to the use of 'carriages' on highways and footpaths apply to pedal cycles?

f) To what extent is a pedal cyclist subject to the restrictions imposed on traffic generally by road markings (i.e. the double white lines)?

(2) Brakes

Brakes on Pedal Cycles Regulations 1954

a) *If any wheel exceeds 18 in. diameter* (to include the tyres when fully inflated), the machine:
i) *having a fixed wheel* (i.e. one which is incapable of rotating independently of the pedals) must have a braking system which acts on the front wheel or both front wheels, if it has two such wheels;
ii) *if of free-wheel type*—must have two independent braking systems, one which acts on the front wheel(s) as in (i) above and the other operating on a rear wheel, but in the case of a tricycle not constructed or adapted to carry goods, both systems may act on the front wheel if it has two rear wheels or on the rear wheel if it has two front wheels.

b) *In any other case*, must have at least one braking system (reg. 4).

OFFENCES—It is an offence:

a) to ride or cause or permit to be ridden on a road any cycle which does not comply with the regulations (reg. 3);

b) if the braking systems are not kept in efficient working order (brakes acting directly on the tyres are not efficient) (reg. 5).

TESTING—A constable in uniform may test and inspect the brakes of any cycle on a road and on any premises where the machine is, if within 48 hours of any accident in which it has been involved and the owner of the premises consents.

EXEMPTIONS—The regulations do not apply to a cycle which has pedals acting directly on the wheels, i.e. where there is no chain or device intervening, or to a cycle brought temporarily from abroad by a visitor to Great Britain if it has at least one efficient brake.

(3) Carriage of persons on bicycles

It is an offence for more than one person to be carried on a bicycle not propelled by mechanical power unless it is constructed or adapted to carry more than one person. 'Person carried' includes the rider (1972, s. 21).

NB: the section is confined to a bicycle (i.e. two-wheeled).

Chapter 20 **Miscellaneous provisions**

In this chapter are included legal provisions relating to road traffic which are of general application or merit separate consideration and for that reason have not been considered particularly relevant to any one of the preceding chapters.

1. Offences not confined to roads

Almost all the offences already noted relate to the use or presence of vehicles on roads or highways (including footpaths) or in public places. A question could well be directed to test a candidate's knowledge of exceptions to this rule. The offence of wanton driving under the OAP Act 1861, s. 35, and offences in respect of parking places off the highway should immediately spring to mind. One section in which no limiting reference to 'road' is made is s. 16 of the 1972 Act which places restrictions on the carriage of passengers on motor cycles, and this might provide a useful subject for debate particularly as the offence re passengers on pedal cycles is expressly limited to roads. Offences which are, without question, of wider application include the following:

a) the prohibition of driving motor vehicles elsewhere than on roads;

b) tampering with motor vehicles on a road or in any parking place provided by a local authority.

(1) Driving elsewhere than on roads

1972 Act, s. 36

It is an offence to drive a MV without lawful authority on to or upon any common land, moorland, or other land of any kind, not being land forming part of a road, or on any road being a footpath or bridleway.

EXCEPTIONS:

a) Driving on any land within 15 yards of a road on which a MV may be lawfully driven for purpose only of parking.

b) Driving on land for purpose only of saving life, extinguishing fire, or meeting other like emergency.

The section does not affect public rights over commons and wastelands, nor confer a right to park within 15 yards of a roadway. See also para. **2 (2)** below.

(2) Tampering with motor vehicles

1972 Act, s. 29

It is an offence for any person, without lawful authority or reasonable cause, to get on to a MV, or tamper with its brake or other mechanism, while the MV is on a road or in a parking place provided by a local authority (£100—compare with **2 (1)** (a) below).

See also Law of Property Act 1925 (below).

2. Other offences

(1) Holding MV to be towed, or getting on to be carried

1972 Act, s. 30

It is an offence:

a) without lawful authority or reasonable excuse to take hold of, or get on to, a MV or trailer *while in motion on a road* for the purpose of being carried;

b) to take hold of a MV or trailer *in motion on road* for purpose of being drawn.

Note absence of 'without lawful authority' in (b).

(2) Driving on wastes and commons

To draw or drive on a waste or common, without lawful excuse, any carriage, cart, caravan, truck or other vehicle, or to camp or light any fire thereon, or to fail to observe any limitation or condition imposed by the Government under this section in respect of such land, is a summary offence (Law of Property Act 1925, s. 193).

3. Notices of intended prosecution

1972 Act s. 179

(1) When necessary

A person *cannot be convicted* of any of the following offences, i.e. reckless, careless or inconsiderate driving or cycling; failing (when driving or propelling any vehicle) to comply with a traffic sign, or with direction of a police officer regulating traffic; leaving a vehicle to remain in a dangerous position on a road; or driving in excess of any speed limit or at less than the minimum speed, *unless —*

a) *he was warned at the time* that the question of prosecuting him for a particular offence would be taken into consideration, *or*

b) *within 14 days of the offence:*
   i) a summons was served on him for the offence, *or*
   ii) a 'notice of intended prosecution' was served on *the driver*, or *the person registered as the keeper* of the MV.

   NB: the day of the offence is not included in counting the 14 days.

EXCEPTION—By an amendment to s. 179 effected by the RTA 1974 the above does not apply (i.e. a warning or notice is not needed) where, at the time of the offence, or immediately thereafter, an accident occurs owing to the presence on the road of the vehicle in respect of which the offence was committed.

NOTES

a) Failure to comply with (b) above is no bar to conviction if the court is satisfied that:
   i) neither the name and address of the offender nor the owner could be ascertained in time with reasonable diligence, *or*
   ii) the conduct of the offender contributed to the failure of the police to comply.

   Archer v Blacker (1965)
   Both driver and owner (if not the driver) must give evidence to prove that they had not received proper notice, and if this is done the prosecutor must prove posting by registered or recorded delivery post, if he can, to the last known address.

b) Compliance is presumed by the court, and the onus of proving the contrary is for the defence.

(2) The warning at the time

The form of warning at the time of the offence (which may be oral or written) has been the subject of many cases and it is advisable that the words of the section should be used, e.g. 'The facts will be reported with a view to consideration of the question of proceedings being taken against you for ...'

Jeffs v Wells (1936)

A verbal warning given on arrival at the scene 35 minutes after the accident when the parties were still present was held to be 'at the time' (2½ hours later has been held to be insufficient where the police had reasonable opportunity of warning him earlier).

Jollye v Dale (1960)

An hour after the offender's arrest for dangerous driving following his pursuit for 30 minutes he was warned for the first time. Conviction was upheld, but the High Court added that where the earliest possible time for warning the driver was several hours later, this would not generally be in compliance.

Sinclair v Clark (1963)

Driver called at station 4 hours after the accident to report same. He was warned re intended prosecution and on appeal this was held to be 'at the time the offence was committed' (i.e. the first reasonable opportunity).

Shield v Crighton (1974)

A verbal warning given some ten minutes after arrival at scene of accident is 'at the time'.

(3) The summons

Proof that the summons was sent by post in time to enable it to be delivered within 14 days of the offence is sufficient proof of service to the court in the absence of any acknowledgement or proof of receipt from the defendant.

When a person arrested for another offence is charged also with one or more of the above offences s. 179 can generally be regarded as having been fulfilled if, when he is charged, a copy of the charges is served on him, but, even so, it is advisable (as a safeguard) to procure service of the summons or notice within the 14 days.

(4) The notice: service and validity

The notice may be served personally upon the driver, owner or cyclist, and will be deemed to have been served on any person if it was sent within 14 days by registered post or recorded delivery service addressed to him at his last known address notwithstanding that it is returned as undelivered or was for any reason not received by him or not received within the 14 days (*Groome v Driscoll* (1969)).

It is to be noted that service by leaving the notice with an adult at the offender's usual place of abode is not good practice because the proof of service by the section applies only to posting the notice. The time, place and nature of the offence must be specified in the notice, which may be served on a Sunday.

Hosier v Goodall (1962)

If the defendant proves non-receipt of a notice said to be left with an adult for him at his last or most usual place of abode within 14 days and not given to any person authorised to accept his correspondence in his absence, the service is not within the provisions of the section. It is therefore good practice to serve the notice either personally or by registered or recorded delivery post.

Stewart v Chapman (1951)

The notice should be sent by registered or recorded delivery post within such time that it would ordinarily be delivered within the 14 days.

R v County of London Appeals Committee (1956)

The police would be wise to take further steps to give notice to the registered owner if the notice is returned by the dead letter office before 14 days have expired.

R v Bilton (1964)

The object of the notice is to ensure that the driver is not taken by surprise long after the offence when his recollection is dulled and witnesses may be difficult to trace.

Phipps v McCormick (1971)

Police sent NIP to home address though they knew defendant to be in hospital after accident. *Held:* notice should be served at place where person would normally expect to receive correspondence, an address with some permanence. The hospital did not satisfy this but the home address did.

Nicholson v Tapp (1972)

A notice posted on the fourteenth day cannot reach defendant until fifteenth day or later and is not, therefore, good service.

NB: when a charge of reckless driving is reduced to careless driving, the defendant may be convicted even though no notice was served in respect of the lesser offence. The serving of notice does not apply to a charge of manslaughter or causing death by reckless driving, and on either charge there may be a conviction of reckless driving.

4. Evidence by certificate

Several statutes enable evidence of certain matters to be given by certificate or written statement instead of calling witnesses to testify in court, providing the prescribed conditions are fulfilled. Those which have particular relevance to road traffic offences are as follows.

(1) Identity of driver, user, and/or owner of MV (certificate)

RTA 1972, s. 181

A certificate in the prescribed form signed by a constable that the person named therein stated to him that on a particular occasion a particular *motor vehicle:*

a) was being driven or used by that person or belonged to him, or

b) belonged to or was used by a firm of which he was partner, or

c) belonged to or was used by a corporation of which he was a director, officer or employee,

is admissible as evidence in any proceedings (summarily or on indictment) for any offence under this Act (with minor exceptions*) or any other Act relating to the use of motor vehicles (not pedal cycles) on a road.

> **Rathbone v Bundock (1962)**
> The section applies to all offences against regulations made under any Act mentioned in the section.

CONDITIONS OF ADMISSIBILITY—A copy of the certificate must be served (as in the case of a summons) at least 7 days before the trial, and provided the defendant has not later than 3 days (or such less time as the court may allow) before the hearing served notice requiring the attendance of the person who signed the certificate as a witness, it will be accepted as evidence in the absence of the witness.

(2) RTA 1960, s. 232

This section makes similar provision to that of the 1972 Act, s. 181 (above) in relation to offences re PSVs, operators' licences, and drivers' hours.

(3) Identity of driver: by his written statement

1972 Act s. 183

On proof (on oath) that the defendant was served with a requirement under this section to give information as to the identity of the driver (or rider of a pedal cycle) concerned in any offence under the RTA 1972, or any other Act (or regulations made thereunder) relating to the use of a vehicle on a road, a statement in writing purporting to be signed by the accused is admissible as evidence (on summary trial only) that he was the driver on that occasion.

---

* Such as weak bridges, obstructing vehicle examiner, goods vehicle driver not present during test, use of GV with unauthorised weight marked.

NOTE
The RTA 1960, s. 243, applies on the same lines concerning offences relating to PSVs, operators' licences and drivers' hours.

(4) Analyst's certificate (drink or drug)

I) UNFIT THROUGH DRINK OR DRUGS—On a charge of driving, attempting to drive or being in charge of a MV while unfit through drink or drug, a certificate purporting to be signed by an authorised analyst, certifying the proportion of alcohol or drug found in a specimen identified by the certificate (and, re a specimen not being blood, the proportion of alcohol or drug in the blood which corresponds to the proportion found in the specimen) is admissible as evidence of those matters and of the qualifications of the analyst (s. 10).

An 'authorised analyst' is one qualified to become a public analyst for purposes of the Food and Drugs Act or other person authorised by the Secretary of State for the purposes of this section (e.g. analysts at the Home Office Forensic Science Laboratories).

II) THE SECTION 6 OFFENCE

a) Section 10 applies also to an offence of driving, attempting to drive or being in charge of a MV with the proportion of alcohol in the blood above the prescribed limit, but the certificate is required to state only the proportion of alcohol found in the specimen of blood or urine, and not, in the case of urine, to certify as well what the equivalent would be in blood.

b) A certificate purporting to be signed by a doctor that he took a specimen of blood from a person with his consent, is evidence of this and of the doctor's qualifications (s. 10).

III) CONDITIONS OF ADMISSIBILITY—As for RTA 1972, s. 181 (see para. (1) above).

(5) Driving instruction

RTA 1972, s. 138

A certificate stating as follows and purporting to be signed by the Registrar (acting for the S of S) is sufficient evidence of the facts stated therein and, unless the defence prove the contrary, that it was signed by him. The facts are that:

a) a person's name was, or was not, in the register;

b) a person's name was entered in or removed from the register;

c) a person was, or was not, the holder of a current licence to give instruction in driving MV for payment;

d) a licence in (c) was granted to a person, came into force or ceased to be of effect.

(6) Plans or drawings

CJA 1948, s. 41

A plan or drawing of any place (e.g. scene of a road accident) and of the relative position of any objects shown thereon (e.g. the vehicles, skidmarks, etc.) is admissible as evidence in any criminal proceedings if certified by the constable or person having the prescribed qualifications who made it that it is correctly drawn to scale.

A 'person having the prescribed qualifications' is a registered architect or member of the Royal Institution of Chartered Surveyors, Institute of Civil or Municipal Engineers or Land Agents Society.

CONDITIONS OF ADMISSIBILITY—The same as for RTA 1972, s. 181 (see para. (1) above).

(7) Service of certificates

The copy of a certificate may be served upon the defendant as in the case of a summons, i.e.:

a) for a corporation—by addressing it to and leaving it at, or sending it by registered post or recorded delivery service to the registered office or the principal office or place of business; or

b) in any other case—by delivering it personally or by addressing it to the alleged offender and leaving it at or sending it by registered post or recorded delivery service to his last or most usual place of abode or place of business.

NOTE
The above instances of proving certain matters relating to road traffic by certificate are exceptions to the general rule that all facts which have to be proved at a criminal trial must be proved by oral evidence given at the trial. For other exceptions which are admissible at common law (e.g. entries in public documents) or by statutory declaration see *Police Promotion Handbook 2: Criminal Evidence and Procedure,* re 'Documentary Evidence'.

(8) Documents connected with licensing, etc.

Statements of certain documents which are authenticated as being part of official records maintained concerning vehicles and licences by the S of S or a licensing authority, as the case may be, copies of such documents and notes of information in those records, are admissible in proceedings (civil and criminal) as evidence of the facts stated to the same extent as oral evidence of those facts would be. The documents which can be admitted in evidence in this way include (in connection with licensing of drivers, registration and licensing and the plating and testing regulations) applications (and documents relating to them), licences, certificates, plates or discs; convictions of offences connected with, and orders relating to, endorsements and disqualifications, and declarations as to exemption from excise duty (1972 Act, s. 182, and Vehicles

(Excise) Act 1971, s. 31). Section 13 of the RTA 1974 added a new subsection (2A) to s. 182 which provides that wherever a statement as is referred to above specifies a previous conviction and the court is satisfied that not less than 7 days' notice was served on the accused (as provided by s. 15 of the Justices of the Peace Act 1949) that the conviction would be put before the court on, or in view of, conviction, then, if the accused does not appear, the court may take account of it as if the accused had appeared and admitted it.

5. Traffic wardens

Section 81 of the RTR Act 1967 authorises the appointments by a police authority of persons (known as 'traffic wardens') to aid the police in duties normally undertaken by the police in connection with the control and regulation of traffic and the enforcement of road traffic law. Wardens are to be under the direction of the COP but employed by the police authority. Traffic wardens cannot be employed on functions other than those declared appropriate by an Order of the Secretary of State. Constables cannot be so appointed.

The Functions of Traffic Wardens Order 1970 provides:

a) Wardens may be employed to enforce the law with respect to the following offences:
   i) vehicles left or parked without obligatory lights or reflectors;
   ii) obstruction, waiting, being left or parked, or being loaded or unloaded in any road or public place unlawfully;
   iii) contravening the Vehicles (Excise) Act 1971;
   iv) offences relating to parking places on highways where charges are made;
   v) drivers or pedestrians failing to comply with traffic directions (1972 Act, ss. 22 and 23).

   Where a warden reasonably believes that any of the above offences has been committed he has the power of a constable under 1972 Act, s. 162 (1) (see p. 174) as to furnishing names and addresses.

b) Wardens may be employed to exercise functions of constables in connection with fixed penalty offences, except
   i) obstruction, or
   ii) leaving in dangerous position.

c) They may be employed:
   i) to act as parking attendants at street parking places*;
   ii) to exercise functions conferred on them by a traffic order or street parking place order, or in connection with the custody of vehicles removed under 1967 Act, s. 20 (see p. 311) or from a street parking place;

---

* Provided by the LA or the S of S.

iii) to act as school crossing patrols;

iv) to control and regulate traffic (including foot passengers) or vehicles (on highway or not) and to carry out other functions of this kind normally undertaken by the police, but this does not apply to a warden who is in a moving vehicle.

d) References to constable include references to a traffic warden in enactments relating to:

i) compliance by drivers and pedestrians with traffic directions, and the power to obtain names and addresses of pedestrians failing to comply;

ii) giving evidence of an admission by certificate.

e) References to constable in s. 161 (production of driving licence and offence of failing to produce) include a warden only where he is employed in connection with the custody of vehicles removed under 1967 Act, s. 20 (see (c) (ii) above), and where he reasonably believes any offence in (a) (ii) has been committed *on a road*.

6. 'Fixed penalty' procedure

RTR Act 1967, s. 80

NOTE

This section applies in any area only if an order by the S of S has extended the section to it. The order may exclude a particular offence.

a) This section relates only to the following offences committed in respect of a vehicle:

i) by its being without 'obligatory' lights or reflectors on a road during the hours of darkness;

ii) by its obstructing a road, or waiting, or being left or parked, or being loaded or unloaded in a road;

iii) by the non-payment of a charge made at a *street* parking place;

iv) by failing to exhibit vehicle excise licence;

v) by contravention of any traffic regulation order prescribing routes to be followed, or roads not to be used, or prohibiting U turns;

vi) by contravention of a C & U regulation specified by an order of the S of S.

b) Where a constable finds any person on any 'occasion' in respect of which he has reason to believe that the person is committing or has committed an offence referred to in (a) above, he may give him the prescribed written notice offering him the opportunity to discharge any liability to conviction by payment of a fixed penalty, which is £6 or one-half of the maximum fine whichever is the less. The amount of £6 can be varied by order of the Secretary of State.

c) If offender is not with the vehicle on the 'occasion', the constable can affix a notice to the vehicle and it shall be deemed to be given to the person liable. Removal or interference with the notice by any person other than the driver, person in charge or person liable for the offence is a summary offence.

d) If the fixed penalty is paid within 21 days of the date of the notice (or any longer period specified in it) or before date on which proceedings are begun (whichever is latest) liability to conviction ceases.

e) No proceedings can be taken until end of 21 days from date of notice (or the longer period, if any, stated in it).

f) The notice must specify the offence and give particulars of the circumstances alleged to constitute the offence, the period during which proceedings will not be taken, the amount of fixed penalty and the justices' clerk to whom penalty is to be paid.

g) Traffic wardens who have been appointed to enforce this section have the same powers as constables in respect of it.

h) Police responsibilities under the Fixed Penalty (Procedure) (No. 2) Regulations 1974 are:

i) to forward to the appropriate justices' clerk (unless he notifies the COP that he does not require it) and to the LA of the area in which the offence was committed (if the LA has notified the COP that it wishes this) a copy of the notice given or affixed;

ii) where proceedings are taken by a constable or a traffic warden, to give notice as soon as practicable to the justices' clerk, who must not, after such notice, accept payment of the fixed penalty.

LIABILITY OF OWNER—By s. 1 of the RTA 1974 liability in respect of offences (a) (i) to (iv) above (except 'obstruction' in (ii)) may be extended to the vehicle owner. The section will apply in these cases if the fixed penalty (FP) notice has been given or affixed and the FP has not been paid within the 14 days. If the s. 1 procedure is carried out it is to be conclusively presumed (in proceedings against the owner) that the owner (even if a corporate body) was the driver and the acts or omissions of the driver were his. To bring this about the prescribed notice must be served by or for the COP within 6 months of the giving or affixing of the FP notice. The notice must give particulars of the offence and the penalty concerned, and provide that unless the FP is paid within 14 days (or such longer period as is stated) the person is required to furnish to the COP:

a) *a statutory statement of ownership*, and

b) *a statutory statement of facts*.

The former is a statement in prescribed form, signed by the maker, stating whether he was the owner at the relevant time and, if not, whether he was the owner before or after this time and, if known, particulars of the person to whom or from whom the vehicle was transferred and the date. The latter is a statement in prescribed form that the person making it was the driver at the time and signed by him, or that the person was not the driver but giving the name and address of the person who was the driver—signed both by the statement maker and the stated driver. Failure (unless the FP is paid in time) without reasonable excuse to furnish the statutory statement of ownership is an offence*, as is also recklessly or knowingly furnishing a statement which is false in a material particular. 'Prescribed' means prescribed by regulations. 'Owner' is the person by whom the vehicle is kept and it is to be presumed (until proved otherwise) that the owner was the person in whose name the vehicle was registered. 'Service' can be by direct delivery, leaving at proper address, or sending by post.

APPLICATION OF ABOVE TO A VEHICLE-HIRE FIRM (RTA 1974, s. 3)—Where a notice under s. 1 (or s. 2 as to excess parking charge) has been served on a vehicle-hire firm and at the relevant time the vehicle was let on hire under a hiring agreement, the firm must furnish the COP (or S of S in case of s. 2) a statement in prescribed form, signed by or for the firm and stating that this was so, together with a copy of the hiring agreement and a copy of a statement of liability (in which the hirer acknowledges liability as owner while the hiring lasts for any FP offence or excess parking charge to which these sections apply) in prescribed form signed by the hirer. If this is done the notice is complied with and s. 1 (or s. 2) applies as if hirer were owner, and as if the statement of hiring were a statement of ownership. Where these copies have been furnished a person authorised by the COP (or S of S under s. 2) may at any reasonable time within 6 months after the service of the notice (on producing authority) require the firm to produce the originals. Failure to do so without reasonable excuse renders the firm liable for non-compliance with the s. 1 (or s. 2) notice. The section applies to a hiring agreement for a fixed period less than 6 months (extendable or not) and the currency of the agreement includes any period beyond the expiry date during which the hirer retained possession as hirer with the consent of the firm.

NOTE
A statutory statement or statement of liability furnished as above and purporting to be signed by the accused is presumed to have been so signed (unless contrary is proved) and evidence of facts therein tending to show the accused was the owner, the hirer or driver at a particular time.

7. Registration and licensing of driving instructors

RTA 1972, Part V

(1) Introduction

The Act authorises the S of S to compile and maintain a register of approved instructors and to make regulations relating to their registration, title, fees, employment etc. The main purpose is to ensure that driving instruction for payment is given only by registered or licensed persons.

---

* But payment of the FP by any person before date of proceedings discharges the liability; conviction of any person for the offence specified in the notice discharges the liability of any other person for the original offence and the liability for failure to furnish; conviction for failure to furnish discharges liability of any person for the FP offence.

(2) Offences

Section 126

It is an offence for any person not in the register of approved instructors or the holder of a current licence under the Act:

a) to give driving instruction for payment of money or money's worth, or

b) to employ an instructor as in (a) above.

Instruction given free of charge by or for a car salesman or dealer to a non-licence holder or provisional licence holder in connection with the supply of a motor car in the course of business is deemed to be payment of money.

DEFENCE—It is a defence for the alleged offender to prove that he did not know and had no reason to believe that he (or the instructor employed by him) was not registered at the time.

EXEMPTIONS (s. 127)—The above offences do not apply to a 'police instructor' giving instructions under arrangements made by the COP, or under the authority of the COP in pursuance of arrangements made by a LA (council of a county, or of a London borough, or the GLC or Common Council of the City of London). 'Police instructor' means

a) a police officer whose duties are (or include or included) the giving of driving instruction to members of a police force, or

b) a civilian so employed by the police authority.

(3) Registration

Section 128

The register is compiled and maintained by a 'Registrar' acting on behalf of the S of S and an applicant for inclusion of his name on the register (subject to the prescribed fee) must satisfy the following conditions:

a) pass an examination (as specified by regulations according to the class of person) of his ability to give driving instruction;

b) be the holder of a current British driving licence or a licence issued in Northern Ireland (not provisional), *and* at no time during the 6 years preceding the application not have held *either:*
i) a current licence (British or N Ireland) as above, or
ii) a driving licence of a country outside the UK authorising driving in that country, *or*
iii) a provisional licence, having passed the driving test;

c) not have been disqualified during 4 years preceding the application for holding or obtaining a licence;

d) be a fit and proper person.

A registered instructor may be required at any time by the registrar to undergo a test of his ability and fitness to give driving instruction.

An instructor similarly registered under the law of Northern Ireland if resident in GB is exempted from the examination in (a) above.

The registrar must give notice in writing of the grounds of his refusal to register an applicant.

(4) Re-registration

Sections 128 and 129

Registration normally lasts *for 4 years* (to the last day of the month of expiry), and at the end of this period a person's name is removed from the register unless he makes application (and pays the prescribed fee) for continued registration and satisfies the registrar that:

a) he has not refused to undergo a test when so required during his period of registration;

b) his ability and fitness to give driving instruction, subject to the result of any test he has undergone, continues to be satisfactory;

c) he holds a current driving licence of one of the kinds referred to in (3) (b) above;

d) he has not been disqualified from holding a licence; and

e) he continues to be a fit and proper person.

NOTES
The retention of an instructor's name on the register is subject to his obligation to undergo a prescribed test if and when so required by the registrar.

The registrar must give notice in writing of a refusal to re-register (and the grounds for refusal) and allow 28 days in which the applicant may make representations with respect to the proposed refusal before it will take effect. If no appeal is made to the S of S the registration ceases 28 days after the day on which the notice was given, but if an appeal is made, only after the appeal is either withdrawn or dismissed. The same considerations and procedure will apply on each occasion that an instructor applies for retention of his name on the register in respect of each successive period of 4 years.

(5) Removal from register

Section 130

The registrar may remove from the register the name of any person:

a) in respect of whom any of the conditions in para. (4) (above) ceases to apply, or

b) who fails to pass a test, or

c) whose registration was obtained or continued by mistake or fraud.

The procedure requires the registrar first to serve a notice in writing of his intention (allowing 28 days in which to receive and to consider any representations made by the person concerned), and then (if he pursues the removal of the name) a second notice in writing specifying the date on which the removal will take effect, again allowing 28 days in which an appeal can be made.

(6) Licences

Section 131

I) GRANT AND REFUSAL—To enable an applicant to obtain practice in giving driving instruction for the purpose of undergoing an examination to qualify for registration, the registrar must grant a licence (subject to payment of the fee and such conditions (e.g. as to duration) as may be prescribed by regulations) authorising him to give driving instruction for payment, if he is qualified otherwise than by passing the test (see para. (3)). If at least two such licences have been issued the registrar may refuse to grant a further licence but must give notice in writing stating the grounds for refusal, and allow 14 days for representations, before the final notice of refusal is given.

II) REVOCATION—A licence may be revoked if the holder:

a) fails to comply with the conditions of the regulations concerning the licence, or

b) is not the holder of any of the qualifying driving licences, or

c) has been disqualified for holding or obtaining a licence, or

d) has ceased to be a fit and proper person, or

e) obtained the licence by mistake or fraud.

The registrar must give notices in writing as in the case of a refusal to renew (see para. (I)).

(7) Appeals

Section 132

All appeals against decisions of the registrar have to be made to the S of S.

The S of S may either allow an appeal or confirm the decision and in each case by order prohibit appellant from applying for a licence or for registration within a prescribed period up to 4 years.

(8) Surrender of licences, etc.

Section 136

The registrar may by written notice require the surrender of a certificate of registration issued to a person whose name is removed from the register or to whom a licence was issued if it has expired or has been revoked. It is offence (£50) if such person fails to return the certificate or licence within 14 days of the day (inclusive) on which this notice is given.

(9) Production

Section 137

A constable or person authorised in writing by the S of S may require the holder of a certificate or a licence to produce it for examination, but failure to do so is not an offence if it is produced *within 5 clear days:*

a) *when so required by a constable*—at such police station specified by the person at the time of request, or

b) *if required by an authorised person*—at such place specified by that authorised person at the time of request.

(10) Seizure

Where the person is the holder of a certificate or licence in respect of which a notice to surrender has been given by the registrar, the constable or authorised person may seize the document upon it being produced and deliver it to the registrar.

(11) Motor Cars (Driving Instruction) Regulations 1977

The regulations provide procedures relating to applications for examination of ability to give instruction, the syllabus for each part of the examination (written and practical), exemptions from examination, and the form of the certificate of registration, which specifies the period of validity of the certificate.

(12) Offences

Section 135

A person is guilty of an offence if he:

a) takes or uses a title prescribed for registered persons when his name is not in the register;

b) wears or displays a badge or certificate or uses any other means implying he is a registered instructor;

c) carries on the business of instructor in driving of MVs and uses any title or description or issues any advertisement or invitation calculated to mislead with respect to his employees or the extent to which registered instructors are employed by him,

unless in each case he proves that he had no reasonable cause to believe that his name, or that of his employee, as the case may be, was not in the register.

NOTE

A corporation may be guilty of an offence under the Act; when committed with the consent of or by neglect of a responsible officer or official of the company, he is liable to prosecution as well as the body corporate.

(13) Evidence by certificate

Section 138

A certificate purporting to be signed by the registrar is admissible in evidence without further proof, unless the defence prove that it is not so signed, and is sufficient proof of the facts stated therein in respect of the holder of a certificate or a licence. For further details, see p. 286.

8. Approval marks

NOTE

This subject is not listed in the syllabuses but is included for general information relating to references to approval marks in other road traffic subjects.

Where an international agreement involving the UK provides for markings on MV parts to indicate conformity with an approved type and acceptance by the law of another country, regulations may be made designating such approval marks. It is an offence under the Trade Descriptions Act 1968 for any unauthorised person to apply such an approval mark or any mark so resembling an approval mark as to be calculated to deceive. An approval mark consists, generally, of a circle inside which appears the reference number allotted to the country in which made, and outside which appears a mark (usually a reference number) enabling the manufacturer to be identified. Approval marks are at present introduced as alternatives to other statutory markings (e.g. obligatory rear lamps can be marked with the appropriate approval mark instead of (inter alia) the British Standard mark BS 2516) but in the near future approval marks will become a compulsory mark on an increasing range of components, e.g.

a) the approval mark for rear lamps will become compulsory on most vehicles made post 1st January 1973;

b) certain passenger vehicles first used after 1st July 1972 will have to display an approval mark to indicate that side doors are fitted with latches and hinges of approved strength, and another mark to indicate conformity with international standards regarding protective types of steering mechanism;

c) direction indicators of vehicles first used post 1st July 1973 will have to bear a specified approval mark, plus a number according to whether it is a front (1), rear (2b), side (3), shoulder (4) or flank (5) indicator.

d) Seats, seat belts and anchorage points will have to bear approval marks according to type, and to date of manufacture, registration or fitting.

9. Proceedings: limitation of time

The general rule for summary offences is that proceedings must be taken within 6 months of the date of the commission of the offence, but in relation to the offences stated below summary proceedings may be brought within 6 months of the date* on which evidence sufficient in the opinion of the prosecutor to warrant proceedings came to his knowledge, but no such proceedings can be brought by virtue of this section more than 3 years after the commission of the offence (1972 Act, s. 180; 1971 Act, s. 28).

1960 Act

s. 233 ⎫
s. 235 ⎬ forgery, alterations and false statements.

1972 Act

s. 99—obtain driving licence while disqualified.
s. 143—use MV without insurance.
s. 169 ⎫
s. 170 ⎬ forgery, alteration, false statements or withholding information, issue
s. 171 ⎭ of false documents, etc.

1968 Act

s. 99 (5)—false entries, etc. in relation to DRBs and DRB registers.

1971 Act

s. 8—unlicensed MV.
s. 16—trade licence (use unauthorised MV or for purpose not prescribed).
s. 18—higher rate of duty payable.
s. 26—forgery or fraud, etc. in connection with vehicle excise licence, registration document or marks.

---

* A certificate signed by or on behalf of the prosecutor stating this date is conclusive evidence of this fact, and shall be deemed to be properly signed unless the contrary is proved.

1974 Act

s.1 ⎱ false statutory statement re ownership in fixed penalty and parking
s.2 ⎰ charges cases.

10. Forgery and deceit

Forgery

RTA 1960, s. 233 and s. 234

It is an offence, with intent to deceive, to:

a) forge, alter, or use, or lend to or allow to be used by any other person any document or thing to which the section applies, or

b) make or possess any document or thing so closely resembling a document or thing to which the section applies as to be calculated to deceive (s. 233), or

c) alter an entry in any record relating to a PSV contract carriage journey (s. 234).

Section 233 applies to any licence under the Act; any document, plate or mark identifying an authorised vehicle under Part V of the Transport Act 1968; any document evidencing an appointment (e.g. examiner) under the said Part V; and any road service licence or permit under the 1968 Act.

RTRA 1967, s. 86

The offences are as set out in RTA 1960, s. 233 (above) but relate to parking meter tickets, any certificate or authorisation under a TRO, or any permit or token issued under a designation order (authorising making charges for parking).

Transport Act 1968

Permits and road service licences issued under this Act are covered by the RTA 1960 (see above).

Vehicles (Excise) Act 1971, s. 26

It is an offence to forge or fraudulently alter or use or fraudulently lend or allow to be used by any other person any registration mark or any trade plate (or replacement) or any licence or registration document under the Act.

RTA 1972, s. 169

Offences correspond to s. 233 of the 1960 Act (see above) and apply to documents or things required by the 1972 Act, e.g. licences, evidence of insurance or of the result of a driving test, any badge or plating plate, and any records required to be kept.

False statements and withholding information: offences

RTA 1960, s. 235

It is an offence, in respect of any licence under the Act, to knowingly make a false statement for the purpose of obtaining grant or variation, or preventing grant or variation, or procuring the imposition of a condition or limitation.

RTA 1972, s. 170

It is an offence

a) knowingly to make a false statement for the purpose of:
   i) obtaining a licence under the Act (for self or another), or
   ii) preventing grant of such a licence, or
   iii) procuring imposition of a condition or limitation, or
   iv) securing registration of any person on the register of approved driving instructors, or
   v) obtaining grant of an international road haulage permit (for self or another);

b) in supplying information or producing any document as required by the Act (or regulations under it) knowingly (or recklessly) to make a false statement*, or knowingly (or recklessly) produce, furnish or otherwise make use of a false document*;

c) knowingly to produce false evidence (or make false statement in a declaration) for purpose of obtaining an excise licence;

d) knowingly to make a false statement in a certificate or declaration under s. 54 as to remedying defects found on test;

e) wilfully to make a false statement in any record required to be kept under the Act or, with intent to deceive, make use of any such entry known to be false;

f) to make a false statement or withhold material information to obtain the issue of a certificate of insurance or security or any document which may be produced in lieu of such a certificate.

RTA 1972, s. 171

It is an offence to issue any document included in (f) above or a test certificate or certificate of conformity which is known to be false in a material particular.

---

* I.e. one false in a material particular.

Personation of authorised person

RTA 1972, s. 174

It is an offence with intent to deceive falsely to represent oneself to be or to be employed by a person authorised to act as an examiner under the Act,

As to powers of seizure see p. 318.

11. Invalid carriages and disabled persons

(1) Definitions and restrictions

a) For the purposes of the RT Acts and the RTR Act 1967 an IC is a MPV specially designed and constructed (not merely adapted) for the use of a person suffering from some physical defect or disability and used solely by such a person, the u/w of the vehicle n/e 5 cwts*.

NOTE

It is important to note that an IC which conforms to specified requirements (see **(2)** below) is not a MV for the purposes of these Acts, nor subject to the lighting requirements of the 1972 Act.

RESTRICTIONS OF PARTICULAR APPLICATION—

a) not to draw a trailer;

b) speed limit is 20 mph;

c) minimum age for driving licence is 16 years, but in this case the u/w limit is raised to 10 cwts.;

d) C & U Regulations apply to width, brakes and wings.

b) For the purpose of the Special Roads Act 1949 and Highways Act 1959 the definition of an IC is the same as in **(a)** above. The Acts relate to motorways, from the use of which an IC is excluded.

c) For the purposes of the Vehicles (Excise) Act 1971 an IC is not referred to or defined, but exemption from duty (though not from registration) extends to a vehicle n/e 10 cwt in u/w and which is adapted, and used or kept, on a road, for invalids.

d) For the purposes of the Chronically Sick and Disabled Persons Act 1970 see below.

---

* 10 cwts for purposes of driving licences and taxation: see p. 278 concerning weights relating to test certificates.

(2) Chronically Sick and Disabled Persons Act 1970

By s. 20 of this Act an invalid carriage complying with prescribed requirements and conditions is *not:*

a) subject to any prohibition or restriction on the use of footways;

b) a MV under the RT Acts or the RTR Act 1967 (though it is a vehicle and within provisions relating to vehicles generally, e.g. as to conformity with traffic signs and signals);

c) whether a MV or not, subject to the RTA 1972 with regard to lighting requirements.

The conditions and requirements referred to above are provided by the Use of Invalid Carriages on Highways Regulations 1970, as follows:

a) the IC is used only by an invalid or by another person in connection with its maintenance and repair;

b) the following conditions with regard to u/w, brakes, speed and lighting are fulfilled.

I) UNLADEN WEIGHT—n/e 250 lbs.

II) SPEED—so constructed as to be incapable of exceeding 4 mph on level under own power.

III) BRAKES—if a MV, must bring vehicle to rest within a reasonable distance and the parking brake must be such that it can be kept 'on' by direct mechanical action, have no hydraulic, electric or pneumatic device in it, and be able to hold the IC stationary on a gradient of at least 1 in 5.
Every part of the braking system and its means of operation must be maintained in good and efficient working order and properly adjusted.
If the IC has no such braking system the alternative is that IC must be so designed and constructed that by using its engine and transmission gear it can be brought to rest within reasonable distance and held stationary on a 1 in 5 gradient.

IV) LIGHTING: OBLIGATORY LIGHTS AND REFLECTOR—as for bicycles, but no lights needed if on carriageway only to cross the carriageway in the quickest manner practicable. The lamps must be kept properly trimmed, lighted and in a clean and efficient condition, and must (with the reflector) comply with the following requirements:

a) *Lamps* (to be marked with BS 3648 and means of identification of maker):
i) *front*—on centre line or offside;
ii) *rear*—centre line or offside, not more than 20 inches from rear, not more than 3 foot 6 inches or less than 12 inches from the ground;

b) *Reflector*—As for rear light, except that lamp marking is AU 40 followed by 'LI' or 'LIA', or the appropriate approval mark.

(3) Local Authorities Traffic Orders (Exemptions for Disabled Persons) (England and Wales) Regulations 1971 (as amended)

I) EXEMPTIONS—DISPLAY OF DISABLED PERSON'S BADGE—The regulations require any traffic order made by a LA which:

a) prohibits waiting of vehicles beyond specified periods, or

b) prohibits the use of any street parking place beyond a specified period, or

c) prescribes charges and time limits for the use of a parking place on any highway,

to include in the order exemptions for vehicles used by disabled persons if the vehicle displays in the 'relevant position' a disabled person's badge issued by *any* local authority.

II) EXEMPTION FOR WHICH BOTH BADGE AND A PARKING DISC ARE REQUIRED—Regulation 3 (1A) and (1B) also provides an exemption in relation to any order which:

a) prohibits waiting during specified periods except for loading and unloading, and

b) does not apply to a bus lane when the bus lane restriction is operating, and

c) is not an order mentioned in para. (I) (a) above.

In this case the exemption applies:

a) where the period of prohibition is 2 hours or less—for the whole period, and

b) if for more than 2 hours—for a period of 2 hours, not being separated by an interval of less than 1 hour from a previous period of waiting by the same vehicle, in the same road (or part), on the same day.

To obtain this exemption not only must the badge be properly displayed on the vehicle, but where the prohibition is for more than two hours duration a parking disc (orange colour and capable of showing the quarter hour period when waiting begins) issued by the LA must be displayed in a 'relevant position' on the vehicle and the driver (or other person in charge) must have marked on the disc the time the waiting period began.

III) RELEVANT POSITION—This means:

a) if vehicle is fitted with a front windscreen—exhibited thereon with obverse side facing forwards on near side of and immediately behind the windscreen, or

b) if no such screen—exhibited in a conspicuous position on the vehicle.

IV) LOCAL AUTHORITY REGISTER—Each LA has to keep a register showing the holders of badges and the vehicles for which each of the badges is held.

12. Type approvals

NOTE
This subject is not listed in the examination syllabuses, but is included in relation to plates on vehicles.

The Secretary of State can by regulations give 'type approval' to particular classes or types of vehicles. The general principle is that a manufacturer may submit to him a type vehicle which conforms with legal requirements relating to design, construction, equipment, markings etc. and seek type approval. If type approval is given for that vehicle the manufacturer can issue in respect of other vehicles which conform with the type vehicle a manufacturer's certificate stating that they conform and specifying requisite weights, which are to be marked on a plate on the vehicle. The Secretary of State can, where there is no manufacturer's certificate, provide the type approval required. See also p. 245 as to the extension of 'type approvals' to EEC vehicles, and exemptions from the C and U Regulations 1978.

Chapter 21 **Various powers provided under the Road Traffic Acts**

1. Summary

The following summary of the main powers provided under the RT Acts is not claimed to be complete but it is designed to provide students with the opportunity of considering the legal position by bringing together all the main powers under one heading. Most of them have been dealt with in earlier chapters, but those which have not been covered earlier and call for greater detail are marked* and are included later in this chapter.

(1) Of the S of S†

a) *To make regulations* in accordance with the provisions of the many sections of the Acts giving him this power.

b) *To be the highway authority* in respect of trunk roads and special roads, e.g. as to speed limits, erection and maintenance of signs, entry on land to remove signs.

c) *To publish the Highway Code*, and to revise it as necessary.

d) *To consider orders for the regulation of traffic* (including pedestrian crossing schemes) made by local authorities and for which his consent is needed (see para (2) below).

e) *To hold public enquiry* where the Acts require it, e.g. on application to modify local restrictions on bus services, on the making of a traffic regulation order.

f) *To remedy default by any local authority,* e.g. in providing, maintaining or removing traffic signs or pedestrian crossings, and to recover costs from the authority as a civil debt.

g) *To appoint officials* for the purposes of the Acts, e.g. to certify officers and examiners in respect of public service vehicles or to approve driving instructors.

---

† Not included in syllabuses.

h) *To authorise examiners* for testing of vehicles and issue of test certificates.

i) *To classify roads,* i.e. in a particular class or as a trunk road.

j) *To make orders* concerning trunk roads and special roads (i.e. motorways).

k) *To promote road safety,* e.g. by disseminating information or advice and providing financial aid to local authorities for this work.

(2) Of local authorities†

NOTE
None of the following relate to trunk roads or special roads, both of which are the responsibility of the S of S.

ALL LOCAL AUTHORITIES EXCEPT COUNTY COUNCILS

a) *Parking places* (see further p. 60):
i) to provide parking places and to make orders concerning their use;
ii) if on a highway, to apply to S of S for a designation order authorising charging of parking fees.

b) *Control of dogs*—to make order creating a 'designated road' (on which a dog must be on a lead).

COUNCILS OF COUNTIES AND DISTRICTS

a) To submit schemes for pedestrian crossings.

b) To make orders for provision of street playgrounds.

c) To make temporary orders (to regulate traffic) necessitated by road works or danger to public.

d) To permit (subject to conditions) a trailer drawn by a locomotive to carry weight in excess of regulations over a road or bridge of which the council is the authority.

e) To cause or permit approved traffic signs to be put on or near any road in their areas.

f) To procure removal of unauthorised traffic signs on or near roads in their areas.

g) To authorise motor vehicle trials on footpaths and bridleways for which they are authorities.

h) To pursue road safety measures including propaganda, training and contributing towards cost of such work by other bodies.

---

† Not included in syllabuses.

COUNCILS OF COUNTIES

a) To give directions by order making 'restricted roads' or de-restricting such roads.

b) To erect, maintain or remove traffic signs in connection with (a) above.

c) To make, with consent of the S of S, traffic regulation orders.

d) To make orders determining highways to be or not to be used by buses and for fixing bus stands.

GREATER LONDON COUNCIL

Powers similar to the above can be exercised by the GLC on roads other than trunk roads within its area, and its powers may even extend to trunk roads with the consent of the S of S.

(3) Of the Commissioners of Police

The Commissioners of Police (of the Metropolis and of London) may, with the consent of the Greater London Council, make regulations for experiments in traffic control in their areas and authorise any person to place on a highway or structure thereon certain authorised traffic signs.

(4) Of chief officers of police*

a) To give directions concerning movements of traffic with reference to pedal cycle races or speed trials on public highways.

b) To authorise any person to place on highways emergency traffic signs.

c) To authorise any person to place on a highway (or structure on it) certain traffic signs.

d) To extend period for which records re goods vehicles are to be kept.

e) To require evidence as to insurance cover.

f) To require information as to the driver of a vehicle on a particular occasion†.

g) To direct duties of traffic wardens and school crossing patrols.

(5) Of constables

a) To control traffic†.

b) To stop vehicles†.

---

* Commissioners of the MPD and City of London and chief constables of other forces.
† Dealt with later in this chapter.

c) To arrest without warrant*.

d) To require the weighing of vehicles*.

e) To inspect vehicles, particularly as regards brakes, steering gear, lighting equipment, etc.

f) To seize certain documents*.

g) In districts where and for offences to which this applies, to give notice offering offenders payment of a fixed penalty instead of prosecution.

h) To eject passengers from buses.

i) To put traffic signs on roads.

j) To require production of various documents (e.g. licences, insurance certificates, test certificate, goods vehicles records, RB etc.).

2. To control traffic and stop vehicles

(1) While on duty regulating traffic

RTA 1972, ss. 22 and 23

1) ALL VEHICLES (S. 22)—It is an offence for any person driving or propelling *any* vehicle, on the direction of a constable for the time being engaged in the regulating of traffic on a road, to neglect or refuse to:

a) *stop*, or

b) make it *proceed in* or *keep to* a particular line of traffic.

NOTES

a) There is no provision that the constable should be in uniform, but in practice some evidence of knowledge of his official capacity would be required.

b) The section goes on to deal with failing to conform to certain traffic signs—see p. 89.

c) If the constable is on duty on a road the section applies to vehicles not on a road (e.g. coming from a field).

d) Section 18 of the RTA 1974 legalises the use of a flare for the purpose of regulating traffic by a constable or other person acting under his authority. A flare is a firework or other device designed to produce light by combustion.

---

* Dealt with later in this chapter.

II) PEDESTRIANS (SS. 23 AND 165)—It is an offence for a pedestrian to proceed across or along a carriageway against the direction to stop of a constable *in uniform* regulating traffic, whether the direction is given to pedestrian only or pedestrians and other traffic (s. 23).

To fail to give name and address on the request of a constable is an offence in the case of a pedestrian committing an offence against s. 23.

As to traffic wardens on traffic duty, see p. 290.

(2) Not on traffic duty (MV and pedal cycles only)

RTA 1972, s. 159

Any person driving a MV or riding a *pedal cycle* on a road commits an offence if he fails to stop on being so required by a constable *in uniform*.

NOTES

The section does not apply to tramcars or trolley vehicles (though s. 22 does) nor to a pedestrian (though s. 23 does).

R v Waterfield (1964)

It is doubtful if the power (not being a duty) to stop includes power to require a stationary car not to move. In this case the driver was held not guilty of assaulting a constable in execution of his duty when trying to prevent a driver moving away because the officer was not acting under a duty by the section.

(3) For traffic surveys

RTA 1972, s. 22A

If such a survey is carried out on or in the vicinity of a road a traffic direction given by a constable for the purposes of the survey is a direction given by him in execution of duty and in the regulation of traffic under s. 22. Traffic direction (for this section) includes a direction to a particular point on or near the road, but does not include requiring any person to furnish information for the purpose of the survey. The traffic direction must not be used so as to cause unreasonable delay to anyone who is unwilling to furnish survey information. As to traffic sign see p. 93.

3. Removal and disposal of vehicles abandoned, etc.

Refuse Disposal (Amenity) Act 1978, ss. 3–5

Empowers a LA to remove and dispose of 'dumped' vehicles and parts of vehicles and trailers, and to recover costs. As to offence of 'dumping' see *Police Promotion Handbook 3: General Police Duties.*

RTR Act 1967, s. 20

Regulations can be made concerning the removal and disposal by the police or LA of stationary vehicles which appear to have been abandoned, or are causing obstruction or danger, or are otherwise offending against specified legal provisions.

Removal and Disposal of Vehicles Regulations 1968

(1) Requirement to remove

Regulation 3*

a) The power relates to *any* vehicle which has broken down, or has been permitted to remain at rest on a road:
   i) in such position, condition or circumstances as to cause obstruction or be likely to cause danger to other road users, or
   ii) in contravention of any offence specified in the Schedule to the regulations.

b) *The Schedule* specifies the following offences: obstruction of highway; failing to conform to traffic signs, including signs placed by police under statutory powers; contraventions of traffic regulation orders; contravention of traffic orders re road works or experimental traffic orders; breaches of motorway regulations or regulations concerning pedestrian crossings; offences re parking places on roads for payment; or any breaches of any local Act similar to the above.

c) A constable may require the owner, driver, or other person in charge or control of any vehicle (as in (a)) to move it or cause it to be moved and include a direction as to any road or position to which it shall not be moved.

d) Failure to comply as soon as practicable is an offence under RTR Act, s. 87.

(2) Power to remove or procure removal

Regulation 4*

This power of a constable applies to any vehicle referred to above and also to any vehicle which from being broken down or from being permitted to remain on a road or on any land in the open air without lawful authority, or from any other circumstances, appears to him to have been abandoned.

NOTE

a) Removal may be by driving, towing or other means thought necessary (reg. 6).

* Regs. 3, 4 and 5 do not apply to the Severn Bridge.

b) The removal may be to a place off the road or to another position on that or any other road.

c) Reg. 5* gives power to a LA to remove (as for constable) but removal must be to place not on a road.

d) The cost of removal is recoverable as a civil debt and, if reasonable care is taken, no action lies for damage caused.

e) *If on occupied land* removal cannot be effected unless notice of intention has been served on occupier, and he has not, within 15 days of service of the notice, objected to the proposal in the manner prescribed by the regulations (Acts and reg. 9).

f) If purpose of removal is (on account of condition) to destroy the vehicle, then, unless the presence of the vehicle constitutes a statutory offence or an obstruction, or is a public danger, a notice of intention to destroy is to be fixed to the vehicle at least 7 days before removal (Acts and reg. 10).

(3) Safe custody

The Refuse Disposal (Amenity) Act 1978 (s. 3) and the RTR Act (s. 20) require a local authority which has removed or made arrangements for the removal of any vehicle to make reasonable arrangements for its safe custody.

(4) Disposal of abandoned vehicles

By RTR Act, s. 53, an apparently abandoned vehicle, which has been or could be removed as above or under an order relating to a parking place, can be disposed of by the COP or LA as thought fit:

a) *if vehicle is one to be destroyed*, at any time if it has no current excise licence displayed, but if such a licence is exhibited, after expiry of licence;

b) in any other case, after taking 'prescribed steps' to find the owner and either:
   i) failing to find him, or
   ii) if he has failed to comply with a notice served on him requiring removal of vehicle within the prescribed period (21 days from service of notice).

The 'prescribed steps' are set out in regs. 11–16 in detail, but are, briefly, as follows:

a) An enquiry with the relevant registration authority to trace the name and address of the owner must be made when the registration mark (if any) is known.

---

* Regs. 3, 4 and 5 do not apply to the Severn Bridge.

b) Notice must be served personally, non personally, or sent by registered post or recorded delivery to the apparent owner of the intention to dispose of the vehicle on or after a specified date unless removed from the place specified in the notice before that date. The specified date cannot be earlier than 3 weeks from date of notice.

c) Where there is no registration mark the authority wishing to dispose (COP or LA) must write to the other one (COP or LA) asking who he (or they) consider to be the ôwner and the address of that person.

d) If the above steps do not produce a claimant, further reasonable enquiries are to be made by the COP or LA as the case may be.

e) If information is received of any one who may be the owner the notice in (b) above must be sent to him.

f) Costs incurred in connection with the removal and disposal of a vehicle may be met out of the proceeds of a sale (if any) and the last owner of the vehicle (if known) is liable for any expenditure not recouped. Any sums in excess of the costs incurred must be reimbursed to the owner, but if not claimed within a year are paid accordingly into the police fund (by the police) or the general rate fund (by a local authority).

NOTES

If before disposal the owner turns up and pays costs of removal and storage he may be allowed to recover possession of the vehicle within the period prescribed (7 days). If vehicle is sold and within one year a person satisfies the authority concerned that he was 'its owner at time' of sale the authority must pay him the sale price minus expenses (within prescribed limits) incurred in removal, storage and sale. When a vehicle has been disposed of by the authority information as to disposal is to be given to specified parties, e.g. licensing authority, Hire Purchase Information Ltd, police, previous owner. 'Authority' is the COP of the area from which the vehicle has been or could be removed.

(5) Charges for removing and storing vehicles

The removal of any vehicle from a road under these regulations or from any parking place (whether free or for which a charge is made) under a designation order authorising the removal of an offending vehicle and its safe custody (see p. 312) introduces liability for the payment of the following charges, i.e.

a) *Removal*—from motorway £24; from place in London £22; in any other case £18.

b) *A charge for storage* of £2 for each 24 hours or part thereof and reckoned from noon on the day after the day of removal (Removal and Disposal of Vehicles Regulations 1968 (as amended), reg. 18).

c) *Disposal*—£6 (reg. 19).

These amounts are payable to the appropriate authority (i.e. the COP or LA, as the case may be) and are recoverable as a civil debt or summarily (if £20 or under). The COP or LA may retain the vehicle in custody until the appropriate charges have been paid.

The person made liable for these charges is—

a) *if abandoned*—the last owner of the vehicle (if known), unless he satisfies the authority that he was not responsible, *in which case liability lies as in (b) below*;

b) *in any other case*—the person driving the vehicle at the time it was left on the road or place.

4. Powers to arrest without warrant

The RT Acts provide powers to arrest without warrant to a constable in respect of *three* classes of offences only, as follows.

(1) Reckless or careless driving or cycling

1972 Act, s. 164

A constable may AWW:

a) the driver of any motor vehicle whom he *sees driving* on a road recklessly (s. 2) or inconsiderately or carelessly (s. 3), *unless* the driver:

   i) gives his name and address, *or*

   ii) produces his driving licence on demand;

b) the rider of a pedal cycle in respect of the same offences committed within his view, unless the rider gives his name and address.

NOTES

a) Where a driver or rider is alleged to have committed one of the above offences and is asked for his name or address *by any person* having reasonable grounds for requiring it, he commits an offence if he refuses to give his name or address or gives a false name or address. There is no power to AWW in respect of this offence only.

b) By the Prevention of Offences Act 1851, there is power to AWW *any* person 'found committing' an indictable offence in the night (reckless driving under s. 2 is an indictable offence).

(2) Drink or drug charges

I) OFFENCES UNDER THE RTA 1972—A constable may AWW for the offences of:

a) driving or attempting to drive, or being in charge of, a MV while unfit to drive through drink or drug—see p. 39;

b) riding a pedal cycle while unfit to so ride through drink or drug—see p. 51.

II) TO IMPLEMENT THE PROVISIONS OF 1972, ss. 8 and 9 (see p. 44)—A constable may AWW:

a) on positive roadside breath test;

b) for failing or refusing to undergo roadside test.

(3) Driving while disqualified

RTA 1972, s. 100

A constable in uniform may AWW any person driving or attempting to drive a MV on a road whom he reasonably suspects of being disqualified for holding or obtaining a driving licence (i.e. not only persons disqualified by courts but also those disqualified on age grounds).

5. Weighing of vehicles

RTA 1972, s. 160 (as amended)

A person authorised by a highway authority (a constable may be so authorised by a police authority or by a chief constable) can require a person in charge of a motor vehicle or trailer drawn thereby (laden or unladen) on a road, to allow it to be weighed at any weighing machine on producing the authority. It is an offence to refuse, but the person cannot be required to unload the vehicle to ascertain the unladen weight. The highway authority are responsible to pay for loss (determined by an agreed arbitrator) caused by the weighing if the vehicle has to proceed more than 1 mile to be weighed and the weight is found to be within the limits authorised by law.

After weighing, a weight ticket must be provided to the person to exempt the vehicle being reweighed on same journey with same load. A certifying officer or vehicle examiner appointed under the Act is empowered to exercise this authority on behalf of the S of S.

NOTE

As to GVs found to be overweight see p. 220, and as to foreign vehicles see chapter 23.

Under s. 14 of the RTA 1974 the following apply by virtue of amendments to s. 160:

a) to the offence of refusal to comply is added one of 'obstructing an authorised person in the exercise of his functions';

b) if an authorised person requires the person in charge of the vehicle to drive it or do anything to the vehicle or its load reasonably required for the weighing, refusal or neglecting to comply is an offence;

c) a weight certificate purporting to be signed by an authorised person and identifying the vehicle is evidence of the matter stated;

d) the driving or doing anything to vehicle or load authorised by the section does not subject the person to liability for loss or damage unless it is shown that he acted without reasonable care;

e) 'road' will include harbour land or land adjacent to a harbour and occupied wholly or partly for harbour operations.

6. Powers to require information

(1) Insurance enquiry

As to duties of owner/driver of MV; see p. 179.

(2) As to registration and licensing

See p. 137.

(3) From supervisor of 'L' driver

See p. 174.

(4) As to identity of driver*

Where a driver is alleged to have committed one of the offences referred to below:

RTR Act 1967, s. 85

a) *The person keeping the vehicle*—shall give such information as to the identity of the driver on that occasion as is required:
i) by or for a COP, or
ii) in case of offence in a local authority parking place—by the COP or, in writing, by or for the LA concerned, and

---

* Includes rider of a pedal cycle.

b) *any other person* (including the driver)—shall, if required as aforesaid, give such information as he can for this purpose.

Gray v Farrell (1969)
It is not necessary for a COP to give separate authority for each case. A general direction from the COP to each member of the force to act on his behalf is sufficient.

Failure to comply is an offence, but it is a defence in the case of (a) if owner satisfies court that he did not know and could not with reasonable diligence have found out who the driver or rider was.

RTA 1972, s. 168

Provisions as for RTR Act above except that the power to require information does not extend to a LA.

RTA 1960, s. 232

Provides similarly (as for RTR Act above), excluding the power of a LA, in relation to offences re PSVs, operators' licences, and drivers' hours.

THE RELEVANT OFFENCES ARE

a) As regards RTA 1972, s. 168 all offences against the 1972 Act (except Part V—driving instruction), and any other enactment relating to the use of vehicles on roads. *Exceptions*—Section does not apply to: offences with regard to obstructing an authorised examiner or other offences relating to testing vehicles on roads; offences relating to the use of goods vehicles under operators' licences*; forgery of documents; falsification of records; false statement to obtain licences, etc.; issue of false documents; promoting, etc., competitions and trials on highways; and driving with uncorrected eyesight.

b) As to RTR Act 1967, s. 85, all offences under the Act except those relating to weak bridges, plying for hire in parking places, removal from vehicle of fixed penalty notice, minimum speeds.

c) As to offences of refusing to give names and address, see:
   i) p. 39 as to cases of reckless and careless driving or cycling;
   ii) p. 310 as to offences by pedestrians failing to comply with traffic directions of constable in uniform.

All provisions relating to production of documents (driving licences, insurance certificates, test certificates, etc.) are for the purpose of making available the information contained in them.

---

* There are two exceptions to this. The section applies to using a goods vehicle without an OL and using a GV while a prohibition (as being unfit) by any examiner is in force.

7. Power to seize documents, etc.

RTA 1972, s. 173

(1) Documents produced to constable

Where any document is produced to a constable *under any legal requirement of the Act* (except records to be carried on goods vehicles†) and the constable has reasonable cause to believe that one of the offences against ss. 169–171 of the Act and RTR Act 1967, s. 86 (forgery, false statements and false documents) has been committed with respect to it, he may seize it. The person from whom taken, unless the document is previously returned, or he has been charged with the offence, must be summoned before a magistrates' court to account for possession. The court can make an order as to disposal of the document and award costs (s. 172).

(2) Other documents or plates

If a constable* has reasonable cause to believe that a document referred to below and carried on a MV or by the driver is one in relation to which one of the above offences has been committed, he may seize it under conditions similar (as to its return and bringing the matter before the court) as those in **(1)** above. The same applies to any plate bearing particulars required to be marked on a GV.

The documents subject to this section include:

a) any document evidencing appointment of an examiner or other officer having powers under the Act relating to goods vehicles (s. 173 (2));

b) any test or plating certificate or any certificate of approval or of conformity;

c) any plate bearing particulars required to be marked on a GV;

d) any record required to be kept by an operator relating to inspection of his GV;

e) international road haulage permits.

NOTE
The power to seize includes power to detach from a vehicle. See p. 213 as to documents, etc. relating to authorised goods vehicles.

---

† These are covered in the next provision.

* The power is given also to a certifying officer or examiner approved in relation to duties in respect of goods vehicles.

Chapter 22 **Supply of information and statements concerning accidents**

The procedure in connection with requests for information from police records relating to traffic accidents and other closely related types of accidents (e.g. injury to pedestrian caused by an irregular paving stone or falling scaffolding, or a cyclist injured because of a road defect) is based on recommendations of a working party on this subject issued in 1966. The recommendations of the working party (with comments added) are as follows.

1. Over-riding discretion of chief constables

Chief constables should continue to have over-riding discretion whether to provide information in individual cases.

2. Range of information to be supplied

a) The practice of providing information about road accidents should also apply to related types of accidents.

b) The police should not, for the purpose of civil litigation, extend the scope of information beyond what they require for their own purposes.

c) The entire contents of accident report books should be provided to parties to proceedings, speculative matter including expressions of opinion only being excluded.

COMMENT

'Entire contents' include:

a) the salient particulars of the accident;

b) witnesses' and parties' statements, whether or not signed;

c) a sketch plan, if made by the reporting officer at the scene, but one should not be specially drawn for the purpose of possible civil litigation.

'Speculative matter' which should not be provided includes matters of conjecture, such as opinion as to responsibility for the accident or how it happened, or recommendations as to proceedings.

The party's recommendation is that information in an accident booklet should be reproduced by photographic or other copying process—speculative matter being concealed.

Where there have been criminal proceedings arising out of an accident the outcome of the proceedings may be supplied at the same time as other information.

Copies of reports and statements obtained by the police in connection with a fatal accident, and supplied in original or by means of copies to HM coroner, may properly be supplied to parties to civil proceedings.

3. To whom information may be supplied

Information about road accidents may be supplied on request to bona fide parties to proceedings or to their solicitors, to insurance companies and to trades unions or friendly societies genuinely acting on behalf of parties.

4. Effect of pending proceedings

All information about traffic accidents should be withheld while police proceedings or inquests are pending, except statements by defendants. Subject to that, all information to be disclosed should be supplied at as early a stage as possible.

5. Statements of parties and witnesses

Statements by *witnesses* should as a general rule be supplied on request to parties to proceedings without obtaining the witnesses' consent.

COMMENT

This completely reverses the previous policy which required the consent of the witness to be obtained. The grounds on which the requirement for the witness's consent may have been thought to be justified were summarised by the working party as:

a) Statements sometimes contain defamatory or personal matter.

b) Witnesses might be less ready to make statements if they knew they could be supplied without their consent for purposes of civil litigation.

c) To act without consent appears discourteous.

To these the working party put the following answers:

i) To (a)—the over-riding discretion of the chief constable provides a sufficient safeguard, but in any case accident statements (unlike crime statements) rarely contain such matter.

ii) to (b)—this consequence is not likely in accident cases, for it is known that the majority of witnesses offer no objection.

iii) To (c)—the trouble saved to the police and to the witness (who may be called upon to deal with a number of requests for his consent) outweighs this.

Statements made by *parties* to the proceedings should be provided on request to both sides and in the same way as in witnesses' statements.

6. Interviews

a) An interview with a reporting officer should not be granted as a matter of course until the stage is reached when it is wished to take a proof of the officer's evidence.

b) The recommendations of the Evershed Committee about facilities for interviews to take proofs of evidence from police officers should continue to be adhered to.

c) An interview with a police officer in an accident case should normally be granted subject to the condition that a copy of any proof of evidence taken should be supplied to the police who are to be free to furnish a copy on request to any other interested party.

COMMENT

The practice of giving almost all information concerning accidents should reduce demand for interviews with police officers, and it is suggested that chief constables might reasonably decline to allow an interview until the stage has been reached when it is allowed for the purpose of taking a proof of evidence, i.e. until after civil proceedings have been commenced. The recommendations of the Evershed Committee may be summarised as follows:

The chief constable may permit an interview with a police officer;

a) *To a party who has had a copy of the police report* for the purpose of amplifying or elucidating points in the report, if this cannot be done by correspondence. The following rules apply:

i) Senior officer to be present to decide what questions may properly be asked and to record the interview.

ii) No police record will be supplied—the interviewer makes his own, which the police officer should not sign.

iii) Questions to be confined to facts and no opinion is to be given, nor should anything precluded from inclusion in the supplied copy report be discussed.

iv) No statement disclosed other than that made to the officer by the party for whom the interview is acting.

v) There should be no marking or filling in of sketch plan.

b) *To a solicitor to enable proof of evidence to be taken for civil proceedings. Requirement:*

i) certificate from solicitor that civil action has commenced (appearance entered, or notice of defence delivered), or

ii) subpoena is served on the police officer.

Matters which can be included: all that are admissible in evidence, i.e. all facts, as well as:

i) statements made spontaneously at time and at scene of accident by the parties (or a servant in charge of a party's vehicle) in one another's presence;

ii) opinion, if within competence of the officer to express it, e.g. as to sufficiency of street lighting;

iii) positions of vehicles on a plan, but only if drawn to scale.

c) *To one representative of the Motor Insurers' Bureau*—this should be allowed when an accident involves an unidentified driver.

NOTES

a) The chief constable may require beforehand a list of questions proposed to be put and indicate those that will not be answered.

b) In case of an accident to a police vehicle, a police officer not involved reporting the accident can be interviewed and can give spontaneous statements made by the police officers concerned (as at (i) above) but police officers involved as drivers or passengers cannot be interviewed.

7. Particular reports

a) *Doctors*—reports prepared by medical practitioners in their professional capacity should not be disclosed, but the name of a medical practitioner who has examined a party after an accident may be supplied.

b) *Vehicle examiners*—reports by expert vehicle examiners may be supplied.

c) *Forensic science*—forensic science reports addressed to the police may be supplied.

8. Method of copying and costs

Report books should normally be reproduced by photographic processes. A costing operation will be necessary to establish the economic charge. (At present costs are generally charged at the rates applied by the Metropolitan Police, which provide a basis for uniformity.)

COMMENT

The above recommendations do not appear to conflict with, nor override, the practice which has been followed since 1948 (following a recommendation of the Evershed Committee) that police officers' notebooks may be shown to counsel (or in county court to a solicitor) in the corridor of the court before the hearing, provided that any expressions of the officer's own opinion in the notebook are effectively covered over.

Chapter 23 Foreign motor vehicles

1. Road Traffic (Foreign Vehicles) Act 1972

(1) Application

The Act relates to foreign goods vehicles and PSVs only. 'Foreign' means brought into GB and not registered in the UK, or in the case of a trailer, one drawn by a MV so brought in and not registered. If no excise licence or trade plate is exhibited the vehicle is deemed, until the contrary is proved, not to be registered in the UK. In the following summary:

a) VE means 'vehicle examiner', i.e. a person authorised to act as such in respect of GVs and PSVs;

b) AP means 'authorised person' having powers under RTA 1972, s. 160 in relation to weighing vehicles.

'Driver' includes any person in charge of the vehicle and, if a second person acts as steersman, that person, as well as any other person in charge of the vehicle or engaged in driving it. In connnection with a trailer it means any person who is the driver (as defined above) of the MV by which it is drawn.

(2) Power to prohibit driving

Section 1

Where a VE is carrying out his statutory functions or an AP is exercising his powers in relation to weighing of a vehicle, he may prohibit the driving of the vehicle on a road either absolutely or for a specified purpose if:

a) the driver obstructs, refuses or neglects or fails to comply with a requirement made by the VE, or

b) it appears
i) to a VE that there is a contravention of any specified statutory provision*, or there would be if driven on a road, or
ii) to the AP that a weight limit under RTA 1972, s. 40 is exceeded.

---

* Re operators' licences; identification plates and marks; hours of driving, records and recording equipment; rules re international journeys; C & U Regulations; and lighting regulations.

(3) Procedure

Sections 1 and 2

a) Where such a prohibition is imposed the VE or AP may direct the driver to remove the vehicle (and any trailer being drawn) to a specified place and subject to any conditions included in the direction—the prohibition not applying to such a removal if the conditions (if any) are observed.

b) The VE or AP must forthwith give notice in writing of the prohibition to the driver specifying the grounds and stating the limits on the prohibition on driving (e.g. on all driving or for specified purposes and/or any time limits).

c) The direction in (a) may be included in the notice referred to in (b) or in a separate notice in writing.

d) The prohibition comes to an end when it is removed, or the specified period (if any) expires, whichever first occurs. An exemption (in writing) from the prohibition may be granted subject to conditions specified in the exemption. The removal of the prohibition is to be notified to the driver in writing by the VE or AP, as the case may be, when satisfied that the faults have been remedied.

(4) Offences

Section 3

The following are offences:

a) driving the vehicle (or causing or permitting this) in contravention of a prohibition, or

b) refusing, neglecting or otherwise failing to comply within a reasonable time with a direction under **(2)** (a) above.

(5) Police powers

Section 3

ARREST—A constable *in uniform* may AWW any person whom he reasonably suspects of having committed an offence in **(4)** above.

DETENTION OF VEHICLE—A constable *in uniform*, on reasonable cause to suspect the driver of having committed such an offence, may detain the vehicle and for this purpose give a direction, specifying an appropriate person and directing the vehicle to be removed by that person to such a place and subject to such conditions as are specified in the direction. Where the detention applies to a trailer being drawn by a MV then, to secure the removal and the safeguarding of the trailer, he may detain the MV as well, and require both to be driven to the specified place. The vehicle can be removed from place to place by further directions.

PERIOD OF DETENTION—The vehicle must be detained in the specified place until a constable* authorises it to be released on one of the following grounds:

a) prohibition under s. 1 has been removed, or

b) appropriate arrangements have been made to remedy fault, or

c) the vehicle is to be taken forthwith out of GB, or

d) the purpose of the detention has been fulfilled.

NOTE

The person in charge of the place of detention is not liable for loss or damage unless it is shown that he did not take reasonable care of the vehicle or its trailer.

'APPROPRIATE PERSON'—means a person licensed to drive vehicles of the class concerned and, if a trailer is to be drawn, to drive with trailer attached. He will not be liable for damages or loss unless it is shown that he did not take reasonable care while driving.

(6) Inspection of documents: prohibitions

Section 4

Where a VE has a legal right to examine documents in respect of a foreign GV or PSV being brought into, or being used in, this country, he may prohibit the driving of the vehicle on a road (either absolutely or for specified purposes) if the driver refuses or fails to comply with any request of the VE to produce, or to permit inspection or copying of such documents. Where such a prohibition is made paras. (2), (3) and (4) above apply.

2. Insurance

(1) MV (Compulsory Insurance) (No. 2) Regulations 1973 (as amended)

1) CHECKS ON ENTRY—The regulations provide for a check on insurance cover in respect of vehicles entering this country from any place abroad except those listed below†, and the prohibition of use in GB if any defect is found. A direction may also be given for the removal of the vehicle to a place of detention on the same lines as under the 1972 Act (para. 1 (3) above). The

---

* The authorisation must be by or for the S of S if the place of detention is in his occupation.

† The territory of a member state of the EEC, of Austria, Finland, Norway, Sweden, Switzerland, Czechoslovakia, Eastern Germany, and Hungary.

offences under reg. 6 are the same as those under s. 3 of the Act (para. 1 **(4)** above). There is one difference, though, in connection with police powers detailed in para. 1 **(5)** above, in that power to arrest is given. The grounds for removal of a detention direction are the same except that ground (c) (removal from GB) must be to a place other than one referred to below*.

ii) CERTIFICATES—The requirement that insurance policies must be issued by authorised insurers and are of no effect unless certificates are issued do not apply to policies issued elsewhere than in the UK for vehicles normally based in countries specified below*.

(2) MV (Third Party Risks) Regulations 1972

PRODUCTION OF CERTIFICATES—In the case of a vehicle normally based in one of the countries specified below* a document issued by the insurer indicating the nature of the insurance, the number or other identifying particulars of the insurance policy issued in respect of the vehicle and the period of cover, may be produced instead of a certificate.

(3) Other insurance provisions

Other provisions relating to foreign vehicles have been included in the chapter on insurance.

3. Particular exemptions

The student should note that exemptions or special provisions (other than those dealt with above) are applied to specified foreign vehicles (including vehicles of visiting forces) in relation to such matters as registration, licensing, construction of vehicles, hours of driving, and keeping of records. These have been incorporated in the text relating to the subjects concerned.

4. The EEC common transport policy

The Treaty of Rome, which governs and sets out the concepts of the European Economic Community, provides that one object of the EEC is to establish a common policy in the sphere of transport, so that the movement of traffic

---

* The territory of a member state of the EEC, of Austria, Finland, Norway, Sweden, Switzerland, Czechoslovakia, Eastern Germany, and Hungary.

between any member state and the others is facilitated. The primary means of achieving this is, of course, by creating greater (and eventually complete) uniformity between the laws of each member state relating to road traffic. The introduction of agreed common policy as part of the law relating to road traffic is effected in the following ways, i.e.

a) *directly—by community law* which becomes part of the law of GB without further enactment in this country, and

b) *indirectly—by Orders in Council and regulations* made in this country to implement, where it is considered advisable, community regulations and decisions (or directions) issued by the EEC Council and Commission. The authority to do this is provided by the EEC Act 1972, s. 2(2), under which legislation based on EEC regulations and directions has been introduced on the following subjects:

    i) insurance—see p. 326;
    ii) type approvals for vehicles and vehicle parts—see p. 245;
    iii) certificates of conformity—see p. 245;
    iv) keeping of records (EEC control book)—see p. 235.

Appendix 1 **Brakes**

MV (Construction and Use) Regulations 1978

1. Brakes on motor vehicles

(1) Invalid carriage

Must have an efficient braking system acting on at least two wheels enabling vehicle to be brought to rest within a reasonable distance (reg. 66).

(2) All motor vehicles, except invalid carriages

Eight general principles apply and the student should know them all but note that only the first four apply to motor cycles.

GENERAL REQUIREMENTS

a) There must be either one efficient braking system with two means of operation *or* two efficient braking systems each with its own separate means of operation.

b) It, or they, must be such that notwithstanding failure of any part (other than fixed member or a brake shoe anchor pin) the driver can still apply to at least half* the number of wheels, brakes which will bring the MV to rest, under most adverse conditions within a reasonable distance.

EXCEPTIONS

i) *Locomotives*
Pre 1st June 1955—only requirement is for one system, brakes of which act on all non-steering wheels, and will stop vehicle within reasonable distance.
Pre 2nd January 1933 and steam propelled—exempt if engine can be reversed.
RR—need have but one system with one means of operation.

ii) *Tractors*
RR or LT—one system and one means. If steam, a reversible engine is such a system but if post 1st October 1943, only if engine cannot be disconnected from any driving wheel except by means requiring sustained

---

* Not more than one front wheel is to be included in half the number of wheels.

GENERAL REQUIREMENTS

EXCEPTIONS

effort of driver. A LT first used post 9th February 1980 must have a system or systems which, on failure of any part, will still have an efficient brake able to stop the vehicle within a reasonable distance.

iii) *HMC*—if fitted with efficient split braking system, two separate systems not needed. If pre 15th August 1928, the only requirement is that the system(s) can bring to rest within reasonable distance under most adverse conditions.

iv) *Motor cycle pre 1st January 1927* if brake acts on one wheel.

v) *WT*—needs but one system and one means.

vi) *Multi-pull* means of operation does not count as one means on HMC or MC registered on or after 1st January 1968 unless it has a specified efficiency (see p. 332).

c) Brakes must conform to percentage efficiency standards provided by the regulations—excepting locomotives and MTs.

PCV and WT

d) The use of one means of operation must not affect the pedal or hand lever operating the other means.

None

e) No system must be rendered ineffective by non-rotation of engine.

i) *MT: HMC or MC (not a PSV)* propelled by steam if engine is reversible and cannot be disconnected from any driving wheel except by sustained effort of driver.

ii) Applies to MT only if post 1st October 1943 and to HMC only if post 1st January 1927.

f) One means must be direct to wheels and not through any hydraulic, electric or pneumatic device.

i) Pre 1st April 1938 MT.

ii) HMC or MC post 1st January 1968 which has a parking brake system independent of its main braking system applied only by direct mechanical action and

GENERAL REQUIREMENTS

EXCEPTIONS
capable of holding MV
stationary on gradient 1 in 6·25.
(i.e. with meter braking
efficiency of 16 per cent).

g) If any one brake shoe is
operated by more than one
means of operation, then every
wheel must have brakes
operated by one means of
operation, provided that a
means of operation if on a brake
shoe additional to those
required by these regulations is
to be disregarded.

i) HMC or MC post 1st January
1968.

ii) *MV with more than 6 wheels*,
four or more being steering wheels,
if one means applies to all except
two steering wheels on opposite
sides of MV (i.e. one pair of
steering wheels).

iii) MV with more than four wheels,
each pair of driving wheels being
driven independently and not
through differential gear between
the axles, if one means applies
brakes to one pair of driving wheels
and the other operates brakes on all
other wheels.

iv) PCV n/e 410 kgs u/w.

v) MCs under 2030 kgs u/w or for
not more than seven passengers if
one means brakes every wheel and
the braking effect on two wheels is
applied on a drive shaft leading to
each wheel without an intervening
gear.

h) One means must be direct (and
not through transmission gear)
to not less than half the number
of wheels.*

i) A MV with more than four
wheels and a braking system as
described in exception (iii) to (g)
above.

ii) MC pre 1st October 1938 with
more than four wheels and with one
means acting on not less than two
wheels other than through
transmission.

NOTE
If a HMC or MC has one means operating brakes on all wheels, any shaft
leading from axle differential gear to a driving wheel is not deemed part of
transmission.

---

* Not more than one front wheel is to be included in half the number of wheels.

EXCEPTIONS

a) All MV with more than three wheels if one means applies brakes to all wheels.

b) Motor cars:
   i) pre 1st October 1938;
   ii) post 1st October 1938 if u/w n/e 1020 kgs, or not for more than 7 passengers or a WT.

(3) Braking efficiency

This applies only to HMCs, MCs and motor cycles and means the maximum 'braking' force obtained by applying brakes measured as a percentage of the weight of the vehicle, including any person (not fare paying or other travelling passengers) or load* carried in the MV at the time.

(4) 'Multi-pull' operation

Many modern vehicles (particularly heavy goods vehicles) have a 'multi-pull' means of operating brakes. This requires the driver instead of applying steady pressure, to apply the hand lever several times (by moving the lever backwards and forwards) to build up the braking efficiency.

On a MV first used post 1st January 1968 a 'multi-pull' means of operation (sometimes called a 'barrell brake') must be able on a first application (i.e. one pull) to operate a hydraulic, electrical or pneumatic device and thus cause the brakes to be applied with an almost instant braking efficiency of not less than 25 per cent. The 'multi-pull' brake which does not operate on only one pull can be neither the service brake nor a secondary brake.

(5) Vacuum or pressure systems

Regulation 14

Every MV first used on or after 1st October 1937 which has a braking system embodying a vacuum reservoir must have *a warning device* readily visible to the driver to indicate an impending defect in the system, but this does not apply to vehicles of 3050 kg u/w or less, provided the braking system is able to stop the vehicle within a reasonable distance if the vacuum system fails.

(6) Parking brakes

Regulation 13

a) *Any MV first used pre 1st January 1968* must have a braking system capable of being set to prevent two of the wheels at least (or one if a three

---

* As regards a plated GV the efficiency must be capable of being produced when the gross weight shown on the plate is being transmitted to the road surface.

wheeler) from revolving when stationary. It can be one of the braking systems required by the regulations for locomotives, MT, HMC and MC.

b) *Every MV first used post 1st January 1968* must have a braking system which:

i) has means of operation, in case of HMC or MC, independent of that operating the primary brakes, i.e., those designed to produce the total braking efficiency of 50 per cent;

ii) maintains the brakes in action by direct mechanical means (e.g. by cable or rod) without intervention of any hydraulic, electric or pneumatic device; and

iii) is capable of holding the vehicle stationary on a gradient 1 in 6·25 without the assistance of stored energy. (This represents a braking efficiency of 16 per cent.)

EXCEPTIONS—The above do not apply to two wheeled motor cycle (with or without sidecar); invalid carriage; L Loco (pre 1st January 1932).

2. Brakes on trailers

Regulation 75

If trailer was manufactured on or after 1st April 1938 its braking system must not be such as to be rendered ineffective by non-rotation of engine of the drawing vehicle.

The remainder of the regulation (below) does not apply to:

a) trailer n/e 102 kgs u/w;

b) LI or LIC drawn by MV;

c) street cleansing trailer carrying only necessary gear and equipment;

d) BDV towed by MV;

e) a pre 1st July 1947 Ag Tlr drawn by MT or LT if laden weight n/e 4070 kgs, it is only trailer drawn, and speed n/e 10 mph; or

f) trailers carrying only gas producing plant, etc., to provide gas for drawing vehicle which is a goods vehicle u/w not less than 2030 kgs or a PSV.

(1) Trailer manufactured before 1st January 1968

Such trailers, and every Ag Tlr whenever manufactured, must have a braking system able to act, when being drawn, on at least:

a) *two wheels* when n/e four wheels;

b) *four wheels* if over four wheels;

c) *half the wheels* if made after 1st April 1938, and so constructed that:
  i) the driver or attendant (on motor vehicle or trailer) is able to apply the trailer brakes*, and
  ii) brakes can be set to prevent two at least of the wheels from revolving when not being drawn whether attached to the drawing vehicle or not.

(2) Trailer manufactured on and after 1st January 1968 (excluding Ag Tlr)

Must have an efficient braking system:

a) capable (when trailer is being drawn) of being applied to all its wheels by the driver using the braking system of the drawing vehicle designed to have the highest braking efficiency*;

b) so constructed that in the case of failure of the system of the drawing vehicle or of trailer (other than of a fixed member or brake shoe anchor pin) brakes can still be applied to at least two wheels of the trailer, or to one wheel of a two-wheeled trailer*;

c) including a parking brake (for use when stationary):
  i) capable of being applied to at least two wheels by person standing on the ground using means of operation on the trailer;
  ii) such that it is at all times maintained in operation by direct mechanical action with no intervening hydraulic, electric or pneumatic device;
  iii) capable of holding trailer stationary on gradient of 1 in 6·25 without assistance of stored energy (which represents a braking efficiency (tested by meter) at 16 per cent).

NOTE
Where a trailer exempt from C & U Regulations by virtue of a certificate of conformity with an EEC directive (see p. 245) is drawn by a MV not so certified (or vice versa), the trailer must, in general, have a braking system conforming with para. (2) (b) above (regs. 75(3) and 76).

(3) Application of brakes on trailers

a) Except in the case of a trailer with overrun brakes, or a broken-down vehicle being towed (and not itself steerable), the driver of the drawing vehicle (or one of the two in the case of locomotive) must be in a position readily to operate the brakes required by regulation on both vehicle and trailer unless another person is carried and in a position and competent efficiently to apply the brakes of the trailer (reg. 126).
b) No person in charge of a MV or a trailer drawn thereby shall cause or permit such trailer to stand detached from the drawing vehicle unless one wheel at least of the trailer is prevented from revolving by setting the brake or by use of a chain (reg. 127).

---

* Do not apply to following if brakes of trailer automatically come into operation on the overrun of the trailer.

PSV—maximum: 12 metres.

Trailers—Maximum 7 metres, excluding towing attachments, but may be 12 metres if:

a) it has four wheels or more and distance between centres of road contact of front and rear wheels is not less than three-fifths of o/l, and

b) it is drawn by MV u/w of 2030 kgs or more.

EXCEPTIONS—Regulation does not apply to:

a) trailers constructed and used for indivisible loads of exceptional length;

b) LI;

c) trailer part of AV;

d) BDV being towed away;

e) trolley vehicle being constructed or delivered;

f) any road works trailer designed to produce tar macadam etc., or being a road planing machine if o/l of MV plus trailer n/e 18·3 m.

Combinations of vehicles—

a) MV plus one trailer: 18 metres;

b) MV* plus two trailers, or one trailer for AIL: 25·9 metres†.

2. Overall width

I.e. width between vertical planes *parallel* to the longitudinal axis of the vehicle and passing through its extreme projecting points.

   'Projecting points' do not include driving mirrors; direction indicators; snow plough attached to front; distortion of tyre caused by weight of vehicle; customs clearance seal container, or (if registered pre 2nd January 1939) the first 105 mm of the projection of a swivelling window for hand signals, *but do include* any device or receptacle on or attached to the vehicle and increasing carrying capacity, except:

a) a side board let down only to facilitate loading, or unloading, or

b) a receptacle to be lifted on or off the vehicle with goods in it, from time to time actually used in ordinary course of business.

Motor vehicles—

a) Loco: 2·75 metres;

b) MT, HMC, MC: 2·5 metres;

c) IC: 2·2 metres.

Trailers—2·3 metres.

---

* MV not to exceed 9·2 m in each of these cases.

† Can be exceeded if Schedule 8 conditions are complied with.

EXCEPTIONS

a) Trailer used by travelling showmen and in use pre 15th January 1931: 2·68 metres.

b) Pre 1st January 1933 trailer if excess over 2·3 metres is caused by conversion from solid to pneumatic tyres: 2·45 metres.

c) If following apply:
    i) all pneumatic tyres;
    ii) drawing vehicle is a Loco, MT or HMC or, if AV, a MC over 2030 kgs u/w;
    iii) drawing vehicle (other than a Loco) has penumatic tyres, and
    iv) does not project on either side more than 305 mm beyond the outermost part of the drawing vehicle,
then: 2·5 metres.

The regulation does not apply to any trailer which is a LI, or a trolley vehicle being constructed or delivered, or a BDV being towed away.

3. Overall height

Of a PSV—maximum 4·57 m.
No other vehicle is restricted as to height by the regulations.

4. Overhang

This is the distance between the rearmost part of a MV and a fixed point towards the front along its longitudinal axis, i.e. along a line joining the centres of the front and the back of the MV. In most vehicles, having but two axles, the forward point is the centre of the back axle. If the MV has more than two axles, then the front (steering) axles are excluded, and the forward point is:

a) *if two non-steering axles*—110 mm to the rear of the centre of a line joining the centres of those axles;

b) *if more than two such axles*—the point at which a line drawn at right angles to the longitudinal axis of the MV passes through the centre of the minimum turning circle of the MV.

NOTE

'Rearmost part' of a MV does not include hood when down, Post Office letter box n/e 305 mm long, fire escape turntable, luggage grid of passenger car (n/e seven passengers), or a towing fitment on a PSV constructed to draw a trailer and n/e 305 mm long.

OVERHANG RESTRICTIONS APPLY TO—

MT—n/e 1·83 mm.

HMC—n/e 60 per cent of the distance from centre of front axle (or of the line joining centres of front wheels) to the forward point from which overhang is measured. *Exceptions:* first used pre 15th August 1928; WT; tipping truck if overhang n/e 1·15 m; street cleansing or refuse vehicle.

MC—as for HMC. *Exception:* first used pre 2nd January 1933; street cleansing or refuse vehicles; WT; if first used pre 1st January 1966, can add 76 mm if distance between foremost and rear axles n/e 2·29 m.

Appendix 5 Motor Vehicles (Competitions and Trials) Regulations 1969

Standard conditions

Schedule 3

(1) Applicable to all events

* CONDITIONS MARKED THUS CAN BE MODIFIED TO A LIMITED DEGREE BY THE APPROPRIATE AUTHORITY AND/OR BY THE RAC.

a) Event to be held in accordance with particulars supplied, subject to any modification agreed with the authorities, or necessary because part of route becomes impassable after the event is authorised.

b) Maximum number of vehicles to be driven by competitors, in night event (10 pm–7 am)—120; otherwise—180*.

c) Rules shall not require any length of public highway (other than motorway) to be traversed more than once during the event*.

d) Starting and finishing points shall not be on a public highway.

e) Rules must not require stopping (or slowing down to solve set problems) within 500 yards of dwelling unless an adult occupant has given permission.

f) Rules to be such that no greater merit accrues to a competitor for visiting certain control points (or reaching one finishing point) rather than others.

g) Checking equipment not to be set up on carriageway or footway nor is any vehicle used to be parked on any carriageway of any highway except in a place provided for parking.

h) Where route contains a road across which there are gates or cattle grids:
i) The promoter must notify the occupiers of the land (other than common land or land fenced off from road) on each side of the road between the gates or cattle grids as the case may be.
ii) Competitors shall not be required to leave their vehicles to open or close gates.

iii) A person shall be posted at each *gate* to make sure that cattle do not pass through and to close gate after last competitor has gone through. With the written consent of the occupiers of the land one person may control several gates; this does not apply to certain gates on or leading to common land.

i) The average speed (calculated by reference to distance travelled and time allowed) which competitors are required to maintain over any part of the route, must not be likely to cause any driver:
i) to exceed a speed limit, or
ii) to drive at dangerous speed.
The average speed required in any case must not exceed:
i) in relation to vehicles not restricted to a speed limit—50 mph on any motorway, and 30 mph otherwise;
ii) in relation to a PSV or large goods vehicle—50 mph on any motorway and 25 mph otherwise;
iii) in case of a car towing a caravan (otherwise than on motorway)—25 mph.

j) Each competitor must declare that he will have in force a policy of insurance or such security as the law requires re third party risks.

k) The promoter must record particulars of each competitor and of each vehicle taking part in the event, and send this information to the appropriate authority.

l) Each competitor must have a rest period after each 200 miles whether he drives continuously or not—the period to be not less than one hour though it may be taken as a passenger in a vehicle taking part.

(2) Additional for time schedule events

a) Rules of event must require competitors to observe timetable such that:
i) *at the start*, interval between first and last competitors;
ii) *at a control point*, interval between arrival of first and departure of last competitor;
iii) *at any point* on route interval of passing of first and last competitor, other than a point on motorway; and
iv) *at the finish*, interval between arrival of first and last competitor, do not exceed 2 hours in night event, and 3 hours otherwise*.

b) No person shall check or record times kept by competitors at the start, finish or control point (other than a rest halt) after $2\frac{1}{2}$ hours in the case of a night event and $3\frac{1}{2}$ hours in any other case, from the time when first competitor left the point (in case of starting point) or arrived in the case of any other point*.

c) At any starting point intervals between starts must not be at intervals of less than one minute*.

d) Time checking or recording points on public highway not to be less than 2 miles apart.

e) Once a competitor has been penalised at a control point, times of arrival and departure at other controls and finishing points must be adjusted so that he will not incur further penalties for failing to make up the time lost.

NOTE

Conditions (a) and (b) do not apply to events for MVs registered pre 1st January 1930 only.

(3) Time limit events and problem solving events

All conditions as in (1) plus condition (c) in (2) above.

Appendix 6 Drivers' Hours (Goods Vehicles) (Exemptions) Regulations 1978

The general rules as to hours of driving and duty under s. 96 of the Transport Act 1968 (see p. 229) may be summarised as follows:

a) Daily hours of driving—maximum: *10 hours*.

b) Break for rest and refreshments—at least: *½ hour*.

c) Maximum working day: *11 hours*.

d) Interval between two WD, at least: *11 hours*.

e) Working week, maximum: *60 hours*.

f) Rest day, weekly, at least: *24 hours*.

Exemptions

In emergency (see p. 230) a driver who on any day does duty to deal with an emergency is exempt:

a) *From* (a), (b) and(c), but if duty time exceeds 11 hours the excess must be for the emergency work only. (NB: if the emergency interrupts (d) this does not prevent his next WD being up to 11 hours (not more than 10 hours in driving) on non-emergency duties if, since his last non-emergency duties he has had two or more intervals of rest totalling not less than 11 hours).

b) *From* (e), but any period above 66 hours must be devoted to emergency duties only.

c) *From* (f), provided, if emergency duty is done during the last 24 hours of the WW, he does not do any non-emergency duties after finishing emergency duty in that period.

FOR SPECIAL NEEDS—The exemptions relate to one or more of the following:

a) *the maximum working day* (WD)—14 hours being substituted for the normal 11 hours;

b) *the maximum working week* (WW), in which 66 hours is substituted for 60 hours;

c) *the weekly rest day* (RD), in which case the conditions of exemption are that the driver has 24 hours off for each WW for which he does not have the s. 96 RD and that this off duty period is taken within 28 days of the beginning of the WW in which he does not have the s. 96 RD and is taken in addition to s. 96 rest day requirements for other weeks;

d) *interval between one WD and the next* (Int) in which case the interval may be 10 hours instead of the usual 11 hours, though for the purposes of s. 96 (calculations) it shall be deemed that he has had the 11 hours.

The cases of special needs to which the exemptions apply are as follows, the exception headings being given in brackets:

a) *Handling of Christmas mail* (WD, WW, RD).

b) *Carriage of food* other than bread, milk, animal fodder or feeding stuffs or drugs—applies during a period immediately preceding the following: Easter (one WW); Spring Bank Holiday (one WW); Summer Bank Holiday (six WW); and also during the WW which includes 1st January and the two preceding WW (WD, WW, RD).

c) *Carriage of bread*—during the period as in (b), plus any Friday or Saturday, and two WD in the week preceding a Bank Holiday (WD*, WW, RD).

d) *Bulk carriage of milk or liquid egg*—(liquid egg only during periods as in (b) above) (WD, WW, RD).

e) *Carriage of animals* (WD, WW, RD, and Int).

f) Animal waste not intended for human consumption (WD, WW, RD, and Int).

g) *Carriage of:*
   i) *fish*, from landing place immediately after landing, or
   ii) *agricultural produce* (other than that of dairy farming of breeding or keeping cattle) from agricultural premises during the harvest period for the produce, or
   iii) anything used for *repairs and replacements* of agricultural machinery (inc. fuel and oil) being used for harvesting produce as in (ii) above, or
   iv) *agricultural lime or animal fodder* or feeding stuffs, or
   v) *trees*, from the place of recent felling (WD, WW, RD).

h) *Collection and delivery of blood for transfusion* purposes—exemptions as for passenger vehicles, see p. 229.

i) *Distribution of newspapers* or periodicals to wholesaler or to premises for retail sale (WD, Int).

j) *Carriage of materials, etc. used for building or civil engineering work*—to or from sites (WD, WW, RD).

k) *Household furniture removal* (house to house or to or from storage) (WD only).

---

* In the case of a Friday or Saturday exemption, if the exemption is used on a Friday it cannot be used on the following day.

l) *Carriage of shop fittings* to or from shops (WD only).

m) *Carriage of explosives, or radioactive substances* or the delivery of *stores to ships* (WD only).

n) *Carrying an AIL* under police escort for the whole journey or the greater part of it (WD†, WW, RD).

o) *Carrying goods on journey involving sea ferry crossing* for which the goods are not removed from the vehicle and having the same driver all the way (WD†).

† Provided the driver is off duty during that day for a period (or total periods) not less than the time by which that WD exceeds 11 hours.

Appendix 7 Model for driver's record book

The model set out below is that prescribed by Council Regulation (EEC) No 543/69 of 25th March 1969 as amended by Council Regulation (EEC) No 514/72 of 28th February 1972 and described by those Regulations as an 'individual control book'. The book must be of standard A6 format (105 mm × 148 mm) or a larger format.

Model Individual Control Book

a) Front sheet

I   INDIVIDUAL CONTROL BOOK
FOR CREW MEMBERS IN ROAD TRANSPORT

II   Country ....

III   Date book first used: ....

                                                       19................

IV   Date book last used: ....

                                                       19................

V   Surname, first name(s), date of birth and address of holder of book:

       ....

       ....

VI   Name, address, telephone number and stamp (if any) of the undertaking: ....

       ....

       ....

       ....

       ....

       ....

VII Operator's Licence No. (goods vehicles only).
Book No. ....

                   (to be stamped or perforated)

---

b) Instructions for use of control book
(These are summarised on page 237.)

c) Daily sheet

1. DAILY SHEET

No

2. Registration No. of vehicle(s)

Operators Licence Nos

3. Day of week and date

8. Place of coming on duty:

9. Place of going off duty:

10. Transport of goods.
Permissible maximum weight of the combination of vehicles – Lorry with trailer or articulated vehicles (where applicable) :

10a. Passenger transport.
System of daily rest selected:

11. Distance recorder:

End of duty: .... km/miles

Beginning of duty: .... km/miles

Total distance covered .... km/miles

	Number of hours
12.	
13.	
14.	
15. Total	
13 + 14	
If applicable.	

16. Remarks and signature:

Book No

d) Example of completed daily sheet

Book No   21

2. Registration No. of vehicle(s) ABC 123 L Operators Licence No: D.123456	1. DAILY SHEET No 11	3. Day of week and date Tuesday 7 September 1972

4. Place of coming on duty: Bristol.

9. Place of going off duty: Nottingham

10. Permissible maximum weight of the combination of vehicles – Lorry with trailer or articulated vehicles (where applicable) 19 tons

10a. Passenger transport. System of daily rest selected:

11. Distance recorded:	End of duty	21230 Miles
	Beginning of duty	21040 Miles
Total distance covered: ...... No. ... Miles		

		12.	Number of hours 12
		13.	6
		14.	3
		15. Total	9
		13 + 14	
		If applicable	

16. Remarks and signatures:

J. Smith

Note 1.

In practice, boxes 10 and 10a will both be completed on the same daily sheet only where a crew member has carried out a passenger transport operation and a goods transport operation on the same day. In box 10a (completed only by crew members of passenger vehicles) the entry should be either "10 h" or "11 h", according to the system of daily rest periods applying to the crew member.

Note 2.

Opposite box 12, if 12 hours is entered as the total period of uninterrupted rest taken prior to going on duty, this means that the driver went off duty at 7 pm on the previous day, because adding the 5 hours from 7 pm to midnight on the previous day to the 7 hours entered in box 4 gives a total of 12 hours.

e) Weekly report

A.		Surname and first name(s) of crew member						
		....						
B.				WEEKLY REPORT				
C.		From .... to .... 19 ..... inclusive						

D.	Days of the weekly period							**J. Weekly total:**
E.	Daily sheet no							
F.	🛏✳							
Hours of occupational activities	G. ⌐							
	H. ◻							
	I. G+H							

K. Remarks: ....

....

....

L. Date of preceding weekly rest period: ....

M. Signature of crew member: ....

N. Signature of employer: ....

Book No ....

Appendix 8 **Projection markers**

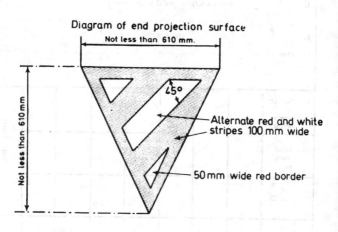

Diagram of end projection surface

Not less than 610 mm.

Not less than 610mm

45°

Alternate red and white stripes 100 mm wide

50mm wide red border

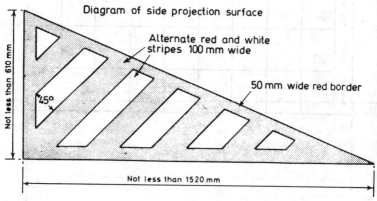

Diagram of side projection surface

Alternate red and white stripes 100 mm wide

50 mm wide red border

Not less than 610 mm

45°

Not less than 1520 mm

Index